Becoming Prominent

Becoming Prominent

Regional Leadership in Upper Canada, 1791–1841

J.K. JOHNSON

McGill-Queen's University Press
Kingston and Montreal

ISBN 0-7735-0641-1
Legal deposit first quarter 1989
Bibliothèque nationale du Québec

Printed in Canada on acid-free paper

This book has been published with the help of a grant from the Social Science Federation of Canada, using funds provided by the Social Sciences and Humanities Research Council of Canada.

Canadian Cataloguing in Publication Data

Johnson, J.K. (James Keith), 1930–
Becoming prominent: regional leadership in Upper Canada, 1791–1841
Includes bibliographical references and index.
ISBN 0-7735-0641-1
1. Ontario – History – 1791–1841 – Biography.
2. Ontario – Biography.
3. Politicians – Ontario – Biography. I. Title.
HN110.Z9E4 1989 971.3'02'0922 C88-090172-1

Contents

Maps and Figures

MAPS

FIGURES

Tables

Acknowledgments

This book has been a long time in the making and over the years I have accumulated many debts. The great number of people who have been helpful at various times, plus a faulty memory, make it unwise for me to try to thank everyone who deserves thanks individually, but I am grateful especially to the staff of the Public Archives of Canada, where most of my research was done, and also for advice and guidance received at the Archives of Ontario, the National Library of Canada, the Metropolitan Toronto Central Library, the University of Western Ontario Regional Collection, and the Queen's University Archives.

The Ontario Historical Society generously published my appeal for biographical information on difficult cases in the *O.H.S. Bulletin* and many local historians and genealogists responded with useful details. The staff of the *Dictionary of Canadian Biography* made my work a good deal easier by sharing their biographical files with me.

Whole generations of colleagues and students at Carleton University have contributed, sometimes unknowingly, to the content of the book and the arguments advanced in it. A grant from the research and publication fund of the Dean of Arts at Carleton covered the cost of the preparation of the maps and figures.

The not entirely anonymous assessors who read the manuscript on behalf of the Social Science Federation of Canada raised some sensible objections which I hope have been adequately met.

One vital contributor to this project does deserve special mention: Doreen Blouin, with extraordinary forbearance, typed all of the bits and pieces of this book on its way to its final form.

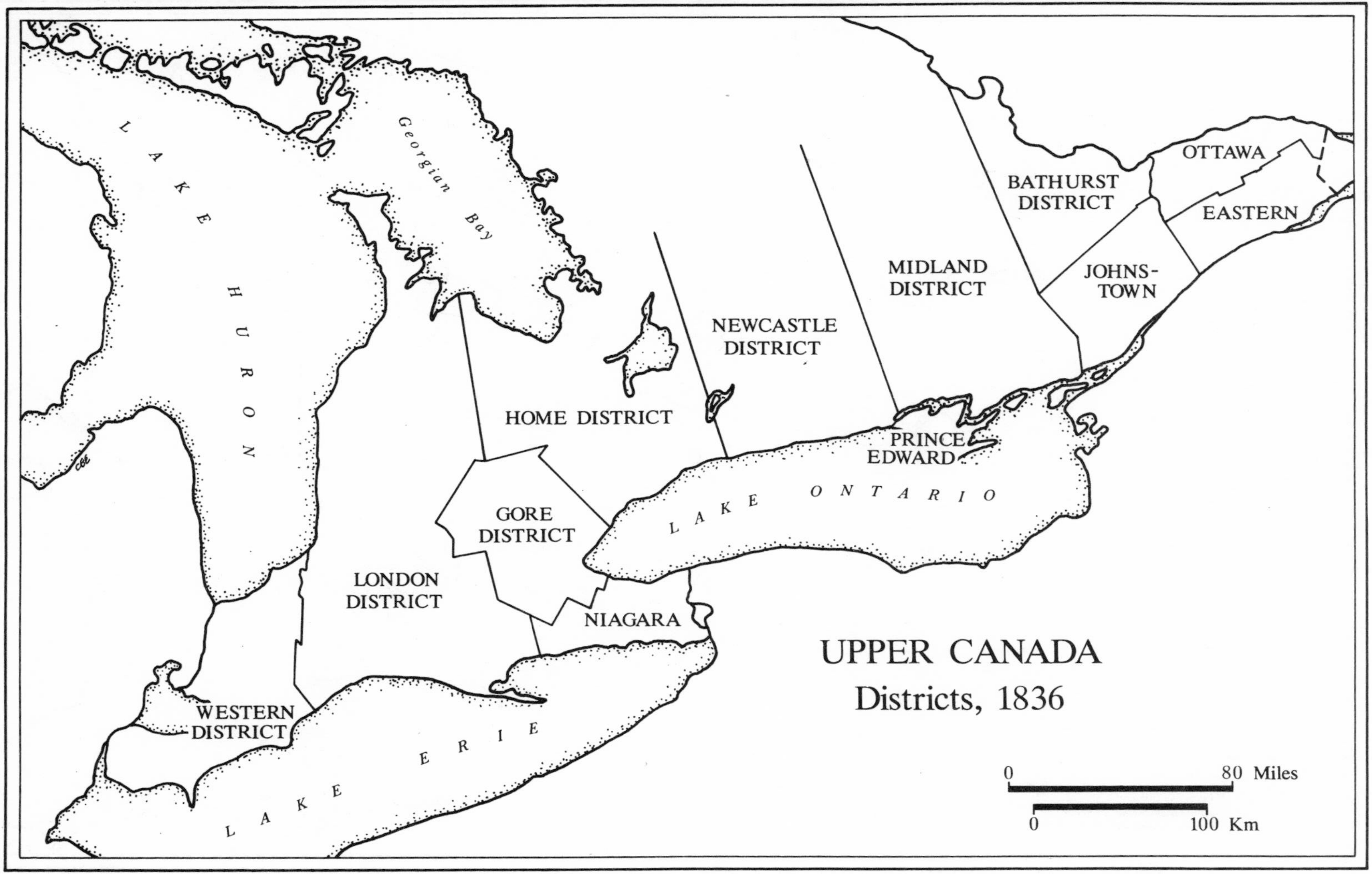
UPPER CANADA
Districts, 1836
LAKE HURON
Georgian Bay
LAKE ONTARIO
LAKE ERIE
OTTAWA
EASTERN
BATHURST DISTRICT
JOHNS-TOWN
MIDLAND DISTRICT
NEWCASTLE DISTRICT
PRINCE EDWARD
HOME DISTRICT
GORE DISTRICT
NIAGARA
LONDON DISTRICT
WESTERN DISTRICT
0
80 Miles
0
100 Km

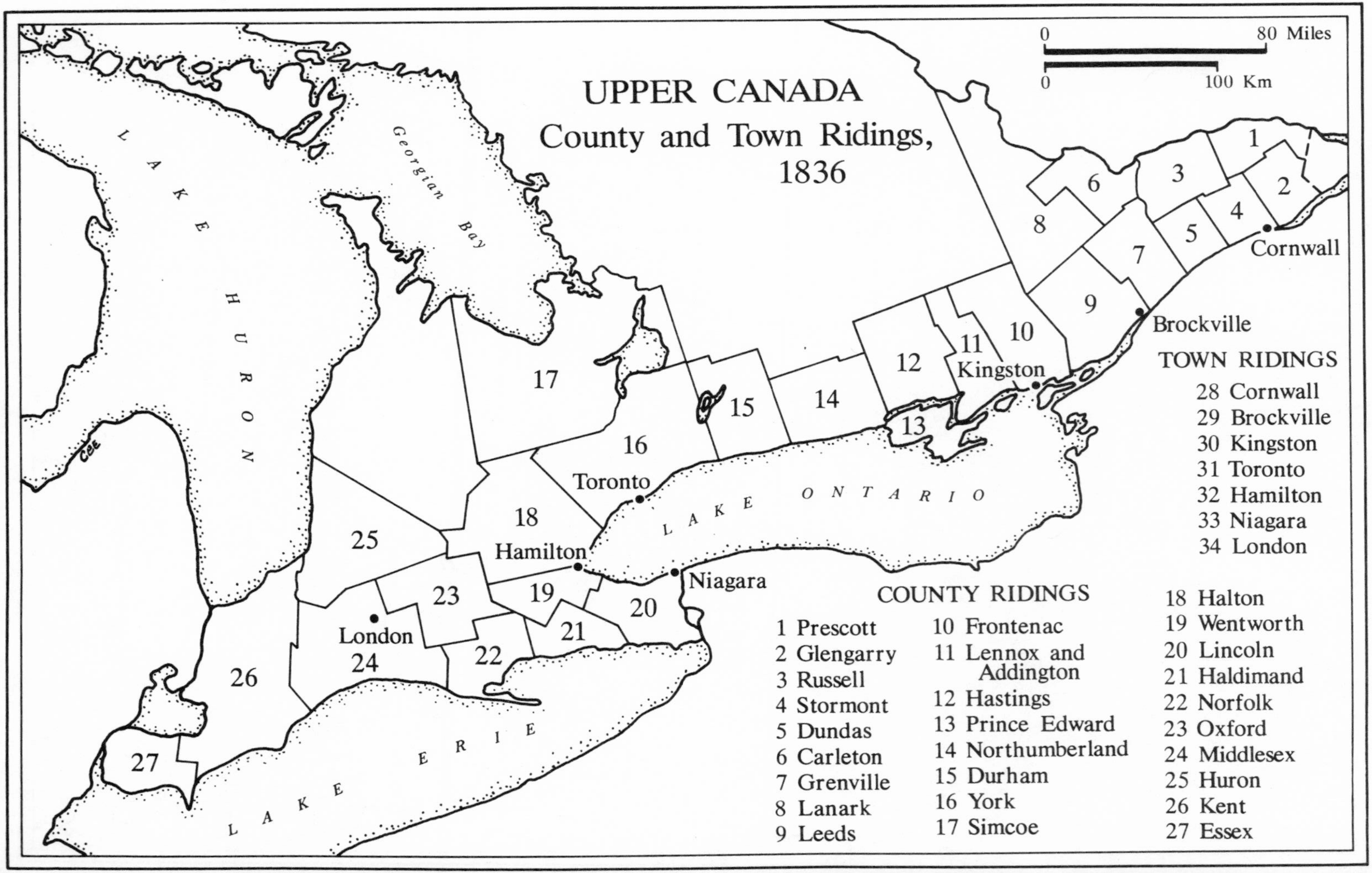
UPPER CANADA
County and Town Ridings, 1836
0 80 Miles
0 100 Km
LAKE HURON
Georgian Bay
LAKE ONTARIO
LAKE ERIE
Cornwall
Brockville
Kingston
Toronto
Hamilton
Niagara
London
1
2
3
4
5
6
7
8
9
10
11
12
13
14
15
16
17
18
19
20
21
22
23
24
25
26
27
COUNTY RIDINGS
1 Prescott
2 Glengarry
3 Russell
4 Stormont
5 Dundas
6 Carleton
7 Grenville
8 Lanark
9 Leeds
10 Frontenac
11 Lennox and Addington
12 Hastings
13 Prince Edward
14 Northumberland
15 Durham
16 York
17 Simcoe
18 Halton
19 Wentworth
20 Lincoln
21 Haldimand
22 Norfolk
23 Oxford
24 Middlesex
25 Huron
26 Kent
27 Essex
TOWN RIDINGS
28 Cornwall
29 Brockville
30 Kingston
31 Toronto
32 Hamilton
33 Niagara
34 London

Becoming Prominent

Introduction

This is a collective biography of 283 Upper Canadians. They are not "ordinary" Upper Canadians, and the reason for studying them is not because they were typical or representative of Upper Canadian society as a whole. What they had in common, besides all being male, was that at one time or another all of them were elected to the Upper Canadian House of Assembly. They were all, in other words, politicians. Despite that fact, this is not a book which is primarily about politics and is not at all about what went on in the legislature. What it is about is prominence – prominence at the provincial level but also and especially local prominence – and about the ingredients – economic, social, and political – of prominence. The reasons for choosing this group of Upper Canadians for such a study are simple. They were a province-wide group whose names and regional (political) affiliation are known and all of whom did at some time indisputably achieve a degree of prominence. They were chosen by the qualified electors of a particular area to speak for them in the provincial parliament.

It cannot be argued that all of these people were the *most* prominent Upper Canadians at any one time or in any one place. Undoubtedly in many cases there were other members of their communities who were in fact better known, better off, or better connected. Nonetheless, the 283 men who were members of the House of Assembly (MHA)[1] have the great advantage as a group of being immediately identifiable. To try to establish just who was at any one time the most prominent person in any district in Upper Canada would require the creation of some kind of workable formula for actually measuring prominence; it would also require sources of information, such as data on income or education, which are frequently unobtainable and would also almost certainly take a very long time to complete. In any case, the MHAS, as will be contended more fully later on, turn out to be quite suitable representatives of prominence, if only in some cases as surrogates for greater prominence. Most of them, before surfacing as provincial politicians, had already achieved certain important local distinctions within their own districts, most commonly by having been appointed as magistrates or by having received commissions as officers of the provincial militia. It has been said that locally prominent Upper Canadians such as magistrates carried a sort of double official stamp of approval: in order to gain such offices they needed the support of both the local "oligarchy" and the central elite.[2] A good many of the MHAS could be said to have had triple approval – of the local and central elites and of the people of their area, or at least of the property-owning portion of them who were entitled to vote.

Some of the MHAS were, even in their own time and certainly since, relatively obscure. Some of them owed their prominence almost entirely to politics and to little else. Some, though not many, had little or no real connection with the ridings they represented. Still, as a group they were of sufficient distinction to make them good subjects for an examination of the nature of prominence. They also exhibit a sufficient degree of uniformity but also a sufficient level of differences relating to time, religion, political alignment, and other factors to provide opportunities for a fair amount of comparative analysis.

The kinds of biographical information collected for this project have been governed by two general considerations: the types of information which seemed likely to be significant for the purposes of collective examination, and the types of information for which sources are available. Since the two are not necessarily the same, the result has been that some categories of data are relatively complete while others are very incomplete indeed. The main headings under which biographical evidence has been sought are: details of birth and death, family relationships, education, religious denomination, occupation, residence, land holding, military service, appointed office-holding, and (of course) provincial political office. The results of investigation into these areas have been assessed in a variety of overlapping ways, but in general under five broad subjects: occupational choice, wealth and land, local office-holding, patronage and status, and the nature of parliamentary representation.

The reader should be warned initially (as the reader will be warned frequently throughout the book) that too much faith should not be placed in the purely statistical results of collective analysis. There are a number of reasons for this, some of which have already been hinted at. The completeness of the data leaves much to be desired, most especially on the question of education but also in a good many other categories including, for most of the period, religious denomination. As well, specific groups within the total number of MHAS such as denominational or national groups, considered over the whole period or especially for shorter periods of time, are often very small, so that slight changes based on incomplete information can produce dramatic but not necessarily real statistical changes. Even when reasonably ample information exists there is a problem of reliability or precision of the sources. In many cases, sources of biographical details such as local or family histories; which must be turned to for want of any official source, are undocumented and often contradict one another on dates or on other matters and are often frustratingly vague. What, for instance, does "born in Canada" mean in the period before 1841? Born in Upper Canada? in Upper or Lower Canada? in any of the British colonies? What does "Methodist" mean? Wesleyan Methodist, and if so Canadian or British Wesleyan? or Methodist Episcopal (i.e. American), or one of several smaller Methodist bodies? These sorts of distinctions are of greater or lesser importance but especially in the case of religion were certainly of considerable importance to the people of the time. They are not, unfortunately, distinctions which it is always possible to make at this distance. The point is that what follows is not a sophisticated quantification of large amounts of presumably valid "routinely generated" data but an attempt, using sometimes fragmentary, sometimes dubious evidence, to identify some trends and collective characteristics which can be applied to the careers of one set of prominent Upper Canadians during a period of about fifty years. The overall question to which an answer has been sought is: how was prominence achieved? What, in other words, were the most significant social, economic, ideological, or other factors which aided or hampered the attainment of prominence? The conclusions which have been reached in attempting to answer these questions, it will be argued, despite the limitations of the data, are, or seem to be, likely conclusions. They are not, and probably cannot be, definitive conclusions.

Some explanatory comments are necessary about terminology and methods. One troublesome area of identification is that of nationality. Essentially the distinctions which have been made are based on place of birth but there are some exceptions to that rule. Three MHAS, Francis and Jean-Baptiste Baby and Jean-Baptiste Maçon, have been designated as "French Canadian." The term has some official status, since it was used in the first Upper Canadian census of 1842, but it also in this case provides a handy label for people whose actual place of birth is uncertain. A more important variation concerns emigrants who came to Upper Canada from what were the Thirteen Colonies and became the United States. Here the important distinction has been taken to be not where someone was born, nor even necessarily when, but when, and for what motives, that person came to Upper Canada. The essential point has been to distinguish between those who belong to a Loyalist group and others who belong to a Post-Loyalist American group, because these labels – and particularly the right to be officially labelled "United Empire Loyalist" – were, it will also be argued, highly relevant to the pursuit of prominence. Thus while one category under the heading of national origin is "Thirteen Colonies," not all of the MHAS who were actually born there are listed as such. To take a couple of examples: Abraham Markle, who was born in New York in 1770 obviously was, strictly speaking, born in the Thirteen Colonies, but since he did not come to Upper Canada until 1802 (and subsequently served with the rank of major on the American side during the War of 1812) his national origin does not appear as "Thirteen Colonies" but as "Post-Loyalist American." Conversely, Mahlon Burwell was born in New Jersey in 1783, well after the Thirteen Colonies had declared their independence, and did not come to Upper Canada until 1796. Nonetheless, since his father was an Anglican clergyman who openly supported the British during the Revolution and since Burwell himself, though never making it onto the official Loyalist List, was in every other way a Loyalist, he has been put among those whose national origins is shown as "Thirteen Colonies." The division is not always a tidy one and has required some judgment calls with which it will be possible to quarrel, but here precise place and time of birth (though they appear in the Appendix) have been judged less significant than the need to establish differences between differently motivated and differently perceived groups.

Aside from the variations just noted no attempt has been made to deal separately with any form of "ethnicity" as distinct from place of birth. Professor D.H. Akenson has argued strongly that it is essential to know not only where people were born but what ethnic group they belonged to, for "ethnicity is a perduring cultural characteristic" which can extend over many generations.[3] This contention may or may not be applicable in Upper Canada and among all its national groups, but unfortunately in too many cases among the MHAS it is simply impossible to say with certainty what the ethnic background of everyone born in North America was. Even when something is known about the family background of individuals, the matter of ethnicity can be complex. The father of James Rogers Armstrong, MHA was born in Ireland. Obviously then Armstrong's "ethnicity" was Irish. But his father emigrated to America as a young man where he married into an old colonial family. James Rogers Armstrong's mother, Mary Rogers, was a sister of Robert and James Rogers of Roger's Rangers who fought against the French in the Seven Years' War. James Rogers Armstrong was born in Quebec (soon to be Lower Canada) in 1787. His Irish father died when he was five, his mother soon after, and he was sent to school in the United States for a period of ten years before finally settling permanently in Upper Canada, where he eventually became a pillar of the Toronto business community. Was his "ethnicity" really Irish, or British, or American, or Canadian? Putting real people into ethnic groups is not always as simple as it might seem.

The fact that the numbers of MHAS elected to the legislature were at first very small and then periodically increased as the population of the province grew creates a problem of numerical balance when trying to measure changes in the nature of elected representation over a period of time because the size of the group being examined changes from one time to another. Seventeen people sat in the first parliament (1792–6), seventy in the thirteenth (1836–41). As a result, in order to create for comparative purposes groups of early and later MHAS of roughly equal size, a certain amount of chronological telescoping has taken place. Two main groups, A and B have been artifically constructed. Group A, the "early" group, contains all the MHAS who were members of the House during the years 1792–1820. (Some of them of course, also sat in later Assemblies.) Group B the "later" group contains all the MHAS who sat in the Assembly between 1830 and 1841, some of whom similarly had served in earlier parliaments. There is in fact an overlap of seven MHAS between the two groups. Group A, though it represents a much longer period of time, contains 103 names, Group B, 138. These two groups, as will be seen, have been used frequently to test for a variety of forms of change over the whole Upper Canadian period. Besides these two main groups, a set of smaller transitional (and, of course, also overlapping) groups have been used to monitor change on a more gradual basis. Group AA (ninety-seven names) consists of all the MHAS who served during the years 1820–30. Group BA (ninety-nine names) consists of those MHAS who served *only* during the period 1830–41. At times as well other smaller groups of MHAS have been used as test groups, such as those who served *only* in the period 1820–30 (forty-nine names) and those who served in the last parliament of 1836–41 (seventy names). There are, needless to say, problems with applying such a system to a fifty-year period and to an expanding number of MHAS. This methodology also is not as neat and tidy as one might like, but it has been adopted as the best of several alternative schemes.

The increase in the number of MHAS between 1792 and 1841 suggests that the period was one of considerable growth and change within Upper Canadian society as a whole, which might also suggest that comparisons, especially between the earliest and latest dates in Upper Canadian history could be unduly artificial and misleading. Certainly the province grew in numbers alone. A population which in 1792 cannot have been much above 10,000 was by 1841 approaching half a million. That growth was reflected in the House of Assembly, most dramatically in 1820 when the number of MHAS rose from twenty-five to forty. Yet in many ways it can be argued that the society itself changed relatively little. The settlement or "pioneer" period, only nicely underway in 1792, was far from over in 1841 when a viable level of commercial agriculture was just beginning to be reached. In 1841 Upper Canada was, as it had always been, a profoundly rural province. Toronto, the capital and largest urban centre, had a population of only 14,249. The entire urban population in that year has been calculated as a mere 11.5 percent of the total population. The kinds of changes which would ultimately make Upper Canada a different sort of place had yet to happen in 1841. The reaper, the train, the telegraph, and a host of other technological wonders had yet to alter forever the pace of Upper Canadian life. Between 1792 and 1841 the landlocked backwoods province of Upper Canada had made progress, but only gradual progress, toward maturity.

Gradual social and economic change was reflected in the province's internal regional divisions. For general administrative purposes, especially for the purposes of local government, Upper Canada had early been divided into districts, each with its own set of district officials centering on a district town. It is primarily these districts, the names of which are largely unfamiliar now but which were once the only common and familiar geographical divisions of Upper Canada, that have been used in this study to denote regional locations and in discussions of regional variations. Just as there was periodic increase in representation in the assembly, there was naturally some increase in the number of districts between 1791 and 1841 and consequent changes in district boundaries. For that reason it has been necessary, in order to avoid endless confusion, to work with the district boundaries as they were at a particular time, to be exact, as they were in the year 1836, at which time there were twelve districts: Western, London, Gore, Niagara, Home, Newcastle, Midland, Prince Edward, Johnstown, Bathurst, Ottawa, and Eastern. One reason for stopping the district clock at 1836 is because in 1837 and 1838 a rash of new districts, eight in all, were proclaimed. Since these new districts, with names like Talbot, Brock, Wellington, and Victoria, would have taken some getting used to, and would not have been well-understood subdivisions of the province even by 1841, they have been ignored, except in necessary specific references, as terms of regional identification. On the other hand in 1836 almost all of the districts as of that date had been in existence for a very long time, Most of them (Western, Niagara, Newcastle, Midland, London, Johnstown, Home, and Eastern) dated from 1798 or earlier and were, for most Upper Canadians most of the time, the accepted and understood regional units. As such they are the most appropriate means of locating Upper Canadians in their own places and in their own time.

A last word about the use of the term "prominence" and of some synonyms for prominence which have been from time to time employed, such as "leadership." These terms are not meant to carry any exact technical meaning but are applied only to denote that the people so described enjoyed greater recognition and played more active roles in the affairs of their communities than did the majority of their contemporaries. Some of them, as has already been admitted, were not all that exceptional even in their own time, while others – John Beverley Robinson may be the best example – were beyond doubt very conspicuous and successful leaders of people and opinion. It is assumed that, taking the MHAS as a whole, "the law of self correcting error" will operate in the normal way.

CHAPTER ONE

Making a Living

Was there a "right" way to make a living in Upper Canada that provided a dependable route to prominence? There were quite a few possible ways of making a living, although none offered total assurance of success or security. The most popular occupations favoured by the 283 prominent Upper Canadians whose careers have been examined in this study, in descending order, were farming, public service, merchandising, milling, law, distilling, land development/speculation, lumbering, shipping, medicine, and surveying, followed by at least twenty-seven other occupations. The complete list, with the number of MHAS known to have been at some time involved in each is as follows:

1. Farmer 143
2. Public servant 112
3. Merchant 100
4. Miller 65
5. Lawyer 47
6. Distiller 24
7. Developer/speculator 21
8. Lumberman 19
9. Shipowner/builder/forwarder 19
10. Doctor 15
11. Surveyor/survey contractor 14
12. Journalist 12
13. Military officer 12
14. Fur trader 11
15. Inn/tavern Keeper 11
16. Businessman 9
17. Manufacturer 8
18. Contractor 7
19. Gentleman 6
20. Ferry operator 5
21. Tanner 4
22. Stage operator 3
23. Brewer 3
24. Auctioneer 3
25. Banker 3
26. Teacher 2
27. Carpenter 2
28. Builder 2
29. Promoter 2
30. Land agent 1
31. Ship's captain 1
32. Tailor 1

33 Quarry operator 1
34 Blacksmith 1
35 Apothecary 1
36 Inventor 1
37 Settlement superintendent 1
38 Sailor 1

Some of these occupational categories perhaps need a word or two of explanation. It could be argued that "gentleman" was not an occupation at all. In each case the label was self-applied and has been included because that was the way in which six people (John Stinson, James Atkinson, Jacob Shibley, Nicholas Lytle, Abraham Marsh, and Walter Freeman Gates) described themselves, and because it suggests that Upper Canada may have contained more people of a leisured class than might have been expected in a pioneer province.[1] "Survey contractor" may be an unfamiliar term. Survey contractors date from 1818, when the government of Upper Canada instituted a system of paying surveyors in land (4.5 percent of the land surveyed). The contractor agreed to complete the survey of a township or townships for which he hired and paid the actual surveyors.[2] Some survey contractors were themselves surveyors, but some, such as George Strange Boulton, Zaccheus Burnham, Thomas Hornor, and Henry Ruttan, were not. An activity which has been linked to survey contracting, land speculation,[3] also requires preliminary comment. (A fuller discussion will be found in chapter 2.) At the moment it is sufficient to say that, although the label "land speculator" has often been used fairly loosely, the relatively few people put into that category here are the result of applying a strict definition by which only those who are definitely known to have regularly acquired land for speculative resale have been included.

The list of occupations suggests a fairly limited range of occupational choices, with quite a bit of "bunching" into five or six main activities, but it also shows that 283 people were in total involved in 690 separate jobs. The striking fact about the working lives of these prominent people is not what occupations they followed, but the extent to which they (evidently in common with similar groups elsewhere) changed or combined them.[4] Throughout the Upper Canadian period, having more than one calling, either in sequence or at the same time, was decidedly the rule rather than the exception. The well-known cases of William Warren Baldwin and John Rolph who practised both law and medicine were not examples of unusual personal energy or personal eccentricity, but in fact their occupational dualism was part of a thoroughly mainstream career pattern. Nor did the trend to multiple occupations decrease much, as might have been expected, as a more complex and more specialized Upper Canadian society evolved between 1791 and 1841. Among the 103

MHAS whose public lives were spent mainly in the period before 1820 (Group A), 77 percent are known to have had more than one occupation. For the later group of 138 who served mainly in the 1820s and 1830s (Group B), the proportion was still about 70 percent.

Two basic kinds of occupational patterns appear to be connected to the fact that so few regional leaders found a single occupation and stuck with it. Some men changed jobs because they hoped to do better financially in another (or in a number of other) lines of work. On the other hand, some simply added occupations to those they already followed, building outward from an initial enterprise either by a process of horizontal growth on the basis of existing assets or credit to add strength to strength or to provide alternative sources of revenue as a hedge against hard times. Both patterns imply a preoccupation with security. The first could be an anxious, even frantic, process of searching for the right route to safe, comfortable circumstances. The second was more likely to reflect a series of calculated risks or the reinvestment of accumulated capital. Both processes could and sometimes did produce ultimate well-being – a steady government job finally acquired after a long period of trying farming or storekeeping or something else; a thriving business complex of stores, mills and shops built up gradually from a small beginning. Both, in the economic conditions of the time, could also end in failure.

The occupational histories of some well-known and some lesser-known Upper Canadian MHAS may help to explain more about the way in which occupations were changed or combined. Peter Robinson, whose Loyalist-soldier/office-holder/lawyer father died when Peter was thirteen, first followed a business career as a fur trader, shipping furs from Penetanguishene to Toronto. He also built a grist mill on the Yonge Street route at Holland Landing and subsequently added an inn near the mill. Early in the 1820s his career took a sharp turn. He became a government employee, first of the British government, supervising the emigration to and settlement in Upper Canada of two Irish groups. At the same time (after serving during the war of 1812 and as an MHA in 1816–24) he was appointed to the Executive Council of Upper Canada and in 1827 became commissioner of crown lands, posts which brought him a handsome combined salary of £1,100 per year.[5] Nevertheless, when he died in 1838 the "unbusinesslike" commissioner left a debt to government of over £10,000, not all of which could be liquidated from his estate; his younger brother, Chief Justice John Beverly Robinson, eventually made up the difference.[6]

Thomas Parke, an Irish immigrant, began his working life in Upper Canada as a carpenter in Toronto and then moved to London where he became a builder and developer and then editor of a newspaper. He too turned for security to government service. After a period in politics, he was surveyor general (1841–5) and then collector of customs at Port Colborne and St. Catharines. The latter position he accepted at age sixty-seven, four years before his death.[7] John Macdonell (Scotus) at age twenty-six joined the North West Company as a clerk. By 1809 he was a partner in charge of the Athabaska River department. He returned to Upper Canada in time to serve in the War of 1812 and then settled on 1,426 acres of land he had bought in Hawkesbury Township. He opened a store in what became Point Fortune and added grist and saw mills. He went into the forwarding business on the Ottawa and along the way served as judge of the Ottawa district court. None of these activities produced ultimate security. In his last years he was heavily in debt from mortgages on his land and from debts owed to Montreal suppliers.[8]

Donald Bethune, son of the Reverend John Bethune, Loyalist and pioneer Presbyterian clergyman, trained in law in the office of Jonas Jones of Brockville and practised first in Kingston beginning in 1824. He quickly became a district court judge of Bathurst District in 1826 and of Prince Edward District in 1834. His ambition outran a legal career. He got into the highly-competitive steamboat business on Lake Ontario in 1833. This took him to Cobourg in 1840, to Toronto in 1843, and to financial ruin by 1848. After a five-year absence in England he returned to Upper Canada, took up his old profession of law at Port Hope, and at length achieved a stable level of prosperity.[9]

Zaccheus Burnham was an even more explicit example of success through steady stages. An American immigrant from New Hampshire, he arrived in the Cobourg area about 1794, where he farmed and, in 1805, opened a distillery. After the War of 1812 he expanded his interests to include mill sites in Otonabee Township and contracted for the survey of several townships. As an additional sideline, he went into the private mortgage and loan business. Public office also came his way. He was treasurer of the Newcastle District for almost thirty years and for a shorter time was a district court judge. His achievements and level of solvency were recognized by an appointment to the Legislative Council in 1837.[10] George Brouse of Matilda Township provides a similar example. The son of a Loyalist private, he inherited 100 acres of land from his father. He farmed it, prospered, and bought more. Some time after 1814 he opened a store on his land. In the 1820s he added steam-driven grist and saw mills, a shingle factory, and a woolen mill. A village eventually called

Iroquois grew up around his enterprises and on its incorporation he was the first reeve. The post office and later the telegraph office were installed in his store. In a comfortable old age, according to local account, he could afford black servants and a race horse.[11]

George Lyon's story was very similar though with a different ending. After service as a British army officer for twelve years, he accepted a grant of land in the military settlement at Richmond. By arrangement with the Quartermaster General's Department, he undertook to build a saw and grist mill for the settlers in exchange for more land. He added in turn a distillery, a fulling mill, a forge, a store, and a potashery. But business was not as good for Lyon in Richmond as it was for Brouse in Iroquois or for Burnham in Cobourg. By the 1840s he was deeply in debt. In 1849, two years before his death at sixty-one, he sought and accepted a lieutenancy in the Royal Canadian Rifles, and immediately sold the commission in order to get his hands on some much-needed cash.[12]

The career of John Clark of Louth Township, Niagara District, is another variant on the kinds of life patterns already described. He was the son of a former army barracksmaster and sheriff of the Niagara District. He was apprenticed as a clerk in the store of Forsyth and Company at Niagara but then went into private business with a partner as an Indian trader and failed. He tried farming, land speculation, and the manufacture of potash and lime. After serving in the War of 1812, in the assembly for six years, and as secretary of the Welland Canal Company, he found his permanent niche at age fifty-two as collector of customs at Port Dalhousie.[13] William Chisholm, the founder of Oakville, was less lucky. After many years spent in building up a personal business empire through storekeeping, milling, and a harbour company, and after acquiring the offices of postmaster and collector of customs of Oakville, he overextended his resources in order to create a manufacturing centre using hydraulic power to be obtained by damming Sixteen-mile Creek. He died a ruined man, his property and other assets seized for the payment of his debts.[14]

As the merest glance at the career of all 283 MHAS will show, the multi-occupational pattern could be illustrated many times over. The Upper Canadian economy provided no certain route to comfort and peace of mind. Many Upper Canadians in whatever line of work would likely have been prepared to apply to their own circumstances the gloomy view of his chosen occupation held by an Ottawa Valley lumberman. "It must be desperation which drives people to lumber, and madness which continues them in it."[15] Making a living was a serious business when cash was hard to come by and when, in most cases, a large family required support and eventually some sort of training or stake in their own futures. Anxiety as much as ambition was likely to be the engine that drove men on in the search for the right path to security.

Among the variety of occupations which prominent Upper Canadians periodically turned to, the most common of all throughout the entire period was farming. Among all of the 283 MHAS just over one-half (143) can be said to have farmed at some time in their lives. It should not come as a surprise however to find that about three-quarters of the farmer–MHAS also at some time or other are known to have followed other lines of work.

It was natural that farming would be an almost universal preoccupation of the prominent and the obscure alike during the initial Loyalist settlement period of the province's history, since there were so few other ways for most people, even those who had been urbanites elsewhere, to make a living. Besides, whatever else the first settlers lacked, they did not lack land. The early leaders especially (many of whom were former officers of Loyalist regiments, plus the few who were brought from the mother country to fill government jobs) were given large amounts of land, far more land in fact than they could possibly use, at least in the short run. Yet the land in the original settlement areas, once the appalling task of clearing some of it had been accomplished, was productive. After a time farming provided at least subsistence and, if markets were available, either at local garrisons or eventually in Europe or Lower Canada for basic products like flour, pork, and potash, it could sometimes yield real rewards.

Farming was in some respects the easiest occupation to enter, requiring only the land and some measure of aptitude for the work, although any hope of success in farming also required some initial investment, in supplies, implements, and stock, which has been said to have been at least £100.[16] For some prominent Upper Canadians, despite the physical demands, or perhaps because of the availability of hired or family help, farming was, and remained, a chosen, satisfying way of life. When the younger William Buell retired after twenty-six years in politics and journalism, mixed with ventures into insurance, real estate development, and a book store, he wanted nothing more than to return to "the peaceful and quiet occupation of an agriculturalist."[17] Though E.W. Thomson was a busy contractor who worked on the Rideau, Welland, and St. Lawrence canals, his attachment to agriculture bordered on the fanatical as an importer and breeder of purebred livestock, founder and president of the Provincial Agricultural Association, president of the Farmer's Mutual Fire Insurance Company, and Canadian representative at two exhibitions in London. His death in 1865 occurred as he might have wished, while walking from his Toronto Township farm (near present-day Dundas and Keele streets) to Toronto to attend a meeting of the Agricultural Association.[18] Peter Shaver of Matilda Township retired from storekeeping at seventy-one but continued to farm his land for at least another thirteen years.[19]

Farming, of course, was not to everyone's taste. "Farming is a losing concern to such as I am," Donald Fraser wrote with feeling from Lanark in 1827, hoping to be given some kind of government job. He had served in the Royal Scots in Europe and America for thirty years; none of this experiences had prepared him for the life of a backwoods farmer on indifferent land.[20] Farming in any case was, among the MHAS, an occupation which declined over time. For them, rural depopulation may almost be said to have begun the day after rural settlement began. Among the mainly pre-1820 Group A MHAS, 64 percent were or had been farmers for a time, but if, as has been suggested, "the leaders of the first Loyalist generation were particularly concerned to escape from the fate of subsistence farming,"[21] the succeeding generations were even more anxious to get off the land. Among the later Group B MHAS, the percentage involved in full- or part-time farming had dropped to 44 percent.

The same point can be made in an even more graphic way by contrasting two early and late groups by place of birth – the Loyalist generation born in the Thirteen Colonies and the native-born whose birthplace was Upper Canada itself. Seventy-eight percent of those born in the Thirteen Colonies were, or were at some time, farmers. Among those born in Upper Canada the equivalent figure was only 43 percent.

There were many reasons why farming declined as an occupation among regional leaders. It was back-breaking work. It was not the work of a gentleman (Though many of the MHAS would not have claimed that title); it represented for some a lowered status compared to former stations in life. Free land became less available, especially to newcomers with no official qualifications, after the government changed its policy to a sale rather than a grant system in 1826.

For many people farming simply turned out not to be very profitable, at least in the short run. As Professor McCalla has put it, farming was long seen as producing "not income, as we might define it, but wealth, as measured in terms of a productive, long-term income-earning farm with a capital value that would be expected to grow as the economy did."[22] Many farmers were not prepared to wait for the long term. And naturally between 1791 and 1841 the number of possible alternative careers greatly increased. Young men could be trained for a profession or given a start in business. Farming declined while, as shall be seen, the professions expanded. In a general way it can be said that the Loyalist leaders were farmers, but their sons were urban dwellers, merchants or lawyers or employees of government. Yet that statement greatly undervalues the continuing importance of farming. Sons of Loyalists continued to farm, and immigrants in the 1820s and 1830s began to farm, at least for a time. A period of change during which farming ceased to be a majority and became a minority occupation among regional leaders certainly occurred, but it occurred less rapidly than might have been expected and less rapidly than some would have liked.

Next to farming, the most heavily favoured occupation or occupational sideline among MHAS was public service. Among the 283 MHAS, 112 of them were able to get some sort of income-producing public appointment at one time or another, not including appointments as magistrate, postmaster, coroner or local appointments such as poundkeeper, pathmaster, assessor, etc. (These have been excluded either because they do not appear to have generated any appreciable income or because reliable records have not been found.) The appointments in question therefore are of five types: the judiciary, principally the Court of King's Bench; positions in the provincial civil establishment at the capital, which could range from executive councillor to a clerkship; district offices such as judge, treasurer, sheriff, or clerk of the peace; county offices, consisting only of registrars of deeds; and positions as collectors in the Customs Department.

It must be said immediately that public service, like other occupations, provided no guarantee of solvency or permanency. Government jobs could sometimes come to an abrupt end, as a result for instance of some form of real or alleged political or other deviance. Joseph Willcocks was an early example of impermanency, being fired by Lieutenant Governor Gore from his position as sheriff of the Home District in 1807 for "general and notorious bad conduct."[23] In 1836 Charles Fothergill was dismissed as king's printer by Sir Peregrine Maitland for criticizing his administration. In 1836 William Warren Baldwin was removed by Sir Francis Bond Head from his position as judge of the Home District court, an office he had held since 1809.

There were other disadvantages to public service. Not all government positions paid well. The income from many positions depended partly, and in some cases entirely, on fees. The fees arising from some appointments in the central bureaucracy, such as that of attorney general, could more than triple the amount of an already substantial salary but such cases were rare. The fees earned on the value of goods and seizures by a collector of customs at a small, little used port could amount to only a few pounds a year.[24] Still it was *possible* to live on the income from even a modest appointment, to be nothing but a district sheriff or treasurer or clerk of the peace, but for most such office-holders the multi-occupational pattern already described also applied. It was quite possible, indeed common, to hold a government office and also to farm or to run a business. Lawyer, businessman, and survey contractor George Strange Boulton of Cobourg was considered a man of substantial wealth, yet he held onto the office of registrar of Northumberland County, acquired at the age of twenty-seven, until his death forty-five years later. (The duties of the office were carried out by a deputy to whom Boulton paid about one-third of the registrar's income.)[25] The office of sheriff of the Home District was held for a period of twenty-nine years by W.B. Jarvis before he handed it over to his nephew. The fees arising from the office, around £500 annually, gave him a secure living, yet he also evidently had the free time to involve himself in a multitude of other activities, business, political, social, and charitable.[26] On the other hand, F.L. Walsh, who was registrar of the Surrogate Court of the London District for twenty-nine years and registrar of Norfolk County for what may have been a record-breaking seventy-four years, seems never to have been much involved in other matters.

While public service was frequently one part of a multi-occupational package, it was also fairly common for one government employee to hold more than one government office either concurrently or one at a time. Among the 112 men who have been identified as having held a public office with some income-producing potential, forty-one, or 37 percent, at one time or another held more than one post and thirty (27 percent) are known to have held two or more offices at the same time. For some, plural office-holding may have been a matter of sheer ambition or even greed, but for others pluralism was more a matter of necessity. An example of the first type, "one of the most respectable barristers in the province"[27] practising in the growing town of Brockville and a successful petitioner for 1,900 acres of land including valuable mill sites on the Ottawa River, L.P. Sherwood was also an indefatigable and highly fortunate applicant for public office. He was appointed collector of customs at Brockville and registrar of Leeds and Carleton counties in 1801, judge of the Surrogate Court of the Johnstown District in 1812, judge of the Johnstown District Court in 1820 and judge of the Eastern District court in 1821. All of these positions he retained until he cashed them in for a senior judicial appointment as a judge of the Court of King's Bench, in 1825. Richard Phillips Hotham, though also a lawyer by profession, had an initial experience of the second kind on the frontier of settlement in the Ottawa District. Locating in the little village of L'Orignal in 1820 to fill the offices of registrar of Prescott and Russell counties and clerk of the peace and registrar of the Surrogate Court of the Ottawa District, he found the combined revenues barely enough to keep him in life and health (which, as it happened, was chronically bad). Eventually, the gradual growth of population and the addition of the offices of clerk of the District Court in 1835 and inspector of licences in 1837 supplied him with the means to achieve a degree of comfort. After twenty years, the proceeds of his five offices permitted him to take a leave of absence and a trip home to his native England. Alas, the "asthmatic affection" from which he had long suffered proved fatal while he was still on the Atlantic, fifteen days out of Québec.[28]

There is no doubt that some forms of public service allowed the incumbents a comfortable living or at the least a useful income supplement. Critics of the provincial administration often alleged that government employees were grossly overpaid or that office-holders concealed the true extent of their incomes. Reform newspapers customarily provided their readers with long lists of officials and their sources of income, culled from the government's own returns in the annual Blue Books. The following examples are from the Brockville *Recorder* of 12 June 1835.

D'Arcy Boulton, Auditor General, (no duties, no salary, was a sinecure of £246 value in 1833) Master in Chancery Legislative Council, £60 ... John Beikie, Clerk, Executive Council, £222 salary; £278 Fees; £222, in lieu of Fees on Patents on lands ... John B. Robinson, Speaker, Legislative Council, salary £400; Chief Justice King's Bench, salary £1666 (In 1833 his income as speaker of the Council was £200, now it is £400) ... Archibald McLean, Speaker, House of Assembly, £200, Clerk of the Peace, E. District, £148, Registrar of Stormont and Dundas, £132, Registrar, Surrogate Court, £11 (Mr. McLean is also Captain on half-pay late Incorporated Militia, £142) ... Henry Ruttan, Sheriff, Newcastle District, fees £1040 (Fees in 1833 £1180, has also 4s. sterling per day as half-pay Lieutenant, Incorporated Militia) ... W.B. Jarvis, Sheriff, Home District, fees, £550. (It is scarcely probable that the fees of the Sheriff of the Home District do not far exceed £550, but we give his own return).

Given the obvious benefits that could arise from holding a government job, it is a little surprising to find that over time public service, like farming, was a declining occupation among regional leadership figures, although in each case the reasons for this decline were likely very different. If we examine the activities of the members of the first few parliaments of the Legislative Assembly of Upper Canada, when the membership was admittedly very small, it is striking how many MHAS were also, that is at the same time, office-holders. In the first parliament nine of seventeen members were office-holders; in the second parliament, ten of seventeen; and in the third parliament, twelve of twenty (for a record high level of 60 percent). Though the figures show a continuing decline thereafter, as late as the sixth parliament (1812–16) half of the members, fourteen of twenty-eight, held offices. For the 103 MHAS in the pre-1820 Group A, the figures for those who held office at any time are 54 of 103, or 52 percent. The corresponding figures for the later Group B are significantly different. Only 48 out of a total of 138, or 35 percent, ever held public office in the period before 1841. Among those who held public office concurrently with elected office, the low point was reached during the tenth parliament (1828–30) when only nine of forty-eight MHAS were also government employees.

Political change of necessity had an important impact on the level of office-holding among MHAS. The appearance by the 1820s of a continuing group of regional politicians who were out of sympathy and out of favour with the provincial administration naturally meant that fewer government jobs went to people of this type. Yet this is not a total explanation. Even in the several parliaments of the 1830s, in which government supporters were definitely a majority, the level of concurrent elected – appointed office rose only marginally. In the last or thirteenth Parliament – which was the result of a Tory landslide, and in which a number of opposition members who abruptly left politics were replaced by true-blue loyalists – only twenty-one of the seventy MHAS (30 percent) who served in that parliament also held office at the same time. Indeed only twenty-three of them had ever held appointed office at any time.

It seems likely that fewer people were able to make a living as government employees as time passed because the number of available positions grew more slowly than the number of potential applicants. Certainly the number of positions grew more slowly than the population as a whole, especially in the 1830s.[29] One office, that of the auditor general of land patents, of which D'Arcy Boulton was the last incumbent, was actually abolished. Much earlier, in 1794, an entire level of the judiciary, the Court of Common Pleas, was done away with by Lieutenant Governor Simcoe, leaving some dozen former judges, among them Benjamin Pawling, Nathaniel Pettit, and John Macdonell (Aberchalder), stripped of their judicial function and of a part of their status in their communities.

There was, of course, some overall growth in the Upper Canadian public service and also some increase in government salaries and fees, reflecting a rising level of government business, a rising population, and a rising cost of living, but so far as potential opportunities were concerned aspirants outside the capital probably had better prospects than those in or near Toronto. The number of district governments increased markedly, especially in the later stages of the Upper Canadian period. The original four districts became twenty by 1841; eight of these were created in 1837 and 1838 alone. Each new district meant a complete new slate of district offices. The competition for these (the main positions were judge of the district court, clerk of the district court, sheriff, treasurer, and clerk of the peace) was understandably keen, but the rising population, fuelled by high immigration in the 1820s and 1830s, meant that inevitably many were disappointed, even those whose credentials and political orthodoxy were never in doubt. The scarcity of offices made no evident difference to the number of applicants, as the correspondence which reached the lieutenant governor or his secretary amply demonstrates.[30] Many prominent Upper Canadians may have given up farming willingly and even eagerly. Their relative withdrawal from public service was a reluctant, and for some no doubt an embittering, experience.

A fairly short list of activities made up the principal business opportunities available to Upper Canadian regional leaders. Storekeeping, milling, distilling, lumbering, and land development were the major forms of business, with storekeeping especially and milling far more common than any of the others. All of these enterprises were expanding occupations among the MHAS, that is they were taken up by a greater proportion of them as the period progressed, except milling, which showed a slight falling off in popularity from 27 to 21 percent. This decline of milling as an occupation among the MHAS is a bit puzzling since milling, particularly saw milling, was generally on the increase.[31] A few possible explanations suggest themselves. Some of the mill sites first exploited turned out to be impractical or unprofitable; the steam mills which began to appear in the 1820s required more capital to set up and maintain.

By 1840 milling could be a complex and specialized business. The census of 1842 lists, in addition to ordinary grist and saw mills, oatmeal mills, barley mills, carding mills, fulling mills, oil mills, and paper mills.[32] But growing diversification did not necessarily mean growing stability or prosperity. The number of mills in the province grew but not at an especially rapid rate, certainly not as fast as most other "economic indicators" such as population growth, cleared land, or bank notes in circulation. Population, for example, increased by more than two and one half times between 1826 and 1841, but the number of grist mills did not come close to doubling in the same period and (if the census figures can be trusted) actually declined in four years. In the 1830s, the number of saw mills increased at a brisker pace but not as rapidly as the general population rate. (Saw mills also show a decline in two years during the 1830s.)[33] It seems likely that grist milling in particular, like farming to which it was economically linked, proved to be an uncertain occupation in the face of fluctuating export demand and fluctuating imperial trade policy. Farmers might be able to survive and even expand their acreage during the 1830s despite "steeply declining volumes of exports to metropolitan markets and declining prices for the basis staple export."[34] It is less clear that millers were in a similar position. As well, milling, like farming, was never a very easy, pleasant, or glamorous way to make a living, and more and more prominent men may have chosen to avoid it.

Storekeeping, which over the whole period attracted the greatest number of adherents after farming and public service, and attracted an increasing number of MHAS (31 percent of Group A and 38 percent of Group B) could vary widely in the scope of the individual business. The modest establishment begun by John Ferguson and his partner in Sydney Township in 1789 to trade "with the Indians and such of the settlers who could pay for the goods they might buy"[35] may have been quite typical of its time, but most mercantile businesses started later or in more promising locations were a good deal more substantial. A small shipment of goods destined for Richard Beasely's store on Burlington Heights was captured by the Americans in 1814; he estimated the goods to have a (possibly inflated) value of £600.[36] In 1821, Anthony Manahan of Anthony Manahan and Company, Kingston, imported in a single shipment 27,744 pounds of "manufactured tobacco" from the United States at a cost of £964.[37] It has been said that it was possible to open a store with a capital of no more than £150[38] but many businesses must have represented investments of a much greater order.

The stores run by people like Ferguson, Beasely, or Manahan were usually genuine "general" stores. Beasely's itemized list of his merchandise lost in 1814 included soap, sugar, putty, wine, cordial, gunpowder, nails, window glass, mustard, snuff, pepper, and tea.

Other similar lists show equal or greater variety. One item of sale was an almost invariable element of storekeeping. Most merchants applied to their local magistrates to become "shopkeepers licensed to sell spirits."

The main "professional" careers open to prominent Upper Canadians were law, medicine, and journalism. Medicine and journalism, although they showed an increase in popularity among the MHAS, were actually practised by so few of them – fifteen doctors and twelve journalists in the entire period – that the only general observation which seems appropriate at this point is that neither of these professions were seen by most prominent Upper Canadians before 1841 as being likely to produce a reliable income or as being the pursuit of a gentleman. They were in fact very often, and in the case of medicine almost exclusively, the pursuit of local political leaders of a Reform or even Radical political stripe, a fact which may have tended to bring not only the men but their occupations into some disrepute in the eyes of the provincial establishment.

The law, on the other hand, was an eminently respectable profession and was also a profession which attracted a growing proportion of the MHAS, though before 1841 the law was by no means a majority profession among regional leaders. Only forty-seven (17 percent) of all of the MHAS in the period 1791–1841 were trained in or practised law. It need scarcely be said, though, that as a group the lawyers had certain advantages over members of other occupations. Except for a very brief period in the province's history, legal training was a mandatory qualification for entry to the judiciary which, especially at the top level (the Court of King's Bench) provided one of the best-paid and most secure government appointments available. The law was also naturally a prerequisite for an appointment as solicitor general or attorney general, frequent stepping-stones to a high judicial appointment. Legal training was not seen simply as a potential form of qualification for the bench, but as the best possible background for a wide range of government jobs. When Upper Canadian public service appointments held by MHAS are linked to the other major occupations it becomes immediately clear how true this was. Of the forty-seven lawyer-MHAS, thirty-four, or 74 percent, also at one time or another held one or more appointed government positions. Among the other main occupations none had anywhere near so high a rate of overlap with public service, the merchants coming in second at 43 percent. It is not difficult to see why many second and third generation Upper Canadians were encouraged to enter the legal profession. It had not become an overcrowded field, there was more and more legal work to be done, and the law could provide a route to other attractive side benefits.

The period 1791–1841 saw the virtual disappearance of some occupations among the prominent and the appearance of some new ones. At one time it was possible to live in Upper Canada and have a military career. John Macdonell (Aberchalder) and his brother Hugh, R.N. Wilkinson, and Hazelton Spencer all served as officers of the Royal Canadian Volunteers garrisoned at Kingston and Fort George until that unit was disbanded in 1802. David Cowan served for seventeen years on the Great Lakes as a lieutenant of the provincial marine until his death in 1808. G.B. Hall also spent many years on the lakes in British ships and as a naval storekeeper before going on half pay in 1814. Thomas McKee held a commission as lieutenant in the Sixtieth Regiment while he was actually employed by the Indian Department at St. Joseph's Island and at Amherstburgh, until he sold his commission in 1806, having been forced to choose between staying in Upper Canada or rejoining his regiment. These were almost the last military politicians in Upper Canada. After their day only J.B. Marks, who sat in the last parliament (1836–41) had a similar career as the long-time and sole custodian of the deserted Kingston dockyard.

In a similar way but for different reasons innkeeping as a way of making a living took a nosedive among the prominent. Pre-1820 MHAS John Fanning, Peter Howard, Thomas McCrae, Benajah Mallory, Abraham Markle, William Terry, and even Peter Robinson had at some point kept inns, but among the later MHAS only Caleb Hopkins and John Chesser are known to have been involved in an occupation which was evidently no longer considered entirely respectable.

A few "new" occupations began to make their appearance on the MHA list around the end of the Upper Canadian period. "Manufacturer" seems the right term for J.R. Armstrong (stoves), J.W. Gamble (cloth), or James Crooks (paper). For others the trend to a multiplicity of commercial and financial activities requires even broader terms. For the affairs of men like W.H. Merritt, A.N. MacNab, Michael Aikman, J.S. Cartwright, C.C. Ferrie, Edward Malloch, or Asa Werden, which included company presidencies or directorships and several types of investment or promotion, "entrepreneur" or simply "businessman" are probably the appropriate labels.

Allan MacNab provides one example of early entrepreneurial activities on a fairly wide scale during the 1820s and 1830s and of the increasing use of other people's money through joint stock corporations and extensive borrowing from banks and individuals. He was involved as promoter, officer, and shareholder in a number of early joint-stock companies, including the Desjardin Canal Company, in which W.W. and Robert Baldwin were also large shareholders, the Grand River Navigation Company, in which two of his associates were W.H. Merritt and Absalom Shade, and a joint stock company formed to provide steamboat service from Hamilton to Niagara and Toronto, a scheme in which he was joined by William Chisholm and C.C. Ferrie, among others.[39] Despite a rate of economic growth that was a good deal less than spectacular, Upper Canadian leaders kept looking for new and more sophisticated ways to make a living and for the best route, or combination of routes, to security.

No occupation guaranteed security nor did any occupation guarantee prominence, but it is safe to say that there were a few occupations (farming, public service, storekeeping, milling, and law) that were by far the most frequent pursuits of the prominent. The numerical line between law as an occupation and the next most common occupation (distilling) in a sharp one. The actual number of MHAS following, at some time, one of the leading five occupations is more than double the number of all other MHAS in all the other occupations. Because most of those who became prominent chose their occupations from quite a narrow range of options, it can be said first, that not all that many promising options existed, and second, that only a few were perceived by most people as being the best way for an aspiring Upper Canadian to rise in the world. Here it is perhaps wise to restate an earlier point about the importance of farming. Although there were clear trends over time among the MHAS toward the increasing choice of commerce or law, throughout the period farming was the basic occupation; a declining occupation, certainly, but it was still taken up at some point by more prominent people than any other, and also significant, over the whole period it was the leading single occupation – that is, there was a higher percentage of known cases (24 percent) of people having only farming as their occupation than for any other occupation. (Law had the next highest rate as a single occupation, 17 percent.) Upper Canada before 1841 was an overwhelmingly rural province, an agricultural province. Upper Canada's regional leaders, as distinct from the leaders of the central bureaucracy, faithfully reflected their rural, agricultural, and only gradually urbanizing society.

Not all Upper Canadian leaders, early or late, were attracted to the range of occupational opportunities in the same ways. There are some distinctions which can be made among the occupations favoured by MHAS, for example on national and denominational grounds. Some national and some religious goups of MHAS can be

TABLE 1
Main Occupations, Groups A and B

	Group A (103)		*Group B (138)*	
	Number	*Percentage*	*Number*	*Percentage*
Farmer	66	64.1	61	44.2
Public Servant	54	52.4	48	34.8
Merchant	32	31.1	53	38.4
Miller	28	27.2	29	21.1
Lawyer	12	11.6	24	17.4

shown to have participated more than others in certain kinds of occupations and (what is perhaps more significant) in some occupations some groups were represented marginally or not at all. Public service is an obvious case in point because some identifiable groups of MHAS, notably Post-Loyalist Americans and Methodists (often the same people) were largely excluded from anything more than the most basic, non-paying public offices, while immigrant Scots and English especially, and the native-born increasingly, were quite evident among those who acquired "higher status" or revenue-producing government jobs. Public service, however, was an occupation which was not so much a matter of choice as of being chosen, by a process of patronage dispensed by a central elite. As such, public service forms the subject of a later chapter on power and patronage, where an attempt is made to examine and explain the apparent criteria, nationality and religious denomination among them, for selection to government posts.

Farming was a different matter. Over the entire Upper Canadian period, farming was primarily the preserve of North Americans, the Loyalist element, as has been seen, being initially mostly farmers for want of much else to do. Their North American immigrant successors, the Post-Loyalist Americans, were also, to a greater extent than was true of any of the other national groups among MHAS, farmers. Even near the end of the Upper Canadian period, in the 1830s, some 52 percent of Post-Loyalist American MHAS were still or had been farmers. Farming too continued to be a popular occupation among native-born Upper Canadians and other British North American-born MHAS. United Kingdom immigrant MHAS were not overall particularly keen farmers; not very many of the Scots especially were farmers, and fewer of them were farmers at the end of the period than previously, although the English MHAS provided an exception to the general pattern. Among seventeen immigrant English MHAS who were in the Assembly in the 1830s, nearly half were or had been farmers, the same proportion than was true of the rather larger group of those born anywhere in British North America (that is, in Upper or Lower Canada, "French Canada," the Thirteen Colonies, or one of the Atlantic provinces), of whom only about 47 percent were farmers. Viewed as a declining occupation among the regionally prominent, it can be said that on a national basis two separate groups were part of a contrary mini-trend by staying in farming longest, immigrants from England and from the United States, but there is a distinction which can be made between the two groups. The English were mainly recent immigrants, using farming as a first, unfamiliar occupation in a new situation; the Post-Loyalist Americans had in general been in the colony longer and were often continuing to do something they or their fathers had done before.

A great deal has been written about the mercantile community in Upper Canada which would lead one to expect that the Scots, especially the Protestant Scots, would be very prominent in it.[40] Such an assumption, so far as the MHAS are concerned, appears to be perfectly warranted. Among the main national groups, the Scottish MHAS had among themselves the highest proportion of merchants, about 46 percent. Although Scots comprised only 13.4 percent of all the MHAS, and among the general population (as of 1842) only 8.1 percent,[41] the Scottish MHAS were decidedly over-represented among merchants. Of the merchant-MHAS sitting in the Assembly in the 1830s, 21 percent were Scottish. But in this case the Scots had a rival national group. Paradoxically, the Post-Loyalist American MHAS, who have just been seen to have been a group which remained prominent in a declining occupation, farming, were at the same time a group which was prominent, and increasingly prominent, in an expanding occupation, merchandising. Overall, about 43 percent of Post-Loyalist American MHAS at some time became merchants. In Group B the proportion of merchants among them exceeded that of the Scots, 52 to 48 percent. Like the Scots, Post-Loyalist Americans made up about 13 percent of all MHAS but in the general population of 1842 the American-born were a considerably smaller group, only 6.7 percent,[42] yet they accounted for exactly one-quarter of the merchants among the MHAS who sat in the 1830s. Many Post-Loyalist American MHAS may have begun life in Upper Canada as farmers, and quite a few continued to farm, but as a group they also had strong commercial ambitions. By contrast the proportion of

TABLE 2
Farming and National Origin

National Origin	*Number of Farmers*	*Percentage of National Group*	*Percentage of Total Farmers*
Total farmer–			
MHAS 143		–	100
Group B 61		–	100
Thirteen Colonies			
Total 59	46	77.9	32.2
Group B 3	2	66.6	3.3
Upper Canada			
Total 53	23	43.4	16.2
Group B 39	17	43.6	27.9
Post-Loyalist American			
Total 37	21	56.8	14.8
Group B 27	14	51.8	22.9
British North American			
Total 23	10	43.5	7.1
Group B 13	7	53.8	11.5
Scotland			
Total 39	13	33.3	9.1
Group B 23	7	30.4	11.5
England and Wales			
Total 33	13	39.4	9.1
Group B 17	8	47.1	13.1
Ireland			
Total 18	4	22.2	2.8
Group B 10	3	33.3	4.9
French Canada			
Total 3	2	66.6	1.4
Group B 1	0	0	0
Unknown			
Total 17	11	64.7	7.7
Group B 5	3	60.0	4.9

merchant-MHAS who were native-born British Americans did not increase at all over time during a period when more MHAS as a whole became merchants. Of course the native-born MHAS constituted the largest number of merchants, because there were so many of them (138 out of the total 283) but as a percentage of *all* merchants their showing was not impressive. Overall they made up about 44 percent of the merchant-MHAS and in the 1830s the percentage was much

TABLE 3
Merchants and National Origin

National Origin	*Number of Merchants*	*Percentage of National Group*	*Percentage of Total Merchants*
Total merchant–MHAS 100			
Group B 53			
Thirteen Colonies			
Total 59	15	25.4	15.0
Group B 3	1	33.3	1.9
Upper Canada			
Total 53	21	38.8	21.0
Group B 39	14	35.9	26.4
Scotland			
Total 39	18	46.2	18.0
Group B 23	11	47.8	20.7
England and Wales			
Total 33	10	30.3	10.0
Group B 17	4	23.5	7.5
Post-Loyalist American			
Total 37	16	43.2	16.0
Group B 27	14	51.8	26.4
British North American			
Total 23	6	26.1	6.0
Group B 13	3	23.1	5.7
Ireland			
Total 18	5	27.8	5.0
Group B 10	2	20.0	3.7
French Canada			
Total 3	2	66.6	2.0
Group B 1	1	100.0	1.9
Other (J. Beikie)			
Total 1	1	100.00	1.0
Group B 0	0	0	0
Unknown			
Total 17	6	35.3	6.0
Group B 5	2	33.3	3.7
All British America			
Total 138	44	31.9	44.0
Group B 56	19	33.9	35.8

smaller, despite the fact that by the end of the 1830s the native-born constituted 54 percent of the general population.[43]

In the other major commercial activity, milling, and in the related fields of distilling and manufacturing, the situation was very similar. In these also the Scots and the Post-Loyalist Americans participated well above the level which their numbers among MHAS and among the general population would have indicated. And here again, although the early Loyalist group had naturally been prominent in milling, toward the end of the Upper Canadian period the native British American element among MHAS involved in these industries was not impressive; they comprised only about 29 percent of millers, distillers, and manufacturers, despite making up 40 percent of the MHAS and, of course, a much larger percentage of the general population.

The one major profession practised by the MHAS, the law, presents some intriguing differences in national origins. The Scots and the Post-Loyalist Americans, so visible in the main mercantile and industrial occupations of the time, were close to invisible in the legal profession. Only three lawyers born in Scotland, Angus Macdonell (Collachie), John Macdonell (Greenfield), and Allan McLean, and three born in the United States, the two Bidwells and G.S. Boulton, served as MHAS during the entire Upper Canadian period (and Boulton was really only of "technical" American birth having been born in New York State to an English father, D'Arcy Boulton, and brought at the age of three to Upper Canada where he was subsequently a student of the Reverend John Strachan). Among the MHAS serving in the 1830s, the only Post-Loyalist American lawyers were M.S. Bidwell and Boulton; no Scottish-born MHA was a lawyer during that period. Who then were the lawyer-MHAS? Two groups were clearly pre-eminent in the law: native Upper Canadians and English immigrants. Together these two groups accounted for about 55 percent of all the lawyer-MHAS. Both groups participated in the legal profession beyond the extent to which their numbers as MHAS entitled them, and the English much beyond their percentage of the general population as of 1842. The English were much more over-represented in law than were Upper Canadian MHAS; 37.5 percent of the English MHAS were lawyers (41 percent at the end of the period) compared to 26 percent of Upper Canadian MHAS (and still 26 percent at the end of the period). English-born lawyers made up 26 percent of the total number of lawyer-MHAS while English MHAS as a group were only 11 percent of all MHAS, and the English-born made up just under 9 percent of the general population in 1842.[44] A majority of the English-born MHAS had received their legal training in England

TABLE 4
Milling, Distilling, Manufacturing and National Origin

National Origin	*Number*	*Percentage of National Group*	*Percentage of Total Occupation*
Total MHAS in occupations 96			
Group B 47			
Thirteen Colonies			
Total 59	18	30.5	18.7
Group B 3	0	0	0
Upper Canada			
Total 53	15	28.3	15.6
Group B 39	14	35.9	29.8
Scotland			
Total 39	17	43.6	17.7
Group B 23	14	60.9	29.8
England and Wales			
Total 33	11	33.3	11.4
Group B 17	3	17.6	6.4
Post-Loyalist American			
Total 37	22	59.4	22.9
Group B 27	14	51.8	29.8
British North America			
Total 23	6	26.1	6.2
Group B 13	2	15.4	4.2
Ireland			
Total 18	2	11.1	2.1
Group B 10	1	10.0	2.1
French Canada			
Total 3	0	0	0
Group B 1	0	0	0
Unknown			
Total 17	3	17.6	3.1
Group B 5	0	0	0
All British America			
Total 138	39	28.3	40.6
Group B 56	16	28.6	34.1

at the Inns of Court, which was evidently an advantage in establishing themselves in their profession in Upper Canada.

Dealing with the question of occupation and religious denomination involves a high degree of uncertainty because the level of

TABLE 5
Law and National Origin

National Origin	*Number of Lawyers*	*Percentage of National Group*	*Percentage of Total Lawyers*
Total lawyers			
MHAS 47			
Group B 24			
Thirteen Colonies			
Total 59	6	10.2	12.8
Group B 3	1	33.3	4.2
Upper Canada			
Total 53	14	26.4	29.8
Group B 39	10	25.6	41.6
Scotland			
Total 39	3	7.7	6.4
Group B 23	0	0	0
England and Wales			
Total 33	12	36.4	25.5
Group B 17	8	47.1	33.3
Post-Loyalist American			
Total 37	3	8.1	6.4
Group B 27	2	7.4	8.3
British North America			
Total 23	6	26.1	12.8
Group B 13	2	15.4	8.3
Ireland			
Total 18	3	16.7	6.4
Group B 10	1	10.0	4.2
French Canada			
Total 3	0	0	0
Group B 1	0	0	0

religious unknowns among the MHAS is very high – about 31 percent. As a result it is impossible to state with confidence even what proportion of the MHAS as a whole adhered to any particular church. What can be said is that most Upper Canadians and most Upper Canadian MHAS belonged to four major denominations; they were either Anglicans, Presbyterians, Methodists, or Roman Catholics, though the Presbyterians and Methodists were split internally into two or more factions. Among MHAS whose denomination is known, the breakdown is roughly; Anglican, 34 percent; Presbyterian, 15 percent; Methodist, 9 percent; Roman Catholic, 7 percent; others,

4 percent, but in view of the high number of "unknowns" such figures are of doubtful validity. Working with the existing numbers, however, produces some interesting if hardly conclusive results. In general, Anglican MHAS appear to have been well- or over-represented in all the main money-making activities in Upper Canada, most strikingly in law, since 64 percent of all the lawyer-MHAS are known to have been Anglicans, and in public service. Presbyterians were well-represented as merchants, farmers, and public servants but were thin on the ground in the legal profession. Roman Catholic MHAS appear to have been highly successful at getting public service jobs, but otherwise their record was undistinguished. The Methodists present the most anomalous case. Those MHAS who are known to have been Methodists were heavily concentrated in farming and in commerce, but in the public service they were almost, and in law, totally, unrepresented, although known Methodists were about 9 percent of all the MHAS, and Methodists of all kinds made up a little over 17 percent of the total population of Upper Canada in 1842.[45]

Putting the very incomplete data on religious denomination together with the fuller but also incomplete information on national origin merely compounds uncertainty, but nonetheless it helps to reinforce in a tentative way some apparent occupational patterns and to suggest some others. Anglican MHAS of all nationalities were active in all the major occupations. Irish Roman Catholic MHAS were so few as to make any generalizations impossible. Protestant Irish MHAS were not all that much more numerous, and consequently it is not possible to detect any pronounced preference or aptitude among them for particular occupations, but it can be said that the Protestant Irish, most of whom were Anglicans, were quite successful in getting government positions. Among Anglicans in general it is noteworthy that Post-Loyalist Americans, who have been shown to have been much under-represented in certain occupations, were likely to be a bit more fortunate in life if they were or became members of the Church of England. Zaccheus Burnham, Absalom Shade, W.H. Merritt, F.L. Walsh, and the aforementioned G.S. Boulton were examples of Post-Loyalist American Anglicans who succeeded as merchants, millers, distillers, public servants and lawyers.

The most interesting overlaps between nationality and religion occur among the Presbyterians and the Methodists. Since only one Methodist MHA (John Willson) ever held a public service position of real status, it is obvious that no other Methodist MHAS of whatever national origin held such an appointment. Willson was also a Post-Loyalist American, but despite this fact, the largest national group of Methodists *not* holding public service appointments were Post-

TABLE 6
Main Occupations and Religious Denominations

Denomination	*Number*	*Percentage of Religious Group*	*Percentage of* MHAS *in Occupation**
Church of England			
Total known	95	100.0	–
Farmers	38	40.0	26.6
Public servants	52	54.7	46.4
Merchants	28	29.5	28.0
Millers	28	29.5	43.1
Lawyers	30	31.5	63.8
Presbyterian			
Total known	42	100.0	–
Farmers	23	54.7	16.1
Public servants	16	38.1	14.3
Merchants	22	52.4	22.0
Millers	10	23.8	15.4
Lawyers	4	9.7	8.5
Methodist			
Total known	26	100.0	–
Farmers	16	61.5	11.2
Public servants	2	7.7	18
Merchants	14	53.8	14.0
Millers	4	15.4	6.2
Lawyers	0	0	0
Roman Catholic			
Total known	19	100.0	–
Farmers	10	52.6	6.9
Public servants	13	68.4	11.6
Merchants	4	21.1	4.0
Millers, etc.	1	5.3	1.6
Lawyers	2	10.5	4.3

* Total MHAS in each occupation:

Farmers	143
Public servants	112
Merchants	100
Millers	65
Lawyers	47

Loyalist Americans, simply because more Methodists were Post-Loyalist Americans than were anything else. None of the four known Post-Loyalist American Presbyterian MHAS was a public servant, though four of the six known Post-Loyalist American Anglican MHAS were. In the legal profession, there were no Methodist MHAS of any national origin. Among Presbyterian MHAS, there was another large national group which was absent from the ranks of the lawyers, the Scots. No Scottish-born Presbyterian MHA was also a lawyer in Upper Canada.

The question of non-selection for public service posts will again be postponed for later and fuller examination in chapter 4 but the non-appearance of Post-Loyalist American Methodist and Scottish Presbyterian MHAS in the legal profession seems to demand some preliminary speculation. To take the Scots first: did prominent Scottish Presbyterians avoid or were they somehow excluded from the practice of law? Of the only three Scottish lawyer-MHAS, two Macdonells were among the early arriving Scottish Roman Catholic Group, and the third, Allan McLean, an Anglican, was also an early Upper Canadian. He and Angus Macdonell (Collachie) were in fact among the first lawyers to practise in Upper Canada, being entered on the books of the Law Society in 1797,[46] and John Macdonell (Greenfield) was called to the bar in 1808.[47] Hence the Scots present a double puzzle. No Presbyterian Scottish-born MHA was ever a lawyer and no Scottish-born MHA of any sort became a lawyer after 1808.

Since Scottish Presbyterians and Scottish Protestants in general were well-represented in the other main occupations, including public service, it is not likely that this is a case of deliberate exclusion or some form of discrimination. The Law Society of Upper Canada admitted to the profession persons licensed to practise in Scotland as well as in England, Ireland, and the other British North American colonies.[48] It is more likely that among the Scots who emigrated to Upper Canada and subsequently gained some prominence there were relatively few lawyers, though there was no shortage of Upper Canadians of Scottish families in the legal profession who received their training in Upper Canada.[49] It may have been that the differences between the Scottish and English/Upper Canadian legal systems raised a certain barrier, but the better explanation seems to be that Scottish lawyers were flourishing where they were and had little reason to emigrate. Among the Scottish professions "there was none, in numbers, wealth, or prestige, to equal the lawyers."[50]

The absence of Methodist MHAS, which is also to say mainly Post-Loyalist American Methodists MHAS, from the law probably requires different kinds of explanation. In this case there is reason to believe that the phenomenon was a general one among the Upper Canadian population. Among the names of all those who qualified as barristers and attorneys in Upper Canada before 1841, only one Methodist has been identified. It is possible that some Methodists coming from predominantly rural backgrounds simply were not able to acquire the kind of education usually associated with a legal career. After 1810 the Law Society required an entrance examination which included Latin, a language taught in Upper Canada only in the district grammar schools and a few private schools.[51] But the fact that Methodist MHAS, unlike those of the other denominations, were also almost totally missing from the ranks of the public service suggests the possibility that other factors may also have been at work; that is, that they may as a group have been judged unacceptable. All law students after 1799 were required to complete an apprenticeship – that is they had to have a "principal" who could agree to give them a place in a law office, supervise their legal education, and support their eventual entry into the profession. This entry was on the basis of "social and ethical criteria"; "testimonials of good character and conduct" were necessary, and these "social prerequisites" became more rigorous with time. In 1828 the Law Society ruled that no one could become a student of law without written recommendations from a bencher or two barristers, and in 1831 a further regulation required "particulars of family residence and connections."[52]

In Upper Canada – a theme which will be developed more fully throughout this study – some Upper Canadians, including Methodists and especially American Methodists, did not have or were believed not to have the right kind of "principles" or the right kind of "connections" to permit them to find places in the legal profession or in other "status" positions, including as servants of the Crown.

CHAPTER TWO

Land and Wealth

Did prominence necessarily imply wealth? Did wealth necessarily precede prominence? The short answer to both questions is no, not necessarily. William Lyon Mackenzie comes immediately to mind as someone who achieved prominence (not to say notoriety) but who was neither wealthy nor much concerned with the pursuit of wealth. Some men, as has been seen, achieved a degree of wealth only to lose it in the end through bad luck or bad management or (in the case of some like Thomas Barnes Gough) through drink.[1]

Still it is not unreasonable to assume that most of Upper Canada's regional leaders were, by the standards of the time, in better-than-average circumstances. The problem lies in assessing just how well-off they were or were not. Wealth, at no time an easy attribute to measure, is particularly elusive during the Upper Canadian period, given the scattered nature and difficulty of interpretation of sources which might serve as indicators of wealth. Business records, always a scarce commodity, are particularly so for the period before 1841. There are quite detailed land records, which show the granting and subsequent disposition of land,[2] but the simple possession of land has never been a sure sign of wealth. Extensive assessment records exist though they are not complete for all areas and all periods. Assessment records are helpful in demonstrating the extent to which an individual possessed those things which were being assessed, such as land, houses, additional fireplaces, pleasure carriages, merchant shops, and mills (people having the latter two were usually those who were assessed at a high value), but in the end the "value of ratable property" cannot be precisely equated with income, or wealth.[3] Consequently there will be no attempt in what follows to establish general standards of wealth or an order of relative wealth, but instead to provide an overall view of the possible sources of wealth and a rather impressionistic survey of the extent and limits of individual wealth.

Wealth is always a relative matter, relative to the economic conditions of the time and to the affluence or non-affluence of other members of the society. There was never any Upper Canadian equivalent of the "handful of great lords" in pre-industrial England, who "received £30,000 a year or more in rent, besides what they might get in government salaries and pensions,"[4] but in the first decade or so of Upper Canada's history, when much of the forest remained to be converted into productive farms, when good markets and cash were hard to come by, any man possessed of a regular income, especially if paid in sterling, may well have been a man of wealth in relation to his contemporaries. Some such lucky individuals would be found holding government jobs in the provincial capital, but for the regionally prominent a more frequent and more significant source of income was military half pay. Many of Upper Canada's early leaders had served as officers of British Loyalist regiments – the King's Royal Regiment of New York, the 84th Regiment, Butler's Rangers – or had been attached to the Indian Department or other units during the American Revolution. When their units were disbanded, these men qualified for half pay, which, depending on rank, entitled the recipient to some £50 to £150 per year.[5] Compared to the very little or no liquid assets enjoyed by the ordinary struggling settler, half pay of necessity bestowed a substantial advantage on those who received it. There is good evidence that those on half pay recognized that advantage and set a high value on it. When in 1806 the Imperial government instituted an enquiry to determine which colonial half-pay officers were also holding civil appointments and gave them a choice of retaining one or the other source "of profit, civil or military under His Majesty,"[6] the reaction was spirited but unmistakable. They wanted to continue to benefit from both, but if the choice had to be made it was half pay all the way. Timothy Thompson, former ensign in the Second Battalion, King's Royal Regiment of New York, at first attempted to pretend that he held no civil appointments "of profit." When it was pointed out to him that he was both district court and surrogate court judge of the Midland District and collector of customs at Newcastle, he readily gave the appointments up to keep his half pay.[7] Protesting that his appointments as clerk of the peace and judge of the district court carried no "paid salary but merely fees of office which are always fluctuating," Ralph Clench of Niagara, lieutenant in Butler's Rangers on half pay, asked to be allowed to keep both his civil and military incomes. After all, he wrote, "at the time of forming and establishing the new settlements in Upper Canada none but Half Pay officers could have been found capable of holding the civil appointments necessary in establishing and forming the different Districts."[8] Thompson and Clench were expressing points of view common to most half pay officers and reflected the extent to which half pay benefited and even helped to create a leadership group. Among seventy-five men who sat in the Upper Canadian Assembly between 1792 and 1812, twenty-six were half-pay officers. In the first two parliaments (1792–6 and 1796–1800) half-pay officers made up exactly half of the membership, sixteen out of thirty-two; in addition they held among them some forty-four offices. In all, between 1792 and 1841 forty-two half-pay officers are known to have sat in the Upper Canadian legislature. By the 1820s and 1830s half-pay officers were by no means as numerous as formerly, but they continued to form a part of the membership of the Assembly, Revolutionary veterans having been replaced by some of the many officers placed on half pay after the Napoleonic Wars. By that time, though, it is unlikely that half pay could be equated with wealth, given the much greater range of economic opportunities available to others, but half pay may still have provided former officers with a margin of respectability which they would otherwise have lacked.

Time and economic change rendered a source of income like half pay less significant, but time and economic change also made the sheer accumulation of capital more and more possible, which also produced a new source of wealth, or potential wealth: inheritance. How many of Upper Canada's second-generation leaders can be put into this category is difficult to be exact about, but some examples come readily to mind. The success of a businessman like J.S. Cartwright owed something to the splendid start provided for him by his father, the pioneer Kingston merchant Richard Cartwright. Few young Upper Canadians were prepared for their professions (in Cartwright's case, the law) by spending three years in England at Lincoln's Inn, but then few Upper Canadians inherited a £10,000 share in an estate.[9] Similarly being the son of another substantial merchant, Adam Ferrie, helps explain C.C. Ferrie's rapid rise in the business world in Hamilton.[10] It is an interesting coincidence that both Cartwright and Ferrie became bank presidents, (Cartwright of the Commercial Bank of the Midland District at age twenty-seven, and Ferrie of the Gore Bank at age thirty-one). The sons of Robert Hamilton, George and the younger Robert among them, were also examples of inheritors of wealth.[11] For W.B. Wells, having a wealthy father had a different kind of advantage. It gave him the ability to pursue a totally "independent" political career, free from government influence.[12]

Some Upper Canadians were said by their contemporaries or have been said by later writers to have been rich men. John Cameron of Fairfield in Charlottenburgh Township was known as "John Cameron the rich" (to distinguish him from his father "John Cameron the wise").[13] A fellow Charlottenburghian, Alexander Fraser, established a 1,600-acre estate which he called Fraserfield and built a house there, long before Sir Allan MacNab built Dundurn Castle, "said to have been at the time, one of the most pretentious in Upper Canada."[14] Asa Werden of Athol Township built a mansion of twenty rooms and was said to have left an estate worth more than $250,000.[15] At his death Zaccheus Burnham was believed to be the richest man in his district.[16] Similar allegations of wealth can be found in references to quite a number of other sometime MHAS, among them Thomas Fraser, Thomas MacKay, Joshua Booth, George Longley, George Rolph, and Absalom Shade.[17]

A further and probably more definite indicator of wealth was the distinction accorded to some few regionally prominent men of being appointed to the Legislative Council of the province, for membership in that body ideally went to "the most worthy, intelligent, loyal and opulent."[18] It is not surprising therefore to find that some of the Upper Canadians already identified as supposed possessors of wealth, such as Zaccheus Burnham, Thomas MacKay, Alexander Fraser, and Thomas Fraser, received that distinction. So to did William Morris, James Crooks, Philip VanKoughnet, John Willson, Jonas and Charles Jones, George Hamilton, and James Gordon. All presumably were or were believed to be "opulent" Upper Canadians.

Contemporary or later assumptions about wealth can of course be misleading. Upper Canadians believed to be "as good as the bank" could turn out to be wealthy only in appearance, as historians of business have discovered. Even professional credit appraisers for such organizations as R.G. Dun and Company often mistook paper assets for real assets and were often wrong about the solvency and credit-worthiness of entrepreneurs.[19] In fact, for contemporaries or for historians it has never been easy to find complete and reliable information upon which an assessment of wealth can be based. Among the main occupations – farming, public service, merchandising, milling, law, etc. – the only one for which it is possible to be specific about income is public service. The annually compiled Blue Books of government statistics contain figures on salaries and fees received by each permanent official inside and outside the capital for the years 1821–41.[20] They therefore provide a complete account of the possible remuneration arising from all of the government jobs to which Upper Canadians could and did aspire. As a source of *total* income they are, of course, not definitive. Even if it was not true, as critics of the bureaucracy alleged, that the income from fees reported was sometimes much lower than the real figures, for many people, government service was only one source of income.

But an ever larger problem has to be faced. Even where income is known, how much income, at any given in Upper Canada, constituted wealth? Within the public service, income levels varied a great deal. The lieutenant governor, whose office no Upper Canadian was allowed to fill, was paid £3,000 per year. His senior advisors, the executive councillors, were paid £100 per year.[21] Did the lieutenant governor enjoy wealth and his colonial colleagues mere subsistence? That might have been true if the lieutenant governor had no expenses of office or if the executive councillors had no other source of revenue, but neither is likely to have been the case. Drawing an income level above which wealth may be said to have resulted is naturally a crude and arbitrary exercise, but some sort of arbitrary level can still be useful as a way of making broad distinctions among people whose incomes are known, such as public servants.

A recent study of the social structure of Upper Canada has concluded that in order to be judged by contemporaries as a member of the "respectable" class a minimum income in the £200–300 per year range was necessary. The principal hallmark of this status was the ability to employ three or more servants and the most likely occupational categories represented were "manufacturer, merchant, wealthy farmer, clergy, barrister, government department head."[22] This description may constitute an accurate formula for respectability but it is doubtful that it accurately describes wealth. If it is assumed that, so far as public service was concerned, it was the intention of the government to provide its senior officers with an income which would convey "respectability" but not wealth, then wealth must have required an income level somewhat higher than the highest government salary, which was the salary of the chief justice of the Court of King's Bench of Upper Canada. In 1821, the first year for which figures are available, that salary was £1,100 per year; by 1841 it was £1,500 per year.[23] In 1821 only the salary of the chief justice himself (who was also paid as a member of the Executive Council and as *ex officio* Speaker of the Legislative Council) and the attorney general (£300 per year plus £1,001 in fees) exceeded the £1,100 level. In 1840 the Chief Justice alone, by virtue of income from extra sources made more than £1,500.[24] As it happens, the attorney general of 1821 was also the chief justice of 1840, John

Beverley Robinson. Robinson has been said to have sometimes "sacrificed material self-interest in the cause of ideology."[25] If so he made his sacrifices from a position of some comfort.

It seems reasonable to conclude that while many public servants enjoyed a comfortable living compared to most of their contemporaries, and had more security than most, their jobs did not make them rich men, but by the end of the Upper Canadian period a handful of other "headquarters" officials – the provincial secretary, the receiver general, the inspector general, the puisne judges, and the solicitor general – had salaries of over £500 per year, which may have equalled comfort, if not wealth. More importantly from the point of view of regional leadership, some officials outside the provincial capital, notably sheriffs of well-populated districts and collectors at major ports, had also passed the £500 mark.[26] Such regional offices however (though anti-administration complaints about high incomes did not mention it) differed from salaried positions in the capital in that they involved outlay as well as income. Sheriffs, collectors, and other office-holders such as county registrars were obliged, by regulations designed to save the administration money, to pay their deputies, bailiffs, messengers, and so forth out of their own fee-generated incomes, so that a gross income of as much as £700 could mean a net income as low as £300 or even £200. The experience of Anthony Manahan, who was appointed collector of customs for the port of Toronto in 1841, is a case in point. The gross annual income arising from the collector's commission on the value of goods entering the port and on seizures was around £450, yet Manahan found that, after paying a deputy, a messenger, and an assortment of informants, and after paying the expense of renting and maintaining an office, what was left to the collector was hardly worth the trouble. After two years he resigned the collectorship owing the government money.[27] Manahan was by no means the only public servant of the time to find that expenses, whether official or personal, often outran income, especially income derived from fees.[28] About all that can be said in a general way about public service incomes is that they undoubtedly conveyed "respectability" to many, but seldom if ever conveyed wealth.

One documentary source which contains some helpful information about the level of accumulated assets of a group of prominent people in several parts of the province at a particular time, but which has not been much used, is the Losses Claims submitted by the many Upper Canadians who had suffered financially as a result of the

War of 1812.[29] For an examination of the affairs of all of the MHAS, the claims are by no means a perfect source. Only 43 of the 283 MHAS (15 percent) made such claims. For those who did, it is possible that some claims were artificially inflated. They are geographically uneven, since most of the damage occurred in the main war zones, especially the Niagara Peninsula and the western section of the province. Two-thirds of the claims were from the Niagara, Gore, Western, Home, and London districts. They do not provide a cross-section of even the five leading occupations, law and public service being decidedly under-represented, presumably since those occupations involved no large amounts of immovable assets which were subject to destruction by enemy, or friendly, hands. (The only "legal" claim was that of William Warren Baldwin for the loss of a silk gown.) Despite these limitations, the losses claims are worth examining because they shed light not on actual levels of wealth, but on levels of assets and levels of investment necessary to acquire those assets for quite a few prominent Upper Canadians. They allow a glimpse of the size and nature of some estates and establishments which had been built up by the time of the war. They are also of some help in pointing to certain occupations as good routes to the accumulation of wealth.

The forty-three claims totalled £57,514; the average size of claim was therefore about £1,337. A suspicious and penny-pinching government cut these claims in half and actually allowed some £28,567 in claims, or an average of about £664 per claim. All but eight of the claims were for £100 or more. Of these, the claims can be broken down by the type of assets which had suffered loss or damage. Such a breakdown, which in many cases includes more than one type of asset per claim, produces the following totals:

Farms and farm products 17
Merchant establishments and merchandise 11
Mills 7
Distilleries 4
Merchant ships 3
Forwarding businesses 1
Lumber business 1

This list conforms reasonably well to what has already been said about the relative incidence of the main (non-professional) occupations but is otherwise not very enlightening on the matter of actual assets or investments. A better idea of the potential upper range of investment in land and businesses which could be found in Upper Canada by 1815 can be gained by looking more closely at those claims, sixteen in number, which exceeded £1,000. In simple order by business or occupation the list is not greatly different from the larger list:

Farms 7	Shipping 2
Merchants 7	Forwarding 1
Milling 6	Lumbering 1
Distilling 3	

But if the top sixteen claims are arranged in order according to the size of the amount claimed, a somewhat different picture emerges. A rank order by size of claim and occupation produces:

1 Miller/distiller
2 Merchant
3 Miller/merchant
4 Miller/foundry owner
5 Farmer/merchant/miller/distiller/shipowner
6 Farm owner (of a rented farm)
7 Shipowner/lumberman/merchant
8 Merchant/farmer
9 Farmer
10 Miller
11 Farmer/forwarder
12 Merchant
13 Miller/distiller
14 Farmer
15 Merchant
16 Farmer

This list demonstrates the familiar pattern of overlapping occupations, but it makes clear that, among this group, the highest level of capital investment was mainly in three activities: milling, merchandising, and distilling. Farming, although as elsewhere a common occupation, did not, at least on the basis of this small group of claims, require so great an investment or involve so great an accumulation of assets.

It may be a worthwhile exercise to narrow the focus even further and to look in even greater detail at the activities as revealed in the claims of some of Upper Canada's biggest war losers. If the financial cutoff point is raised to take in only claims of £3,000 or over, the claims of eight prominent Upper Canadians remain. What kinds of assets had they accumulated which merited so high a level of compensation?

The largest claim was submitted by Robert Nichol. While serving with distinction as lieutenant colonel and quartermaster general of militia for Upper Canada, his "mercantile establishment" in Woodhouse Township was first occupied by British troops and then burned by the enemy in May 1814. His claim for £6,684 described the loss of grist and saw mills, a distillery, his house, a workman's house, a barn and stables, a storehouse for flour, plus fences, houses, and other items. The value of his mills he put at £2,500 and the distillery at £1,250. He was allowed £4,204, about 63 percent of his claim.[30]

James Crooks, then Captain Crooks of the First Regiment of Lincoln Militia, suffered the double indignity of being captured and losing a large quantity of goods on the same day, 27 May 1813, during the capture of Niagara by the Americans. His claim in the amount of £6,394 on behalf of himself and his partner and brother William Crooks (who submitted a separate claim of £581 for damage to his mills, distillery, and other property at Grimsby) was mainly based on the loss of merchandise, but included one unusual item, the amount of a debt owed to Crooks by an Aaron Stevens, a man who had been hanged for treason. Crooks was careful to point out that as foreman of the jury which sent Stevens to the gallows, he had put duty before business, knowing that Stevens would not be in a position to pay his debts. He hoped that a grateful government would repay the money owed by the late Mr. Stevens. The government proved quite impressed by the altruism of James Crooks, awarding him almost 70 percent of his claim.[31]

The claim for £5,402 of James McGregor on behalf of the former firm of John and James McGregor reflects not only occupational but geographical variation. Included in the claim were a large grist and saw mill complex in Chatham Township on the Thames, burned by the British during Procter's retreat in 1813; two houses and two stores in Sandwich, damaged by British troops; and a farm and large house at Amherstburgh, damaged by the enemy. Like Crooks, McGregor was also a prisoner of war for a time in 1814. McGregor was awarded about 60 percent of his claim, £3,191.[32]

The next-highest claim, that of Robert Randall, has its own unusual aspects. Randall did not spend the war in the active defence of his province. Like Crooks and McGregor he was a prisoner, but not of the United States. Between 1809 and 1815 he was in prison in Montreal for debt. Despite that technicality, he sent in a claim for £5,000 for the destruction of the Bridgewater works at Niagara Falls, a milling-foundry complex he had begun to develop about 1800. Not surprisingly, the government of Upper Canada rejected his claim outright, the works having been seized and sold during his absence. In fact, the Niagara firm of Clark and Street (not Samuel Street the MHA but his nephew) were compensated for the destruction of the works and for other loss to the amount of £4,970, marked down from a claim of £7,785. Robert Randall's only successful claim netted him £4 10s for destruction of some fence rails.[33]

Richard Hatt's claim reflected the wide range of his enterprises established at the village of Dundas on Spencer's Creek since about 1804 and in Ancaster and Flamborough West townships. His losses included a sawmill, a sixty-ton schooner, four houses, a printing press, 1,200 acres of hardwood trees, two storage buildings, and a good deal of merchandise and farm produce and livestock. His claim was for £4,738; the schooner alone he valued at £1,250. He was allowed only £1,220, about 26 percent of his claim, partly because his claim for the ship was ruled "inadmissable."[34]

The claim of George Hamilton for £3,704 was the only one among the sizable claims which was concerned mainly with farm-related losses. As well as the value of the houses, furniture, barns, lodges, stables, outbuildings, and fences destroyed on his Queenston property, his claims included the loss of rent which he had previously collected. Hamilton, having moved in 1811 to the location of a village which was to bear his name, left his Queenston land occupied by tenants. A rare example of landed gentry enjoying a part of his income from rents in early Upper Canada, he was well treated by the government, receiving over 70 percent of his claim.[35]

Number seven in order of the size of his claim was Richard Pattison of "River Thames" and Sandwich. In common with his fellow western Upper Canadian, James McGregor, his claim demonstrated the range of endeavours and places which could be involved in the pursuit of profit. His losses included a one-third interest in the schooner *Thames*, sunk on Lake Erie; damage to large quantities of cut and standing pine, cedar and oak timber; ballast stone; a house; two large storehouses; a slaughterhouse; a fowl house, and a stable at Sandwich, plus a house, a barn, and flour taken by General Hull's troops from his property on the Thames.[36]

Richard Beasely's claim, which has already been referred to, was for exactly £3,000, and was also testimony to the fact that assets (and hence losses) were often of more than one kind or in more than one place. In his case, he had suffered damage to his farm at Burlington Heights at the hands of British troops and the loss of his merchandise in a ship captured by the Americans on Lake Ontario.[37]

The evidence contained in eight or sixteen or even forty-three claims for war losses does not provide a basis for hard-and-fast conclusions about wealth in Upper Canada. Some limited observations can be advanced. It is possible to say that by 1812 some leading Upper Canadians had managed to amass sizable assets of several kinds, mainly through milling, distilling, storekeeping, and farming, and even if the claimants put too high a cash value on their own possessions, a none-too-generous government was prepared to admit that in most cases some 60 to 70 percent of their assets had been real. The size and value of the largest "establishments" also implies the previous accumulation of considerable capital to be invested in them or the ability to obtain credit on a fairly large scale. It can be suggested as well that although farming was what most Upper Canadians did most of the time, it is again evident that it was not a major preoccupation of the largest entrepreneurs, who thought that there were better ways to wealth, such as milling and storekeeping. It can be added that the fierce dedication with which prominent early Upper Canadians sought out and sometimes competed for eligible mill sites is testimony to the importance which they attached to milling as a potentially money-making occupation.[38] It is also worth noting the apparent importance of distilling. It is true that distilling was almost invariably an occupation carried on in connection with other activities, primarily milling, but it may have been a significant ingredient in the accumulation of wealth. Both of the largest losses claimants among the MHAS, Robert Nichol and James Crooks, were distillers among other things as was Richard Hatt and another claimant-MHA, Benjamin Hardison, who was allowed £1,224 for his losses.[39] At least three of the men earlier identified as being among the ranks of Upper Canada's allegedly wealthy, Zaccheus Burnahm, Absalom Shade, and William Morris, also numbered distilling among their enterprises.

A similar observation, although one which emerges less obviously from an analysis of the losses claims, might be made about what may loosely be called "the lumber business." Lumbering, it may be remembered, ranked eighth (distilling was sixth) among occupations known to have been followed by Upper Canadian MHAS. Among the claimant-MHAS, the most conspicuous example of participation in lumbering was Richard Pattinson. His claim, which, as has been seen, included damage to standing oak timber, sheds some light on the ways in which money could be made from lumbering, at least in wartime near a British naval and military establishment. Pattinson's timber that had been destroyed had been squared pine and white oak ship timber, undoubtedly to have been used by the British to build additional ships for service on Lake Erie or on the upper Great Lakes, plus cedar poles that he had contracted to supply for the fortification of the British garrison at Amherstburgh.[40] Among other claimants, it may be noted that all of the millers operated saw mills as well as grist mills and that five other claims referred specifically to losses of valuable standing timber or of quantities of piled lumber.[41] Thomas Smith's claim, with remarkable precision, listed the loss of a "copse" measuring exactly 7,785,720 square feet and containing exactly 34,603 oak trees.[42] Smith, Pattinson, and a number of other MHAS who were involved in lumber at the time of the war, such as William Crooks (15,000 feet of boards destroyed) and Samuel Street, were also operating in parts of the province which have not generally been considered as centres of lumbering.

As with distilling, connections can be made between lumbering and other supposedly well-to-do Upper Canadian MHAS who were not losses claimants, most of whom were, as might be expected, from the eastern part of the province. The wealth that gave W.B. Wells his political independence was the result of his father having done "a large and lucretive [sic] business in lumber."[43] Wells' MHA brother-in-law, George Longley of Maitland, was also said to be "possessed of much wealth acquired in the lumber trade."[44] Local and family historians believe that George Brouse's wealth was based primarily on lumbering.[45] Brouse's fellow MHA for Dundas, John Cook, "engaged rather extensively" in lumbering and in so doing founded a lumber business whose operations eventually stretched from Quebec City to Muskoka.[46] Lumbering was also an ingredient in the sources of wealth of Asa Werden, the reputed quarter-millionaire.[47]

A final comment needs to be made arising from a characteristic which was shared by a number of losses claimants. It is plain that some of these people moved from time to time from one location to another or had "establishments" in two or three places. This might suggest a relatively high level of transiency among the prominent, which, as recent quantitative studies of rural and urban Upper Canada have argued, ought to have operated adversely on their ability to accumulate wealth. This apparent contradiction is probably just that: apparent, not real. Thirty-two of the losses claimants (74 percent), as far as is known, spent all their adult lives in one place. (Nine are known to have moved once and two to have moved twice.) In fact if the entire group of 283 MHAS is examined on this basis, a similar impression of permanence emerges. Based on (admittedly incomplete) evidence of known locations over time, it can be said that most of Upper Canada's regional leaders exhibited a proper degree of immobility. For some 63 percent of them only one location has been found, and even among those who moved, most of their moving was done within the same district. Only 54 out of the 283 MHAS (19 percent) are known to have moved outside of their original districts. It is unlikely that many of them, like George Brouse, stayed so close to home that they could be said to have died "on the very spot" where they had been born,[48] but unlike so many other Upper Canadians they had not made the mistake of equating "moving on with moving up."[49]

F.H. Armstrong has written that the principal ways of becoming wealthy in Upper Canada were by "holding offices and gathering the perquisites of office," by "the accumulation of land," and "through the continued advance of commerce and later finance and manufacturing."[50] The evidence of the losses claims might suggest some modification and extension of these means to wealth, but as has been admitted those claims involving significant levels of assets are neither very numerous nor very representative of the province as a whole. To test Armstrong's categories and to explore further the question of the acquisition of wealth in general, a list of MHAS, most of whom have already been referred to, who are known to have been or who have been alleged to have been wealthy has been compiled for further investigation, using as a basis four criteria: known high income, reputed wealth, appointment to the Legislative Council, and, from the war losses claims, claims over £1,000. These criteria produce a list of thirty-eight names.[51] Obviously it is far from being a definitive list of wealthy Upper Canadians or even wealthy MHAS, nor is it certain that all of the "wealthy" retained their wealth indefinitely, but it does provide a basis for some conjecture about sources of wealth. Unlike the losses claims this list of the wealthy has reasonable regional distribution, having at least one representative from each of the Upper Canadian districts except the Ottawa District.[52]

By occupation the thirty-eight "wealthy" MHAS, demonstrating numerically the usual pattern of occupational overlap, break down as follows:

Merchants 22
Public servants 21
Farmers 20
Millers 17
Distillers 7
Lumbermen 6
Land developers/speculators 6
Shipowners/builders/forwarders 5
Lawyers 5
Businessmen 4
Fur traders 2
Bankers 2
Manufacturers 2
Military officers 2
Contractors 2
Ferry operator 1
Tanner 1

This list conforms reasonably well to Armstrong's description of the wealthy, except that milling and distilling ought perhaps to be included along with public office, landholding, and commerce as main roads to wealth. "Finance" is evident in the form of two bankers and four "businessmen," but "manufacturing" (except for milling and distilling) is not really an important factor in this group.

What other characteristics can be attached to these thirty-eight allegedly wealthy MHAS? Ranked by national origin the order is:

Scotland 9
Thirteen Colonies 8
Upper Canada 8
England and Wales 4
Post-Loyalist America 4
British North America 3
Ireland 1
Unknown 1

A list by religious denomination produces:

Anglicans 10
Presbyterians 9
Methodists 3
Roman Catholics 1
Lutherans 1
Unknown 14

Combining those whose national origin and religious affiliation is known gives this result:

Scottish/Presbyterian 5
Upper Canadian/Anglican 4
Thirteen Colonies/Presbyterian 3
Thirteen Colonies/Anglican 2
Post-Loyalist American/Anglican 2
British North American/Anglican 1
Upper Canadian/Presbyterian 1
Upper Canadian/Methodist 1
Thirteen Colonies/Methodist 1
Post-Loyalist American/Methodist 1
English/Anglican 1
Scottish/Roman Catholic 1
Upper Canadian/Lutheran 1

If these small numbers and the very high level of religious unknowns permit any valid conclusions, they are fairly obvious and straightforward. Anglicans and Presbyterians clearly predominated. Among national groups the Scots and, collectively, native British Americans were most numerous. The best combination of religion and nationality was to be Scottish and Presbyterian.

Since among MHAS whose religious affiliation is known, Anglicans were by far the most numerous, it is not surprising to find Anglicans heading a list of the well-to-do; but as the leading national group, the Scots are quite different. There were in total only thirty-nine Scottish-born MHAS; nine of them are on the "wealthy" list – a rather remarkable record compared to the two next highest groups (eight of fifty-three MHAS born in the Thirteen Colonies and eight of fifty-four born in Upper Canada). Some possible reasons for Scottish pre-eminence among the wealthy and in other ways will be canvassed at a later point in this study, but as the most successful national group on the "wealthy" list it is of some immediate interest to return to the matter of occupation to see how the Scots were making a living and striving to make their fortune. By single occupation among the Scots, the order is:

Merchant 7	Ferry operator 1
Public servant 7	Banker 1
Miller 4	Military officer 1
Distiller 3	Contractor 1
Farmer 3	Businessman 1
Shipowner 2	Land developer 1
Manufacturer 1	

In fact, all of them followed more than one calling, usually at the same time. Five were, among other things, merchants and public servants at the same time. Three of these merchant/public servants were also millers and distillers. For the Scots, at least, the principal keys to wealth would seem to have been commerce, public service, and milling or distilling, commonly carried on in combination with one another.

A few other known attributes of the entire group of thirty-eight presumed wealthy people are of some note. Among those few to whom a firm political label has been attached the Conservatives had a definite edge: thirteen Conservatives to six Reformers. On the question of transiency versus persistence, the persisters were once again well in the lead. Twenty-eight of the group, or 74 percent, are believed to have spent their working lives in only one location. Eight others moved once after a short period in an initial location. One moved to Toronto from Brockville in middle age after being appointed to the Court of King's Bench.[53] In fact, in the entire group there was only one who can really be called transient at all. Oddly enough, this was Robert Nichol, who submitted the largest war losses claim of any MHA. He began his business career at Niagara about 1792, had moved to Amherstburgh by 1797, was located in the Fort Erie area in 1803–6, moved before the war to Woodhouse Township, and left in 1821 for Stamford Township after being appointed a Niagara District judge.[54] Nichol was surely a classic case of an exception which proved the rule. The pattern of the group as a whole was to find a promising location and, having found it, to stay in it.

There is the possibility of a suggestion that inherited wealth was of some importance, or was coming to be, among MHAS who sat in the 1830s. Six of the thirty-eight MHAS have been identified as having been sizable inheritors. But a much more important potential factor in the achievement of wealth may have stemmed from a somewhat opposite circumstance; being early and long in the province. Seventeen of the "wealthy" (45 percent) arrived in the province as Loyalists or arrived as adults and were established in the province before 1800. An additional nine were the children of Loyalists and were born before 1791. These two groups together make up about 84 percent of the total. The implication is twofold; that being on the spot before a great many others was an advantage, and that wealth took some time to accumulate.

If, as one historian has concluded, land was the key to a "rise to independence" in Upper Canada,[55] Upper Canada's regional leaders held that key firmly in their hands, for as a group they acquired in one way or another an impressive amount of property. Better still, most of their land was obtained either cheaply or free, as grants from the crown. At least 236,600 acres are known to have been granted by a generous government to men who were or became MHAS, of whom 216, or about 76 percent, got land, receiving an average grant of 1,095 acres each, and if the amount of "family lands" granted to heads of families on behalf of their wives and children were included, the total would be very much higher.[56] Larger than normal grants of land were handed out as a matter of routine to anyone who could claim status or prominence. Land was originally given to Loyalists and their sons and daughters and also to government officials and military officers. By a series of further precedents, extra amounts of land were also given to petitioners who were deemed to be eligible "as a barrister," "as a magistrate," "as a merchant," "as a Member of the Assembly," "as a very worthy and well informed man," and even "as a settler" who had already "improved" a grant of land.[57] The land-granting system from the beginning was, and was intended to be, inequitable, in order that the "respectable classes"might be endowed with suitable estates on the British model, but the fact was that anyone who was prepared to take an oath of allegiance and could get a magistrate to certify that he was reputable could apply with every prospect of getting the basic grant, which for most of the Upper Canadian period was two hundred acres. For leading Upper Canadians and their children, a grant of land from the crown came to be seen as almost a matter of right, mainly because the Executive Council, wearing its other hat as a land committee, was highly liberal in its application of the land regulations when it came to "deserving applicants." When Charles Fothergill, "late of the City of London ... a gentleman of an ancient and respectable North of England family" appeared in Upper

Canada in 1817, bringing letters from the colonial undersecretary, Henry Goulborn, and dropping the name of his cousin, Baron de Montalembert, the council hastened to grant him 1,200 acres at Rice Lake, plus "a competent reserve" set aside next to his grant for his family and friends.[58] (In fact Fothergill was something of a ne'er-do-well who had failed at everything he had tried to do in England, a pattern which was not to change in Upper Canada.)[59] William Hamilton and his three brothers, "late of Liverpool, merchants and co-partners in trade," in need of land near their lumber mills at Hawkesbury "to form a settlement for the supply of labour," were given 1,200 acres each in 1816.[60] A similar grant had been made earlier to Richard Hatt who, wishing to bring to Upper Canada from England his father, brothers and sisters, and their servants "to farm on a large scale and to build mills," was granted 1,200 acres for himself plus 200 acres for each other member of his family.[61]

People petitioned for land not only because they wished to farm it, or put settlers on it, or make a profit on its sale, but simply because it was there to be had. In somewhat the same way that the arrival of a child in contemporary Canada implies an automatic application for family allowance payments, so for Upper Canadians being "upwards of twenty-one years" almost guaranteed the submission of a petition for land. It is highly unlikely that all of the sons and daughters of Loyalists or the barristers or merchants or magistrates who received land could scarcely wait to start farming it. John Beverley Robinson, who, as has been seen, was unusually well paid as attorney general and later chief justice of the province and not in great need of additional rewards, collected 1,700 acres of free land as the son of a Loyalist, as a senior government official and as a lieutenant of militia during the War of 1812.[62] His political enemy Robert Baldwin, who was also comfortably placed in life, with a father who already owned a large amount of land, and who as a Reformer might conceivably have opposed the unequal distribution of land in Upper Canada, nonetheless applied shortly after his twenty-first birthday for the land "usually granted to barristers."[63]

The level of land granted to prominent Upper Canadians shows, as one would expect, a decline over the fifty-year period, especially, as one would also expect, after 1826 when the government stopped making grants to "ordinary grantees." An analysis of the land granted to MHAS on the basis of the groupings employed earlier into chronological groups A and B demonstrates this change quite graphically. Of the 103 MHAS in the mainly pre-1820 Group A, no fewer than 100 (97 percent) received grants of land, totalling 159,420 acres or an average of 1,594.2 acres each. Of the later 138 MHAS in the mainly post-1830 Group B, only 83 (61 percent) received land totalling 50,804 acres, an average of 612.1 acres. A third transitional group of forty-nine MHAS, whose political service was in the 1820s only, averaged 677.8 acres to thirty-nine grantees (80 percent of the group). The large discrepancy between the early and late groups is striking but not surprising. The first group was heavily loaded with Loyalists and their sons and with official and military claimants, and they were in the province while land was still being routinely granted rather than being sold. There were some among the later Group B (C.C. Ferrie, R.R. Hunter, R.S. Jameson, Edmund Murney, Henry Sherwood, and W.B. Wells, for example) who were too young or who arrived in Upper Canada too late to apply for land in the period when its acquisition from the crown was almost automatic. These considerations aside, it is clear that both the proportion of prominent people petitioning for land and the amount of land granted declined as the initial government liberality was gradually replaced by a somewhat more systematic approach, as the amount of land the government had to give away began to be perceived as no longer inexhaustible, and as the number of means to potential wealth and respectability which did not involve the possession of land increased. The fact remains, though, that, as long as possible, most prominent Upper Canadians continued to take the trouble to petition for and to be granted land.

What did they want with all that land? Undoubtedly land was seen as patrimony. The average number of children known to have been born into the families of Upper Canadian MHAS works out to a little over seven children per family. Providing all those children with property, for whatever purpose, was a likely reason for many people to get their hands on as much of it as possible. But basically land was for farming, either immediately or in the future. The fact that more than half of the MHAS are known to have farmed at some time, and that at least thirty-four of them are not known to have done anything else, suggests that land was acquired and valued for its agricultural promise.

But to return to the original point, did, or could, farming equal wealth? It could in the right circumstances. Still another look at some aspects of the 1812 losses claims illustrates the scale on which by that era farming could be carried on and the level of investment and reward involved. Six losses claimants among the MHAS reported farm losses of over £1,000. Robert Hamilton's claim included, among much else, sixty hogs killed and the labour of forty-five yoke of oxen lost on his farm at Queenston.[64] An even more dramatic example of the possibilities of wealth through farming is provided by the case of Matthew Elliott. Elliott did not survive the war to make a personal claim, but according to his widow his "extensive, well cultivated estates" of over 3,000 acres in Malden Township provided an income of "at least £600 a year," which rendered his "small salary" as Indian superintendent at Amherstburgh irrelevant. This income was derived from a contract to supply the British garrison at Fort Malden, dating from at least 1802, when he provided 10,000 pounds of flour. When Procter evacuated Amherstburgh in 1813 the Elliott family abandoned their "estates," taking with them only their silverplate and "other most valuable portable effects" in nine wagons, drawn by thirty horses.[65]

It is apparent that one factor which could affect the degree of success in farming was location. Substantial farm operations like those of Matthew Elliott, Robert Hamilton, Samuel Street, Thomas Smith, or Richard Beasely may have suffered the misfortune of lying in the path of war in 1812–14 but they had previously enjoyed the advantage of being close to rising urban areas, especially areas like Niagara and Amherstburgh which had British garrisons to provide early and sizable local markets for flour, pork, and beef. (The importance of location in a different kind of enterprise is also demonstrated in the losses claim of Thomas Smith whose demolished tavern Belleperche House had been situated "on the public road between Sandwich and Amherstburgh.")[66]

Substantial wealth through farming in the right circumstances was always possible, but it is less certain that it was prevalent. Contemporary references and local lore provide few actual examples of conspicuous success through farming alone. Merchants, millers, and distillers were sometimes described as "opulent" but farmers, even prominent farmers, were more likely to be called "practical" or "honest." Some early Upper Canadian leaders such as John Cameron and Alexander Fraser, as has been said, were alleged to be rich men and were also farmers. Thomas Fraser was said to be a farmer of wealth as early as 1791.[67] Such cases of wealth drawn almost exclusively from farming, though, are not numerous at any time and seem to get fewer with time. The search for conspicuously affluent farmers is not very rewarding. Colonel E.W. Thompson was a farmer and a reputed man of means but, it will be remembered, he was also for a long time an active contractor. John Willson farmed in Saltfleet Township for sixty-three years, but left a total estate in 1860 of only $6,000,[68] hardly a mark of unusual riches even then.

Land could produce revenue in ways other than by farming it, especially by buying and selling it at a profit – in other words, through speculation. It was once confidently asserted that land speculation was so widespread in Upper Canada that it could almost be called "the Upper Canadian national game."[69] The validity of that statement depends to some extent on how the game is defined. (Not all Canadians, after all, are hockey players.) The problem lies in deciding what constituted speculation. In a study of land speculation in the Western District of Upper Canada before 1825, John Clarke has used a formula under which the possession of at least 400 acres of land implied speculation on the grounds that that amount of land, or more, was greater than "most individuals could expect to clear in their lifetime." Such a definition makes instant speculators out of a great many Upper Canadian regional leaders since, as has been shown, the 283 Upper Canadian MHAS were given by the government an average of 1,547 acres each. The average is misleading of course; some were granted as much as 5,000 acres and others none at all. When actual individual land holdings are considered, combining known government grants and what has been found out about additional land acquired by purchase (which the reader should be aware is certainly far from a complete record of such purchases), the figures are more modest though by no means insignificant. On this basis, if the 400-acre test is applied to all the MHAS, 190 of them, over two-thirds, qualify as speculators. Perhaps Clarke's cutoff point is too low. If the barrier is raised to 1,000 acres, however acquired, 127 MHAS or 45 percent became, by that arbitrary standard, speculators, which may be a more reasonable proportion, especially since the acquisition of land by grant is a lesser indication of speculation than the acquisition of land by purchase. Among the thirty-eight reputedly wealthy MHAS discussed earlier, twenty-three, or 61 percent, are known to have acquired one way or another more than 1,000 acres.What is known about land purchases by the MHAS is, as has been admitted, fragmentary but it is still possible to say that some of them bought a lot of land. Fifty-nine of the MHAS are known to have bought more than 500 acres of land and thirty-nine bought more than 1,000 acres.

It cannot be said that all or any of these men were necessarily speculators. The simple possession of 500 acres or 1,000 acres or more than 1,000 acres does not prove speculative intent. It could mean, as has been suggested, the accumulation of land for family members, and no arbitrary acreage level is therefore really satisfactory.

As R.W. Widdis has correctly pointed out, what matters is not just the scale of operation of a landowner, but the motivation for land acquisition. Did the acquisition of land involve real speculation "the assumption of a business risk in hopes of procuring gain"? Although

Widdis's own proposed method for identifying speculators is too cumbersome for use on a large scale and is based on data which is not complete for the whole province, his point is a valid one.[70]

Only on an individual basis can it confidently be said that some leading Upper Canadians were speculators on a considerable scale, especially in one of the most common of sources of speculative land, United Empire Loyalist or military rights, a commodity popular throughout the entire Upper Canadian period. Many Loyalists or their children and (after the War of 1812) militiamen were happy to dispose of some or all of their grants by assigning their rights to a purchaser for cash. The reason that rights were so popular with speculators was because they were cheap. Once acquired, purchasers had to go through a process of applying to government, in the face of continually changing regulations, to have the rights assigned to them confirmed and turned into actual patented land, but despite a good deal of red tape the process was evidently considered worth the trouble and a brisk trade in rights went on.

Among the MHAS, Samuel Street seems to qualify as a speculator. He petitioned the executive council in 1798 to be given title to 9,800 acres of land which had been assigned to him by a series of individuals.[71] Alexander Fraser's land dealings also look highly speculative. Among the 2,200 or more acres in Loyalist rights and other purchases which he accumulated were two lots in Sydenham Township.[72] The distance of these lots (about 360 miles) from Fraser's home in Charlottenburgh Township would suggest that he and his children didn't plan to farm them. The frequency with which Edward Malloch applied to the government to have Loyalist rights and other land purchases regularized in his own name suggests that for him the buying and selling of land was close to a full-time occupation.[73] As early as 1799 R.I.D. Gray successfully applied to have patents issued to him for 9,700 acres made up of forty-three "sundry deeds of bargain and sale from sons and daughters of United Empire Loyalists to R.I.D. Gray Esq."[74] Since Gray was unmarried, he for one was not acquiring land for any (living) children. Other MHAS at various times "located" lands, mostly Loyalist rights, in much greater amounts: Darcy and H.J. Boulton, 31,000 acres; G.S. Boulton, 12,700 acres; G.H. Detlor, 20,400 acres; Allan McLean, 18,000 acres; John Crysler, 60,200 acres.[75]

Large amounts of land could be amassed in ways other than by buying up rights. Richard Beasely bought 94,012 acres of land from the Six Nations Indians in 1798, which eventually became Waterloo Township.[76] R.S. Jameson bought suburban land west of Toronto in the area of the street which now bears his name, as well as 15,200 acres in Loyalist rights.[77] John Beverley Robinson, previously identified as the recipient of a substantial salary and a substantial amount of crown land, also invested in three town lots and a park lot in Toronto, and also accumulated over 1,000 acres in York County, plus land in Simcoe, Peel, and Ontario counties and "some 29 parcels elsewhere."[78] William Morris had 4,120 acres for sale in 1830[79] but it seems not to have been selling briskly. Ten years later he expressed his willingness to give away fifty acres of land to prospective buyers if they would agree to buy adjacent land.[80] W.B. Jarvis at the same time had enough land on hand to actually donate 1,600 acres to an early land consortium, the Canada Emigration Association, in the hope of attracting imigrant settlers with the bait of small amounts of free land.[81]

The cases of Jarvis and Morris raise the question of whether land speculation was in fact a profitable line of business to be in. As usual it is difficult to give a definitive answer to the question. The fact that so many leading Upper Canadians appear to have been involved in it to some degree suggests that it was a way in which many people *hoped* to make money. It is also easier to link land speculation to leading Upper Canadians who have been identified, however reliably, as being wealthy than to make similar links between the other land based activity, farming, and wealth. Thus Thomas Fraser (died 1821) may have been a prosperous farmer, but he is also known to have owned over 20,000 acres of land, a suspiciously large farm for the time. Other prominent men of presumed wealth, such as Asa Werden, George Rolph, or Absalom Shade are also known to have been part-time speculators. Yet it is not easy to associate speculation directly with wealth, partly because land speculation was almost never the sole occupation of any of the MHAS and partly because there isn't much evidence in the Upper Canadian period of unusual sudden wealth acquired through speculation. Sir Allan MacNab's biographer, who describes him as "one of the leading practitioners" of land speculation, contends that at certain favourable times MacNab made large profits from land sales, especially in the town of Hamilton where land prices rose dramatically in the early 1830s. In MacNab's case, however, it is impossible, as it is so often, to isolate the contribution of land speculation to his overall income from the many other business operations in which he was involved, all of which were in any case actually financed through borrowing from banks and other sources.[82] A recent study of land speculation in the Niagara Peninsula argues that for those who speculated in land on the largest scale the object was not quick profits but long-term gain. For Robert Hamilton, father of the MHAS Robert the younger and

George, "in 20 years your *ideal* wealth is to produce a hundred fold."[83] It was probably hard to lose money on land if the owner could afford to keep it, since the demand went generally up as the province grew, but the demand wasn't very strong for a long time and it was possible to get stuck with a lot of land that couldn't be turned into cash. Before the 1850s, there is no obvious land "boom" period in which dramatic windfall profits could be made. Land speculation undoubtedly helped some people to accumulate wealth in the long run; it is less certain that land speculation alone routinely produced wealth in the period before 1841. Land was more or less valuable depending on its quality and (especially) its location, but even the classic source of wealth through speculation – turning former rural land got cheap or free into urban building lots – cannot be said to have produced any *known* remarkable cases of wealth in the Upper Canadian period. George Hamilton at Hamilton[84] and Francis Baby at Sandwich,[85] and perhaps the Jessups in Prescott and the Buells and Joneses in Brockville, benefited financially from being lucky enough to have land in the right place at the right time. They were all members of distinguished Upper Canadian families, but the extent to which they were wealthier than most of their contemporaries is open to some doubt. There is no reason to think that the second generation of Buells, who have been examined with care by Ian MacPherson, derived any extensive benefits from the fact that their father had once owned and had subdivided the land which became downtown Brockville.[86] For the seller, land eventually loses its value once it is sold.

Can anything concrete be said about wealth in Upper Canada? Perhaps not much, but perhaps, based on the scattered bits of information which have been pulled together about those among the MHAS who were supposedly well-to-do, this much: that wealth was most likely to be associated with some form of mercantile activity; that wealth was very likely the result of a combination of activities which could include non-business activities such as public office; that Scots seem to have been better equipped than other nationalities to successfully acquire wealth; and that it was best to arrive early in the province and then to stay in one advantageous spot. This last observation suggests an additional factor which may have been significant in some cases – the achievement of some form of "monopoly" situation. It was because Matthew Elliott and not someone else had the contract to supply the garrison at Fort Malden that he was able to amass those "valuable effects" which filled nine wagons. Richard

Hatt's carefully chosen location and multiple enterprises at Dundas put him "virtually in a monopoly position"[87] and the same was likely true of quite a few other multi-faceted entrepreneurs in early strategic locations, such as George Brouse at Iroquois, James Crooks at Crook's Hollow, Absolom Shade at Shade's Mills, or George Longley at Maitland. For a time, for some longer than others, theirs were the only game in town.

CHAPTER THREE

The Building Blocks

The possession of much land or much wealth, especially wealth acquired through a range of activities which touched the lives of many local people, was no doubt important in the achievement of regional prominence, but land or wealth alone was not a guarantee of high community esteem or of public status recognized by higher authority.

There were two principal initial and often overlapping roads to public recognition in Upper Canada, one civil and one military, both eagerly sought after by ambitious or public-spirited men throughout the province. Two kinds of commission demonstrated that, in the eyes of the already regionally prominent and in the eyes of the central elite, recognition was merited and a requisite basic level of status had been achieved. The commissions were a commission of the peace and a commission in the provincial militia. Most MHAS held both.

The importance of the office of justice of the peace or magistrate (the terms were used interchangably) has been repeatedly stressed by Upper Canadian historians. F.H. Armstrong has written that being appointed a magistrate "while not quite a sort of local 'patent of nobility,' indicated that [the appointee] or his family earlier, had received recognition" and that the office was "a touch-stone of membership in the ruling class." The magistrates, Colin Read has written, were "the linchpins of district government." Their influence, J.H. Aitchison concluded, was "all pervasive." G.M. Craig called them "the real basis of local government throught the history of the province."[1] There is no doubt that all of these statements are perfectly accurate. Becoming a magistrate did imply that status had been conferred. Magistrates customarily added "esquire" to their names as a sign that they had received the local colonial equivalent of "a patent of nobility." Becoming a magistrate also involved, if the position was taken seriously in a proper spirit of *noblesse oblige*, a very wide range of mainly thankless duties.

The functions of the magistracy have been frequently described elsewhere, but it may be useful to restate some of them at this point, particularly since their actual judicial role has not received a great deal of attention. The magistrates were charged with the responsibility for "keeping the peace" in their districts at the lowest levels of the Upper Canadian court system. They dealt mainly with petty crimes and petty debts. It has been said that "Upper Canada was not seriously threatened by crime,"[2] but it is hard to believe that the magistrates would have agreed. They were not short of business. If anything there were often too few magistrates to meet the needs of justice. At the most basic level, the magistrates presided over the Courts of Requests which existed in divisions of the districts, covering usually two or three townships, with two or three magistrates empowered to act as commissioners of the courts. These courts heard "small causes" for the recovery of debts (until 1833 the maximum debt over which they had jurisdiction was £5) but they were held frequently, on the first and third Saturday of every month. They were somewhat casual in their procedures, meeting in private homes or taverns where the magistrates did not always receive much respect, being sometimes exposed to "insult, uproar and contempt of legal authority on the part of the suitors and visitors." They were "governed by no strict rules of law," and the magistrates acted entirely on their own, unassisted by a clerk or bailiff. At this level of justice the magistrates often made up the law as they went along, "sometimes in opposition to every principle of justice, sometimes taking it on themselves to decide points which courts of higher jurisdiction would hesitate to decide upon."[3] It should be kept in mind that no magistrate at any time was required to have even the slightest legal training.

Proceedings at the next level of the court system, the Court of Quarter Sessions, were a shade more formal. Here the magistrates gathered four times a year at the district town, one of their number being elected to preside as chairman, surrounded by district functionaries – the sheriff and his deputy, a court crier, one or more constables, a coroner, and the indispensible clerk of the peace who recorded the proceedings. The courts disposed, with the aid of juries, of the backlog of alleged crimes which had built up since the previous sessions. Upper Canadians were not gentle people. The overwhelming majority of the cases concerned assault and battery,[4] with petty larceny a clear but distant second category of crime. The other crimes which came before the magistrates showed great variety, embracing selling liquor without a licence, breach of the peace, nuisance, "swindling," and many other minor charges. Even in this court one suspects that at times the law was being created on the spot, for some unusual charges such as "cutting down corn in a field and lying in wait" or "breaking a door" can be found in the records of the courts.[5] The law's concerns seem also to have varied somewhat from district to district. The London District magistrates in particular were periodically much concerned with moral crimes: "swearing one profane oath," "breaking the Sabbath," "bastardy," "living in a lewd state," or "gambling."[6]

The correct official name of the courts, "The General Quarter Sessions of the Peace," is potentially misleading in two ways. It might be supposed that the magistrates met on four days of the year only, and it might be supposed that their proceedings, unlike those of the Courts of Requests, were conducted in customary formality and decorum. Neither of these was true. The court met in January, April, July, and October but sat each time on a irregular schedule until all the business before the magistrates was disposed of, which meant that the court could meet as many as fifteen or more times over one, two, or three months, so that one quarter could and sometimes did follow another with no real break in between. As for decorum, consider as an example an incident which took place at the London District court house on 13 March 1805:

John McCall, is brought into Court, in Custody of The under Sheriff, charged with high crimes and misdemeanors by William Hutchison Esquire. John McCall the Prisoner, asked William Hutchison Esquire, what he wanted with him, William Hutchison Esquire, in answer, Said, to find Bail for the Peace and Good behaviour, and your appearance at the next Assizes; the Prisoner Said, will you take Land, or Horses, or money, or Dogs for Security, I have two goods Dogs; William Hutchison Equire answering Said, No none but personal Security will do.

Benajah Mallory Esquire appearing at the Bar, William Hutchison Esquire threatened to Send him to Goal [sic] and demanded Bail for his good behaviour which Benajah Mallory Esquire positively refused to give, Said he had done nothing, and plead priviledge [sic], as being a member of Parliament.

The Prisoner, John McCall Said, Speak up, Captain Mallory, you are a Gentleman, you are the only Gentleman in the house or in the District, I am not quite certain which.

William Hutchison Esquire, Said if you open your mouth again, I will order you to be put in the Stocks; the Prisoner then gaped his mouth wide open and Said, I shall want some more Whiskey. William Hutchison Esquire, then ordered the Prisoner to be put in the Stocks, and the under Sheriff commanding assistance took the prisoner out of the Court Room and reported upon Oath, with the Oath also of the High Constable, that the Prisoner was Resqued [sic] out of their hands by Philip Fonger, Constable of Charlotteville, Joseph Miller, of Charlotteville, Miller, Peter Combs, of Charlotteville, Carpenter, Robert Monro, of Charlotteville, Farmer, and many others, and by the Oath of Henry Bostwick, and the Under Sherriff, that Anthony Sells, of Charlotteville labourer, being Commanded to assist in putting the Prisoner, in the Stocks disobeyed those orders and fled.[7]

What kept the magistrates busy over longish periods of time at each meeting of quarter sessions was not just their never-ending battle against crime. They had, as is well known, sweeping administrative responsibilities for the entire functioning of local government in Upper Canada. This part of their work, the subject of much discussion by others,[8] will only be summarized here, though even summarizing their duties satisfactorily is not an easy matter. The magistrates controlled the finances of their district, set the rate of local taxation to meet estimated yearly expenditure, appointed and supervised a district treasurer, and supervised the tax assessors and collectors. They arranged to have built and administered the district public buildings, the courthouse and jail, and were responsible for their upkeep and repair. They issued licences and certificates of good character to the many tradesmen, tavern keepers, petitioners, and others who needed them. They regulated and set rates for public ferries. They made regulations for the public markets. They supervised the work of all the township officers such as pathmasters, wardens, and poundkeepers. All such matters and many more were dealt with at the meetings of quarter sessions, interspersed with the court's judicial activities.

Outside of quarter sessions, the magistrates (acting singly or as "any two" of them) also had a wide range of duties. They administered the oath of allegiance to all local officers. They issued warrants for the holding of township meetings. They approved the apprenticeship of orphan children. They were almost perpetually involved in the supervision of the building of roads and bridges. Acting in divisions which usually corresponded to the divisions of the Courts of Requests, they were road commissioners for a section of their district – two, three, or four townships at a time. And they assumed many other small responsibilities which are impossible to describe succintly. Professor Aitchison was right. At the local level they were all-pervasive. They were also totally unrepresentative, owing not the slightest responsibility to the people whose affairs they administered, holding office only by appointment of the provincial government.

It might be supposed that given the number of public duties which being a magistrate involved, such appointments might have been frequently avoided rather than sought after. Certainly the nature of the magistrates' duties were unlikely to make them popular among all members of their communities. They sometimes handed out sentences which not only involved punishment but could include public humiliation. The Midland District magistrates for example dealt firmly in April 1790 with a man convicted of stealing "a shear coulter and bolt." (One wonders why he didn't just steal a whole plough.) The magistrates ordered that he receive "thirty-nine lashes on his bare back at the public whipping post, suffer one month's imprisonment and ... be set in the stocks one day in each week of that month with the label of *Thief*."[9]

It is true that the government often had trouble in finding enough suitable, competent people to act in all the townships in the districts; it is also true that some magistrates neglected or mishandled their duties or acted arbitrarily.[10] But by and large it is abundantly evident that the appointment was considered highly desirable, not just for the local power thereby acquired and certainly not for the remuneration, which was negligible, but for the status conferred. The only thing worse than not being appointed a magistrate at all was being appointed a magistrate and later being removed from the list. This was a way in which the executive government of the province or its local advisors in the districts or both could punish behaviour perceived as unbecoming to a public officer. After the Gourlay incident of 1817–18, for example, some magistrates who had taken too active a part in his meetings found themselves stripped of their "local patent of nobility" or did not receive it until they had recovered from their delusions and were sufficiently contrite. Richard Beasely, who has already been encountered as a merchant-miller-developer, who was also a colonel of militia, a veteran of both the Revolution and the War of 1812, who had been a magistrate in Upper Canada since 1796, was struck off the "Commission of the Peace" for seven years before finally receiving that distinction again.[11] Several other Gourlayites who had served with distinction during the War of 1812, such as John Brant and Thomas Coleman, never became magistrates, while William Chisholm had to wait until 1829.[12] Donald Fraser, a former British officer who had served under Wellington, although he had nothing to do with Gourlay, found that, while he had been made a magistrate of the Johnstown District in 1821, on moving to the Bathurst District he was not put on the list of magistrates for his new district. He was worried about this oversight – not, he professed, on his own account, but because it might be seen by the local populace as "a mark of disfavour" which would weaken their respect for and deference to their social and political betters. His argument was accepted and the mistake corrected with all deliberate speed, three years after he had complained.[13]

Professor Armstrong has used the term "building block" in relation to the magistracy.[14] It is an apt phrase, because usually an appointment as a magistrate came first in an Upper Canadian's public career, before going on (if at all) to other and more prestigious appointments. Becoming a magistrate was one very important way of signalling that the minimum requirements for public status and recognition had been met. Among all the 283 Upper Canadian MHAS, 185, or about 65 percent, were magistrates. This is not perhaps as high a proportion as might be expected. In fact quite a few prominent Upper Canadians were never magistrates at all because they were examples of "accelerated promotion." They skipped the lowest rung on the ladder of status and power and went directly into higher or better-paid offices. This could occur through the intervention of an authority even more powerful than the provincial executive. S.F. Wise has described "The Rise of Christopher Hagerman." who was never a magistrate, as a result of his favourable standing with the British military command.[15] Other Upper Canadian office-holders were simply parachuted into an unsuspecting province from afar. John White, brought from England to be the first attorney general, was an early example of this type; he was followed periodically by people like Judge Henry Allcock and Judge Robert Thorpe. The pattern was still in vogue when R.S. Jameson was brought out to be attorney general in 1833. More frequently, the provincial executive conferred a swift rise to higher prominence on people already in the province who were seen as possessing special ability or special claims. An English barrister, D'Arcy Boulton, went straight into the office of solicitor general without holding any lower office. Two of his sons followed similar paths; H.J. Boulton also began in government service at the level of solicitor general, while G.S. Boulton's first office was as registrar of the County of Northumberland. R.I.D. Gray, like the two Boultons, started as solicitor general at the age of twenty-five. The best known example of really early preferment was John Beverley Robinson, whose exceptional legal powers were recognized by an appointment as acting attorney general at age twenty-one. Altogether, of the ninety-eight MHAS who were never magistrates, forty-four never occupied the "building block" office simply because they were originally given other offices of greater status instead.

On the other hand, some MHAS did not become magistrates or anything else for the opposite reason – that is, because they were considered unfit to be awarded status. The rise of a political opposition from the 1820s onward produced people who were prominent in their regions but who were not considered safe by the provincial administration. While it is not quite true (as G.M. Craig believed) that "very few" Reformers were magistrates, it is certainly true that a higher proportion of Conservative than Reformer MHAS were magistrates (a subject which will be dealt with more fully in a later chapter). Of seventy-one MHAS serving between 1828 and 1841 who have been identified as Reformers, thirty-four, or 48 percent, were magistrates. The comparable Conservative figure is 71 percent. This ideological bias helps to explain the fact that the overall proportion of MHAS who were magistrates declined over time. Of the early Group A of 103 MHAS, 74 percent were also magistrates. For the later 138 MHAS in Group B the figure is 64 percent – a decline, though not really a dramatic decline. In the very last parliament of Upper Canada (1836–41) only forty-four out of seventy MHAS had received appointments as magistrates, for almost exactly the same percentage – 63 percent.

For those not seen as being either over- or under-qualified to be magistrates, the "building block" process can be readily demonstrated. Among 104 magistrate-MHAS who are known to have held other government office as well, 72 percent were magistrates prior to receiving the other office or offices. For those whose qualifications or ambition took them some way up the scale of preferment, the usual way was first to become and satisfactorily perform as a magistrate. It should also be noted that the magistracy was normally a prelude to elected as well as appointive office. Out of the 185 magistrate-MHAS (1792–1841), 118 were either magistrates prior to their election or were appointed (16 of them) in the year of their election. The percentage of MHAS whose appointments as magistrate preceeded their election (64 percent) is therefore very similar to the equivalent figure for those who later held higher appointed office. The progress from magistrate to MHA can be demonstrated in a second way. The average age of appointment to the magistracy was 38.3 years. The equivalent age of first election was 39.2 years. And if these figures are compared to the average age for first appointment to *any* civil office (35.5 years) the difference is even greater.

Some form of public recognition of suitability bestowed from above in the form of a government position usually came before elected office. Of course the MHAS were popularly elected, and there were even numerous cases of residents of townships trying to "elect" their own magistrates by submitting petitions to the lieutenant governor nominating certain individuals who had been chosen at a kind of local informal primary election,[16] but in the main, regional political prominence was not a phenomenon which emerged from the bottom up. In the majority of cases, prestige, prominence, and status were bestowed from afar by the central elite, with or without the advice of local worthies who had themselves already achieved prominence.

Appointment as a magistrate was the basic way of conferring civil status and civil power. But status and power were not exercised by nor confined to the leadership of the civil society alone, for Upper Canada was not just a civil or civilian society. Upper Canadians, especially prominent Upper Canadians, saw themselves as part of an important defence organization, almost (it is possible to say) as living in a permanent armed camp. Any view of Upper Canadian society in general and Upper Canadian leadership in particular that ignores this fact is a distorted and misleading view, which fails to take into account some fundamental lessons of Upper Canadian history.

It has been said that Upper Canada's provincial leaders felt their province to be "under a state of permanent siege"[17] and as a result developed a kind of garrison mentality. The enemy was, of course, the United States. The perceived threat was by no means purely military; it was also economic and above all ideological, and for many the threat was not only external but also in the midst of Upper Canadian society itself, among a partly American and possibly Americanizing population. A genuine military threat, though, was never, and was never allowed to be, very far below the surface. It needs to be kept in mind that Upper Canada began as the result of a war which was a civil war as well as a revolution, and that the Loyalist losers who came north to found the new province left in bad blood, bringing lasting, bitter resentments with them, leaving behind the victors who were and remained contemptuous of the beaten "Tories." It has been said that this state of enmity began gradually to ease as personal and business relationships were re-established across the border, and there is some evidence to show that this occurred in some cases.[18] But students of Upper Canadian history are in agreement that the War of 1812 exerted a very powerful influence on Upper Canadians to turn them once more into staunch anti-Americans and at the same time to implant the first seeds of real nationalism among a population which believed, or had been told, that the inhabitants of the province, had "repelled its invaders, slew or took them all prisoners, and captured from its enemies the greater part of the arms by which it was defended."[19] Upper Canadians were prone to dating events as being before or after "the late war." The War of 1812, a military event, may well have been the most significant single occurrence in Upper Canadian history.

The War of 1812 occurred within scarcely more than a generation of the American Revolution. Quite a number of Upper Canadians fought in both; military threat and military experience were contemporary. In fact the whole period, as Wise has pointed out, was one in which British forces were almost constantly in action against the rebellious Americans and against the French, in which the British Empire, which included Upper Canada, could be interpreted as fighting a long holy war against the forces of revolutionary evil.[20] The War of 1812 demonstrated that the threat was indeed within as well as without. There *were* Upper Canadians who sympathized and even collaborated with the enemy, some of whom were hanged for their treasonable activities. Two MHAS, Joseph Willcocks and Abraham Markle, defected to and served with the enemy, as did a former MHA, Benajah Mallory.

Twenty-three years after the war, Upper Canada's third military event, the Rebellion of 1837, occurred. The rebellion was a small, brief affair which presented relatively few opportunities for conspicuous military accomplishments, but it could once again be used to demonstrate the reality of the threat. There *were* disloyal, violent, revolutionary elements among the people which had to be put down by military force. Again, some local leaders, MHAS or former MHAS William Lyon Mackenzie, Charles Duncombe, Finlay Malcolm, David Gibson, and Samuel Lount, were in actual arms against the government of Upper Canada and a good many others came under a cloud of suspicion. Again during the period of border raids which followed the United States was perceived as the enemy, harbouring rebels and providing a breeding ground for secret anti-Upper Canadian societies and secret conspiracies and a launching pad for raiding parties which had to be militarily repulsed. Even if they had wanted to, Upper Canadians were never allowed to forget that for them military preparedness was a necessity and that military service and military leadership were therefore vital to the well-being of the community.

Across the province Upper Canadians were broadly exposed to military presence and military experience. If some Upper Canadians had a garrison mentality, they also had actual garrisons to go with it. It would be laughable to suggest that Upper Canada was ever, even in war, heavily defended, but the province was garrisoned and fortified more or less consistently at quite a number of places, such as Kingston, York/Toronto, Niagara, Fort Erie, Chippawa, Amherstburgh, Bytown, Prescott, Penetanguishene, Michilimackinac (until 1796 and during the war), Drummond Island (until 1828), Grand River, and London. There were always British regular troops in Upper Canada, sometimes quite a few of them, a visible reminder of the need for defence against the enemy without.[21] In times of emergency, as in 1812–14 and 1837–8, their numbers increased dramatically, but in peacetime also a series of British regular regiments (including the Fifteenth, Twenty-fourth, Sixty-eight, Seventeenth, Seventy-first, Seventy-sixth, and Seventy-ninth) made their headquarters in Kingston, York, or Niagara and provided one or two companies or small detachments for the smaller centres. From 1796 to 1802, as has been seen, two of the principal fortified areas, Kingston and Niagara, were garrisoned by a regiment raised in the colony among veterans of the Revolution, the Royal Canadian Volunteers.

After the War of 1812 the British military presence in Upper Canada was increased in a number of official and unofficial ways. The Rideau Lakes area in particular received an infusion of disbanded officers and men whose initial settlement was paid for by Great Britain, as were members of the Corps of Sappers and Miners who helped build the Rideau Canal. The period of peace after 1815 also saw the arrival of quite a few officers, now on half pay, who settled, often in small groups, in areas like the Rideau Lakes, around Peterborough or Woodstock, or elsewhere. As many writers have pointed out, their immigrant experience was rarely happy but they had, by virtue of their former profession, instant status in Upper Canada. They were welcomed gladly by the provincial executive as officers and gentlemen whose presence would raise the tone of provincial society and dilute the unfortunate American character of the population. Men such as Donald Fraser, Robert Rollo Hunter, James Wickens, Alexander Chisholm, John Kearns, George Lyon, or John Alexander Wilkinson, none of whom had held a commission in the British army above the rank of lieutenant, were quickly showered with land grants, appointments to the magistracy, militia commissions, and other offices, even though their competence in these new roles did not always turn out to be very great.

All ordinary Upper Canadians in the province who were male, able-bodied, and between the ages of sixteen and sixty[22] were under an unavoidable military obligation. They belonged automatically to the provincial militia. Service in the militia was not normally a very onerous duty, though the possibility of active service, and of being disabled or killed was always there and sometimes, as in 1812–14, turned out to be real. Most of the time, for most people, service in the militia was confined to the annual muster of each regiment for a day of rudimentary drill, which no one except some of the officers took very seriously. Mrs. Jameson's well-known account of such an event is probably an accurate enough description of most such musters. The officer "made himself hoarse shouting out orders which no one obeyed" and "the parade day ended in a drunken bout and a riot."[23] (Officers of militia, like magistrates, sometimes received very little respect.) It would be pointless to pretend that militia service was a frequent preoccupation for the rank and file, but then most of the time soldiers everywhere, even those who are paid, spend most of their time waiting for something to happen. The annual militia muster served the purpose of a periodic reminder of a continuing duty and a continuing belief in the possibility of war.

Each Upper Canadian county, of which there were originally nineteen, had at least one militia regiment. Before the Rebellion of 1837 there were already sixty-four regiments, eight in York County alone, and the rebellion produced an absolute explosion in militia expansion. By 1838 the number of militia regiments had reached 111, 16 York and 13 Gore regiments among them, plus a variety of independent rifle and artillery companies and troops of cavalry. So many regiments required a good many officers. Each regiment when at full strength, had a colonel, a lieutenant colonel, a major, and at least five and as many as ten each of captains, lieutenants, and ensigns, as well as a quartermaster and (if one could be found) a surgeon.[24]

Service in the militia was compulsory; service as a militia officer was not. Militia commissions could be refused and they could be resigned. By and large, they were rarely refused and only reluctantly resigned, sometimes under great pressure. Militia commissions were undertaken as a matter of duty by prominent men in their areas. They were also an almost indispensible mark of local status and were eagerly sought. Particularly when the command, that is the colonelcy, of a regiment was involved, they could be bitterly contended for. "I have learned by dear-bought experience," John Prince wrote to the adjutant general of militia in 1841, "that the Command of a Militia Regiment in this Country entails upon one (if one does one's duty) Envy, hatred and malice, and all uncharitableness."[25] One example of what Prince meant, involving three men who were also at some point in their careers MHAS, may usefully serve as an introduction to the idea of the militia as status symbol, and to how such status was achieved.

In 1832 the colonel of the First Regiment of Stormont Militia, Albert French, wrote to the adjutant general of militia at the provincial capital to say that he was suffering ill health and wished to resign his command.[26] French's wish to be replaced was soon known in the area, and three candidates for the colonelcy emerged: Donald Aeneas Macdonell, lieutenant colonel of the regiment, Philip VanKoughnet, lieutenant colonel of the Second Regiment of Stormont militia, and Archibald McLean, colonel of the Second Regiment. It may seem puzzling that a man who was already colonel of a regiment would wish to be transferred to the command of another. McLean's motives were partly sentimental; the First was the senior regiment and had once been commanded by his father, Neil McLean.[27]

Faced with three strong claimants, all about the same age, all of whom had held requisite civil and military appointed and elected offices, all of whom had been pupils of the Reverend John Strachan, and all of whom were well known to the provincial bureaucracy, the government (that is the lieutenant governor in consultation with the adjutant general) did nothing for as long as possible, which turned out to be four years. French died in 1836 not, as it happened, from ill-health, but by being beaten to death by two canal labourers.[28] In the meantime, the three would-be commanding officers had had plenty of time to state their own cases and to disparage the claims of the others. Macdonell had an advocate inside the provincial administration, his uncle, John Beikie, clerk of the Executive Council. (Coincidentally, Beikie, like Macdonell, McLean, and VanKoughnet had once served as MHA for Stormont.) Beikie stated his nephew's case in a letter to the lieutenant governor's military secretary. Macdonell was "true and deserving ... a gentleman by birth as well as behaviour." "By birth" he was the son of Miles Macdonell and the grandson of John Macdonell, both of whom had been officers of the King's Royal Regiment of New York and both of whom had also been colonels of the First Regiment of Stormont Militia.[29]

But other unrecorded representations had also been made to the lieutenant governor. Macdonell soon heard unofficially that he would not get the appointment; it was going to be given to McLean. Deeply mortified, Macdonell submitted his resignation from the regiment, to take effect if "Mr. McLean or any other person" became colonel. He gave up his "post of honour" because he believed the government was playing favourites. "I observe," he observed, "that a person can walk from one regiment to another, if they please, if possessed of influence."[30]

Macdonell was right in suspecting that the fix was in. The nature of the plan became clear when French actually died, but meanwhile a complication had arisen; the lieutenant governship had changed hands. The new man, Sir Francis Bond Head, had his attention drawn by Philip Vankoughnet to "the arrangement made by Sir Peregrine Maitland during his administration which was that Mr. McLean was to succeed to the command of the First Regt. as soon as the vacancy ensued and I was to succeed to the Second Regt."[31] Head was not necessarily going to be bound by his predecessor's decisions and took the view that the lieutenant colonel of a regiment ought to be promoted to a vacant colonelcy "unless good reasons can be shown to the contrary."[32] The fight was now on in earnest. Appointing Macdonell, VanKoughnet argued, would be "a great injustice" to himself and McLean because they were "many years his senior" in the militia. This happened to be true. McLean had already been a colonel and VanKoughnet a lieutenant colonel back in 1822 when Macdonell was commissioned a major. VanKoughnet had an even stronger reason for opposing Macdonell. In politics Macdonell was a Reformer. If Macdonell were to be promoted over VanKoughnet's head, *he* would resign, "for I *never* will bring myself to serve under the command of a person possessing the Revolutionary principles that he does."[33] Macdonell, perhaps informed that his loyalty had been cast into doubt, restated the services of his family in the Revolution and his own in the War of 1812, in which he had served as an officer of a British regular regiment "with which corps he was present in several general actions and was severely wounded." He was still, he added, a British officer on half pay.[34]

Archibald McLean, after also reminding Head of Sir Peregrine Maitland's promise, was prepared to match his war record with anyone's. He too had been "severely wounded" at Queenston Heights while serving as a militia Lieutenant. He had recruited and commanded a company of incorporated militia on the Niagara frontier. He had fought at Lundy's Lane. He too was on half pay, as a captain. Besides he had "rendered important services" in a civil capacity since the war.[35] Macdonell was only too well aware of that. McLean was "already loaded with profitable offices ... but it appears that this is not sufficient to satisfy this individual, he must at the expense of your petitioner's feelings be gratified by stepping over his head to fill a situation in which there is no profit."[36]

On the question of War of 1812 service, VanKoughnet was the most vulnerable. Macdonell scoffed at "his imaginary service in time of the war," claiming that VanKoughnet had resigned his lieutenant's commission in the militia during the war, which "ought to operate against him." VanKoughnet had not "done his duty." He was "not distinguished for bravery in defence of his country."[37] In his defence, VanKoughnet had no battle service to point to and no wounds to show, but he was able to produce certificates to prove that he had not resigned his commission during the war. The stories of his resignation had come from "an envious and grovelling mind."[38]

Eventually the question of the colonelcy of the First Regiment of Stormont Militia was resolved to the satisfaction of McLean and VanKoughnet and to the total dissatisfaction of Macdonell. VanKoughnet received his promotion to colonel of the First Regiment. Then, by agreement with McLean and Sir Francis Bond Head, he and McLean exchanged commands, VanKoughnet stepping aside so that McLean might take command of the regiment "so long under his father."[39] Macdonell resigned from the militia altogether to protest an act of injustice done to him "in placing an individual over my head who I considered had no claim."[40]

This unedifying glimpse of the petty squabbling of three "gentlemen" over the command of a regiment of militia suggests a number of observations which might be made about the way in which the militia was perceived by prominent Upper Canadians, some of which can be shown to have had more than individual validity. Appointments in the militia were keenly sought after. They were not "offices of profit" but "posts of honour." Seniority of militia service as an officer was considered important. Stress was placed on family continuity in a militia regiment. It was important to be able to establish a record of past loyalty, especially to have "done one's duty" during the War of 1812. It was necessary to be "a gentleman" to hold a commission. Being a Reformer could be a handicap but was not a total barrier to a career as a militia officer.

The degree to which these statements can be given general application, or can be quantified varies quite a bit. It must be realized, to begin with, that the completeness of the available militia data, especially when compared to that for civil offices, leaves much to be desired, since consistent militia officers' registers only begin in 1824. As a result, total available figures on militia commissions are probably lower than they ought to be. But that militia commissions were much coveted can scarcely be doubted. Among all 283 MHAS, 196 (69 percent) are known to have held commissions in the militia. It should be noted that these figures are slightly higher than those for the number of MHAS who were magistrates (185 or 65 percent). If total military service by MHAS is taken into account, including service below officer rank and in the British regular forces, the result is even more impressive. Of the MHAS 230, or 81 percent, could claim some military service, a level of participation slightly higher than the total number of MHAS holding any kind of civil appointment (225 or 79 percent). Among Upper Canada's regional leaders it can be said that military service, especially in the militia with commissioned rank, was seen as a duty which had of necessity to be performed.

If the office of magistrate was a "building block" to which other or greater responsibilities could be added, military service was a parallel, if not more fundamental, starting point. The average age at which first militia commissions were obtained (*not* including commissions issued during the War of 1812, when a considerable number of people were commissioned at an abnormally early age) was 30.9 years, compared to 35.5 years for first civil appointment of any kind, 38.3 years for first appointment as a magistrate, and 39.2 years for first election to the legislature. The extent to which military service was customarily undertaken prior to other offices can be made clear in at least two other ways. Among 191 MHAS whose career included both military service and civil office-holding, 158 (83 percent) had done military service before holding any civil office, and of the 230 MHAS who did some form of military service, in 208 cases (90 percent) military service had already been performed prior to being elected.

It is not surprising, of course, that young men might be trusted with the burden of military leadership at an age when they would not likely be trusted with judicial or legislative duties. The point is that military service was evidently a necessary prerequisite for other civilian service. In war or peace military service was a duty which Upper Canadians expected their prospective leaders to assume.

The fact that military service was usually begun at a tender age makes it understandable that a good deal of fuss would now and then be made over who had the longest record of service, and at what rank. During the War of 1812 boys like George S. Boulton, George S. Jarvis, Allan MacNab, and W.H. Merritt saw action at the age of fifteen. Even in peacetime getting an early start in the militia was common. At least six of the MHAS had peacetime militia commissions before they were twenty. Most first commissions were obtained between the ages of twenty and twenty-nine. It should not be supposed, though, that militia service was simply a young man's game. Service beyond the age of fifty was frequent. Some men, including Peter Shaver, H.J. Boulton, Robert Nelles, John Kearns, J.B. Marks, William Thompson, the Frasers (Thomas, Alexander, Isaac, and Richard Duncan), John Crysler, James Cotter, John Clark, Zaccheus Burnham, and John Beikie, were still soldiering, mainly as commanding officers of militia regiments, in their sixties.

Continuity of military service within families, exemplified by the rival family claims of Donald Aeneas Macdonell and Archibald McLean, was, as might be expected, a recurring phenomenon. Among the 230 MHAS who had done military duty, at least 76 were the sons of men who had also had military careers. (Considering that in 69 of those 230 cases no relevant information has been found about the fathers, the rate of father-and-son military service may well have been higher.) The fact of widespread participation in the War of 1812 by former, serving, and future MHAS can also be readily shown. Some gave their lives – Thomas McKee, Matthew Elliott (at the age of about 75), Joshua Booth, and John Macdonell (Greenfield). (Joseph Willcocks was also killed, but while fighting on the wrong side.) Quite a few besides Donald Aeneas Macdonell and Archibald McLean were wounded, including George Lyon, Richard Hatt, Henry Ruttan, John Bostwick, Francis Caldwell, William McCormick, the younger William Buell, John Campbell, Thomas Dickson, Alexander McLean, and Donald Fraser. For all of the MHAS (after deducting those who were already dead, or were too young or too old to be involved, or had left or had not yet come to the province, or were prevented from serving for some other reason) 189 men are left who had no apparent reason for avoiding service. Of these, 150, or 79 percent, are known to have seen military service during 1812–14 in some capacity. This percentage is almost exactly the same as the overall percentage of all MHAS who saw military service at any time, which might suggest that a high proportion (that is about 80 percent) of Upper Canadian regional leaders could be expected to be involved in military activities in peace or war.

Having responded to the call of duty during 1812–14 at a suitably high level, Upper Canada's actual and aspiring local leaders used that response in future years as one strong mark of their fitness for popular or official recognition. Having "done one's duty" was a basic requirement; not "having done one's duty" was a serious stigma. The examples of Donald Aeneas Macdonell and Archibald McLean using their war service as a means to gain favour in the eyes of the lieutenant governor, were by no means unique, nor was Macdonell's use of VanKoughnet's alleged "lack of bravery in defence of his country" as a means of blackening another's name. In a dispute over ownership of land, James Young, who served as both an MHA and a militia officer during the war, reacted contemptuously to the claims of a man who "never did his militia duty during the late war and ... was considered by ... Lt. Colonel Bell and Major McNabb of the Hastings Militia as a suspicious character."[41] Petitions for land, or for anything else after 1814, routinely included an account of war services by those who could claim them. After the war, in fact, it became official policy to require that even the sons and daughters of Loyalists, who had ordinarily received their 200 acres as a matter of routine, had to prove "that the Parent retained his Loyalty during the late War, and was under no suspicion of aiding or assisting the Enemy – and if a Son, of Age, that he also was loyal during the late war, and did his duty in defence of the Province—and if a Daughter of an U.E. Loyalist married, that her Husband was loyal, and did his duty in defence of the Province."[42]

It is worth re-emphasizing that military duty was not something which was taken up, or peaked, in times of crisis, but was a continuing – indeed an increasing – commitment, reflecting a sense of threat and a consequent sustained need for vigilance. Among forty-seven Revolutionary War veteran-MHAS, thirty-one or 66 percent continued to serve in the provincial militia after coming to Upper Canada. Similarly, of the 145 MHAS who served in and survived the War of 1812, 92 or 63 percent also held militia commissions in the period of peace which followed. In both periods they were joined by new men, seventy-one between 1784 and 1812 and sixty-eight between 1815 and 1841, who were commissioned for the first time and who kept the overall number high. It is significant that, in comparing the two chronological groups A and B, the level of military service among MHAS actually went up in the later period. Seventy-five percent of Group A and 81 percent of Group B had seen some military duty. Militarism was not on the wane in Upper Canada in the 1820s and 1830s. The possibility that the War of 1812 might be the last to be fought on Upper Canadian soil does not appear to have occurred to prominent Upper Canadians at all.

The question of whether political leanings had a bearing on the likelihood of men acquiring or seeking militia commissions will be part of a larger discussion of politics to follow in chapter 5. Briefly, it can be said that there are some political distinctions which can be made in the case of military service. Among ninety-one MHAS who have been identified as Conservatives who served in the legislature between 1828 and 1841, eighty, or 88 percent, occupied or had occupied military positions. The equivalent figures for Reformers in the same period are fifty-one of seventy-one, or 72 percent. Reformers were less active militarily, but as a group could hardly be accused of shirking their duties. Even in the most radical of Upper Canadian parliaments (1828–30), when the proportion of MHAS who were magistrates or were holders of some higher office or were of Loyalist antecedents plummeted, the level of those who could claim some military service stayed high at 81.2 percent. (See Figure 2.)

Among Reformers themselves, however, at least one observation is appropriate. It is evident that militarism and radicalism did not often go hand in hand. On the list of fifty-five MHAS who are not known to have ever seen military service of any kind are two of the earliest political malcontents (Judge Robert Thorpe and William Weekes), two who defected to the United States during the War of 1812 (Abraham Markle and Joseph Willcocks), two "Gourlayites" (Barnabas Bidwell and Willet Casey), four suspected rebels of 1837 (M.S. Bidwell, T.D. Morrison, W.B. Wells, and Reuben White), and three actual rebels (David Gibson, Samuel Lount, and W.L. Mackenzie).

It could be argued that it is unwise to put much stress on the importance of military service, especially as an officer in the militia, since the functions of a militia officer were ordinarily more ceremonial than arduous, in contrast (for example) to the many essential functions performed by the magistrates. It could be argued too that the revolution, the war, and the rebellion created an artificial situation which made a peaceable society more than usually warlike in outlook. These are valid arguments, up to a point. The duties of a militia officer were less demanding and far less frequent than those of most civil officers, although it may again be remarked that such offices did not involve the possibility of having one's head blown off. Nonetheless most civil offices had the advantage of returning some financial compensation, however slight, in the way of salary or fees for services rendered. A militia commission was not only not "an office of profit," it was likely to be an office of loss. After 1839 a militia commission involved the payment of a fee by the recipient.[43] Some officers, particularly dashing young captains of cavalry companies, spent money on uniforms and equipment. When the York Dragoons, commanded by George Taylor Denison, were disbanded in 1839 after active service during the rebellion, three of Denison's sons outfitted the troopers at their own expense with "shakos, sabres, sabre belts, ammunition pouches and jackets" so that the unit and the family's honour and image might be maintained.[44] Officers were expected, it nothing else, to treat the men at the annual muster. Except in time of war, militia service at any level was unpaid. A militia commission conveyed a measure of power but it assumed rather than bestowed a degree of wealth. Nor was the possession of power over others always an unmixed blessing. Colonel Josias Tayler, commanding the Third Regiment of Lanark Militia, expressed a not-uncommon sentiment when he complained that he had to cope with "a bad set of officers," including "an old gentleman" who "cannot be altogether right in the upper story." (The "old gentleman" was also a magistrate.) Weary of the responsibilities of command, Tayler wished himself at "a respectful distance from such a set of yahoos as I have to deal with here."[45]

Whether being a militia officer or holding a civil post was more or less thankless or more of less time-consuming is in the end somewhat beside the point, because more often than not (as in the case of "the old gentleman") both kinds of positions were held by the same people wearing different or, it might be said, overlapping, hats. Yet there is still a sense, as has been shown, in which military service can be said to have taken precedence over civil appointments. It was more widely sought and earlier sought than any other public duty. A commission in the militia was a status appointment.[46] As J.W. Gamble put it, a militia commission tended "to produce a certain degree of respect and deference from the mass, towards those who may hold superiority of station or rank."[47] The evidence suggests that a militia commission was *the* basic status appointment, almost an indispensible requirement for anyone hoping to assume a regional leadership role.

As for the fact of revolution, war, and rebellion producing an artificially military attitude in Upper Canada, it needs only be said that, while in the great cosmic scheme of things the situation may have been abnormal, the point is that at the time it *was* the situation, and there would be no use in pretending that it should have been otherwise. Upper Canadians lived with war, or the rumour of war, or the expectation of war. Canadians have been described as an "unmilitary people." If the behaviour of most of their leaders is any indication, Upper Canadians were a military people who, as time passed became more, rather than less, military.

There was then not one "building block" office but two, both of which were essential prerequisites to greater things, both of which were "local patents of nobility" conferred from on high. Both positions could be onerous, both were basically thankless tasks, yet both were in demand, because local status, local prestige, local prominence were impossible if these offices at least could not be obtained.

CHAPTER FOUR

Power and Patronage

Most MHAS also held civil and military office. Holding the two basic offices, as a magistrate or as a militia officer, conveyed status which could be increased by acquiring other or more responsible civil offices or by promotion in the militia. Civil office-holding also implied the possibility of security. An appointment to the central bureaucracy, to the judiciary, to one of the district, county, or customs positions, or to some combination of small offices could produce a livable income or, if combined with other activities, a reliable nest egg which constituted a margin of safety in an uncertain world. Office-holding always conferred status; it sometimes produced security. It could also involve the exercise of power.

Not all offices gave the incumbents much real or direct power over others. Some offices (clerk of the peace, district treasurer, or county registrar for example) were largely just matters of recording or accounting. And no doubt not all office-holders enjoyed such opportunities as they had for the exercise of power. Certainly there are instances enough of the neglect of duties, especially by magistrates but also by more exalted officers. Yet the potential for the exercise of power always existed, and power, in various degrees, was routinely exercised, sometimes responsibly and sensibly, sometimes ignorantly and arbitrarily.

It is not difficult to understand how power belonged to those who were senior members of the provincial administration. Executive councillors not only deliberated regularly upon matters of "state" but also on matters of land. They decided who got land and in what quantities. An early land petitioner, Levy Solomons, a member of a Montreal merchant family, writing from Cornwall in 1798, was given an abrupt answer which left no doubt about the council's power over land granting: "Jews cannot hold land in this province."[1] Much less exalted officials had their own kinds of power. In the ports a collector of customs was empowered to seize goods in any quantity which he suspected had entered the province illegally, the onus then resting with the owner to show that the collector had acted wrongfully.[2] At the district level, the powers of the sheriffs were thrust upon them as servants of "the King's Courts of Justice" and were not always calculated to make them popular. They sold land for non-payment of taxes, made arrests, kept the jails, and conducted hangings as required.

The most numerous district officials, the magistrates, as has been seen, were possessed of powers which, if limited by provincial legislation, were very broad and included the power to set the rate of taxation, to appoint or dismiss the district treasurer, to grant or refuse licences and certificates, to remove and replace township officers, and to impose fines on assessors for submitting inaccurate returns. That the powers of the magistrates were real is attested to by the number of times they were accused of exceeding or abusing them. Captain John Matthews, MHA for Middlesex, himself a magistrate and certainly no shrinking violet, complained to the provincial executive that a brother magistrate was partial, arbitrary, and unjust and "neglects and exceeds his duties."[3] Charles Waters of L'Orignal also annoyed his fellow magistrates, R.P. Hotham among them, by an excessive use of power in 1832 when he released some prisoners from the district jail on his own authority.[4]

In the ordinary way, a militia commission did not convey an excess of raw power, though the officers were always part of a chain of command and could and did impose peacetime discipline on militiamen who were derelict in their duty through militia courts martial, and the commanding officers routinely imposed fines on men who did not attend the annual muster. For militia officers to have more real power, unusual events such as war or civil disturbance were necessary, at which times power, whether looked for or not, could be real indeed. No doubt the exercise of actual military command was in the main a grim business, but there is good reason for thinking that the exercise of military power was sometimes carried out with keen zest and even with a certain degree of malice. Colonel Allan MacNab, leading his triumphal sweep through western Upper Canada in search of rebels in December 1837, and on the Niagara frontier encamped opposite Navy Island, enjoyed his stint of command no end and bitterly resented attempts to supersede him even by a senior British regular officer.[5] "Power-mad" might be a better description of the state of mind of Colonel John Prince when he ordered five American invaders to be shot in cold blood on 4 December 1838.[6] It is likely also that the militia officers who were responsible for the post-rebellion arrests of Samuel Lount, Joseph N. Lockwood, Reuben White, Finlay Malcolm, T.D. Morrison, and Elias Moore derived a certain satisfaction from their work. For that matter, the same can probably be said for those MHAS who voted to expel their former colleagues W.B. Wells, John Rolph, Charles Duncombe, and David Gibson from their midst, for emergency military situations increased the power of civil authority as well. The young John Beverly Robinson, prosecuting the government's case against alleged traitors at the Ancaster "Bloody Assizes" of 1813, was an example of such unexpected power. So were the fourteen sitting or former MHAS who in 1814 were appointed "Commissioners to Arrest Persons suspected of High Treason."[7]

An individual illustration of the extent and nature of personal power enjoyed by certain office holders may be drawn from the career of Christopher Alexander Hagerman who, in a series of posts – collector of customs, lieutenant colonel of militia, provincial aide-de-camp to Lieutenant General Sir Gordon Drummond during the War of 1812, solicitor general, attorney general and judge of the Court of King's Bench – had ample scope for the exercise of power. Hagerman, in and after his time, has been pointed to as an example of someone who used power in a crude and vindictive way. According to Charles Durand (son of James Durand, MHA, and brother of the younger James Durand, MHA) Hagerman was a heartless man whose "Star Chamber" treatment of accused rebels in 1837–8 demonstrated "dreadful cruelty."[8]; Durand may have overstated the case, but his view of Hagerman is not without some basis in fact, as a couple of incidents involving other sometime MHAS will help to show. In 1821, Hagerman was collector of customs for the port of Kingston. In July of that year, Anthony Manahan, then a newly-established Kingston merchant, bought 136 kegs of tobacco in New York and had them shipped to Carleton Island in the St. Lawrence River near Kingston. The tobacco was seized on Hagerman's orders and impounded on the grounds that the goods had been imported into Upper Canada without going through a regular port of entry. In fact, a joint British-American commission under the Treaty of Ghent was then in the process of sorting out the ownership of the St. Lawrence Islands and had already agreed that Carleton Island was a part of the United States, though that decision was not formally proclaimed until 1822. Protesting innocence, Manahan went to court and finally won a partial victory. The court admitted that Carleton Island was outside its jurisdiction and Manahan got his tobacco back. All of it had become unfit for sale in the meantime, which meant a loss to

Manahan of his entire initial investment plus legal costs. (On the other hand collectors of customs received one-third of the value of all seizures over £40.) For the next twenty-five years, off and on, Manahan tried to obtain compensation for his loss. In all that time Hagerman never backed down even slightly from his original view that his actions in 1821 had been entirely legal and proper. He continued to insist, despite the contrary opinion of the governments of Great Britain and the United States, that in some peculiar way Carleton Island was still a British possession, though "not situated within the line that separates Upper Canada from the United States." This opinion may have been eccentric but it was enough to ensure that Manahan never received so much as a penny for his losses.[9]

In 1834, when Hagerman was solicitor general, he was asked to give a legal opinion as one of the law officers of the crown on a land case involving a fellow MHA, Charles Duncombe. Shortly after coming to Upper Canada from the United States, Duncombe bought a 999-year "Brant" lease for land on the Grand River. The land had originally been leased by Joseph Brant to Benajah Mallory, afterwards a defector who fought on the American side during the War of 1812, but conveyed by Mallory to other parties from whom Duncombe bought the lease. Having been in possession of the land for sixteen years and having made extensive "improvements," Duncombe applied to the executive council to have his lease changed to an ordinary title "in fee simple," as had already been done in the case of some other Brant leases. Hagerman's response to this request from an American immigrant of advanced political views was violently negative. Not only was he opposed to giving Duncombe what he wanted, but thought he should be stripped of the land altogether since it had once belonged to a traitor and ought therefore to have been forfeited to the crown. In Hagerman's eyes, Duncombe deserved no consideration whatsoever, having, he believed, knowingly bought a lease once held by a traitor. Duncombe later appealed over the heads of the provincial authorities to the colonial secretary, alleging "party" bias on Hagerman's part, and received a sympathetic reply, so it is possible that had the Rebellion not intervened Duncombe might eventually have got title to the land, but if he had it would have been only over the implacable and powerful opposition of Hagerman.[10]

Since civil and military office-holding offered status to all, power to many, and security to some, it is not surprising that most ambitious Upper Canadian regional leaders sought and obtained both civil and military positions. How such positions were obtained is therefore a matter of some importance. The nature of office-seeking in Upper Canada, or more accurately of its opposite, patronage, has been the subject of a number of studies which have dealt mostly with local oligarchies and their connection with the central political elite.[11] As well, there is an excellent, concise discussion of the entire provincial system of patronage by S.F. Wise in his article "Upper Canada and the Conservative Tradition". Crown patronage is described by Wise as a system of personal "interest" or "clientage," in which those most firmly entrenched in power in the central administrative elite dispensed patronage with the advice of local oligarchies with whom they shared friendships and an ideological viewpoint, on grounds which "had little to do ordinarily with forms of merit other than the political."[12] Wise's description of the essential principles upon which the patronage system worked can scarcely be improved upon, but it is possible to show by individual cases involving some of the MHAS how the system worked in practice, and to explore at somewhat more length the kinds of overt and also unstated non-merit qualifications that a successful applicant was required to have. While it is undoubtedly true that if one were not in favour with the right people no combination of characteristics could produce a position, it is possible to discern some common desirable and undesirable attributes among job seekers which could be used, if for no other purpose, to publicly justify appointments, or to justify withholding appointments, and it is possible by reasoning backwards, to suggest some kinds of attributes which could be evinced as barriers to official favour.

The way in which the patronage system worked can rarely be illustrated in a well-documented way since it was natural, given the personal nature of the process, that much that was done in order to obtain preferment was done in ways which were, and were intended to be, unrecorded, but the highly personal nature of the process cannot be doubted. Consider an example from the Brockville area, where the local-central patronage network has been examined with some care.[13] On 24 August 1838 David Jones, former MHA for Leeds and Brockville, wrote to the lieutenant governor's secretary to apply for the position of registrar of Leeds County, vacant due to the death of his brother, Sir Daniel Jones, who could truthfully be said to have been scarcely cold in his grave, having died only the previous day. With only slightly less unseemly haste, Henry Sherwood, the sitting MHA for Brockville and a member of an equally old-established Loyalist Leeds County family, wrote on 27 August to solicit the appointment on behalf of his younger brother, George Sherwood.[14] Within a month a decision had been made. David Jones got the job. But how was this outcome arrived at? The truth is that there is probably now no way of knowing for sure. No written evidence has been found to explain David Jones's success, and probably little if any written evidence ever did exist. The curious historian can only indulge in some freehand speculation on the possible factors and actors involved.

Both candidates were lawyers; both were militia officers; both were Tories. On the face of things, though, the Sherwood family ought perhaps to have had the advantage. Henry Sherwood was on the spot in Toronto to plead his brother's case, having moved his law practice there in 1835. He enjoyed political popularity, having defeated the same David Jones in 1836 for the Brockville seat. Henry and George Sherwood's father was Levius Peters Sherwood, a justice of the Court of King's Bench, as was their uncle Jonas Jones, and Jonas Jones was a member of a rival set of Brockville Joneses which had long supported the Sherwoods against the family of which David Jones was a part. What did David Jones have going for him? He had held elective and appointive office. He had been judge of the Eastern District court since 1825 and was a major of militia while George Sherwood was only a captain. He was also older, at forty-six, than his twenty-seven-year-old rival. None of these were remarkable achievements that would necessarily have tilted the scale in his favour and, as has been pointed out, his family had previously been losing out steadily in patronage battles with the rival Joneses and Sherwoods.[15]

Only an entirely personal, individual explanation is possible. The lieutenant governor, Sir George Arthur, who was brand new at the job, decided or was convinced by someone (perhaps by his private secretary, John Macaulay of Kingston, who was even newer to his job but scarcely new to Upper Canadian politics and patronage) or by some other unknown advisor that David Jones had the better claim. Perhaps the decision was even influenced by what might be called sentimental factors, so that the office might stay in the Jones family and with the family of the man who had been the very first Upper Canadian to receive a knighthood (for reasons which were never very clear then or since.)[16] The point is that the results of the patronage game were never entirely predictable.

It has been said that single individuals exercised enormous personal influence over patronage matters – Peter Russell and Chief Justice William Dummer Powell in turn, and after them the Reverend John Strachan[17] – but even then the system was not automatic because influences tended to conflict. In 1819, Donald Macdonell exchanged the office of registrar of Glengarry for that of sheriff of the Eastern District "chiefly if not entirely" through the aid of Powell, who had "exerted his interest" on Macdonell's behalf. Donald Macdonell's brother Duncan hoped to succeed to the resistrarship and also appealed to the chief justice. Though he could "easily obtain signatures from gentlemen from this place," he "did not think it necessary, being known to the gentleman whose interest I solicit." He was right in thinking that it was central, not local, influence that mattered most, but he didn't get the position, which went to a member of another branch of the family. Captain John Macdonell became registrar "in consequence of a promise made by Mr. Administrator Smith."[18] At times forces even beyond the provincial capital could intervene to affect the futures of individuals. It was by attracting the favourable attention of Sir George Prévost, the governor in chief, that Christopher Alexander Hagerman emerged from the War of 1812 no longer a mere law student and lieutenant of militia but a lieutenant colonel, provincial aide-de-camp and collector of customs.[19] An even longer arm reached into Upper Canada to elevate Hugh Macdonell (Aberchalder) out of colonial obscurity. In 1805 "the extreme benignity of His Royal Highness the Duke of Kent" obtained for him the office of assistant commissary general at Gibraltar, from which he went on to be the British consul at Algiers.[20]

By the 1830s, during the administrations of Colborne, Head, and Arthur, no obvious single long-standing powerful advisor held sway, but the key remained always access not to local notables (though that could be helpful) but to the seat of genuine power at the capital. Some people some of the time could get what they wanted from government merely by asking. In 1833, James Crooks, legislative councillor and former MHA for Halton, wrote to the lieutenant governor's secretary recommending the appointment of two local men as notaries public. Letters were sent out the next day advising the two nominees that they had been appointed.[21] It has already been demonstrated that, in local militia affairs, Archibald McLean and Philip VanKoughnet were able to arrange matters to their own satisfaction over the protests of Donald Aeneas Macdonell. In 1839, the other Donald Macdonell, who has just been shown to have benefited from the "interest" of William Dummer Powell in 1819, hoped again to be favoured by the government with the command of one of the battalions of incorporated militia then being organized. It was not to be. "The superior interest however at Toronto of Col. VanKoughnet prevailed and he was ... appointed over me."[22]

It should be noted, on the subject of the militia, that the process of militia appointment and promotion was ordinarily much more straightforward than the system of civil patronage, since appointments and promotions were almost always made automatically on the recommendation of the commanding officer. Deviation from this pattern was rare, but there are signs that the conventions of militia appointment were also beginning to loosen somewhat by the 1830s under the impact of new forms of "interest," to the indignation of militia colonels like Charles Jones who commanded the Second Leeds Regiment. "I perceive, by the *Gazette*," he wrote to Richard Bullock, the adjutant general of militia, "that Ogle R. Gowan Esqr. has been appointed a Captain in the 2nd Reg't Leeds Militia, which Reg't I have the Honour to command. Hitherto I believe it has been required by the Government, that in every case an appointment to the Militia should be preceeded by a recommendation from the Officer Commanding the Regt. I am not aware that I have in this case recommended Mr. Gowan to the appointment. I will thank you to inform me under what circumstances and to whom he is indebted for the appointment."[23] Bullock in reply denied the universality of the appointments procedure described by Jones.[24] Exceptions to the rule could be made, in this case for the leading Orangeman in Upper Canada. As has been seen in the case of the command of the First Regiment of Stormont Militia in 1836, a vacant colonelcy also produced an exceptional situation in which the usual pattern of militia promotion did not always apply, and no holds were barred in attempts to secure the vital "interest" of the central elite.

To get (sometimes even to keep) a government job or a militia commission, it was necessary to have "interest." It was also necessary, or was said to be necessary, to meet certain other kinds of qualifications. Colonel Philip VanKoughnet, whose own success in patronage matters has been noted, had definite views on what these qualifications were or were not. In 1838 he wrote to the adjutant general to secure the dismissal of one of his militia officers, Captain Charles Farrar. What were Farrar's defects? His loyalty was questionable. He was "a most confirmed Radical" who had "done much mischief by the dissemination of his Republican principles." It was said that he had had "to fly from Ireland during the Rebellion for the part he took." "It is all important," Vankoughnet believed, "that appointments in the militia should be conferred upon persons only of undoubted loyalty." In addition to his political shortcomings, Farrar was also, according to VanKoughnet, of bad moral character having "been living for a number of years in a state of adultery with another man's wife."[25] Farrar lacked two qualities which VanKoughnet valued highly, loyalty and respectability. (And, sure enough, the notation "removed" shortly appeared beside Captain Farrar's name in the militia register.)[26]

An example of successful civil patronage may help to expand the broad categories of loyalty and respectability somewhat. John Willson, a much-respected MHA for Wentworth, afterwards a member of the Legislative Council, wrote to Edward McMahon, private secretary to Sir John Colborne to recommend a number of Gore District men as likely magistrates, among them one sitting and one future MHA, Absalom Shade and Michael Aikman. Shade was "of good character, large property, good morals and altho new came [sic] into this province a short time after the late war, possesses sound principles toward the government." Aikman also had "a substantial and good property [and] unblemished morals," was "active, intelligent and industrious," and also held "the soundest principles toward the government." Aikman had the extra advantage of living less than a mile from the district town[27] and (although Willson didn't mention it) of being John Willson's son-in-law.

What VanKoughnet meant by "undoubted loyalty" and Willson by "sound principles toward the government" were part of the same concept. As S.F. Wise has pointed out, loyalty was neither simple adherence to crown and empire nor simple political allegiance but also, and more significantly, a reaction against, indeed a total rejection of "the manners, politics and social arrangements of the United States."[28] A person who held "republican principles" could not, by definition, be loyal, though one who was "new came into this province" (from the United States), to his credit, could be. Respectability, like loyalty, was a compound concept. It included "good character," which implied not only "unblemished morals" but other virtues – piety, sobriety, honesty, industry, and tangible evidence of material success ("substantial and good property.")

It is fair to say that it was always the intention of the provincial government that only applicants of "undoubted" loyalty and respectability should receive appointments; human nature dictated that these ideal requirements were not always met. If they had been, Charles Farrar would not have been commissioned in the militia in the first place. It has been noted that the chronic shortage of magistrates meant that some were appointed whose industry and competence were open to question, and the same was at times true of the militia. As well, it is clear that "respectability" did not always, in individual cases, actually denote the possession of *all* the desirable qualities preferred (for instance) by John Willson. As H.C. Pentland observed, "respectability rather than competence was the foundation of social approval and public advancement until about 1840."[29] In other words, "competence" was a desirable but not a necessary component of "respectability." Two of Toronto's distinguished early families, the Jarvises and the Robinsons, provide illustrations of this point. John Beverley Robinson enjoyed a lifelong reputation for intelligence and good judgement. He was thus "respectable" in the broadest sense, but his brother Peter, while also "respectable," has been seen to have had some problems in coping with responsibility and temptation. As commissioner of crown lands he has been charitably described as "unbusinesslike" since "a marked discrepancy" was discovered between the amount of money he collected and the amount he turned over to the receiver general of the province.[30] Similarly W.B. Jarvis and his brother George served their government with faithfulness and energy in a variety of capacities for many years, in some contrast to members of another branch of their respectable family. William Jarvis was "so little a man of business that one cannot trust anything to his care,"[31] yet despite his "almost sublime incompetence"[32] he served as provincial secretary until he died in office after twenty-six years. His son S.P. Jarvis filled the office of chief superintendent of Indian Affairs until forced to give it up following charges against him of "immoral behaviour," "blatant favouratism," and "irregularities" in his accounts,[33] but he continued all his life to be a member of "respectable" Toronto society, living off the sale of family lands.[34] Incompetence and even moral deviance or dishonesty, so long as they were not too flagrantly displayed,[35] could be compatible with "respectability" and certainly with the possession of office.

Even loyalty, though by and large a quality more consistently demanded in a public office, could be subject to some qualification. Being a Reformer was not a total disqualification for office. Even a political radical could become a magistrate in certain circumstances. R.D. Fraser, whose own Conservative principles were never in doubt, was willing to recommend Milo McCarger – "A respectable farmer a McKenzieite against him but the best to be found in that quarter."[36] The importance of being thought "respectable" is highly relevant in McCarger's case, for besides his politics he was illiterate and when he was an MHA was said to be out of his depth.[37] Conceivably the fact that both Fraser and McCarger were long-standing members of the Masonic Lodge had something to do with Fraser's tolerance of McCarger's deficiencies.

In general it can be said of the way in which patronage worked in Upper Canada that there were professed principles of selection and established channels through which "interest" was exerted, but the patterns were never entirely rigid and the rules could always be broken if there was cause or need to do so. Patronage, after all, *was* power, the power to reward or to withhold rewards. Those who were in a position to dispense patronage or whose patronage recommendations were usually acted upon held a large and increasing power, and the further up the ladder of government or official favour, the greater that power became. Power could be exerted wisely but also partially, and, on occasion, capriciously, It is worth bearing in mind that one of the most bizarre appointments ever inflicted on the unsuspecting people of Upper Canada came from the very top of the power ladder, – the appointment by the imperial government as lieutenant governor of that "damned odd fellow," Francis Bond Head.

The professed grounds upon which Upper Canadians were selected for civil or military positions can be reduced to the possession of *a sufficient degree* of loyalty and respectability. S.F. Wise, after studying the entire system of patronage in Upper Canada, concluded that the real main underlying principle of selection was political,[38] that is, that the applicant had to be a supporter of the central administration, which of course was one version of "loyalty." Is it possible to go beyond or behind these general criteria to ask if there were other kinds of guidelines which were consciously or unconsciously applied in making appointments? Political opposition to the government, as has been demonstrated, did not constitute a total disqualification for office, especially for the basic positions in the magistracy and the militia. Among seventy-one MHAS who served during the tenth, eleventh, twelfth, and thirteenth parliaments (1828–41), who have been identified as Reform or opposition members, fifty-three or 75 percent held some kind of "status" appointment, mainly as magistrates and militia officers. It is true that the equivalent number of Conservative or "government" members during the same period holding "status" appointments was quite a bit higher – ninety out of ninety-one or 99 percent; nonetheless Reformers as a group were by no means systematically excluded. Some "form of merit other than the political" was in fact being recognized and rewarded at the basic office-holding level.

Political considerations were not paramount in all patronage appointments, but they were in some cases, especially when offices of greater "status" than the "building block" offices were concerned. When the government did not have to take the best candidate "to be found in that quarter" because of a shortage of competent people, or when offices that actually promised some financial rewards were at stake, the picture was totally different. By and large the rule was "only Conservatives need apply." In the four parliaments referred to above, at some time fifty-seven MHAS held offices that can be called "higher status" appointments, ranging from clerks of the peace, sheriffs, county registrars, and customs collectors to members of the Legislative and Executive councils. Of these fifty-seven, forty-four (77 percent) has been identified as Conservatives and only thirteen (23 percent) as Reformers. (Two of those thirteen, Robert Baldwin and John Rolph, qualify only by having served as members of the Executive Council for a period of three weeks in 1836.) The conclusion is unmistakable: when offices of more than ordinary status, and particularly when income-producing offices, were concerned, having the "right" political views was almost a total necessity.

But were "sound principles toward the government" the only requirement? Or, putting the question the other way around, was the possession of "wrong" political views the only serious barrier to preferment in Upper Canada? One way of getting a first grip on this problem is to look closely at thirty-two rather unusual individuals among all of the 283 MHAS, unusual because they are not known to have held, and conceivably never even sought, any status position either civil or military.

MHAS who held no status appointments:

Barnabas Bidwell
Marshall Spring Bidwell
Malcolm Cameron
Willet Casey
John Cawthra
Joshua Cornwall
David Cowan
John Fanning
Moses Gamble
David Gibson
Thomas Barnes Gough
Solomon Hill
Jesse Ketchum
Joseph Lockwood
Samuel Lount
Angus Macdonell (Sandaig)
John McIntosh
William Lyon Mackenzie
Abraham Markle
Elias Moore
Thomas David Morrison
Paul Peterson
Robert Randall
John Roblin
Jacob Rymal
William Terry
William Weekes
William Benjamin Wells
Reuben White
Walter Butler Wilkinson
James Wilson
Dennis Woolverton

Did these thirty-two people singly or as a group exhibit any particularly undesirable characteristics which might help to explain their atypical lack of status or which might be used as a basis for further examination of differing status among the rest of the MHAS? Again the political connection is immediately apparent. Among the office-less thirty-two, at least twenty-three can be readily identified as having been some sort of "opposition" politician. The usual suspects are there – rebels and radicals like the Bidwells, William Lyon Mackenzie, David Gibson, Samuel Lount, Jesse Ketchum, and Robert Randall, and from an earlier period, the traitor Abraham Markle, the Gourlayite Willet Casey, and the malcontent William Weekes. Politics alone could explain the presence of these people and the other Reformers (Cameron, Cawthra, Lockwood, McIntosh, Moore, Morrison, Peterson, Roblin, Rymal, Wells, White, Wilson, and Woolverton) on the list of undesirables, but politics alone has been shown to be an insufficient deterrent to all office-holding. Markle's fellow traitors Joseph Willcocks and Benajah Mallory held offices; other rebels and radicals such as Charles Duncombe, Finlay Malcolm, John Rolph, Caleb Hopkins, John Matthews, and Hiram Norton held offices. Are there avenues other than the political that should be explored? A further look at the "non-status" MHAS raises some possibilities worth pursuing. For example, Markle, William Terry, and John Fanning had all been innkeepers. Jacob Rymal was a carpenter. Besides William Lyon Mackenzie, Malcolm Cameron and W.B. Wells had been journalists and John McIntosh had been a sailor. Did some occupations impose a stigma? Or was religion a factor? Among the thirty-two, dissenters are well-represented with six known Methodists (Ketchum, Lount, Morrison, Peterson, Roblin, and Wilson) two Quakers (Casey and Moore) one Baptist (Woolverton) and one who professed to have no religion at all (White). There is also the question of nationality or, more accurately, place of birth. The list of thirty-two includes five (M.S. Bidwell, Gamble, Lount, Norton, and Woolverton) who were born in the United States and six (B. Bidwell, Ketchum, Markle, Moore, Randall, and White) who, though born in the old Thirteen Colonies, were Post-Loyalist immigrants. Two, Gough and Weekes, were from Ireland and eight, Cameron, Morrison, Peterson, Rymal, Terry, Wells, and Wilkinson (raising the possibility of bias against the home-grown) were born in Upper or Lower Canada. Finally it may be observed that, with perhaps four exceptions (Terry, Cornwall, Macdonell, and Wilkinson), the "non-status" MHAS had no discernible ties, especially of blood, to any of the major centrally or regionally prominent Upper Canadian families. Could a lack of patronage result from being born into the wrong family?

There is good reason to believe that family connections were decidedly helpful. Among the thirty-two "non-status" MHAS, only one, W.B. Wilkinson, whose father was a district court judge, is known to have been connected by family ties to anyone in a position of really significant authority, and his presence among the gang of thirty-two is probably a fluke due to his early death at twenty-six, before he had time to begin acquiring his own offices. On the other hand, a look at the information which has been collected (in passing) about family relationships among the 251 MHAS who did hold status appointments produces interesting if not overwhelming results. Seventy-one cases readily come to light in which the MHAS in question had a relative (father, brother, uncle, father-in-law, brother-in-law, or cousin) who held office above the basic status level, as a member of the Legislative or Executive Council, as a senior public servant, or as a judge. If senior military service by a relative, either as a Loyalist or other British officer, is added, a further seventy-five such family relationships emerge. Since these figures are based on no systematic attempt to trace family relationships in detail, they are probably quite a bit too low, but it hardly requires a feat of mental daring to surmise that having a relative already established as a person of consequence was useful to an aspiring local leader. Michael Aikman might have been appointed a militia officer and a magistrate on his own merits in due course, but his father-in-law's recommendation probably speeded the process up somewhat.

The question of "right" or "wrong" occupations is much less clear-cut. Upper Canadians, and Upper Canadian MHAS, followed at times a fair range of occupations including some which might seem not to have been the pursuits of a gentleman. Some MHAS were blacksmiths, sailors, innkeepers, tailors, or carpenters, but with the exception of the one known blacksmith, Samuel Lount, and William Terry, a sometime apothecacy, none of these occupations can be linked to the non-holding of status offices among MHAS in *all* cases. About all that can be said is that the practitioners of certain occupations were more successful than others in acquiring offices above the basic status level. The highest percentage figure of this type among MHAS is for surveyors/survey contractors, of whom 77 percent were also public servants, but since there were only thirteen of them altogether the statistic is not very meaningful. Among lawyers, as previously noted, the connection is solid: thirty-five of forty-seven or 74 percent also held government jobs. Aside from the lawyers, the figures for other leading occupations do not seem especially significant: 11 of 24 distillers (46 percent), 39 of 98 merchants (40 percent), 27 of 63 millers (43 percent), and 46 of 143 farmers (32 percent). In general it would appear that Upper Canadian occupational diversity and the pattern of having multiple occupations by which a possibly less respectable occupation could be replaced by a more acceptable one ruled out any widespread rejection of candidates for office on the grounds of what they did or had done for a living.

Two other possible assets in the search for patronage demand brief attention. Having been a student of the Reverend John Strachan has often been said to have conferred a powerful advantage in the world of Upper Canadian politics and government. A former Strachan pupil had "a passport to preferment."[39] Nonetheless, even John Strachan could not teach school in every part of the province at once, so that his students were limited to those who came from the areas around Cornwall and (later) Toronto or those who were sent as boarders. Strachan liked to boast about the number of his protégés who were in positions of influence and claimed that "all my pupils" are "now the leading characters in many parts of the province,"[40] but in all among the MHAS only twenty-seven have been identified as Strachan's students.[41] It must be acknowledged that, among that small number, most of them eventually achieved public office well above the basic status level and some, of course, like the Robinsons (John Beverley, Peter, and William Benjamin), Charles and Jonas Jones, Henry John Boulton, Archibald McLean, Philip VanKoughnet, Robert Baldwin, and Henry Sherwood, had quite notable careers, as did a good many of Strachan's former students who were not members of the Assembly. Still, Strachan's influence must be measured in quality and not in quantity.

Another association shared by some MHAS, the significance of which is even more uncertain, was membership in the Masonic Lodge. The numbers involved are a bit higher than the number of Strachan's pupils; at least fifty-seven MHAS are known to have been Masons.[42] Was membership in the lodge used to help achieve appointed or elected office? Masonic historians have claimed that during the early history in Upper Canada the lodge attracted "some of the most distinguished men of the period" who went on to take "foremost positions ... as jurists, legislators, educationists, ministers of the gospel, military men, architects, artists, merchants, journalists, etc."[43] A recent study of skilled workers in Hamilton has concluded that "a clear majority" of Masons "belonged to a social stratum distinctly removed from the world of the skilled workingman."[44] Thomas Dalton, in an attack on C.A. Hagerman in 1824, alleged that Hagerman had become a Mason "with the end of being elected a Member of Parliament," implying that he expected the support of other Masons.[45] John Ross Robertson in his *History of Freemasonry in Canada* told the story of how W.L. Mackenzie was refused membership in a Toronto lodge. Would his political course have been different if he had been admitted to an "establishment" institution?[46] The possibility has been raised that membership in the Masonic Lodge may have been helpful in particular patronage cases. The problem is that in discussing the possible political and patronage advantages of being a Mason, there is only slight and inferential evidence to work with. It is true that quite a number of prominent Upper Canadians were Masons. Three lieutenant governors, (Simcoe, Maitland, and Arthur) were Masons, as were chief justices Powell and Campbell, Provincial Secretary William Jarvis, Receiver General J.H. Dunn and legislative councillors Richard Cartwright and Thomas Clark. Among the fifty-seven MHAS who were Masons there were also some well-placed individuals such as L.P. and Henry Sherwood, Sir A.N. MacNab, W.H. Draper, R.S. Jameson, C.A. Hagerman, and James Crooks. Taken as a group, however, the fifty-seven Masons lack any real homogeneity. While some of the Masons such as Henry Sherwood, W.B. Jarvis, and Donald Bethune are also to be found on the list of Strachan's students, three others (Jesse Ketchum, W.B. Wilkinson, and M.S. Bildwell) can be found on the list of those MHAS who never held any offices. In addition the list of Masons who were MHAS contains quite a few names of people who were seldom if ever in favour with the provincial elite – Bidwell, Ketchum, the Duncombe brothers, John Rolph, Milo McCarger, Abraham Markle, Harmannus Smith, and the two William Buells. The most that can be said about membership in the Masonic Lodge is that it may in some cases have been useful in obtaining an office or getting elected, that it reflects the overlapping nature of regional and central leadership relationships in Upper Canada, and that the whole subject could do with much closer study.

A matter on which it is possible to write with somewhat more precision, if scarcely with total authority, is religious affiliation and patronage. The statistics on religious denominations are neither complete nor entirely reliable. Biographical sources do not always agree, and as well it is known that some people changed churches at some point in their lives, making it difficult to apply a single denominational label to them. This "tendency to move between various religious groups" has been described in the case of the Buells of Brockville, who went from Anglicanism to Presbyterianism.[47] Other examples are not hard to find. Michael Aikman began life as a Methodist but joined the Church of England in the 1840s.[48] Zaccheus Burnham also embraced the Church of England, having previously been a Presbyterian.[49] (Were these examples of rising

TABLE 7
All MHAS by Denomination

Denomination	*Number*	*Percentage*
Church of England	95	33.6%
Presbyterian	42	14.8
Methodist	26	9.2
Roman Catholic	19	6.7
Quaker	4	1.4
No religion	3	1.1
Lutheran	2	0.7
Unitarian	1	0.4
Baptist	1	0.4
Congregationalist	1	0.4
Unknown	89	31.4
Total	283	

respectability?) Captain John Matthews, eccentric in religion as in all else, was first a Roman Catholic, then an Anglican, and finally a Unitarian.[50] Besides the doubtful nature of some denominational identifications, there is the problem of no identification at all. Of the 283 MHAS, to only 194, or about two-thirds, has it been possible to apply even a tenuous religious label.

However partial or doubtful the data, 194 cases are better than none, and some conclusions which are probably valid in a general way can be extracted from them. To begin with, a simple breakdown by denomination over the entire period produces quite interesting figures, shown in Table 7.

It is immediately obvious that among MHAS members of the Church of England were by far the most numerous; that Presbyterians, Methodists, and Roman Catholics were a distant second, third, and fourth; and that no other denominations were significantly represented. But what do these figures mean? Was the Church of England wildly over-represented and the Methodists, for instance, under-represented with regard to their numbers among the general population? It is easy to assume that this was the case, since it was generally believed at the time and has been since that, at least until the 1830s, the Methodists were the largest denomination in Upper Canada.[51] Unfortunately there are no statistics with which to verify this belief. The first more or less reliable statistics on denominational adherence in Upper Canada appear only with the census of 1842 when the percentages were as presented in Table 8.

If these two sets of figures are at all comparable, the Church of England was indeed over-represented (among those MHAS whose

TABLE 8
Religious Denominations in the General Population, 1842 Census

Denomination	*Percentage*
Church of England	22.1
Presbyterians	19.9
Methodists	17.1
Roman Catholics	13.4
Lutheran	0.9
Quaker	0.1
Baptist	3.4
Congregational	0.9
Others	5.5
No denomination given	16.7

religious affiliation is *known* the Anglicans account for just under half) and all the other denominations under-represented among elected politicians in Upper Canada. But obviously the percentages are not strictly comparable. The religious makeup of the population in 1842 cannot be assumed to have applied to the whole period from 1791 to 1841, or to any period much earlier than the time at which the census was taken. In order to achieve a higher degree of comparability, it is necessary to examine only those whose cases apply to a time period closer to 1842. For this purpose the 138 MHAS of Group B who served in the 1830–41 period have been used on the grounds that the group is not so small as to be meaningless and their period of activity not too far away from the census date. Group B has one other advantage: the level of religious unknowns among them is relatively low; in fact it is comparable in percentage terms to the 1842 census itself. Of the 138 MHAS, a religious affiliation has not been established for 21, which works out to 15.2 percent compared to 16.7 percent of unknowns in the census. For the 117 MHAS whose denomination is known (or in some cases strongly suspected) the breakdown is given in Table 9.

Among the four main denominations, Presbyterians, Methodists, and Catholics appear to have been under-represented politically, though perhaps not alarmingly so, but the Anglicans were decidedly over-represented. There were almost twice as many of them as there ought to have been on the basis of their percentage of the population. It was not so much a question of certain denominations being discriminated *against* as of a particular denomination being heavily discriminated *for*. If the figures mean anything, it is that being an Anglican was a very great political advantage.

TABLE 9
MHAs in Group B by Denomination

Denomination	*Number*	*Percentage*
Church of England	58	42.1
Presbyterian	24	17.4
Methodist	19	13.7
Roman Catholic	11	7.9
No religion	2	1.5
Lutheran	1	0.7
Quaker	1	0.7
Baptist	1	0.7
Unknown	21	15.2
Total	138	

TABLE 10
Denomination and All "Status" Appointments in Group B

Denomination	*Number*	*Percentage*
Church of England	56	44.1
Presbyterian	20	15.7
Methodist	15	11.8
Roman Catholic	11	8.6
Lutheran	1	0.8
Baptist	1	0.8
No religion	1	0.8
Unknown	22	17.3
Total	127	

There are a number of ways in which the analysis of religious affiliation can be refined and extended and more closely linked to power and patronage. An examination of the personnel of each of the thirteen parliaments of Upper Canada makes additionally clear the consistent dominance of members of the Church of England among elected representatives. In every parliament but one, the fifth parliament of 1808–12, (known) Anglicans easily outnumbered (known) members of the other denominations. In eight parliaments, half or more of the MHAs whose religion is known were Anglicans.

Among the 127 MHAs in Group B who held some form of "status" civil or military appointment, Anglicans are again well out in front, and similar results are obtained by subdividing these people into the number of MHAs in Group B who held militia commissions (105) and were magistrates (88) (Tables 10–12).

TABLE 11
Denomination and Militia Commissions in Group B

Denomination	*Number*	*Percentage*
Church of England	47	44.7
Presbyterian	16	15.2
Methodist	10	9.5
Roman Catholic	10	9.5
Lutheran	1	0.9
No religion	1	0.9
Unknown	20	9.1
Total	105	

TABLE 12
Denomination and Magistrates' Appointments in Group B

Denomination	*Number*	*Percentage*
Church of England	33	37.5
Presbyterian	16	18.2
Methodist	12	13.6
Roman Catholic	9	10.2
Lutheran	1	1.1
No religion	1	1.1
Unknown	16	18.2
Total	88	

If only those in Group B who held a "higher status" appointment are considered the numbers become dangerously small, for there were only forty-eight of them, but as Table 13 shows the Anglican advantage varies only in that it increases while the Methodists show marked decline. There is even some doubt about including the one "higher status" Methodist, John Willson of Saltfleet Township, because he too eventually became an Anglican.[52]

These results suggest that the farther up the ladder of power and preferment one went in Upper Canada, the more likely one was to be an Anglican and the less likely one was to be a Methodist, while Presbyterians and Roman Catholics maintained their share of places more or less at the same level regardless of the degree of status involved. A similar situation existed so far as higher status in the militia was concerned. Among all of the MHAs there were ninety-six who reached the top of the militia ladder as colonels commanding their regiments (Table 14).

A final demonstration of the same general denominational phe-

TABLE 13
Denomination and "Higher Status" Appointments in Group B

Denomination	*Number*	*Percentage*
Church of England	29	60.4
Presbyterian	9	18.7
Methodist	1	2.1
Roman Catholic	5	10.4
No religion	1	2.1
Unknown	3	6.2
Total	48	

TABLE 14
Denomination and Militia Colonelcies

Denomination	*Number*	*Percentage*
Church of England	39	40.6
Presbyterian	13	13.5
Methodist	1	1.1
Roman Catholic	15	15.6
Lutheran	1	1.1
Unknown	27	28.1
Total	96	

nomenon can be made based on land-holding, in this case those who are known to have had lots of it, over 1,000 acres. This was a sizeable group of 130 (Table15).

The prizes of land, and especially of place, that Upper Canada had to bestow on its regional leaders went very freely to members of the Church of England, apparently more or less fairly to Presbyterians and Roman Catholics, and very sparingly to Methodists and others.

Indications of a certain dominance of elected and appointed positions in Upper Canada by members of the Church of England and a corresponding lack of representation in these positions by Methodists will not come as a complete surprise to students of Upper Canadian society, but perhaps the evident extent of that dominance and that lack of representation may be surprising. F.H. Armstrong has written that, from about 1829 on, "the modern Canadian phenomenon of a sort of composite state church in which several denominations hold privilege and prestige was already making its

TABLE 15
Denomination and Landholding Over 1,000 Acres

Denomination	*Number*	*Percentage*
Church of England	45	34.6
Presbyterian	19	14.6
Methodist	8	6.2
Roman Catholic	12	9.2
Quaker	2	1.5
No religion	1	0.8
Unknown	43	33.1
Total	130	

appearance," and that in the later Upper Canadian period "religion was progressively no bar to admission to the ruling class." In the 1830s, he writes, "appointment of Methodists to the magistracy became frequent."[53] There is some statistical evidence that Methodists were making the kind of progress that Armstrong suggests they were at the basic level of status. Among the 103 early-period MHAS in group A there were six known Methodists (5.8 percent) while among the later Group B there were nineteen out of 138 (13.7 percent). Among magistrate-MHAS the corresponding figures are: Group A, Methodists, four (3.9 percent); Group B, Methodists, twelve (8.7 percent). On the basis of the evidence, it can be concluded that Methodists were being elected and appointed to the "building block" office in greater numbers, but two comments should be made. There are far more religious unknowns among the early group (46.6 percent as compared to 15.2 percent in Group B), which casts some doubt on the comparability of the two sets of figures. Beyond that, the level of elected and appointed success reached by Methodists in the 1830s, while possibly higher than at a previous time, was not really very high. If the MHAS were at all representative of leading men in the province generally, the Methodists were still underrepresented even at the lowest level of "the ruling class." So far as "higher status" positions were concerned there is almost no evidence at all of upward mobility on the part of Methodists. The only MHA who is known to have been a Methodist who rose above the basic status level during the Upper Canadian period was John Willson, whose denominational purity, as has been seen, is in some doubt. In any case his appointment to the Legislative Council can hardly be said to represent a growing recognition of Methodist merits during the 1830s. In fact, his was the very last appointment ever made to the Legislative Council of Upper Canada, in December 1839. He was not reappointed to the new Legislative Council of Canada in 1841.

"The ruling class" did impose barriers to membership against Methodists and other dissenting denominations. Exclusion on religious grounds among the MHAS themselves was at times quite overt. In the first parliament (1792–6) Philip Dorland was not allowed to take his seat because as a Quaker he refused to take the oath, and his fellow members refused to accept his affirmation. (Efforts to permit Quakers to sit without taking the oath were blocked either in the Assembly or the Legislative Council until 1833, when the local legislature was overruled by British legislation.)[54] During the fifth parliament (1808–12), which contained an unusually high number of Methodists (five known), two of them were got rid of by an interpretation of clause 21 of the Constitutional Act forbidding clergymen from sitting in the House, on the grounds that James Wilson and John Roblin were Methodist lay teachers.[55] They were voted out by two-to-one majorities. The Methodists and the electorate in general appear to have got the message. No Methodist is known to have been elected to the next parliament (1812–16) and only one to the parliament of 1816–20.

However the situation may have changed, or begun to change, in Upper Canada being a Methodist was not helpful to anyone interested in achieving regional or provincial prominence. Anglicanism, on the other hand, was. Even among the MHAS of the period before 1830, when Anglicans have been assumed to have been thin on the ground, they still far outstripped, on the basis of available evidence, all other denominations. There were more than twice as many MHAS (thirty-nine) who are known to have been Anglican as there were Presbyterians (nineteen), their nearest rivals in that period. It seems safe to say that, at all times and at all status levels, Anglicans enjoyed a share of power and patronage well beyond their due on the basis of their numbers alone. So far as the MHAS were concerned, it has been seen that their election (that is, their achievement of some prominence at the provincial level) was in a majority of cases preceded by the attainment of a status office bestowed from above. Since so many of the people in this process were Anglicans, it must be concluded that their selection was based, at least in part, on one "form of merit other than the political." They also got merit points for attending the "right" church. Of course in most cases political orthodoxy and Anglicanism went happily hand in hand, but then so did political orthodoxy and (Church of Scotland) Presbyterianism and Roman Catholicism, but those denominations were not over-represented in positions of status and influence. Anglicans got special treatment.

What was no special about being an Anglican? It was not, or certainly not entirely, a matter of faith or dogma. More likely it was a matter of respectability. The Church of England was the "best" church, the "safest" church, because of its several favourable associations – with the crown, with the empire, with the mother country, and (perhaps most of all) with all that was "correct," that was free from suspicion of religious, social, or political deviance. The central "elite of power" was itself heavily Anglican. R.E. Saunders has identified eight men who were members of the Executive Council of Upper Canada whom he claims "were in effective control of the province between 1820 and 1837."[56] Every one of them was an Anglican. There is no doubt that the provincial elite used its patronage power to reward Anglicans far more than members of any other denomination and rewarded them moreover with the largest share of the best jobs available.

A further personal factor which requires discussion in connection with matters of patronage is place of birth. Statistically the situation is considerably better than for religion; only seventeen of the 283 MHAS have resisted birthplace identification. The overall unknown percentage (6.1 percent) consequently compares favourably with the closest census data of 1842 for the whole population, which had a 5.6 percent unknown component. For the MHAS in Group B, the percentage is even lower than the census figure at 3.6 percent so that it is possible to tell with a fair degree of accuracy how the national makeup of the assembly, especially the later assemblies, corresponded to the national distribution of the population as a whole.

Not much has been written about nationality/ethnicity and leadership in Upper Canada. In 1839, Lord Durham, in his famous *Report*, claimed that nationality played a role in matters of power and patronage, alleging that "the power of office and the emoluments of the professions" were mainly in the hands of "native-born Canadians" who worked to keep power away from immigrant newcomers.[57] More recently, J.H. Aitchison argued that "the better class" of emigrants from the United Kingdom was given special treatment by the Upper Canadian establishment, being welcomed with open arms because of the need to fill local positions, especially in the magistracy, with competent people. Indeed Aitchison demonstrates that in some cases appointments to the magistracy were deliberately delayed in the hope that the next year's westbound ships would bring

TABLE 16
Group BA: National Origin

National Origin	*Number*	*Percent*	*Percentage of General Population (1842 Census)*
English Canadian	41	41.4	50.8
French Canadian	1	1.1	2.9
Total Native-born	42	42.4	53.7
England and Wales	14	14.1	8.3
Scotland	18	18.2	8.2
Ireland	8	8.1	16.1
Total UK	40	40.4	32.6
Post-Loyalist American	14	14.1	6.7
Europe	0	0	1.3
Unknown	3	3.1	5.6
Total Group BA	99		

a suitable complement of qualified emigrants from the British Isles.[58] F.H. Armstrong's even more recent view is that ethnicity was one factor in the formation of elites in Upper Canada; that probably the Scottish Lowland Protestants, in proportion to their numbers, were the most successful ethnic group in the governance and commerce of the colony, but that "in the rise of various individuals to power ... ethnicity played a rather secondary role."[59]

If the MHAS were at all typical of the society as a whole, it is not difficult to show that, on the relationship between power and nationality, Lord Durham, as on most other Upper Canadian subjects, was seriously misinformed. A process of chronological head-counting of overlapping groups starting with Group A through Group AA, (those who served in the 1820s) to Group B and ending with Group BA, the ninety-nine MHAS who served only in the 1830–41 period, produces an unmistakable decline in the successful participation by the native-born both in electoral politics and in acquiring appointed positions. Before 1820, native-born British Americans (mostly Loyalists born in the Thirteen Colonies), were a sizable majority, making up 60 percent of the MHAS. From then on it was mostly downhill; among the MHAS who sat during the 1820s, they were about 55 percent of the total; among all MHAS who sat in the 1830s, they were down to 41 percent; and among those who sat only in the 1830s, they were in virtually the same position at 42 percent. On

TABLE 17
National Origin: Percentages in Selected Categories, 1791–1841

National Origin	*All* mhas		*Militia Colonels*		*Land over 1,000 acres*	
	No.	*%*	*No.*	*%*	*No.*	*%*
Native-born	138	48.8	49	51.1	69	53.1
Scotland	39	13.8	21	21.9	23	17.7
England and Wales	33	11.7	8	8.3	17	13.1
Ireland	18	6.4	7	7.3	6	4.6
Post-Loyalist American	37	13.1	5	5.2	9	6.9
Other	1	0.3	1	1.1	1	0.8
Unknown	17	6.1	5	5.2	5	3.8
Total	283		96		130	

the other hand immigrants from the United Kingdom experienced a steady increase among MHAS, from 25 to 27 to 36 to 40 percent of the total, and the Scots, as Armstrong suggested, made the most dramatic gains. When the figures for the group of ninety-nine MHAS who served only in 1830–41 are compared with the breakdown by birthplace in the 1842 census, the picture at the end of the Upper Canadian period becomes even clearer (Table 16).

In relation to their share of the general population, the native-born were under-represented by almost 12 percent. This is not perhaps a glaring discrepancy, but it does represent a consistent loss of ground. Three immigrant groups (the Scots, the English/Welsh and the Americans) are over-represented, the Scots and the Americans to an extent more than double their numerical due. Only the Irish among immigrant groups are under-represented; among the ninety-nine MHAS, they were represented by about half of the proportion that their numbers in the general population warranted.

The slippage within the power structure of the native-born, the disproportionate dominance of the Scots (and, to a lesser degree, of the English), and the exclusion of the Irish can all be demonstrated in a variety of other ways by raising the "status level," using the same kinds of tests already applied in the area of religious denomination. For the whole period the native-born held their own in some categories (Table 17).

Among the ninety-six MHAS who served as colonels of militia, the native-born percentage was a little above their overall figure, but the

Scottish colonels were well above their percentage in the whole group. The test involving the 130 MHAS known to have acquired more than 1,000 acres of land yields a similar result. The Scots lead the immigrant groups, followed by the English. The Irish and especially the Americans both fare poorly.

The patterns become rather more interesting when the "basic status" and "higher status" positions in the patronage system are examined from a national point of view over time (Table 18).

As the tables indicate, the native-born share of all positions declined generally between the earliest and latest group/period and the decline was consistent except for one or two variants. Conversely, the share of positions held by immigrants from the United Kingdom went more or less steadily up. But it is in the "higher status," most prestigious patronage and power area that the most dramatic changes occurred. By the 1830s, the native-born share of "higher status" positions was actually *lower* than that of the immigrants. The native-born percentage was 44 percent while the combined immigrant percentage was 52 percent. United Kingdom imigrants alone held 48 percent of "higher status" positions. And of these, as usual, the lion's share belonged to the Scots, who held 24 percent or exactly half of the United Kingdom total.

The proportional dominance of the Scots is all the more remarkable when the figures for Group BA (the MHAS chronologically closest to the end of the Upper Canadian period) are compared to the actual Scottish percentage of the population (8.2 percent) as revealed in the census of 1842. As elected politicians, the Scots had more than double their share of positions. Among Scottish elected politicans, those holding appointed "status" positions constituted a group even further out of line with their overall numerical rank among national groups. The point to note is that the further up the ladder of preferment, the more the Scots were over-represented. And the Scots were not the most successful immigrant group only at the end of the Upper Canadian period. They outstripped the others from the beginning to the end of the province's history. It is conceivable that at times before 1842 they were a somewhat larger national element in the population as a whole, giving them a greater numerical "entitlement" to positions, but there is no reason to suppose that matters were ever very different. Available statistics suggest that the Scots always emigrated in the smallest numbers compared to the Irish and the English.[60] It is hard to escape the conclusion that the emigrant Scots were, early and late, a collection of over-achievers.

Everything that is known about Irish immigration to British North America up to 1841 points to the conclusion that "the Irish were the

TABLE 18
National Origin and Status Positions by Chronological Groups

Group	*Magistrates*		*Militia Officers*		*"Higher Status" Positions*	
	No.	*%*	*No.*	*%*	*No.*	*%*
Group A (103)						
Native-born	51	67.1	45	61.6	28	50.0
Scotland	7	9.2	11	15.1	11	19.6
England/ Wales	4	5.3	5	6.8	8	14.3
Ireland	2	2.6	1	1.4	3	5.4
Post-Loyalist American	6	7.9	4	5.5	4	7.1
Other	1	1.3	1	1.4	1	1.8
Unknown	5	6.6	6	8.2	1	1.8
Total	76		73		56	
Group Aa (97)						
Native-born	34	56.7	44	55.7	26	56.5
Scotland	7	11.7	7	8.9	6	13.1
England/ Wales	4	6.7	7	8.9	5	10.9
Ireland	4	6.7	5	6.3	3	6.5
Post-Loyalist American	6	10.0	9	11.4	5	10.9
Unknown	5	8.3	7	8.9	1	2.2
Total	60		79		46	
Group B (138)						
Native-born	37	42.1	48	45.7	22	45.8
Scotland	17	19.3	17	16.2	10	20.8
England/ Wales	7	7.9	12	11.4	7	14.6
Ireland	7	7.9	7	6.7	2	4.2
Post-Loyalist American	15	17.1	16	15.2	5	10.4
Unknown	5	5.7	5	4.8	2	4.2
Total	88		105		48	
Group Ba (99)						
Native-born	26	41.3	37	48.1	11	44.0

TABLE 18 (continued)

Scotland	14	22.2	15	19.5	6	24.0
England/ Wales	6	9.5	10	12.9	5	20.0
Ireland	6	9.5	5	6.5	1	4.0
Post-Loyalist American	8	12.7	7	9.1	1	4.0
Unknown	3	4.8	3	3.9	1	4.0
Total	63		77		25	

single most [numerically] important group of migrants to British North America,"[61] yet their statistical record among MHAS and among all the other more exclusive subgroups of MHAS who held "status" positions is precisely the reverse of the Scots. Though the actual percentage of MHAS who were Irish increased somewhat, (from 4.8 percent in Group A to 8.1 percent in Group BA) their share, even of elected positions was never a large one. Among MHAS who were colonels of militia, they made up 7.3 percent of the total; among large landowner-MHAS they made an even poorer showing, at 4.6 percent. As magistrates and militia officers, their numbers among the MHAS, while always small, can be said to have shown some slight proportional improvement, but as holders of more prestigious or better-paid positions they appear to have lost ground over time. In any case, all of the percentage figures for the Irish which are nearly comparable to the census of 1842 show them to have been woefully under-represented in comparison to their numbers in the whole population. In 1842 they made up 16.1 percent of the population. The percentage of MHAS who were Irish at the end of the Upper Canadian period was about half that figure. Among those MHAS, the percentage who held "higher status" positions was 4 percent, or about one-quarter of their actual proportion of the total population.

The position of the English (including the Welsh) was certainly much more favourable than that of the Irish and, by the end of the Upper Canadian period, they, like the Scots, seem to have been somewhat over-represented, in all categories, especially in "higher status" positions, but their degree of over-representation was a good deal less even there than that of the Scots. In view of Aitchison's claim that the government of Upper Canada had "a bias in favour of newcomers from Great Britain"[62] in the appointment of magistrates, it is interesting to see that among MHAS who were magistrates that bias cannot be said to have operated in a notable way in favour of the English. Their proportion of magistrates' positions was never very high, though it increased gradually. At the end of the Upper Canadian period, 9.5 percent of the English MHAS were magistrates, a figure only slightly higher than their standing of 8.4 percent of the general population in the census of 1842.

The only immigrant group of any size which did not come from the United Kingdom was the American-born, almost all of whom, among the MHAS were Post-Loyalist Americans who had come into Upper Canada before the War of 1812. Given the original strain in the relationship between Upper Canadians and Americans arising from the revolution, which was reinforced by the War of 1812, they made quite a reasonable showing electorally, but otherwise, towards the end of the period especially, American-born MHAS appear to have been a shrinking element so far as "status" positions were concerned. Where it mattered most, in "higher status" jobs, the American-born MHAS in the 1830s-only group (Group BA) held only 4 percent of the positions, below the level of their actual percentage of the population (6.7).

Putting national origin and religious denomination together to produce a set of composite numbers and percentages relating to office-holding is, as always, not really very satisfactory or enlightening. The number of unknowns is even higher than for religion alone, and the resulting figures are of necessity fairly small and of doubtful general application. The unknown factor becomes much smaller toward the end of the period, but since the 1842 census was not broken down into cross-connected religious/birthplace categories there are no general population figures to use as benchmarks. A simple listing of the combined groups produces no real surprises.

Since, as of 1842 at any rate, native-born Canadians and Anglicans are known to have formed the two largest national and denominational groups in the society as a whole, as they did among the MHAS, it is natural to find native-born Anglicans making up the largest combination among all the MHAS, followed distantly by English-born Anglicans, native-born Presbyterians, Scottish Presbyterians, native-born Methodists, Scottish Catholics, and seventeen other national-religious groups (Table 19).

Faced with an unknown level of more than one-third, it would be hazardous to draw any hard and fast conclusions from such a set of figures, but some general observations may be offered. To begin with, it would seem that (with some possible exceptions to be noted shortly) being of the "right" or "wrong" denomination was more important than being of the "right" or "wrong" national origin. Being an Anglican could make up for other disabilities, such as being a

TABLE 19
All MHAS and Office-holders by Denomination and National Origin

Denomination/National Origin	*All* MHAS	*"Status" Office Holders*	*"Higher Status" Office Holders*
Anglican/Native-born	46	45	26
Anglican/England Wales	21	21	12
Presbyterian/Native-born	20	17	10
Presbyterian-Scotland	16	13	7
Methodist/Native-born	13	10	0
Roman Catholic/Scotland	11	10	8
Methodist/Post-Loyalist American	10	8	1
Anglican/Post-Loyalist American	9	7	5
Anglican/Ireland	8	8	3
Anglican/Scotland	6	6	4
Roman Catholic/Native-born	5	5	3
Presbyterian/Post-Loyalist American	4	2	0
Roman Catholic/Ireland	2	2	0
Lutheran/Native-born	2	2	0
Quaker/Native-born	2	1	1
No Religion/Post-Loyalist American	2	1	1
Methodist/Ireland	1	1	0
Quaker/England/Wales	1	1	1
Quaker/Post-Loyalist American	1	0	0
Unitarian/England/Wales	1	1	0
Baptist/Post-Loyalist American	1	0	0
Anglican/Other	1	1	1
Methodist/England Wales	1	0	0
Congregationalist/Native-born	1	1	0
Unknown	98	87	17
Total	283	251	99

Post-Loyalist American. Being a Methodist imposed penalties where important patronage posts were concerned, regardless of nationality. It might be argued that in the case of the Irish Roman Catholics national origin was more significant than denomination; Roman Catholics generally were quite successful, even in the "higher status" category, but the very small number of Irish Roman Catholics makes any such generalization unwarranted. In any case, the Irish, both Protestant and Roman Catholic, will be discussed in more detail a little further on. Presbyterian Post-Loyalist Americans would also appear to be a case of national origin outweighing negatively the advantages which other Presbyterians evidently enjoyed. Here, however, an additional factor must be taken into account. It was possible to be the "wrong" kind of Presbyterian. In addition to those Upper Canadian Presbyterian churches "in connection with the Church of

Scotland" (often referred to as the Kirk of Scotland) there were quite a number of other Presbyterian groups of varying size,[63] many of which had an American background or American connections and whose members were sometimes accused of having "connections ... to what may be called the radical party."[64] Presbyterians of American origin, then, could labour under a double disadvantage, coming from the wrong place and coming from or adhering to the wrong kind of Presbyterianism. The actual biographical evidence on this point is unfortunately very thin, since most of the time only the general term "Presbyterian" appears in the sources. In fact for only nine of the total of forty Presbyterian MHAS has it been possible to make this kind of distinction,[65] and none of those nine was a Post-Loyalist american. Nonetheless, the existing evidence suggests that, for themselves and their contemporaries, there was an important difference between belonging to the Kirk and belonging to other Presbyterian bodies. Of five known members of the Kirk (Malcolm Cameron, R.G. Dunlop, C.C. Ferrie, Thomas McKay, and Archibald McLean) all but Cameron were Conservative in politics and three (Dunlop, McKay, and McLean) held "higher status" offices. As for those who are known to have been Presbyterians but not members of the Kirk (David Gibson, John McIntosh, Gilbert McMicking, and David Thorburn), all were Reformers, none held "higher status" positions and two, Gibson and McIntosh, held no civil or military appointments of any kind.

It should, of course, be added that there were similar divisions, some of them internal, within most Protestant churches of the time that may have had a bearing on the careers of their members. Certainly there were many varieties of Methodism[66] and it is possible, for instance, that British Wesleyans were viewed with somewhat more favour by the central elite than were members of Methodist churches with American antecedents, but where patronage posts were concerned there is little sign that among Methodist MHAS there were believed to be some who were of the "right" variety.

The list of MHAS by denomination and national origin presents the opportunity to make some comment on Armstrong's contention that among ethnic groups it was Scottish Protestant Lowlanders who succeeded best, "disproportionate to numbers."[67] It has been seen that Scots, while low in numbers generally and among the MHAS, were the most successful immigrant groups where it mattered most, but being also divided religiously, they are not in the most prominent positions in a national-denominational list. So far as Lowlanders are concerned, it is not possible to write with much authority, the evidence on birthplace location being pretty scarce. Among Scots MHAS for whom both a denominational and a Highland or Lowland birthplace identification has been established, Protestant Lowlanders are in a slight majority over Roman Catholic Highlanders (eleven to eight) but not much weight should be given to such small numbers. If the question of Highland versus Lowland region is ignored, however, and the question is reduced simply to one of Scottish Protestants versus Scottish Roman Catholics, the numbers are a bit larger and the picture somewhat clearer. The religious affiliation of thirty-three of the total or thirty-nine Scottish MHAS is known. Of these, twenty-two were Protestants and eleven were Roman Catholics. Even these figures do not convey the real extent of the advantage enjoyed by Scottish Protestants. The Scottish Roman Catholics were really only a significant factor in politics and, within their political group, in patronage in the early years of Upper Canadian history. Among the Scottish MHAS who sat in the period before 1820 (Group A) there were seven Roman Catholics and only three known Protestants (two unknowns). The seven Roman Catholics were all members of Loyalist families, most of which settled in eastern Upper Canada and were all named Macdonell: Alexander Macdonell (Collachie) and his brother Angus, Angus Macdonell (Sandaig), Hugh and John Macdonell (Aberchalder), their nephew John Macdonell (Greenfield), and John Macdonell (Scotus), son of "Spanish John" Macdonell who had been a captain in the King's Royal Regiment of New York. By the 1820s this Roman Catholic Scottish Loyalist group was no longer a numerically significant political force, nor was it ever one again in Upper Canada. Following the Scottish Roman Catholics and Protestants through the four overlapping chronological groups previously employed produces clear Protestant ascendancy after 1820, and among these Scottish MHAS the same early Catholic and subsequent Protestant numerical superiority was reflected in the "higher status" patronage positions they held (Table 20).

Among Loyalists and other early Scottish arrivals, the Roman Catholics leaders were a majority, largely owing to the number of Roman Catholic Scots who had emigrated to America just before the revolution and had taken military roles as officers on the British side. By the 1820s, the tide of immigration, as reflected in the political and patronage systems at any rate, had turned in favour of Scottish Protestants. Even the Scottish Roman Catholic enclave in eastern Upper Canada was forced to share power with about equal numbers of Scottish Protestant leaders. By the time of the 1842 census, Presbyterians outnumbered Roman Catholics in the Eastern District. Elsewhere, prominent Scottish Roman Catholics were a rarity.

TABLE 20
Scottish MHAS: Denomination and "Higher-status" Appointments by Chronological Group

Denominational Group	*Group A*	*Group Aa*	*Group B*	*Group Ba*
All Scottish MHAS				
Protestant	3	8	16	13
Roman Catholic	7	2	5	3
Unknown	2	0	2	2
"Higher Status" Office-holders				
Protestant	3	4	7	5
Roman Catholic	6	2	3	1
Unknown	2	0	0	0

Among immigrant groups, Scottish Protestants (mainly Presbyterians plus a few Anglicans) were a successful and favoured group. English Protestants (almost all Anglicans) were also quite fortunately placed. The Irish, on the other hand, whether Protestant or Roman Catholic, were less so. Though the Irish at the end of the period, and probably for some time before that, were the largest immigrant group, as MHAS they appear (as Irish Anglicans) only some way down the overall combined national-denominational list. Irish Roman Catholics are even further down, tied in numbers with native-born Lutherans, native-born Quakers, and Post-Loyalist Americans of no denomination. If, for purposes of comparison with the census of 1842, the ninety-nine MHAS who sat only in the 1830s are analyzed in national-religious terms, the numbers are naturally smaller but the rank order changes little. Irish Protestants rank fifth in a field of nine: Irish Roman Catholics are eighth. In fact no Irish Roman Catholic was elected to the Assembly until 1836, the last election held in the Upper Canadian period. Before that date, Irish Roman Catholic penetration into the world of elected politics and patronage had been exceeded or equalled by just about every possible national-denominational group, including native-born Quakers and Lutherans. The number of Irish Roman Catholics in Upper Canada in 1842 can be estimated to have been about 26,000. In the census of 1842 Lutherans of all origins numbered 4,524, and Quakers of all origins 5,200.

The Irish Protestants were not markedly better off among MHAS. In 1842 their total numbers in the province were about 52,000, a larger group than the English and Welsh (40,684), the Scots (39,781), or the American-born (32,009) regardless of religious affiliation in each case.[68] Yet so far as successful participation even in elected politics in the 1830s was concerned, the largest Irish Protestant group, the Anglicans (there was also one Irish Methodist) ranked numerically lower among immigrant groups than English-born Anglicans and Scottish Presbyterians and was only tied with American-born Methodists. Here there may well be a genuine exception to the theory of the greater importance of denomination. Being Irish in Upper Canada, regardless of denomination, does not seem to have been a good thing.

The question of the position of the Irish Roman Catholics in the Upper Canadian power structure has some particular historical interest because they provide a rare example of a group which alleged at the time that there was a policy of systematic discrimination in operation against them. In 1838, Anthony Manahan, "the leading member of the Roman Catholics"[69] in Upper Canada, in a long memorial to Lord Durham (then in Canada on his famous mission) complained of widespread anti-Irish Roman Catholic bias. The problem was "the absence of liberal and enlightened men" among "the notorious Family Compact in Toronto." Manahan alleged that although Irish Roman Catholics made up 20 percent of the population of Upper Canada, not one of them held "any office of profit or emolument under the Crown."[70] Despite their subsequent appearance without question or comment in Durham's *Report*, neither of these claims was strictly true,[71] but there is no doubt about the general validity of Manahan's statement. In relation to their actual numbers Irish Roman Catholics *were* considerably under-represented in politics and government. Did Manahan's charge have wider application to Upper Canadian history? Was Upper Canada a place where rampant discrimination against (or for) particular religious or national groups regularly prevailed?

It would be gratifying to be able to say that the information which has been gathered together about the Upper Canadian MHAS and their times throws a strong, clear, unambiguous light on that question. Unfortunately that is not the case. Beyond a doubt, some groups were, in relation to what is known about their share of the population, over- or under-represented. Discrimination, in a strictly mathematical sense, was a fact. But was it deliberate discrimination? Or did it simply reflect some of the realities of Upper Canadian life?

It would be helpful if information were generally at hand about the amount, quality, and type of education which the MHAS received, since the Scots in particular have frequently been said to have benefited from the advantages of a superior educational system. Unfortunately, education is a matter on which research has proved more than usually fruitless. Presumably the MHAS had at least a basic elementary education (though one or two are said to have had almost none)[72] but the fact is that for most of them, there is simply no information on their education at all. Only about one-quarter of all the MHAS are known to have had some form of education (most often in the law) above a rudimentary level. Only five are known to have attended a university. Among themselves, those who had some higher education were relatively successful in patronage matters: nearly two-thirds of them held a "higher status" appointment. That does not necessarily mean, though, that advanced education was by any means a prerequisite for all offices, since 53 percent of all "higher status" office-holders are not known to have had an education beyond a basic level. Certainly legal education quickly became a necessity for an appointment to the bench, but for other positions their degree of education may not have been very relevant. John Willson, for example, is said to have had "little formal education,"[73] but he became a legislative councillor, and at least six MHAS who had more than an elementary education (all but one of whom had legal training) held no public office of any kind.[74] What is known about education at a higher than elementary level among the MHAS reveals no particular Scottish pre-eminence, but it must again be said that the information is really too fragmentary to permit any theorizing on the point.

Occupational statistics provide some background to political and patronage positions. It has been shown, for example, that the Scots among the MHAS were also dominant in relation to their numbers in some of the leading revenue-producing occupations such as milling, distilling, storekeeping, and public service (but not law or farming), while the Irish were under-represented in all leading occupations. These factors, however, simply push the question one step further back. How did the Scots come to penetrate these occupations so thoroughly, and why were the Irish so thoroughly outclassed? There has been no lack of explanations for Scottish successes. Frequent instances of youthful poverty; national habits of "frugality, thrift, and a hardy, self reliant nature"; a school system that required a school in every parish; the existence of a Scottish international commericial network; a Scottish preference for dealing with each other and advancing each other's interests; a higher-than-average level of per capita wealth among Scottish immigrants; and even a willingness to use business methods that were "often dubious, sometimes downright illegal," have been suggested as reasons why Scots excelled in the new world.[75] No doubt there is some truth in all of these; no doubt also they did not apply in all cases. Certainly not all Scots came with capital,[76] and not all Scots in a position to do so always advanced the careers of other Scots. Upper Canada's best-known Scot, the Reverend John Strachan, possessed great influence, especially during the administration of Sir Peregrine Maitland. "The power of rewarding modest worth," he once wrote, "is perhaps the sweetest blessing that attends rank and authority, for our Great Master tells us it is more blessed to give than to receive,"[77] but on the whole Strachan seems to have found "modest worth" embodied in members of the Church of England, of whatever background, more often than among his fellow Scots.[78] If the extraordinary level of Scottish prominence owed little to the assistance of someone as well placed as Strachan, their achievement is even more remarkable.

If the Scots have been assumed to have profited from a range of fortunate attributes and circumstances, it has generally been alleged that the Irish, especially the Roman Catholic Irish, were in an opposite situation and suffered from some collective disadvantages. In a great deal of nineteenth-century literature and in much subsequent historical comment, Irish immigrants to Upper Canada have been described as a group of unskilled, impoverished, pugnacious semi-savages. A recent study of Upper Canadian society has summarized the stereotypical view of the Irish Roman Catholic of the time. They were seen as "careless, improvident, dirty, disorderly and proud."[79]

This view of the Irish has been vigorously challenged by Donald Akenson. Rather than the ignorant, shiftless peasants which many of their contemporaries and later historians have said they were, Akenson argues, from Irish sources, that the Irish immigrants were not a landless, poverty-stricken group but came from the "relatively prosperous areas of the country." In the period 1815 to 1845, before the great Irish famine, Akenson believes that Irish migration to British North America "consisted chiefly (but by no means entirely) of individuals who were above the subsistence line and who came to the new world with resources and ambitions intact."[80]

If Akenson is right – and he presents a forceful case – a number of questions about the Irish in Upper Canada immediately arise. If the Irish were not really substantially different from other immigrants in economic and social background, their lack of success in politics, patronage, and more general areas of Upper Canadian life is even more difficult to explain. One might ask, although the question goes well beyond the bounds of this study, why, if most of the Irish arrived "with resources and ambitions intact," they made up, well before the famine years, such a large proportion of the unskilled labour force on public works projects such as the canals? Why did they figure prominently in jail and penitentiary statistics? Why were they so frequently involved in "riotous proceeedings"?[81] It is likely that some of their notoriety was simply a result of their numbers, they being the largest of the immigrant groups, and as such they may have seemed to constitute some kind of threat to other, smaller groups. However, it might have been expected that at some point those very numbers ought to have begun to operate for, rather than against, their chances of advancing in the social, economic, and political scales.

Two possible avenues of explanation suggest themselves in connection with Akenson's arguments and the position of the Irish in Upper Canada in general. First, it is likely that where there was so much nineteenth-century smoke there was at least some fire: that is, that while Akenson may well be right in claiming that the Irish were not all so poor or so unskilled or so unsuited for farm work as their contemporaries believed, there were still enough of them who did appear to fit those categories to make the stereotype understandable and easy to apply. Recent studies of the "Irish" township of Montague in eastern Upper Canada show clearly that, while the Irish had no trouble adapting to pioneer farming, they were as a group less well-off than their non-Irish contemporaries, were willing to put up with worse land and worse conditions for longer periods of time, and (particularly among the Irish Roman Catholics) had a higher level of illiteracy.[82] They may have had some resources, yet as a group they had less than other immigrant groups. It is also likely that as a group they had fewer helpful connections within the power structures of either the colony or the mother country. The typical Irish immigrant undoubtedly did not deserve H.C. Pentland's description: "a primitive man – half a tribesman still,"[83] but it is possible that compared to other national groups the Irish started from a position of greatest disadvantage.

The second potential line of explanation involves a return to the difficult question of discrimination. There is a good deal of evidence to show that many non-Irish Upper Canadians thought of the Irish as their inferiors. Examples of anti-Irish prejudice are common in nineteenth-century newspapers and in travel and immigrant literature.[84] That being so, it would be hardly surprising to find that non-Irish Upper Canadians in a position to do so sometimes discriminated against individual Irish people, nor is it surprising to find that some of the Irish, like Anthony Manahan, complained about it. The Irish were thought of – rightly or wrongly, consciously or unconsciously – as unskilled, unlettered, quarrelsome, shiftless people. It was a difficult stereotype to escape, and even the Irish who were far from personally fitting the stereotype found, or alleged that they found, their way up the ladder made unduly difficult. Politically, despite their numbers, they did not rise as quickly as others. It was not that there were so qualified Irishmen, including Roman Catholic Irishmen,[85] and it was not just that they didn't often get elected to public office. They were not often candidates for office, which is also to say that they were not encouraged by other members of their society to become candidates. They were not often considered for electoral or appointed office because they were assumed to be unsuitable for such offices. Anti-Irish, especially anti-Roman Catholic Irish, prejudice *did* exist.

A final anomaly requiring some tentative explanation concerns those Upper Canadian MHAS who were born in the United States (as distinct from the Thirteen Colonies) and who as a group formed an increasing political element in the Assembly, achieving by the 1830s a level of participation almost twice as high as their actual (1842) numbers would have warranted. Such electoral success appears all the more surprising since not only had American immigration into Upper Canada been officially discouraged after 1815, but the growing stream of immigrants from Great Britain had rapidly outnumbered the earlier Post-Loyalist American population. Some of the American-born probably benefited at elections from the fact that they ran in areas like the London, Niagara and, Gore districts where there was a sizable population of American origin.[86] More importantly, as Fred Landon pointed out long ago, the success of Americans in achieving prominence in Upper Canada owed much to the fact that many of them "were people with capital, and what was of equal importance, with technical expertise."[87] There are plenty of examples of the type of individual Landon had in mind among the American-born MHAS: Charles Duncombe and John Gilchrist, physicians; M.S. Bidwell, lawyer; William Hamilton Merritt, entrepreneur and promoter; Hiram Norton, carriage manufacturer and stagecoach operator; Absalom Shade, miller, merchant and land speculator; Richard Woodruff, merchant and miller; Charles Ingersoll, merchant; Henry Jones, merchant. Merely as MHAS, the American-born seem to have had some of the same characteristics as the Scots, bustling and successful out of proportion to their numbers. Their success, however, unlike that of the Scots, had definite limits. Beyond elected office, the American-born did well (if less well than the Scots) in acquiring the "building block" positions in the militia and the magistracy, but when it came to "higher status" government positions, they suffered badly unless they became members of the Church of England, being under-represented, in the 1830s below their apparent numerical share, and indeed evidently acquiring a diminishing share of such offices. The American-born may well have had capital, expertise, and ambition in levels equal to those of the Scots, but unlike the Scots they could not penetrate the patronage and power system to any real effect. Like the Irish, they were excluded by the provincial establishment from "the elite of office." Neither group was trusted to exercise power well or to execute it wisely.

CHAPTER FIVE

Parliaments and Politicians

It was customary for the Upper Canadian establishment to look upon the members of the House of Assembly with a certain disdain. The first lieutenant governor, John Graves Simcoe, set the tone when he expressed his often-quoted fear that the first House would turn out to be made up of "men of the lower order, who kept but one table, that is who dined in common with their servants."[1] Simcoe's surveyor general, D.W. Smith, added another view of that initial group which would also become a common complaint of the executive. "Our House of Assembly for the most part have violent levelling principles which are totally different from the ideas I have been educated with – The neighbouring states are to [sic] often brought in as patterns & models, which I neither approve or countenance."[2] Throughout the political history of Upper Canada, lieutenant governors such as Gore, Maitland, or Head periodically found the people's representatives lacking in social graces, education, and parliamentary skill and much too democratic in their views. After the first major opposition victory in the elections of 1828, Sir Peregrine Maitland reported to the Colonial Office that men "whose principles were notoriously disloyal, and whose characters as individuals are really detestable, are now degrading the legislature of the country by their presence."[3] General Brock, in a time of military crisis, suspected them (in some cases rightly) of actual disloyalty due to the "great influence which the vast numbers of settlers from the United States possess over the decisions of the Lower House."[4] The Reverend John Strachan thought that the Assembly of 1808–12 was "composed of ignorant clowns" but had hopes that the future election of a good number of his former students would bring about a marked improvement.[5] One of his former students, John Beverly Robinson, once described radical members of the Assembly as "scum."[6]

There is no doubt that the low opinion held by Simcoe or Maitland or Strachan or Robinson of the social and educational level of the MHAs was sometimes justified. In the session of 1807, Ebenezer Washburn, member for Prince Edward, was described as "no scholar" and as being "rather too deep in drink" in the House. According to his "particular friend" Judge Thorpe, Joseph Willcocks, MHA, "did not possess a sufficiency of brains to bait a mouse trap."[7] Certainly the ranks of Upper Canadian parliamentarians contained some who held radical political views. Even in the last parliament, (1836–41), which was about as conservative a body as the province had ever seen, at a time by which the general population, much swollen by British immigration, had reached some 400,000, there were still quite a few members who were said to have "Yankee republican principles" (some of whom were, of course, to be real or suspected rebels in 1837), and there were still some who were without formal education and who were "out of their depth" in the House.[8] Nonetheless, though the level of debate in the Upper Canadian House must certainly have been somewhat below the standard ofWestminster, it is possible in each of Upper Canada's thirteen parliaments to find a good many members of some talent and common sense. As well, it is possible to argue that most of the time the House of Assembly reflected far more accurately the prevailing sentiments of the people of Upper Canada as a whole (what Receiver General Peter Russell once called "the low ignorance of the Electors")[9] than did the more exclusivist views of members of the Upper Canadian establishment such as Strachan or Maitland. Peter Perry may have been one of those who could not "read, write, or spell a sentence of their own, or any other language, correctly,"[10] but the voters of Lennox and Addington who elected him four times running did not find his lack of polish a liability. The fact is that each Upper Canadian parliament was different from the others, becoming more or less "democratic" and more or less "respectable" as the membership periodically changed.

It has been said that, in both Upper and Lower Canada, the provincial governing elite found it difficult to get members of its own circle elected to the lower house, and was thereby at times prevented from having the government's programs properly presented in the Assembly. "After 1800 ... the Governor and his advisers were unable to devise any electoral machinery for the creation of enough government seats for the men in whom they did have conficence."[11] This is something of an exaggeration. The government of Upper Canada was unable in only two parliaments, the fifth (1808–12) and the seventh (1816–20), to get one or both of the law officers of the crown elected to the Assembly. The attorney general was a member of eight parliaments and the solicitor general of five, and both of these government officials sat together in three parliaments. The government was in fact most successful in having one of its nominees elected to the Assembly when it became most necessary, that is, after the emergence in the 1820s of a consistent opposition movement within the House. From the eight parliament (1820–4) on, including "the most radical of all Upper Canadian assemblies"[12] (1828–30), the attorney general was always a member of the house and the solicitor general as well was a member in the last three parliaments (1830–41). As S.F. Wise has pointed out, the people's representatives, whether Reform or Conservative, did not always give government initiatives a sympathetic hearing,[13] but it was not for lack of government spokesmen – John Beverley Robinson, Henry John Boulton, Christopher Hagerman, and W.H. Draper among them – who were there to take the government side. In fact it has been demonstrated that Robinson in particular was quite successful in achieving major administration goals through the device of joint legislative committees, which put in place a provincial commitment to a large-scale public works program and the heavy provincial borrowing necessary to finance it.[14]

There are a number of ways in which it is possible to analyze the changing nature of Upper Canada's political personnel, for instance, by the familiar categories of national origin, religion, occupation, or civil or military office-holding, or by age at election, length of political service, or education. Some of these categories have in fact been explored to a degree in earlier chapters dealing with occupation and with office-holding. It has been shown that over the entire period some occupations (farming, milling, and public service) declined in frequency among MHAS, while others, (law, medicine, journalism, distilling, and store-keeping) became more popular. It is known that the proportion of MHAS who held appointments as magistrates also declined, but that their participation in the militia showed some increase. It would be possible to examine each of the thirteen parliaments of Upper Canada separately, using some or all of the potential categories, thereby refining and extending the general trends already identified. It is doubtful, though, that such a minute examination would be either very enlightening or very accurate. The numbers involved, especially in the early parliaments, are very small, and the number of "unknowns" in many categories, is very high, which means that small changes among a small group, using very incomplete data, could produce dramatic but probably misleading statistical results. To take an extreme example, that of educational level: the percentage of MHAS known to have had "more than rudimentary" education was 20.8 percent in the fourth parliament but dropped to 3.5 percent in the fifth parliament. That there may have been a drop of some kind is quite possible; that it was so drastic a drop is unlikely. What is likely, indeed certain, is that the available information on the educational background of the MHAS is woefully lacking.

Rather than a blow-by-blow examination of each parliament, a division of the thirteen parliaments into periods has been adopted to try to establish some general tendencies within the membership over time. As it happens, two parliaments in particular provide convenient breaking points in the whole fifty-year period. The fifth and the tenth parliaments are, on a number of scores, the most anomalous among the thirteen parliaments, and it is useful therefore to use them as yardsticks against which to measure the rest of Upper Canada's parliamentary history.

What was so special about the fifth and tenth parliaments? From the point of view of the provincial elite they were low points, when the House of Assembly least resembled the type of body they wished it to be. No member of the provincial administration was elected to the fifth parliament. The known level of education among the members was at an all-time low, as was the number of members who had had or were still involved in military service. The proportion of MHAS who held government appointments was also at its lowest point to that date. Religiously the Fifth Parliament, compared to its predecessors, also presented some intriguing differences. Before 1808, only three Methodists are known to have ever sat in the house. The fifth parliament alone included at least five Methodists. There were even more (known) Methodists in the fifth parliament than (known) Anglicans, an unheard-of circumstance up to that time, and two other dissenters, a Quaker and a Lutheran, had also been elected.

The tenth parliament exhibited similar characteristics. It set an Upper Canadian record for most known Methodists in a single parliament (ten or 21 percent of the total membership), for the lowest proportion of its members holding a concurrent appointment as a magistrate or other government appointment, and for the lowest incidence of representation from families of Loyalist background. The tenth Parliament, along with the fifth, marked the greatest degree of religious and civil deviation from the ideals of the elite (Figures 1 and 2).

It is time to backtrack. If the members of the fifth parliament

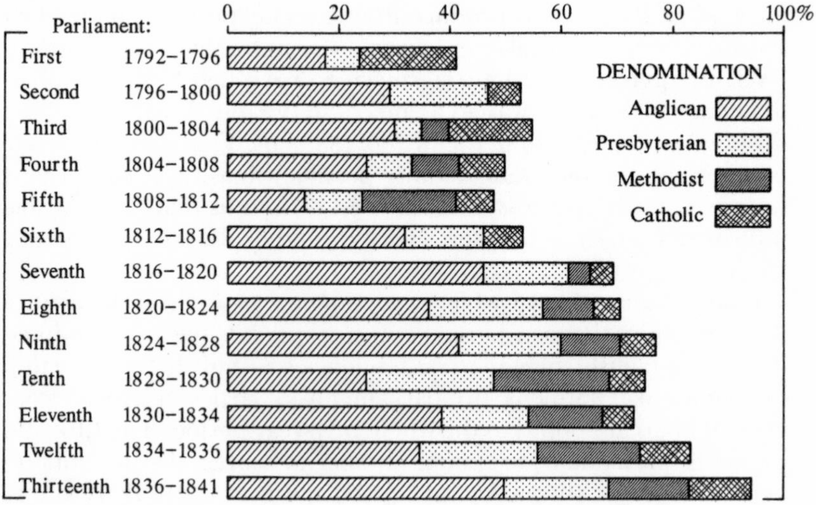

Figure 1 MHAS by Known Principal Denominations, 1792–1841

reached a first peak of deviance, what were they deviating from? The first two parliaments of Upper Canada (1792–1800) were both very small and quite similar in composition. Loyalists in general, and Loyalist half-pay officers in particular, predominated. In the first parliament, nine out of seventeen members were on half pay from Loyalist regiments. John and Hugh Macdonell had been officers of the King's Royal Regiment of New York, as had Jeremiah French and Hazelton Spencer. Alexander Campbell and Ephraim Jones were half-pay officers of Jessup's Rangers. Both Philip Dorland and Peter Vanalstine, who succeeded to Dorland's seat in 1793, had been lieutenants in Colonel Cuyler's Loyalist Refugees, and Benjamin Pawling had been a lieutenant in Butler's Rangers. The first parliament was rounded out by men whose loyalty during the revolution had been manifested in non-military ways (Nathaniel Pettit, Isaac Swayze, Parshall Terry, William Macomb, and Francis Baby), and by two government placemen, the attorney general, John White, and the surveyor general. D.W. Smith.

The second parliament was equally loyal, D.W. Smith being the only non-Loyalist in the group. Loyalist half-pay officers were only slightly less evident. Eight of them (John Macdonell, R.N. Wilkinson, and Timothy Thompson of the King's Royal Regiment of New York; Edward Jessup, Thomas Fraser, and Solomon Jones of Jessup's Rangers; Christopher Robinson of the Queen's Rangers; and Thomas Smith of the Indian Department still made up almost half of the membership of seventeen. There were, though, signs that a subtle change in attitude on the part of the Upper Canadian elec-

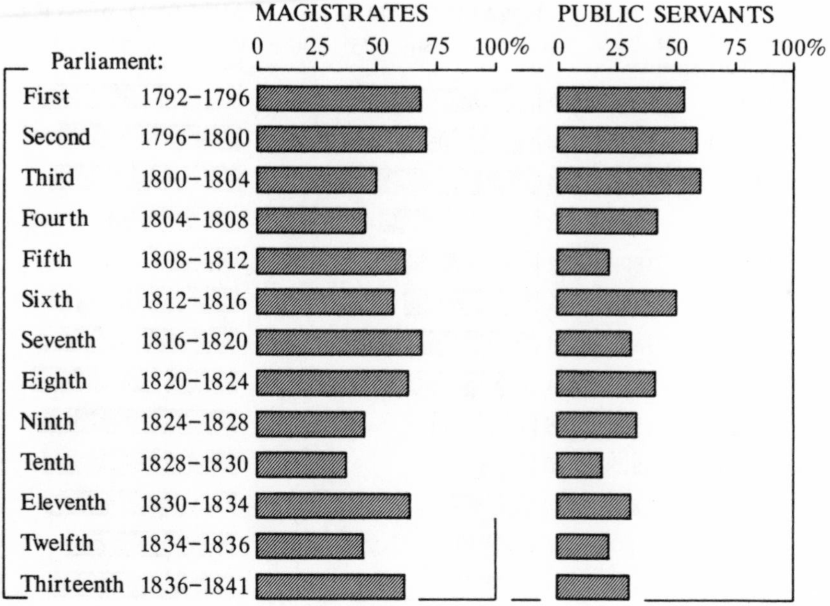

Figure 2 Magistrates and Public Servants

torate toward their leaders may have been in process. In a by-election in 1799, the attorney general, John White, was defeated in the riding of Addington and Ontario by "an illiterate young man of their own level & neighbourhood"[15] (in fact William Fairfield, a second-generation Loyalist) despite White's election expenses having been paid from the funds of the lieutenant governor's office.[16] In the general election the following year, the proportion of Loyalists elected slipped marginally (in percentage terms from 94 to 85) but the Loyalist half-pay presence was sharply reduced to a little over one-third, seven out of a total of twenty. The fourth parliament continued these trends. The Loyalist contingent of all kinds dropped to about 67 percent of the membership, (sixteen of twenty-four) and the number of Loyalist half-pay officers fell even more dramatically to only five of twenty-four. The fifth parliament, the first "bench-mark" parliament, extended the trend a bit further. Loyalist participation remained about the same (nineteen out of twenty-nine, or 65 percent) but the number of Loyalist half-pay officers dropped to only four. The Loyalist officers and, to a degree, Loyalists as a whole were losing their position in the Assembly. The proportion of successful government candidates, as has been seen, also decreased. The solicitor general, the surveyor general, and, for a few days, the chief justice, sat in the third parliament. The solicitor general (ac-

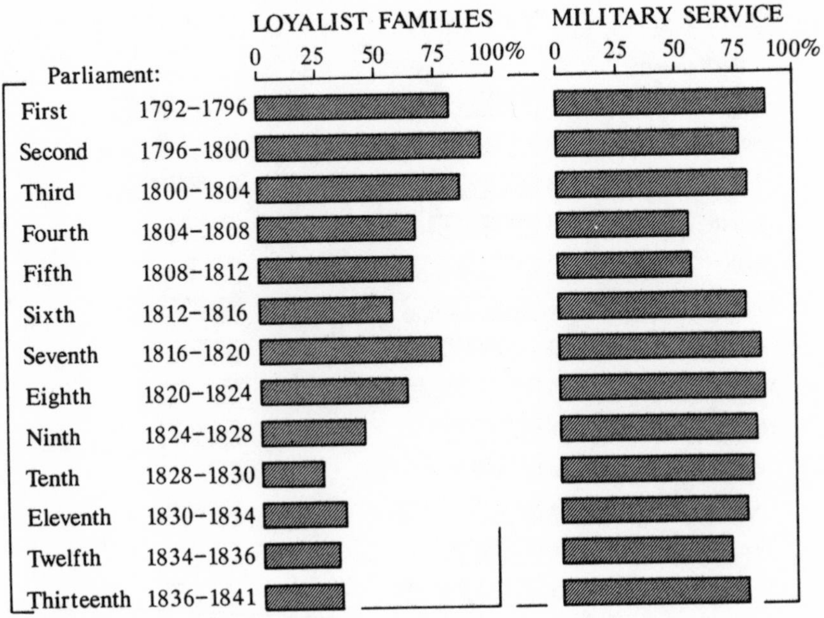

Figure 3 Loyalism and Military Service

tually two of them in turn, R.I.D. Gray and his successor D'Arcy Boulton) sat in the fourth parliament. No government nominee was a member of the fifth parliament. The new element consisted of non-administration, non-Loyalist immigrants. William Weekes, Robert Thorpe, Joseph Willcocks, and T.B. Gough were recent arrivals from Ireland; David Cowan, James Durand, and James Wilson had come from England, while Benajah Mallory, Thomas Mears, Philip Sovreign, and John Willson were Post-Loyalist immigrants from the United States.

The movement toward a more pluralistic and democratic House shows up over the first five parliaments in several other ways already alluded to. The proportion of MHAS also holding government appointments held relatively steady during the first three parliaments, in the range of 53–60 percent. In the fourth parliament the figure was 42 percent and in the fifth parliament 21 percent. The percentage of MHAS who were also magistrates declined in the same period, with some fluctuations dropped from 82 to 62 percent, and those holding concurrent militia commissions from 88 to 55 percent. (See Figures 2 and 3.) There can also be discerned an apparent religious trend based on known religious affiliation. While the participation of the state-supported denominations in politics was fairly stable, with Anglicans always in the lead, the Methodists, the most prominent dissenting group, made notable gains. There were no

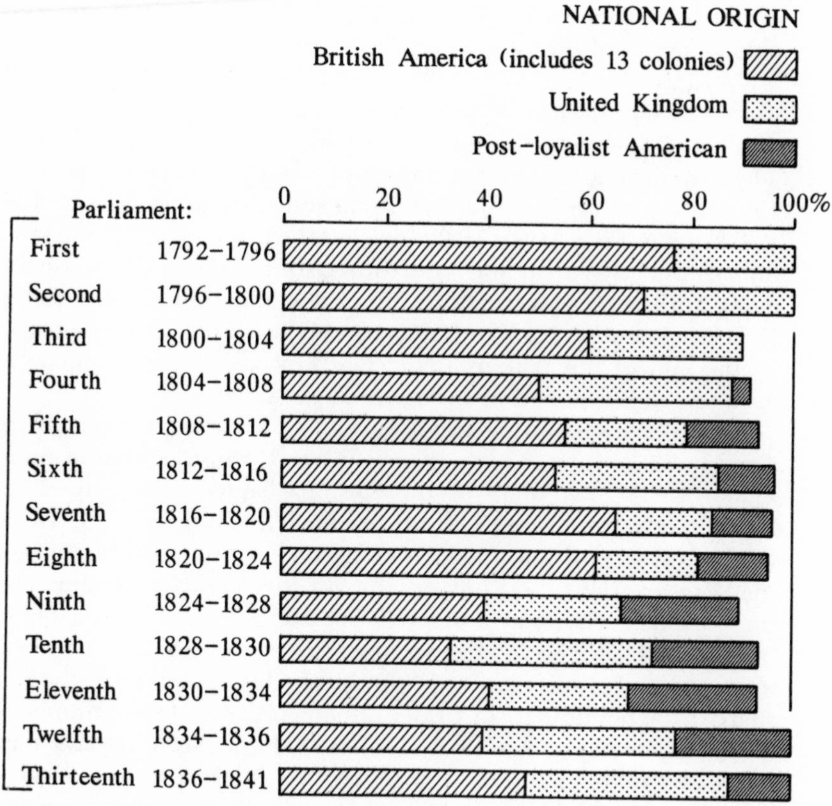

Figure 4 MHAS, by Main Known National Origin, 1792–1841

known Methodists in the first two parliaments, one in the third, two in the fourth, and five in the fifth. (See Figure 1.) Lastly, though people of North American background had always been in a majority in the House, in the fourth and fifth parliaments there was some increase in the proportion of members whose place of origin was North America, particularly the United States, rather than Europe. (See Figure 4.)

On the basis of these various kinds of "indicators" and despite a lack of complete data in all areas, there is not much doubt that some sort of "levelling" process was going on within the Upper Canadian House of Assembly during the years 1792–1812. The people of Upper Canada showed an increasing tendency to reject as their representatives members of the civil, military, and even religious establishments, to send to the provincial capital in increasing numbers men whose social (and probably educational) backgrounds more closely reflected the mainly agricultural population as a whole, and even to elect men such as Willcocks, Weekes, and Thorpe who were voluble critics of the ruling elite.

Some changes had taken place, but it would be unwise to attach too much significance to them, or to make too strong a claim that a process of "democratization" or "Americanization" was underway. The Loyalist half-pay group was destined to pass from the political scene in any case. Christopher Robinson died in 1799 and R.N. Wilkinson in 1804. Hugh Macdonell left the province about the same time, never to return, and his brother John died in 1809. Among other former Loyalist officers, Matthew Elliott, Ephraim Jones, Hazelton Spencer, Thomas McKee, and Edward Jessup were all dead by the end of the War of 1812. The Loyalist officer group were losing its numbers and its influence at the same time.

The appearance of Methodism as an increasing political force should also be treated with some caution. It must be kept in mind that, with the exception of the fifth parliament, the Church of England was always the best-represented denomination, and that Methodists were often no more numerous, or were less numerous, than Presbyterians and Roman Catholics. (See Figure 1.) In any case, the presence of one, two, or even five Methodists was probably to be expected since Methodists were said to be increasing in numbers in the years before 1812.[17] If the Methodists deserved to have a share in the political life in Upper Canada because of their numbers, the members of the Assembly as a whole do not seem to have seen the matter in that light. It was after the five Methodists were elected that two of them, John Roblin and James Wilson, were expelled from the House in 1810 as "Ministers, Priests, Ecclesiastics or Teachers" of their church. The expulsion of Roblin and Wilson showed how little most of the members were concerned with the need for some recognition of the presence in Upper Canadian society of religious dissent. The vote was two to one for expulsion.[18]

If there must be some question about the extent to which the Assembly had come by 1812 to reflect change in the religious makeup of the population, there is even greater reason to question the extent of any "Americanizing" or "North Americanizing" trend. Between 1792 and 1812, the population of Upper Canada was fundamentally transformed. The original nucleus of perhaps 7,000 Loyalist settlers was overwhelmed by the arrival of thousands of Post-Loyalist Americans. An American visitor to Upper Canada in 1812 estimated that these settlers from the United States made up about 60 percent of the population. G.M. Craig's modern estimate was a good deal higher. Post-Loyalist Americans, he believes, "outnumbered the old Loyalists and the few residents who had come directly from Britain by about four to one on the eve of the War of 1812" – that is, they made up about eighty percent of the population.[19]

Though the precise proportion of Americans within the population is uncertain,[20] if these estimates are even roughly correct they should have been represented in the fifth parliament, on a strictly numerical basis, by at least seventeen and possibly as many as twenty-three members out of the total of twenty-nine. As has been seen, there were actually only four Post-Loyalist Americans who sat in the fifth parliament. There were, of course, reasons (other than political reasons) why they did not make a greater impact in the House before 1812. They were relative newcomers; they were not a homogeneous group; they did not come with a built-in leadership element, as the Loyalists had; and they were not evenly spread among the ridings, being hived mainly into the Niagara, Home, and London districts,[21] but as an undoubted majority of the population they were grossly under-represented in the Assembly, and the "old Loyalists and the few residents who had come directly from Britain" were to an equal extent over-represented in the most "democratic" Assembly elected before 1812.

The War of 1812 produced a distinct ripple effect in the parliamentary history of Upper Canada. At first there was a definite anti-democratic, pro-establishment reaction, quite natural under the circumstances, which was most marked in the first two post-war parliaments (1816–20 and 1820–4) but began to subside in the ninth parliament (1824–8) and bottomed out dramatically in the tenth (1828–30) as the impact of the alien question and other grievances appear to have produced a counter-reaction to the original reaction.

The Loyalist influence, which had been declining before the war, recovered strongly in the seventh parliament (1816–20) with the appearance for the first time of a large contingent of Loyalists' sons, who outnumbered, and from then on continued to outnumber, Loyalists themselves. Together thirteen Loyalists' sons and seven Loyalists made up 77 percent of the membership of the seventh parliament. Second-generation Loyalists were also well represented in the eighth parliament. There were twenty-six of them, plus one original Loyalist, making up 61 percent of the total of forty-four members. But another Loyalist decline had set in. The Loyalist share of the membership of the ninth parliament fell to 44 percent and to an all-time low of 27 percent in the tenth parliament. (See Figure 3.)

The Loyalist pattern of "come-back" and decline was not unique. The proportion of members of the House who were also magistrates followed a similar curve. In the wartime Assembly of 1812–16, 57 percent of the MHAs were also magistrates. The percentage jumped to 69 in the seventh parliament, slipped a bit to 64 percent in the eight, and then headed sharply downward to 46 percent in the ninth and 38 percent in the tenth parliament (that was also to be an all-time low). The evidence relating to the number of MHAs who also held higher public service appointments during the 1812–30 period is somewhat but not entirely different. In the sixth parliament (1812–16) the proportion of such members was exactly 50 percent. For the succeeding parliaments the figures are: seventh parliament, 31 percent; eighth parliament, 41 percent, ninth parliament, 33 percent; tenth parliament, 19 percent (also an all-time low). On the whole, although the numbers are less neat, the same general trend as in the case of magistrate-MHAs is apparent: an increasing (if, in this case, fluctuating) support of candidates who were also government officers for about ten years after the war, followed by a rapid loss of support for people of this type in the period 1824–30. (See Figure 2.)

Similar but reversed rises and falls in representation can be seen in the cases of the Methodists and the Post-Loyalist Americans, both of whom may be said to have been under a cloud immediately after the war from which they later began to re-emerge. In the sixth parliament (1812–16) there are not known to have been any Methodists and in the seventh parliament only one. From then on, though, the trend was again steadily upward to a high point at the election of 1828. (Coincidentally, that was the year in which the evidence taken by a parliamentary committee demonstrated that most prominent Upper Canadians believed that Methodists were the most numerous denomination in the province.)[22] There are known to have been four Methodists in the eighth parliament, five in the ninth, and ten in the tenth. Again however it is well to remember that, so far as is known, Methodists were almost always less numerous than Anglicans in the Assembly and were usually less numerous than Presbyterians. (See Figure 1.)

In the same way Post-Loyalist Americans, who had only begun to be visible in the fifth parliament just before the War of 1812, went into a not surprising postwar decline in the sixth and seventh parliaments, in each of which only three of them were elected, making up in each case about 11 percent of the membership. Like the Methodists (although they were not, with the exception of one member, John Willson, the same people) the Post-Loyalist American membership in the Assembly rebounded somewhat in the eighth parliament to 14 percent, to 23 percent in the ninth, and to 21 percent in the tenth. Here too, however, it is necessary to inject some notes of qualification. While Post-Loyalist Americans were making some political gains, they were not the only national group to do so in the same period. The percentage of MHAs from the United Kingdom also increased especially in the ninth and tenth parliaments. (See Figure 4.) More significant than the increase in representation by either of these groups was the increase in the number of members who were native-born Canadians, that is, born after the revolution either in Upper Canada or in another British North American colony. There were no native-born Canadians elected before the sixth parliament, mainly because there hadn't been time for them to achieve any real level of prominence. In the election of 1812 three native-born Canadians were elected, including the first native-born Upper Canadian elected, Alexander McMartin. After that the increase was rapid, if erratic.There were five native-born Canadians elected to the seventh parliament, the astonishing number of twenty to the eighth, fifteen to the ninth, and fourteen to the tenth parliament. By 1828, native-born Canadians were routinely making up around one-third of the membership of the Assembly. (See Figure 5.)

What little is known about the educational background of the MHAS suggests an apparent steady rise in their educational level in the sixth through tenth parliaments (1812–30), the most noteworthy change appearing in the last three of these parliaments, when the known proportion of members possessed of more than rudimentary education was about 30 percent. This could suggest (especially if the data were reliable) a trend, contrary to those so far described, for Upper Canadians to increasingly opt for a group of leaders of a higher and less democratic class. The problem with this notion is that an apparently high level of education continued unchanged in the most radical of all the assemblies, the tenth. What is more likely is that by the 1820s immigration from the United Kingdom was beginning to have some effect on the education level of the MHAS as a whole. Of the fourteen MHAS in the tenth parliament who are known to have had some higher education, six had been born in the United Kingdom.

It should also be realized that the radicalism of the tenth parliament was by no means a North American, or purely North American, phenomenon. In fact, the representation in the House of members from the United Kingdom went up sharply in the tenth parliament reflecting the presence of a large Reform element of British origin which outnumbered British-born Conservatives by eleven to eight.

By far the most striking phenomenon to emerge among the MHAS in the period following the War of 1812 was a change, undoubtedly brought about directly by the war itself, in the rate of participation in the Assembly by members of a military bent. In the last prewar parliament (1808–12) members who were serving or had served in

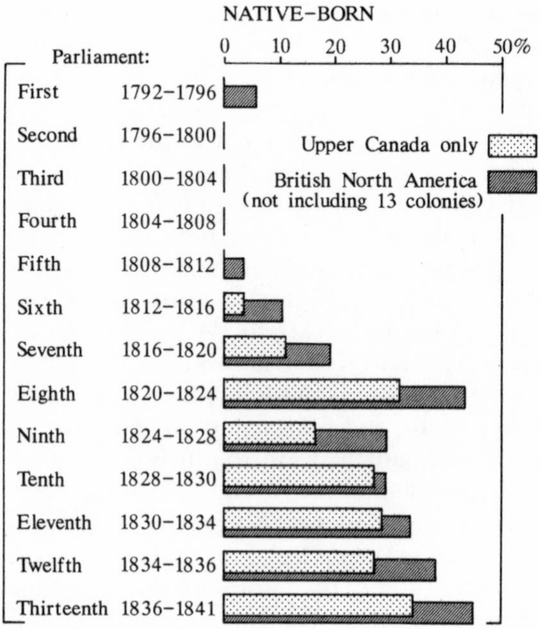

Figure 5 Native-born MHAS

a military capacity made up 55 percent of the membership in the House. In the sixth parliament (1812–16) the equivalent figure was 79 percent, and in the seventh, eighth, ninth, and tenth parliaments it varied between 81 and 86 percent. (In fact, it never fell below 70 percent in the period up to 1841; see Figure 3.) There can be no doubt that military service came to be seen as a critically important virtue and an almost indispensible requirement by the voters of Upper Canada, whatever other merits candidates may have possessed. A willingness to personally resist present or future dangers from the United States was consistently associated with electoral success.

The last three parliaments of Upper Canada, covering the years 1830–41, showed rather more consistency than was true of the two earlier periods. The twelfth parliament (1834–6), in which there was a majority of members usually in opposition to the executive, provided some evidence of variation, primarily on a political basis, a subject to be discussed more fully at the end of the chapter, but anomalies where they occurred were not very great. Certainly there were discernible trends. Loyalism, now primarily second-generation Loyalism, whose influence had waned somewhat in the tenth parliament, rebounded in the last three parliaments, remaining at around 32 to 36 percent of the known membership of the House. (See Figure 3.) There was an increase in the proportion of members who were United Kingdom immigrants, who had made up about 38 percent of the membership in the last two parliaments. This increase was accompanied by a waning of American influence. The Post-Loyalist American element among Upper Canadian MHAs declined in the last three parliaments from 25 to 23 to 13 percent. (See Figure 4.)

The religious composition of the last three parliaments, while apparently fairly stable, can also be shown to have been heading in a couple of different directions. Anglicanism, which had almost always been the leading denomination among members whose affiliation is known, continued to be dominant through the last three parliaments and in the thirteenth parliament (1836–41) eventually reached the extraordinary level of 50 percent of the membership. On the other hand, (known) Methodists, who had been just behind (known) Presbyterians for third place among denominations in the eleventh parliament (1830–4), slipped back a bit more in the twelfth (Reform) parliament, and lost even more ground in the thirteenth, retaining their status as the third largest denomination but dropping from 18 to 14 percent of the membership. (See Figure 1.) It should be noted that in the last parliament (1836–41) changes in personnel stemming mainly from the replacement of actual or suspected rebels produced a net loss of two Methodists and a net gain of two Anglicans and one Presbyterian. Though these changes altered the overall denominational standings slightly, they did not change the relative positions of the three leading denominations: the Anglicans, the Presbyterians, and the Methodists.

The strongest signs of stability, and conceivably something close to normalcy among the MHAs as a group, to emerge during the last three parliaments are revealed in the patterns of civil and military office-holding. In the tenth parliament (1828–30) the proportion of MHAs concurrently holding a public service appointment dropped suddenly from a previous level of around 35 percent to 19 percent. In the eleventh parliament, the equivalent figure returned to 31 percent; it dipped somewhat in the twelfth parliament to 21 percent and returned to 30 percent in the thirteenth parliament. The relationship between MHAs and the magistracy was very similar. The proportion of MHAs who were also magistrates had been at an all-time low point in 1828–30 at 38 percent. Again the figures show a return in the eleventh parliament to something much closer to an overall norm at 64 percent; again there is a dip in the twelfth parliament to 45 percent and a return in the last parliament to a "normal" 63 percent. Finally, the close connection between membership in the House of Assembly and the possession of a militia commission or other military service, which did *not* drop off in the tenth parliament, continued at a high level, standing at 78 percent in the eleventh and thirteen parliaments, with the same slight dip to 71 percent in the twelfth. (See Figure 3.) It would be rash to suggest that there was ever an entirely normal leadership profile at any one point, but the last three parliaments probably represent something close to a contemporary, and to some extent future, stable state among the elective leadership – predominantly Anglican and military (but North American), with a lingering Loyalist legacy, and a strong connection between the elected political community and the office-holding establishment, especially the magistracy.

The thirteenth parliament provides an opportunity to make some specialized comparisons on the basis of national origin and religious denomination between the makeup of the elected political leadership of Upper Canada at the very end of the Upper Canadian period and the population as a whole as revealed in the first census of 1842. There are some obvious dangers in making such comparisons. Seventy people sat in the thirteenth parliament, while 487,053 people lived in Upper Canada in 1842. It could hardly be expected that seventy people, however selected, would share the exact characteristics of the population as a whole. Also it is surprising to find that, in this instance, the level of unknows among the MHAS of 1836–41 was actually much lower than for the census itself. The religious affiliation of 20.7 percent of Upper Canadians ("other denominations" plus "not given") is unknown in the 1842 census, compared to 2.8 percent of the MHAS, and the census figures show 5.6 percent of the population as of unknown national origin, while the national origin of all the MHAS is known. The difficulties notwithstanding, it is of some interest to compare the two sets of figures, not because they produce any large surprises but because the differences where they occur are in some cases so very distinct and reinforce conclusions already reached elsewhere.

The most obvious anomaly is religious (Table 21.) Of the four major denominations, the Presbyterians, Methodists, and Roman Catholics show no serious deviation from the positions they should have occupied on a strictly numerical basis, though the Methodists were furthest from their "correct" proportion and lost even more ground after the removal of three of their number (Hiram Norton, T.D. Morrison, and Charles Duncombe) from the House. The extraordinary figure, as always, is that of the Anglicans. According to the 1842 census, 22.1 percent of Upper Canadians were Anglicans, but exactly half of the MHAS who served in 1836–41 were members

TABLE 21
The Four Major Denominations, 1836–41
(percentages)

Denomination	*13th Parliament*	*1842 Census*
Church of England	50.0	22.1
Presbyterian	18.6	19.9
Methodist	14.3	17.1
Roman Catholic	11.4	13.4

of the Church of England, so far as can be determined from incomplete data. Anglicans had always been the "best" denomination so far as electoral success was concerned. The thirteenth parliament, the only one for which almost complete denominational identification has been possible, provides indisputable evidence of the extent to which the Church of England was the "right" church among Upper Canadians aspiring to local and provincial leadership. It might be suggested that the high number of Anglicans in the last parliament reflected new and heavy immigration into Upper Canada from the United Kingdom during the 1830s, but if that was true, it was only partly true. Among the thirty-five Anglicans of 1836–41, twenty-two were of British North American origin, and only eight came from England, four from Ireland, and one from Scotland.

In comparing the national origins of the members of the thirteenth parliament to the equivalent census figures (Table 22), no anomalies quite so obvious as the over-representation of Anglicans appear, but there are some familiar discrepancies.

Among immigrants, the English were somewhat above their numerical entitlement, but the Scots once again stood out, being over-represented by more than a factor of two. The Irish, as is known the largest immigrant group, were once more the most under-represented and were under-represented regardless of religious affiliation. Working from the premise that Protestant Irish immigrants outnumbered Roman Catholic Irish immigrants by about two to one,[23] there ought, on the basis of proportional representation, to have been at least seven Protestant and at least three Roman Catholic Irish members in the House of 1836–41. Instead there were actually five Protestant Irish and two Roman Catholic Irish, the two Catholics, as has been seen, being the first Irish Roman Catholics ever elected to the House. Even the American-born, the smallest of the main "foreign" elements in the Upper Canadian population in 1842, were better represented in the House than the Irish (nine Americans to

TABLE 22
National Origin, 1836–41 (percentages)

Group	*13th Parliament*	*1842 Census*
English Canadian	47.2	50.8
French Canadian	0	2.9
Ireland	10.0	16.1
England and Wales	12.8	8.4
Scotland	17.1	8.1
United States	12.9	6.7

seven Irish) and were almost as much over-represented as the Scots compared to their actual numbers in the population.

Upper Canadians themselves were probably under-represented in the House of Assembly of 1836–41. The 1842 census classifications for the native-born had only two categories, "English-Canadian" and "French-Canadian," which makes it impossible to know whether the "English Canadians" were actually born in Upper Canada or elsewhere in British North America. If it is assumed that "English Canadians" meant "Upper Canadian," then 51 percent of the population in 1842 was Upper Canadian-born. In the House of 1836–41, 34 percent of the members had been born in Upper Canada. The situation looks better if the Upper Canadian MHAS are combined with those born elsewhere in British North America, including two old-timers, Peter Shaver and Mahlon Burwell, who had been born in the Thirteen Colonies during the revolution; together they made up 47 percent of the membership of the House. This brings them close enough to the "English Canadian" percentage in the census but leaves them still somewhat below the actual native-born percentage of the 1842 population, combining French and English Canadians, which was 54 percent. It is worth noting also that the proportion of MHAS of strictly Upper Canadian origin (34.3 percent) was lower than the proportion of immigrants from the United Kingdom (40 percent) and much lower than the total percentage of "foreign" born (52.8 percent). At the end of the Upper Canadian period, Upper Canadian regional leaders were a colonial minority even in their own province.

Just when partisan politics may be said to have begun in Upper Canada is a matter of some difficulty to decide. Strictly speaking, there never were political parties in Upper Canada – that is parties which had acknowledged leaders, met in caucus to decide on political courses, accepted party discipline, or consistently attempted to organize mass party membership on a provincial basis. It has been shown that there were some attempts to create political organizations on the part of the Reformers in the 1830s, and that the provincial executive had its own built-in provincial political network resulting from the system of government patronage,[24] but neither of these reflected or led to the existence of parliamentary parties as such. Nevertheless there were, from an early date, political groupings in the House, which, while they lacked much real organization or consistency of voting behaviour, can be said to have existed in the sense that within the House there were MHAS who more often than not supported the policies of the administration and others who more often than not opposed them.[25]

The election of 1824 has been said to have been a landmark in the political history of Upper Canada, a significant point in a transition from general concern with purely local issues to "province-wide political awareness," producing an Assembly that was able to "focus and articulate the growing sense of grievance with the existing order."[26] Certainly in the House of 1824–8, there were a good many MHAS who were critical of the administration, some, like M.S. Bidwell, Peter Perry, John Rolph, John Matthews, and J.J. Lefferty, making their first appearance on the provincial political stage. The study of political dissent could therefore well be begun in 1824, or indeed at a number of earlier points, but for several reasons the discussion of evolving partisanship which follows begins with the tenth parliament (1828–30). The tenth parliament was, more than any previous parliament, a point of departure. It was the first parliament to contain a clear majority of members who most of the time were in opposition to the provincial executive. It was the first in which the speakership was held by an unmistakable Reformer, M.S. Bidwell. It featured most of the Reform "stars" who were to become well known for their political activities in the ensuing period: Bidwell, Rolph, Perry, William Buell, the two Baldwins, Jesse Ketchum, Mackenzie, and Robert Randall. From 1828 on, the major players had appeared and the political behaviour of others can be measured against theirs. There are also a couple of practical reasons for beginning a political analysis in 1828. First, the amount of information available about the members is somewhat greater than for earlier periods. Second, beginning in 1828 makes it possible to deal with a fairly balanced political situation – two parliaments which can be labelled Reform and two which were Conservative.

Between 1828 and 1841, 162 MHAS sat in four parliaments. Deciding which of them belongs in a Reform and which in a Conservative group is not always a straightforward exercise. There are some easily identified, clear-cut cases, but many which are much less so. Indeed reading the *Journals* of the Assembly in order to try to establish some patterns of consistent political behaviour on the part of individuals or groups can be an exercise in extreme frustration; voting records frequently follow no discernible pattern of any kind. There were a number of contemporary attempts by newspaper editors to clarify the members' political leanings. W.L. Mackenzie's periodic "black lists" are of some help. His lists, published before elections, divided candidates into those he recommended ("Independents") and those he did not ("Ministerialists"), but to some candidates he attached no label at all, or classed them as "undecided."[27] Conservative papers such as the *Kingston Chronicle and Gazette* published rival "white lists," but these too were incomplete or ill-informed, the editor once admitting that the political opinions of some members were "only partially known" and classing as "Constitutionalists" members who did not support Mackenzie, "though they call themselves Reformers."[28] Hard and fast political identifications are difficult to make and in some cases probably not really appropriate. Nevertheless a division into two overall political camps has its uses and has been made, using in doubtful cases the working rule that those who opposed government measures at least 75 percent of the time were Reformers, and those who supported such measures at least 75 percent of the time were Conservatives. The results may well be arguable in some cases. Some members, if they were alive to do so, might protest that they have been put in the wrong camp, or that they should not properly have been put in any camp at all, but the general division is probably accurate enough to provide a basis for further analysis.

The most obvious difference between Conservative and Reform MHAS during the years 1828–41 is one of numbers; there were far more Conservatives than Reformers who sat in the last four parliaments. The discrepancy stems from the fact that when the Conservatives won elections they won big majorities, while Reform majorities were often much smaller. The political classifications used in this study give the Reformers a large edge in the 1828–30 parliament, thirty-five to thirteen, but in 1830–4 the Conservative majority was almost equally large, forty to nineteen. In the twelfth parliament (1834–6) the Reformers had an advantage of thirty-seven to twenty-nine, but in the last parliament they were again snowed under, forty-eight to twenty-two. The Conservative group altogether adds up to ninety-one MHAS, the Reformers to only seventy-one.

Were there genuine differences between these two groups of people? The answer is a definite yes; they appear to have had some quite distinct characteristics. Religiously they diverged significantly. All of the Conservatives whose denomination is known belonged to the top four churches; that is, they were Anglicans, Presbyterians, Roman Catholics, or Methodists, but Anglicans easily outnumbered all the others. Over half of the Conservatives, forty-seven or 52 percent, belonged to the Church of England, compared to those who are known to have been adherents of the other churches (twelve Presbyterians, nine Roman Catholics, and four Methodists). By contrast, the Reformers were more denominationally diverse and their numbers more evenly spread among the churches. Besides those who belonged to the four main denominations, their ranks included one who professed no church affiliation at all, two Quakers, and one adherent each of the Lutheran, Baptist, Congregational, and Unitarian churches. Few Reformers (four) were Roman Catholics, but the three major Protestant denominations were fairly equally represented. In percentage terms the largest group was the Methodists (23.9 percent), followed by the Anglicans (21.1 percent) and the Presbyterians (19.7 percent). It is significant that at least four of the latter, David Gibson, John McIntosh, Gilbert McMicking, and David Thorburn, were members of Presbyterian congregations not "in connection with the Church of Scotland."[29]

On a national basis the differences were less marked. The comparative percentage figures for the English- and Scottish-born (13–15 percent in each case) show a strong similarity, but among the Irish-born there was a definite Conservative tendency. Eight out of a total of ten Irish members were Conservatives. The two Groups were also quite similar so far as their respective proportions of the native-born were concerned. The Reformers were a somewhat more indigenous group, by 49.3 percent to 46.1 percent. As might be expected, the American-born were a great deal more evident among the Reformers than among Conservatives. Of a total of sixteen, ten of the American-born were Reformers.

Other differences, if also not all that surprising, are revealing. 77 percent of Conservative MHAs were also magistrates compared to 48 percent of Reformers. Of the Conservatives, 88 percent had military experience compared to 73 percent of Reformers. Forty-eight percent of the Conservative MHAs also held a government office other than that of magistrate. For Reform MHAs the equivalent figure is only 18 percent. Among non-office-holders there was an equally clear distinction. Eighteen of the seventy-one Reformers did not hold a public office of any kind, but only one of the ninety-one Conservatives is known never to have held any civil or military position. Being a friend to the administration did pay dividends. Being a critic of government did impose penalities.

Most other identifiable differences between Conservative and Reform MHAS are less sharp or less subject to easy interpretation. Proportionally more Conservatives were Masons and more were former pupils of the Reverend John Strachan, but in each case the total numbers are too small to be very meaningful. A higher proportion of Conservatives than Reformers were of Loyalist stock, but the difference was not sufficiently great (36 percent compared to 25 percent) to bear much significance, except to show that Conservatives had no monopoly on Loyalism. Conservatives as a whole entered electoral politics at a slightly younger age, perhaps because of better economic circumstances and better family and other connections. Most Reformers entering politics were bunched in the middle years from thirty to forty-nine. Conservatives, besides starting younger, covered a wider age spectrum, including two, Alexander Thom and James Wickens, who began their electoral careers when over the age of sixty. These age differences are not very great but do point to the conclusion that, regardless of age and experience, it was generally easier to be elected as a Conservative than as a Reformer.

On the other hand there is some reason to believe that, once elected, Reformers were more successful in retaining the support of their constitutents. The average length of parliamentary service of Conservatives and Reformers was almost equal – about six years in both cases – but the comparison is hardly a fair one, since the two parliaments in which Reformers were a majority were short, two-year parliaments, the only short parliaments in Upper Canadian political history. In the circumstances, Reformers could be said to have had greater political longevity. It can also be argued that the Reformers were a more genuinely "grassroots" political group, that is, that they drew their support more directly from the people, than was true of the Conservatives. One kind of evidence to support this assertion rests on a distinction between Conservative and Reform MHAS who were also magistrates, and the order in which their elected and appointed offices were acquired. Among Conservative magistrate-MHAS, it was usual to acquire their "local patent of nobility" – an appointment to the magistracy – before being elected to the House of Assembly, and in fact 68.7 percent of them followed that pattern. Their prestige had already been conferred and "signalled" to the local populace by the central elite. The Reform case was quite different. Among Reform MHAS who were also magistrates, only 43.7 percent were magistrates first and MHAS second. Reformers received their status, as MHAS, from the people of their constituencies and only later (if at all) had that status confirmed by the provincial government. Here again there is an illustration of the fact that in seeking to rise in the world, Reformers were forced to do things the hard way.

There are some interesting comparisons which can be made on the basis of occupation. As was true of religious denomination, there was a bit more occupational diversity among Reformers – twenty-five occupations among seventy-one Reformers, as opposed to twenty-three occupations among ninety-one Conservatives. As well, Reformers were to be found in some "low status" occupations where Conservatives were not. Two Reformers, Thomas Parke and Jacob Rymal, had once been carpenters. Robert Alway may have been a teacher, while Samuel Lount was a blacksmith and John McIntosh was a sailor and lake ship captain. One occupation which was an almost exclusive Reform preserve was that of medical doctor. Ten of the twelve doctors among the MHAS in the 1828–41 period were Reformers. That among leading Reformers quite a few were doctors is, of course, well known. W.W. Baldwin, John Rolph, Charles Duncombe, and T.D. Morrison come readily to mind as examples. Doctors in Upper Canada often found themselves on the outside of the political and patronage systems. Theirs, among most Conservative MHAS at least, was evidently not a respectable calling, perhaps because medical practice in the early nineteenth century was neither particularly profitable nor highly regarded. The level of medical knowledge was not high, nor was the level of success in curing disease, especially in the face of great public epidemics such as occurred in the cholera years of 1832 and 1834. One contemporary newspaper view of the worst examples of the medical profession described them as going "from house to house like pedlars, dealing out their poisonous pills and herbs and holding out to the gaping ignorant the advantages of a republican government." Quite a few Upper Canadian doctors were suspect in the eyes of the Upper Canadian elite because, like the Duncombe brothers or John Gilchrist, they had come from or been trained in the United States.

Another occupation almost totally shunned by Conservative MHAS but heavily favoured by Reformers was journalism. Eight of the nine journalist-MHAS of the 1828–41 period were Reformers. By Conservatives most journalists were apparently viewed as being no more and perhaps less respectable than doctors. Theirs too was an itinerant, often unprofitable trade, and (even more deplorable) journalists were often prone to be outspoken public critics of the provincial administration. There were, of course, Conservative journalists, but they attracted less notoriety and (needless to say) got into less trouble with the provincial executive. Even those journalists, and there was a long series of them, who were also the king's printers very often felt compelled to point out the administration's shortcomings, and just as frequently found themselves no longer king's printer.[30]

Among the main "respectable" occupations there are some suggestive distinctions which can be made. Conservatives were far more heavily involved in public service positions than Reformers, reflecting their closer personal and ideological connections to the central elite. They were also about twice as heavily involved in the legal profession. In the mainstream of commercial activity there were no significant differences; Reformers were about as likely to be merchants as Conservatives, more likely to be involved in another common business pursuit of the time, land development or speculation, and as likely to be millers or lumbermen (though less likely to be distillers). In only one of the major occupations did the Reformers have a clear predominance, the most common occupation of all, farming, where in proportional terms about 10 percent more of the Reformers were or had been farmers than had Conservatives. This Reform attachment to a "traditional" way of making a living had an intriguing counterpart. They were much less involved in "modern" activities such as manufacturing, or in those careers which have been lumped together under the general term "businessmen." There were very few Reformers of this period whose business careers paralleled those of entrepreneurs such as Charles Bochus, Zaccheus Burnham, J.S. Cartwright, C.C. Ferrie, Benjamin Ewing, W.H. Merritt, A.N. MacNab, or Asa Werden, whose business scope included directorships and presidencies of banks and other joint stock corporations, loan companies, brokerages, and a variety of promotional ventures including canals and early railways. Michael Cross, writing about W.L. Mackenzie and the Family Compact, has argued that they shared a common vision of an Upper Canada "that was agrarian, that was devoted to values that were non-capitalist." Whether this was in fact entirely true of the Compact is debatable, but in any case the evidence suggests that, well before the advent of men like Hincks and Macdonald who were (for Cross) the first politicians "devoted to the interests of a new capitalist order," some Conservatives had already firmly rejected a "non-capitalist" society and had opted for the view that "what was good for business was good for the country."[31] Of course there were Reformers of a similar type, but fewer of them. Perhaps the explanation is simply that as a group they began with fewer resources, opportunities, and helpful connections, but there was also a genuine ideological commitment involved. Mackenzie really did believe that the "honest yeoman" was the backbone of an ideal society, that "labour was the true source of wealth." Few Reformers would follow Mackenzie so far as to accept his belief that "paper currency" and "vile banking associations" should be "swept from among you,"[32] but there were plenty of Reformers who had doubts about the benefits to be gained from the Welland Canal. Robert Baldwin, the quintessential moderate Reformer, was committed absolutely to fundamental political reform of both provincial and local government, yet he could also be described as "the most Conservative public man in U. Canada,"[33] who deplored the trend away from personal or family enterprises toward the modern and impersonal joint stock corporation.[34] Politically, Reformers believed themselves to be "in the van of history." but occupationally they reflected more closely a traditional rural past – and of course their own heavily rural constituencies from which they drew most of their support.

To the extent that the MHAS may be said to have represented their society, Upper Canada was a place where by 1841 changes could be said to be underway toward Canadianization, urbanization, professionalization, and commercialization, but where many old patterns also persisted, including reliance on agriculture as a basic occupation, dominance by established groups and families, anti-Americanism expressed through continued or increasing militarism, and adherence to Conservative political principles. Of course political change was also in the wind. Despite the devastating electoral defeat of 1836, a permanent Reform movement was established long before 1840 and indeed could be said to have been the way of the political future after 1848 in the Province of Canada and after Confederation in the Province of Ontario. In 1841 that was by no means clear. There could be no doubt that Conservatism as a political force was still in the ascendent, and that public figures who opposed in some way the prevailing groups and their prevailing beliefs could still be said to be deviating from the norm. Do the collective backgrounds of Reform MHAS help us to understand how such deviance, not in ideological but in concrete practical terms, could come about? The answer is no, not completely, but some speculation is possible. It goes without saying that for some Reformers no explanation for political "deviance" is necessary. Some (William Lyon Mackenzie, as always, comes first to mind) were natural-born oppositionists. Even if he *had* been accepted by the Masons, it is clear that Mackenzie would never have been a member of the "establishment." "He was instinctively suspicious of the great ones of this earth."[35] Other prominent Upper Canadians such as William Warren Baldwin or Barnabas Bidwell evidently arrived in the province with their political ideas already formed, derived from exposure or experience elsewhere or from strong family influences. Yet for some Reformers there must have been some kind of conversion process, leading individuals who were politically "normal" or politically neutral into private and ultimately public opposition to the state of government and society as they were. It has been customary to point to the much-discussed grievances of which Reformers complained as sources of discontent, but these clearly did not turn all prominent Upper Canadians into opponents of the provincial administration. What *were* the roots of Reform?

It is perfectly possible, although almost impossible to prove, that in some cases the cause of disaffection was highly personal – some real or imagined slight, perhaps, dealt out by an unthinking bureaucracy. There is the question of loyalty. It has been seen how bitterly someone like Donald Aeneas Macdonell resented any suggestion that his or his family's loyalty was in any way suspect. Some other examples help to expand this point. John Kilborn, who demonstrated his loyalty as a militia sergeant during 1812–14, cannot have been pleased that his grandfather who "suffered imprisonment and loss of property" during the American Revolution, was nonetheless classed as "not privileged" as a Loyalist because he "did not join the Royal Standard." (He *had* served on the British side in the Seven Years' War).[36] In 1818, Matthew Clark, who was to succeed Barnabas Bidwell as MHA for Lennox and Addington in 1823, petitioned the lieutenant governor and council to be put on the Loyalist list. In 1783, at the age of twelve, he had joined his Loyalist father, Robert Clark, a pioneer millwright of the Engineer Department at Kingston, to help with the building of the first Kingston mills. This service, Matthew Clark believed, qualified him for the honour of being able to sign himself Matthew Clark, UE, and would also (as he admitted), make it possible for each of his twelve sons to qualify for a grant of 200 acres of land as the sons of a Loyalist. His petition was refused for lack of evidence. Over many following years Matthew Clark submitted further petitions, presenting additional evidence and arguments, the last of which was sent in only a year before his death at the age of seventy-eight. The government never relented.[37]

Charles Waters of L'Orignal had what appears to have been a considerably stronger claim to Loyalism, but got no better satisfaction. His father, Abel Waters, had also served the crown in both the Seven

Years' War *and* the American Revolution, in the latter as an officer of the King's American Dragoons. He made the mistake, however, of going first to settle in the Gaspé region, only coming to Upper Canada about 1800, at which point he and his son Charles were declared too late to qualify for Loyalist land. In this case, too, repeated petitions were of no avail.[38] Such unsuccessful dealings with the central administration may have had something to do with the fact that Kilborn, Clark, and Waters eventually became part of a political opposition.

Despite such examples, it has been shown that there were quite a few people who came to be Reformers whose Loyalist credentials were unquestioned. Nonetheless the matter of Loyalism and political persuasion bears some additional comment. In fact there were real differences between Loyalist Reformers and Loyalist Conservatives in one important way. Most Conservatives who belonged to Loyalist families were, or by the 1830s were likely descended from, original Loyalists of the military officer class. Reformer Loyalists were much more likely to be, or be descended from, "ordinary" Loyalists, or the military rank and file. To be precise, the division among the eighteen Loyalist Reformers of the period 1828–41 was six (33.3 percent) officer class to twelve (66.6 percent) other ranks. The figures for the Conservative Loyalists were twenty-three of thirty-three, (70 percent) officer class to ten (30 percent) other ranks. One of the factors influencing political choice among Upper Canadians of Loyalist families was likely former military rank, which no doubt also reflected previous social rank. There were, in other words, two kinds of Loyalists, the leadership group and the "ordinary" Loyalists; in military terms, those who gave orders and those who obeyed them. Politically most representatives of the leadership group were firm adherents to the social and political *status quo*, while "ordinary" Loyalism expressed politically was much more likely to be critical of entrenched ways and established leaders, and to advocate political and social change.

Some Upper Canadians, Loyalist or otherwise, who became Reformers clashed in a number of ways with various levels of the establishment. Dr. John Rolph carried on a long feud with the government, still unresolved as late as 1845, over the sum of £378 13s 2–3/4d which it was alleged he had overspent as a militia paymaster during 1813–15.[39] His brother George Rolph experienced more direct evidence of official disapproval. Because his personal life was believed by the local elite to be immoral, he was dragged from his bed at one o'clock in the morning of 3 June 1826, and tarred and feathered by a disguised gang, one of whom was likely A.N. MacNab.

The government declined to launch a criminal prosecution or even an investigation of the case. George Rolph brought an unsuccessful civil action against ten local worthies and, for his pains, was dismissed from his post as clerk of the peace of the Gore District.[40] Dr. Charles Duncombe's rather sudden conversion to radicalism and ultimately to revolution appears to have been stimulated in part by his dispute with the law officers of the crown referred to earlier in chapter 4 over his title to a Brant lease on the Grand River.

The evidence is slight and the connection tenuous, but it is also possible that in some cases grievances began or were reinforced as a result of dissatisfaction over War of 1812 losses claims, especially when the amount of compensation allowed to some claimants is compared to that allowed to others. William Warren Baldwin's whole claim was ruled inadmissable because his possessions were stolen rather than damaged or destroyed.[41] Caleb Hopkins was allowed only 10 percent of his claim; Peter Shaver, 42 percent; John Cook, 37 percent; the elder William Buell, 16 percent; and Finlay Malcolm, 25 percent.[42] The average among all claimant-MHAS was almost exactly 50 percent, but some received much more, including William Buell's near neighbour and business and political rival, Charles Jones, who was allowed 81 percent of his claim.[43]

A source of discontent which has been often suggested as a cause of Reform was the uneven workings of the patronage system, which has been said to have increasingly excluded able applicants. "Too frequently" S.F. Wise has written, "men of real ability were passed over, and became permanently embittered. Robert Nichol, William Warren Baldwin, and an assortment of Ridouts, Jarvises and Smalls were given jobs of a demeaning kind, either in terms of their competence, or in terms of their personal measurement of their merits; such incidents had something to do with the making of a few reformers.[44] Wise may be right about patronage in a general sense, though his examples do not help his case very much. Most of the people he refers to did not hold particularly demeaning jobs, and two of them, Baldwin and George Ridout, lost patronage jobs which they had been given *after* becoming known Reformers.[45] Actually it is rather difficult to find good examples of "the making of reformers" as a result of patronage denied. James E. Small could be one example, since he is said to have been disappointed at not succeeding his father as clerk of the Executive Council, but he too was given status appointments as a magistrate and colonel of militia, which were then taken away in 1836.[46]

Another possible case of discontent over patronage, though again over loss of patronage, could be that of the radical Reformer Dr.

T.D. Morrison, who (according to the testimony of the Reverend George Ryerson) was fired as a clerk in the surveyor general's office "without a single cause of complaint alleged against him" because "from conscientious motives" he had left the Church of England and become a Methodist.[47] It is easy to see how his dismissal might have soured Morrison's attitude toward the provincial administration, but the reason for his dismissal, if true, had nothing to do with ability being passed over but with his choice of the "wrong" religious denomination, which raises once more the vexed question of discrimination for and against certain groups in Upper Canadian society. For whatever personal circumstances may have affected political decisions, the fact is that most of the people who wound up in an opposition political camp had some kind of disability in the eyes of the provincial establishment which excluded them from full membership in an elite. Most of the Reformers just referred to bear out this point. The Buells of Brockville were Loyalists and Anglicans, but, like Morrison left that church, in their case for the secessionist Presbyterianism of the Reverend William Smart. Similarly, Finlay Malcolm, John Cook, Philip Shaver, and Caleb Hopkins all came from Loyalist families but in religion chose dissenting denominations. Malcolm was a Congregationalist, Cook a Lutheran, and Shaver and Hopkins were Methodists. William Warren Baldwin had anglicanism, wealth, and education on his side, but his Irish background, which in his case included an inherited belief in "the rights of parliament and people, the responsibilities of ministers of the crown,"[48] made him politically suspect. The Duncombe brothers, Charles and David, were American-born and were Methodists. John Gilchrist was also of American birth. All three were doctors, as were (some of the time) John Rolph and W.W. Baldwin.

There can be no doubt that discrimination, however conscious or systematic it may or may not have been, was routinely practised in Upper Canada by people in a position to confer status, privilege, and government jobs. This was by no means merely a political matter; it was true of the Upper Canadian period before anything resembling "party" politics emerged, and could apply to those whose politics were entirely orthodox or simply neutral. It has been argued that the Family Compact had only a "fragile grasp of power," because the power of the local executive really rested on its association with an imperial official, the lieutenant governor.[49] Be that as it may, there is little evidence to show that the lieutenant governor and his advisors ever varied much in their notions of who in Upper Canada was or was not entitled to be favoured or ignored. Among those who had aspirations to prominence, especially prominence above the "basic status" level, certain attributes were simply barriers to advancement. To be Irish (particularly Roman Catholic Irish), to be American-born, to be Methodist or of any other dissenting or Americanized denomination was also to be, with very few exceptions, excluded from all but the lowest rungs of the ladder of power and preferment. Since in acquiring prominence or status, it was more important that it be conferred from above rather than earned from the bottom up, it is clear that the central elite, however fragile their collective or individual grasp of power, were exercising their power to confer status within certain consistent "guidelines," guidelines which were far from purely political. In this context it is in a way misleading to argue, as Donald Akenson has, that some groups in Upper Canada, such as the Irish, were not really different from others – that is, that they were not less competent or less rural or less well-to-do.[50] The point is that they were *treated* differently. The picture we have inherited from our ancestors of the immigrant Irish is not a recent historian's invention based on "anecdotal" evidence or on a borrowed American stereotype; it is an accurate reflection of nineteenth-century reality. If the Irish were not inferior to other groups, and since they were in fact the most numerous among immigrant groups, they ought to have been *more* prominent than other groups in politics and appointed offices, but they were not. Anthony Manahan had it right in 1838. "The notorious Family Compact in Toronto," lacking "liberal and englightened men," did practice discrimination against Manahan's "fellow Catholics from Ireland,"[51] and against a good many others on the basis of ideology, respectability, family, national origin, and religion. So far as politics was concerned it is apparent that not everyone who belonged to a "wrong" group wound up as a Reformer. But for some people who had aspirations to prominence, their membership in such groups may have made them Reformers almost by default, since they were not likely to be made welcome by "the notorious Family Compact in Toronto."

The geographical distribution of political support in Upper Canada is not a clear-cut matter. Only a few areas can be said to have been consistently and distinctly Reform or consistently and distinctly Conservative over any great period of time. It has been said that "the core of Tory support was in the eastern counties, the area of major Loyalist settlement, and in the towns."[52] The part about the towns is true enough, as will be seen, but the eastern counties' Loyalist association with Conservatism is much less demonstrable. It would be just as true, perhaps if anything a bit more true, to say that this area formed the core of Reform support. The eastern Loyalist region (that is, the Eastern, Johnstown, Midland, and Prince Edward districts) very frequently elected such Reform stalwarts as M.S. Bidwell, Peter Perry, Peter Shaver, John Cook, William Buell, Paul Peterson, James Wilson, John P. Roblin, Hiram Norton, W.B. Wells, Donald Aeneas Macdonell, William Bruce, George Brouse, Matthew M. Howard, Milo McCarger, and others, and most of them, except Bidwell, Wilson, Norton, Wells, and McCarger, were from Loyalist families. Among twenty-seven Loyalist-derived MHAS elected in the eastern Loyalist region between 1828 and 1841, fifteen were Conservatives and twelve were Reformers. Overall, in all the general elections, by-elections, and contested elections which occurred in the eastern-Loyalist region between 1828 and 1841, Reformers (not all of whom came from Loyalist families, obviously) were elected, or awarded a seat after the incumbent was unseated, a total of forty-five times, Conservatives a total of forty-two. If there is a pattern of Conservative political support in that area which helps to explain "the political geography of twentieth-century Ontario," it cannot safely be said that the pattern had its beginnings in "colonial Upper Canada."[53] (In fact, the pattern isn't all that clear in the following Union period either. Combining Paul Cornell's political identifications for 1841–67 produces a Reform majority of seats in the eastern Loyalist area in the first, fifth, sixth, and eighth parliaments of the United Province of Canada and a tie in the fourth parliament, or a slight overall Reform advantage.)[54]

What can be said with assurance about the geographical distribution of political support in Upper Canada is a bit more complex. (Table 23.) Conservatives were consistently strong in the Western District, where, in the 1828–41 period, only one Reformer was ever elected, in the Bathurst District, which only elected a Reformer twice, and Conservatives had a considerable advantage in the Newcastle and Gore districts. Reformers had real dominance only in the Home and London districts (the most populous and, in the case of the London District, the most "Americanized" district) although they never came close to shutting out the Conservatives in either area. In the other districts (Ottawa, Eastern, Johnstown, Midland, Prince Edward, and Niagara) both political groups were able to maintain a nearly equal level of electoral support, with the Conservatives having a slight edge in the Ottawa and Niagara districts and the Reformers a similar small advantage in the Eastern, Johnstown, and Prince Edward districts, with the balance in the Midland district about equal.

What appears to have tipped the overall political scales decidedly

TABLE 23
Political Divisions by District, 1828–41

District	*Conservatives*	*Reformers*
Eastern	12	14
Ottawa	5	4
Bathurst	14	2
Johnstown	12	13
Midland	14	14
Prince Edward	3	5
Newcastle	11	5
Home	9	16
Gore	12	7
Niagara	14	12
London	11	20
Western	13	1
Total elected	142 (91 MHAS)	113 (71 MHAS)

in favour of the Conservatives was their ability to win elections in two quite different settings: the urban ridings and the thinly-settled, newly-developed or remote sections of the province. Only two (moderate) Reformers, Robert Baldwin and J.E. Small, were ever elected in town constituencies. Both were elected for brief periods in York/ Toronto and were subsequently defeated. On the other hand, no one but a Conservative was ever elected in the other urban ridings – Cornwall, Kingston, Brockville, Hamilton, London, and Niagara – and in York/ Toronto Baldwin and Small were easily outmatched by the success records of J.B. Robinson, W.B. Jarvis, and W.H. Draper. In town constituencies, it was not uncommon for a Conservative to be unopposed for election or (more likely) to be opposed by a fellow Conservative in a "factional" election.[55] Conservative strength in the "fringe" areas of the province was as striking as it was in the towns, and could produce the same phenomenon of factionalism.[56] In the western, northern, and eastern ridings of Essex, Kent, Huron, Simcoe, Lanark, Carleton, and Russell, the Conservatives were nearly invincible.

Since some distinctions have been noted between the two groups of regional political figures, it is worth asking whether those distinctions can be found reflected in the composition of the general population in particular regions from which one or other of the two political groups drew significant political support. The census of 1842 permits some limited speculation on this point, looking back from the end of the Upper Canadian period, in two categories, national origin and religious denomination, since for both of these the census provided a breakdown by districts (though not unfortunately by riding). Did areas where there were sizable concentrations of Methodists or Americans or native-born Canadians tend to vote more often for Reformers? Did districts which were heavily Church of England or Roman Catholic or foreign-born (especially Irish-born) consistently support Conservative candidates? By and large, the answer in fact is no. No such neat patterns can be identified, but there is some intriguing evidence to suggest that in certain cases, if some or all of these kinds of factors were present in sufficient concentration, the national origin or religious affiliation of voters did make a difference. Two small Upper Canadian districts were in their own ways very different sorts of "political laboratories." Prince Edward District, separated from the Midland District in 1834 but one of the oldest original Loyalist areas in the province and a separate political riding (or county) since 1800, had, in 1842, some striking population characteristics. It had by far the highest level of native-born Canadians of any district in the province (76.4 percent) and, conversely, the lowest level of British immigrants (14.3 percent). Religiously, Prince Edward had the highest concentration of Methodists in Upper Canada (33.9 percent), the lowest proportion of Presbyterians (7.7 percent) and a low (but not the lowest) proportion of Anglicans (16.7 percent). Politically, in the four elections between 1828 and 1836, Prince Edward (a two-member riding geographically identical to the district) elected five Reformers to three Conservatives. In fact, Prince Edward's Reform associations extended in both directions beyond that period. Two of the Reformers, James Wilson and Paul Peterson, had previously been elected in 1820 and 1824. A third Reformer, John P. Roblin, elected in 1830 and 1834, also represented Prince Edward in the first two Union parliaments. Among six successful candidates in the 1828–36 period (Roblin and Wilson were both elected twice), four were Methodists, including a Conservative, James Rogers Armstrong, and four were native-born, including Armstrong and another Conservative, Charles Bochus.

The Huron District, created out of a part of the London District only in 1838 but a county for electoral purposes from 1835, was Prince Edward's opposite in a number of ways. Most of the district was in the Canada Company's Huron Tract, which, for a variety of reasons, including its relatively remote location, was still an under populated frontier area of the province in 1842.[57] It was the smallest of all the Upper Canadian districts, with only 7,190 people (Prince Edward had 14,495 in 1842). Huron District in 1842 had the highest proportion of British-born residents in the province (54.2 percent), and the largest group of those (24.5 percent of the total population) were Irish. Naturally, native-born Canadians were scarce in the Huron District, at only 27.5 percent, the lowest such figure in any Upper Canadian district. Huron also contained the highest percentage of Anglicans (38 percent) and the lowest percentage of Methodists (6.4 percent) in the province. Huron did not have a long political history, but such as it was it was consistent. In the only two Upper Canadian elections held in the riding, a Conservative, R.G. Dunlop, was elected. Dunlop was not a member of the largest immigrant group in the district (Irish) nor of the largest religious group (Anglican), but as a Scot and a Presbyterian he represented the second largest group in each case. Like Prince Edward, Huron retained its political consistency after 1841; its voters elected Conservatives, Dunlop's brother "Tiger" Dunlop and William Cayley, in the first three parliaments of United Canada.

Outside of Prince Edward and Huron districts it is difficult to find close or clear relationships between Conservative and Reform politicians and their constituencies on national or religious grounds, probably because the levels of concentration of denominations or nationalities, or combinations of both, were not generally sufficiently high to produce strong consistent voting behaviour. Religion and nationality, and no doubt personality, appeals to loyalty (as in 1836), and a host of other purely local factors may have cut across one another in ways which prevented particular elements of the population from voting on mainly religious or national grounds. There are hints that here and there in the province, aside from the Prince Edward and Huron districts, religion or nationality may at times have had political significance, but there are always also exceptions and counterindications. It is possible for example that the relatively high proportion of Methodists in the Midland and Johnstown districts (about 23 percent) may have been generally helpful to the Reform cause. Similarly, the London District, a Reform stronghold, was also the home of the most former Americans (14.3 percent American-born in 1842), but in the next most "Americanized" region, the Niagara District (11.3 percent American-born), Conservatives had a small political lead during 1828–41. The Ottawa District had the second highest proportion of native-born (71 percent), but invariably voted Conservative. The fact that the Ottawa District also had the highest percentage of Roman Catholics (42.5 percent) and the highest percentage of French-Canadians (28 percent) may be part of the explanation of that area's voting pattern, but nearby in the Eastern District, which had the second highest proportion of

Roman Catholics in the province (30 percent), Reformers were elected more often than Conservatives. Even predominant Anglicanism was not a sure indication of Conservative political strength. In most parts of the province, districts with a high level of Anglicans in the population in 1842 (such as the Newcastle and Bathurst districts) also leaned toward Conservative candidates, but in the Home District, which was tied with the Bathurst District for second place among Anglicans at 30 percent, and in which Anglicans easily outnumbered all the other denominations, Reformers nonetheless were able to maintain a definite political edge.

It is not, then, in most cases possible to make clear-cut connections between religion and nationality (in 1842) and voting behaviour in the period 1828–41. No doubt both political groups benefited at times and to a degree from the presence of certain population mixes, but there is little geographical consistency on that basis. Otherwise, however, the composition of the Reform and Conservative constituencies in general terms throughout the province is fairly clear. The Reformers drew their support from the older-settled, well-established agricultural areas, essentially the areas of pre-1812 Loyalist and Post-Loyalist American settlement. Unfortunately for them, they shared that constituency more or less equally with their political opponents, and in addition they made almost no headway in the towns or in the emerging areas of Upper Canada.

Any complete explanation of electoral success or failure would involve the consideration of a complexity of factors and (perhaps most important) the examination of a great many purely local situations. A few general observations, however, may be appropriate. In the older rural areas, where the opposing political forces were roughly equal, Conservative appeals to loyalty and their greater ability to get political results may have constituted a counterbalance to Reform advocacy of rural grievances. So far as the towns were concerned it seems likely that the urban property owner voter identified strongly with the economic outlook of local Conservative candidates and with that of the provincial elite, which included strong support for improvement of the Laurentian transportation system and the expansion of credit facilities. As S.F. Wise has put it, the elite was "responsive to the interests of the provincial mercantile community, and to the larger needs of St. Lawrence commercialism."[58] The office-holders, merchants, professionals, clerks, and artisans who made up the bulk of the electorate of the mercantile centres[59] proved duly grateful. Reformers, on the other hand, who expressed mainly rural concerns about such matters as land, roads, and bridges, had much less urban appeal and even opposed such commercially popular government undertakings as the Welland Canal, and, in the extreme case of Mackenzie, opposed the very existence of banks.

Conservative success in the most remote areas of Upper Canada was clearly a different matter. With the exception of Essex County, which had a long history of settlement but was still thinly populated and underdeveloped before 1840,[60] the regions in question were Upper Canada's frontier in the 1830s, and as such the case study of Conservative dominance in Carleton County by Michael Cross probably provides a good foundation for a general explanation. On the frontier, men of education or wealth or position or even leisure were readily accepted as local leaders for their usefulness in promoting regional needs by a population largely preoccupied with a relentless battle against the forest, whether for purposes of agriculture or lumbering itself.[61] If life in the Upper Canadian pioneer areas imposed a kind of rough democracy on the society, in which everyone struggled on equal terms against the forces of nature, the people of the frontier nonetheless continued to ignore "democratic" candidates where they appeared, and to send Conservative merchants, office-holders and half-pay officers to be their representatives.

CHAPTER SIX

Being Prominent: Staying Prominent

Summarizing the nature of prominence in Upper Canada as represented by the MHAS, how it changed, and how it varied from district to district, is no easy task. A composite Upper Canadian MHA of the whole period would probably have been an Anglican and would have been, or would at some time have been, a farmer, but would also likely have done something else for a living, most probably some form of government service. He would have been a magistrate and an officer in the militia, would likely have been born in a British colony either before or after the American Revolution, and politically would probably have been a Conservative. Such an amalgam of characteristics, though, would disguise some genuine variations and some discernible trends. Variations in occupation across the province, for instance, were not particularly marked (and in any case the small numbers involved in particular occupations in any one area at one time make accurate comparisons difficult.) But if there were an anomalous region in this regard it was the area centring on the provincial capital itself. In general it has been noted that, among the major MHA occupations, farming and public service declined while storekeeping and law became increasingly common. Among the MHAS of the Home District, over time farming and milling went up and law went down, and the decline in public service occupations, while following the general provincial trend, showed a steeper rate of decline than the average, starting higher and ending lower. What had happened in the Home District was a change in the nature of political representation. For a time, the provincial urban professional/bureaucratic establishment in the capital was evidently able to control the electoral politics of the district quite successfully, but eventually a kind of rural hinterland resistance in the York and Simcoe county ridings set in. This expressed itself partly in frequent support of Reform and even Radical candidates (accounting for much of the sharp decline in public service as an occupation) but also of candidates, Reform or Conservative, who were closer, by occupation at least, to the people of a rapidly expanding rural region. Bureaucrats and officials like Judge Henry Allcock, Peter Robinson, and Thomas Ridout were replaced after 1828 by "men of the people" such as Mackenzie, Jesse Ketchum, or David Gibson.

Denominationally also, Anglicanism, though generally the dominant religious persuasion among MHAS – Anglicans were more numerous at all times in nine of the twelve districts – was not universally so. In the Ottawa District, Roman Catholics had a numerical advantage among those MHAS whose denomination is known, and in Prince Edward District, as has been seen, Methodism was the favoured denomination. Anglicans were also in a minority in the Eastern District, running a poor third to Roman Catholics and Presbyterians, who more or less shared the religious leadership. Anglicans and Presbyterians nonetheless were overall more prevalent across the province among the prominent than other denominations. At least one Anglican is known to have been elected in every district in Upper Canada at some point, and at least one Presbyterian in every district except one, Prince Edward. The Methodists and Roman Catholics were much more restricted in their regional representation. The Methodists were only really a political force in Prince Edward and to a lesser degree in the London District, as were the Roman Catholics in the Ottawa District and the Eastern District, where, it will be recalled, eleven Macdonells were elected, and (partly because of the only three French-Canadian MHAS) in the Western District. No Roman Catholic is known to have been elected in six of the districts (Bathurst, Johnstown, Prince Edward, London, Gore, or Niagara), and no Methodist in three districts (Ottawa, Bathurst, and Western).

It has been shown that, on the whole, the MHAS were not very diverse in their religious preferences, the great majority of them belonging to one of the four leading churches, but here too there were some regional variations. In some districts the range of religious pluralism among MHAS was very narrow. In Prince Edward, only Methodists (five) and one Anglican are known to have been elected. The Johnstown District returned only Anglicans (nine), Presbyterians (five), and one Methodist; the Western District elected Anglicans (eight), Catholics (four), and one Presbyterian. In the Gore District as well only three denominations are known to have been represented: Anglicans (nine), Presbyterians (three), and Methodists (three). Elsewhere the four main denominations were all present to some degree, with a few additional regional variants. The Eastern

District, reflecting the presence of German Loyalists in Dundas County, provided two Lutherans. Quakers were elected in the Midland, Newcastle, and London districts. The only known Baptist was elected in the Niagara District, the only known Unitarian and the only known Congregationalist in the London District. The London District, in fact, was easily the leading example of Protestant diversity, electing (at least) six Anglicans, four Methodists, three Presbyterians, one Quaker, one Congregationalist, one Unitarian, and one MHA who claimed to have no church affiliation at all. There is not much evidence which suggests that the pattern of denominational adherence was anywhere in a state of significant change; in fact the most obvious conclusion to be drawn about church affiliation is that Anglicans in all areas were holding their own or increasing their presence among the ranks of the prominent.

Variations in the national origins of the MHAs were somewhat less clear cut. Native-born Upper Canadians and native-born British Americans in general were a steadily increasing element among the MHAs, but immigrants from the United Kingdom, who had always made up around 30 percent of the membership of the House, maintained their share of the total, and, at the end of the period, could even be said to be on the increase. The only national group to show eventual decline, after a long period of gradual increase peaking in the election of 1830, was the American-born. Here too, however, there were notable regional differences. The American-born, in fact, while in the 1830s in retreat as a provincial political force, maintained to the last a strong presence in the London and Niagara districts (areas of relatively high levels of American-born population as of 1842) and, to a lesser extent, in the Gore District. The area of the province which by the 1830s was producing a predominance of Upper Canadian-born MHAs coincided with one of the areas of earliest settlement, the Eastern, Johnstown, Midland, and Prince Edward districts, all of which had been settled in part from 1784 by United Empire Loyalists. It was appropriate that the first Upper Canadian-born MHA, Alexander McMartin of Martintown, Charlottenburgh Township in the Eastern District, was the son of a Loyalist officer in the King's Royal Regiment of New York. Away from the old Loyalist areas, though, Upper Canadians had still to make a significant impact on their own political system by 1841, except to some extent in the Gore District, where in the 1830s the numbers of Upper Canadian and British-born MHAs were about equal. In developing areas of the province such as the Bathurst and Ottawa districts, no Upper Canadian was ever elected before 1841, and at the other end of the province, in the Western District, only one native-born Upper Canadian was ever elected. In both areas, United Kingdom immigrants were and continued to be politically dominant, and, while the fringes of the province had yet to become politically Upper Canadianized by 1841, the province's central area was not entirely different. In the Newcastle Districft only two Upper Canadians were ever elected. In the Home District, native-born Upper Canadian MHAS were more common but were nonetheless greatly outnumbered by immigrants even at the end of the Upper Canadian period.

To some extent it is possible to provide simple explanations, based on birthplace figures, to explain these variations in the origins of the MHAS. The old Loyalist areas had, as of 1842, much higher levels of native-born (up to 76 percent in the Prince Edward District) than was true of the Newcastle and Home districts, neither of which were even 50 percent native-born areas at that time. Clearly the central area of the province reflected in its political representatives the large-scale immigration of the post-1815 period, which had bypassed much of the already-occupied Eastern region, just as the London District continued to reflect the vestiges of the prewar Post-Loyalist American immigration. Population figures for Upper Canada, however, in no way explain the numerical superiority of United Kingdom immigrant MHAS in the Ottawa, Bathurst, and Western districts, all of which had native-born 1842 populations of over 50 percent. Here it may have been that the relative newness and smallness of population, previously suggested as factors which contributed to the success of political Conservatism, were also reflected in a form of local deference to the supposedly superior gifts of officers and gentlemen from the British Isles.

No matter what corner of the province they represented, it is likely that most MHAS saw themselves as being entitled to some measure of deference. As a group, they could have claimed a certain degree of respectability; some, as has been seen, even claimed the title of "gentleman." The majority of them after all were possessed of large quantities of property; they had had the local equivalents of a "patent of nobility" bestowed on them in the form of a magistrate's or militia officer's commission, and some 40 percent of them had been given the further reward of a revenue-generating public appointment. It is true that on the whole they would not have met the ideal standards of the provincial "gentry" as identified by R.L. Fraser – those "set apart by gentle birth, education and good breeding" – nor is it likely that they would all have shared a vision of "a hierarchical ordering of a landed society" in which "gentlemen were the proper rulers in society rather than merchants, businessmen or farmers."[1] There were, of course, representatives of the gentry view among the MHAS (John Beverly Robinson, Christopher Alexander Hagerman, Jonas Jones, and a few others) but it is clear that very few of the MHAS at any time, even in "Tory" parliaments, agreed with Hagerman that "what was most essential to the happiness and good government of any people" was "an aristocracy."[2] Still, despite the tendency of the "gentry" to sneer at the "scum" who were sometimes elected to the lower house (and there were MHAS who by any standard were no gentlemen), as a group they had earned a general collective right to local distinction. Their resemblance, however, to the gentry ideal of a system of landed hierarchy, which was never very strong, became even less so over time. "Genteel decline" set in. The extent to which property was acquired and the incidence of office-holding (which, R.L. Fraser has argued, could be in Upper Canada a substitute for landed estates)[3] both declined, as has been seen, while commercial and entrepreneurial activities increased. This is not to suggest that the MHAS toward the end of the Upper Canadian period were becoming a more "democratic" group. The mere facts that the election of 1836 was won so convincingly by the administration side and that the American-born formed a dwindling element among MHAS point to the fact that conservative ideology was still dominant. One symptom of change, however, among the membership of the Assembly can be identified in an early stage. A species of political animal which would be more easily recognizable in the post-1848 period as a "businessman-politician" was already in evidence and on the increase in a limited way before 1841. Such Upper Canadian politicians as George Hamilton, John Prince, William Chisholm, C.C. Ferrie, Absalom Shade, A.N. MacNab, Donald Bethune, W.B. Jarvis, and Malcolm Cameron, as well as W.H. Merritt, are examples of the new breed.

A final aspect of local prominence which was sufficiently common to be worth brief notice is family interconnection. In the whole period of 1792–1841, eighty-two people who served as MHAS were related to others who were also past, current, or future MHAS. Altogether they represented thirty-seven families and made up 29 percent of all Upper Canadian MHAS – and these figures are for MHAS *only*. A good many MHAS were also related to influential people who were not members but were holders of senior civil or military offices.

There was a slight decline among interrelated MHAS over the whole period, but it was not marked. There were thirty-six such cases in Group A (35 percent) and also thirty-six in Group B (26 percent). The most obvious family dynasty was that of the Macdonells of the Eastern and Ottawa Districts – there were a total of nine Macdonell

MHAS who were related to at least one other political Macdonell, plus two more Macdonells who cannot be definitively linked by family connection – but there were many others: four members of the family of Ephraim Jones, four Robinsons, three Sherwoods, three Boulton, and three Cornwalls. There were thirty-one other cases in which two members of the same family (usually father and son or brother and brother combinations) were both members of the legislature. It is not surprising that this pattern of family dominance was also most pronounced in the old, settled, eastern Loyalist areas, especially in the Eastern, Johnstown, and Midland districts, where the Loyalist founding families continued for a long time to enjoy political success. The Johnstown District provided a striking example of this phenomenon. For most of the Upper Canadian period politics in this district was largely the preserve of a few Loyalist families: the two Jones families, the Sherwoods, the Buells, the Howards, the Burritts, and the Jessups.

S.F. Wise has argued convincingly that there is a degree of political and ideological continuity between the Upper Canadian period and twentieth-century Ontario.[4] Is it possible to claim, from the example of the Upper Canadian MHAS, a similar kind of continuity in leadership patterns, in the nature of prominence and how it has been achieved? Perhaps it is, although any claim for formative influence over so long a time must of necessity be highly speculative and subject to much qualification. What can be suggested is that in some respects and for whatever reasons, some things about Ontario (and Canadian) society do not seem to have changed very much in well over a century. When in 1965 John Porter published his ground-breaking study of social class and power in Canada, *The Vertical Mosaic*, he concluded that being an Anglican and being a member of the "British Charter group" were still very important assets in a society "relying heavily on its elite to make major decisions," in which "ethnic and religious affiliation ... have always had an effect on the life chances of an individual."[5] To an historian of Upper Canadian society, it has a decidedly familiar ring.

It is not necessary, though, to make elaborate and probably unsupportable claims about the importance of Upper Canadian history for an understanding of present-day society to establish the fact that some forms of continuity beyond the Upper Canadian period itself were very real. One form of continuity which can be illustrated using the Upper Canadian MHAS was family continuity. In the parliaments of the United Province of Canada, and in the post-Confederation federal and Ontario parliaments, names such as Ridout, Cartwright, Merritt, Prince, Boulton, Robinson, Powell, Morris, Burnham, Crooks, Burwell, Jarvis, and many others, representing succeeding generations of Upper Canadian leadership families, continue to turn up. In Leeds and Grenville counties, for example, those few families, the Joneses, Sherwoods, Buells, Jessups, and Burritts, remained for a long time a prominent part of the leadership group. Some families provide particularly striking versions of continuity. John David Smith was MHA for Durham in 1828–30. His son James was MPP for Durham in 1848–54 and for Victoria in 1854–7. Another son, John Shuter Smith, was MPP for Durham East in 1861–7, and his best-known son, Sidney, was MPP for Northumberland West in 1854–61, member of the Legislative Council for Trent Division (1861–3) and postmaster general (1858–62.)[6] One of the sons of William Thompson, MHA for York and Simcoe (1824–8), H.H. Thompson, was mayor of Penetanguishene (1887–96) and an unsuccessful candidate for the Ontario legislature in 1883 and 1888. William Thomson's grandson, Alfred Burke Thompson, was MLA for Simcoe Centre in 1898–1902 and 1905–19, and MP for Simcoe East (1925–35).[7] The family connections of John Cook, MHA for Dundas (1830–41), included three nephews, J.W. Cook (MPP, Dundas, 1857–61), S.S. Cook (MLA, Dundas, 1867–75), and H.H. Cook (MLA, Ontario, 1879–82; MP, Simcoe North, 1872–78, MP, Simcoe East, 1882–91).[8] In the case of some other families such as the Roblins, the long-term dynasty of leadership figures was not even confined to Upper Canada or Ontario.

There is a more concrete way of demonstrating that for some time Upper Canadian leadership norms and trends continued little altered into a later Ontario period for a collective biographical study of a similar but later group of leadership figures has been done and can readily be used for comparative purposes. In his PHD thesis "The Personnel of Politics, A Study of the Ontario Members of the Second Fereral Parliament,"[9] Donald Swainson analyzed the background of the ninety Ontario MPs who sat in the House of Commons during 1872–4. As a group they had, as Swainson observed, a couple of fortunate attributes. They were fairly evenly divided politically into forty-seven Liberals, thirty-seven Conservatives and six "political deviants." They were also in office at a convenient time, just after the taking of the first Dominion census in 1871 which allows for a quite accurate assessment of how they compared to the profile of Ontario society as a whole. Swainson's conclusions about his ninety MPs are valuable and interesting in their own right. They are also quite intriguing when compared with what has been discovered about the earlier generation of Upper Canadian public figures. It must be admitted, of course, that the two groups are not completely comparable. Swainson's MPS were fewer in number and served over a far more restricted time period than did the Upper Canadian MHAS. It could also be objected that federal politicians should not be compared directly with provincial politicians. These objections have some merit, but there are at least two reasons for proceeding with a comparison nonetheless; first, in each case, locally prominent people were aiming for the highest form of elective office open to them; and second, Swainson's study is the only one of its kind available which makes possible any form of comparison between the Upper Canadian MHAS and a similar but later group.

Swainson himself noticed, looking backward, the phenomenon of family linkage. At least eight of his MPS had one or more ancestors who had sat in the Upper Canadian House of Assembly.[10] There were as well among the MPS of 1872–4 some other echoes of their earlier counterparts. Loyalism, which had been a continuing but diminishing factor among Upper Canadian MHAS (about one-third of the members in 1841), continued its downward trend but was still of some significance. About 12 percent of all the 1872–4 MPS and 25 percent of the native-born MPS were of Loyalist descent.[11] Occupational characteristics also illustrated the extension of some earlier trends. Of the MPS, 73 percent had followed more than one vocation;[12] in that respect nothing had changed. Changes had occurred in choice of occupation but in ways which could have been expected. Farming and public service had been declining occupations among the Upper Canadian MHAS. By 1875, public service had virtually disappeared as an occupation among Ontario MPS and people who farmed made up only 16 percent of the group. Business and law, on the other hand, which were "growth" occupations among Upper Canadian MHAS, had by 1872 come into their own. Businessmen now led the list at 47 percent, followed by lawyers at 22 percent. Other unpopular occupations of the Upper Canadian period such as medicine (4 percent in 1872–4), journalism (4 percent) or teaching (2 percent) were still equally unfavoured.[13]

There are four other biographical categories of information in Professor Swainson's thesis which make for useful comparisons with the background of the Upper Canadian MHAS: birthplace and ethnicity, religious denomination, local office-holding, and Liberal-Conservative differences. Table 24 presents Swainson's birthplace percentages with equivalent figures for the province as a whole.

The most obvious comment to be made about this table is the degree to which native-born Canadians had *not* improved their

TABLE 24
Birthplace of Ontario MPs, 1872–4

Country	*Percentage of Ont.* MPs	*Percentage of general population (1871 Census)*
Canada	50	73
Scotland	20	6
Ireland	11	9
England & Wales	10	8
USA	7	3
France	2	1

Source: D. Swainson, "The Personnel of Politics: A Study of the Ontario Members of the Second Federal Parliament," (PHD thesis, University of Toronto, 1968), 449

standing as a politically prominent group. At 50 percent of the membership they were only slightly more evident than their counterparts in the last Upper Canadian parliament (47.2 percent) and in fact they had lost ground, for the native-born proportion of the general population had gone sharply up and the level of immigration during the 1850s and 1860s had dropped off. Ontarians, like Upper Canadians before them, continued to show a colonial preference for non-Canadians as their representatives.

So far as particular immigrant groups were concerned, it is possible to say that the position of the Irish-born had improved to the point where they were represented in proportion to their share of the general population and that they had more or less caught up with the English, but the outstanding immigrant group was still the Scots, who were still greatly over-represented. But in addition to birthplace, Swainson was able to supply information on the related question of the ethnic background of his MPs (Table 25.) Here again the Scots emerge the clear winners and in this case the Irish are still losers. Having an Irish heritage continued to be something of a disadvantage in 1872–4.

Swainson's findings about the distribution of religious denominations among the Ontario MPs (Table 26) are also worth some comment. Here the most significant development to be noted concerns the Anglicans who, so far as is known, were always the leading denomination among the MHAs in Upper Canada; in the last Upper Canadian parliament they had made up exactly half of the membership. The proportion of Anglicans in the general population had dropped a bit (it was 22.1 percent in 1842) and the Presbyterians

TABLE 25
Ethnic Origin of Ontario MPs, 1872–4

Country	*Percentage of Ont.* MPs	*Percentage of General Population (1871 (Census)*
Scotland	36	20
England and Wales	30	27
Ireland	27	35
France	1	5
Other	7	11

Source: D. Swainson, "The Personnel of Politics: A Study of the Ontario Members of the Second Federal Parliament," (PHD thesis, University of Toronto 1968), 450.

had increased (19.9 percent in 1842), but as a leadership group Anglicans had lost ground. If this loss was real and not a temporary aberration of the 1872–4 period, it strongly suggests that the degree of Anglican prominence in the Upper Canadian period had always been artificially inflated by the favouritism of the provincial and local establishments. Nonetheless, in 1872–4 Anglicans were still over-represented, as were the Presbyterians, who were still internally split. As for the Methodists, compared to their situation in the last Upper Canadian parliament they can be said to have made some gains (they composed 14.3 percent of the MHAs in 1836–41) but they were still under-represented. Roman Catholics had lost ground and were more under-represented than ever.

Swainson did not cross-tabulate his data by birthplace and denomination, but it is not difficult to do using his biographical sketches. As had been true at the end of the Upper Canadian period, native-born Anglicans were the largest combined group, but only by a slim margin. There were fifteen of them out of the total of ninety (there were fourteen Scottish-born Presbyterians). The Scottish-born, including three Scottish Anglicans and one Baptist, had not only continued but extended their position among prominent Ontarians. The only other national/denominational groups of any size were the native-born Presbyterians (nine) and the native-born Methodists (eight). No other combined group was represented by more than four MPs. The Irish-born appear only well down the list (three Irish Presbyterians, two Irish Anglicans, two Irish Methodists). There was only one Irish-born Roman Catholic in the house. Again, it all has a familiar ring.

Swainson's comments on the differences which he found between

TABLE 26
Religious Denominations of Ontario MPs, 1872–4

Denomination	*Percentage of Ont.* MPs	*Percentage of general population (1871 Census)*
Presbyterian	36	22
Anglican	32	20
Methodist	20	29
Roman Catholic	6	17
Baptist	3	5
Lutheran	1	2
Other	2	5

Source: D. Swainson, "The Personnel of Politics: A Study of the Ontario Members of the Second Federal Parliament," (PHD thesis, University of Toronto, 1968), 452.

Ontario Liberals and Conservatives of 1872–4 were not extensive but also suggest some further points of continuity. His Conservatives on the whole were wealthier and of higher social status and education, and had a higher proportion of Anglicans and a lower proportion of native-born Canadians among them than did the Liberals, although he did not find important occupational differences, both parties being dominated by businessmen and lawyers.[14] Finally, Swainson found that the old pattern of previous office-holding at the local level (though no longer on an appointed basis) and of active involvement at the officer level in the local militia were still normal prerequisites for higher levels of prominence. Some 74 percent of his MPs had held local office or militia commissions, and holders of militia commissions alone still comprised 30 percent of the MPs of 1872–4.[15] More than thirty years after the end of the Upper Canadian period, prominent "unmilitary" Ontarians were still, in considerable numbers, standing on guard against the enemy which might yet appear.

Attempting to find points of continuity between one period and another, or one group of prominent people and a later one, is not an exercise which should be pushed too far. Certainly it is possible to detect Upper Canadian echoes in 1872 or at any time since, but there were also evident departures from Upper Canadian norms which developed fairly quickly. The same families did not remain prominent, or at least politically prominent, indefinitely, and the really sharp distinctions among national, denominational, and even political groups began to blur somewhat with time. The political game, after all, was altered fundamentally and forever after 1841. No longer was it possible for an entrenched, irremovable group of powerful administrators to decide, using criteria of their own, who was to receive or to be denied status and favour. Still, an argument for the importance of Upper Canada as a critical starting point – "as she began" – can be made. Much that was Upper Canadian lived on in varying degree, if not always in the ways which historians have thought. A society in which prominent people sought prosperity through a multiplicity of routes but opted increasingly for commerce and law, a society in which local office and military activities were normal preludes to greater prominence, a society in which there were clear differences between those who wished to conserve and those who wished to reform that society, a society in which certain national and denominational groups received greater sanction and success than others cast a long shadow from which Ontario has not yet entirely emerged. Gerald Craig was right. In a lot of ways the years before 1841 really were "the formative years."

Abbreviations

AO	Archives of Ontario	*Hs/SH*	*Histoire sociale/Social History*
b	born	HP	half pay
BNA	British North America	JP	justice of the peace
Bttn	battalion	MG	Manuscript Group
CCHA	Canadian Catholic Historical Association	MHA	member of the House of Assembly
CHA	Canadian Historical Association	MTCL	Metropolitan Toronto Central Library
CHR	*Canadian Historical Review*	OA	Ontario Archives
Co./Cos.	county/counties	*OH*	*Ontario History*
Cols	Colonies	OHS	Ontario Historical Society
CW	Canada West	PAC	Public Archives of Canada
d	died	*q.v.*	which see
dau	daughter of	RG	record group
DCB	*Dictionary of Canadian Biography*	Regt	regiment
		Twp.	township
DHB	*Dictionary of Hamilton Biography*	UC	Upper Canada
		UE	United Empire Loyalist
Dist.	District	WO	War Office

Appendix
Biographical Data

The entries in this Appendix are not intended to be complete biographical sketches of the MHAS but contain the basic categories of information gathered for the purposes and period of this study. About one-third of the Upper Canadian MHAS are the subjects of articles in the *Dictionary of Canadian Biography*. If this is the case, a reference to the relevant volume of that admirably thorough series has been given in lieu of any other sources. In all other cases, a list of primary and secondary sources consulted is included, both to provide the origin of the information which appears and to act as a partial guide to further research.

Throughout the entries square brackets have been used to indicate that, while there is good reason for thinking that the information or identification enclosed by the brackets is correct, the evidence is not sufficiently complete or reliable to allow for an unqualified statement of fact.

Political labels (some of them also in square brackets) have been attached only to those MHAS who sat in the last four Upper Canadian parliaments (1828–41) and precise details relating to provincial parliamentary careers have not been included. For information on elections, ridings, Parliaments, sessions, etc., the reader is referred to F.H. Armstrong, *Handbook of Upper Canadian Chronology* (Dundurn Press: Toronto and London 1985). Debra Forman, ed., *Legislators and Legislatures of Ontario*, (Toronto: Legislative Library 1984) and, of course, to the *Journals* of the Upper Canadian House of Assembly.

ADAMS, Gideon, *b* 1754 or 1755, Conn., 13 Cols; *d* 20 June 1834, South Gower Twp., UC. Son of capt. Samuel Adams, UE; *m* Mary Ann Snyder (*dau* William Snyder, UE, ens., Loyal [Jessup's] Rangers); six sons, two daughters. [Presbyterian]. Farmer. Granted 2,000 acres. Lived in (1) Edwardsburg Twp., (2) S. Gower Twp., [1818]–34. Served 1776–83; ens., 9 Aug 1777; lt., Jessup's Rangers (HP 1783); capt., Grenville Militia by 1807; maj., 2d

Reg., Grenville Militia, 1812–14. JP, Eastern Dist., 1 July 1796. MHA, Grenville, 1812–16.

See PAC, RG 1, L 3, vol. 2, A 3/30; vol. 5, A 10/48; vol. 6, A 11/32; VOL. 12, A 18/78; vol. 16, A, Misc/10; RG 5, A 1, vol. 5, p. 2078; RG 8, C 634 A, p. 1717; RG 9, IB 5, vol. 6; RG 68, General Index to Commissions; MG 21, B 167, p. 104; T. Leavitt, *History of Leeds and Grenville* (Brockville 1879), 109, 134; W.D. Reid, *The Loyalists in Ontario* (Lambertville, NJ 1973), 2.

AIKMAN, Michael, *b* 9 Dec. 1797, UC; *d* 21 Mar. 1881, Barton Twp., Ont. Son of John Aikman and Hannah Showers (*dau* Michael Showers, UE); *m* Ann Willson (*dau* John Willson, *q.v.*); three sons, three daughters. Methodist. Farmer, businessman. Lived in (1) Barton Twp. (2) Hamilton. Ens., 3d Regt., Gore Militia, 19 Apr. 1823; lt., 27 May 1830; capt., 4 Oct. 1837; capt. commanding special detachment, Niagara frontier, June 1838. JP, Gore Dist., 2 Apr. 1833. MHA, Wentworth, 1836–41. Conservative.

See PAC, RG 9, IB 5, vols. 1, 6; RG 68, General Index to Commissions; MG 12, WO 13, vol. 3682; Hamilton *Spectator* 22 Mar. 1881; *Dominion Annual Register*, 1880–1; W.D. Reid, *The Loyalists in Ontario* (Lambertville, NJ 1973), 288.

ALLCOCK, Henry, *b* 1759, Birmingham, England; *d* 22 Feb. 1808, Quebec City. Son of Henry Allcock and Mary Askin; *m* Hannah ——— ; one daughter. Anglican. Lawyer, public servant. Granted 1,200 acres. Lived at York (Toronto) 1799–1806. Judge, Court of King's Bench of UC, Nov. 1798; chief justice, 14 Oct. 1802; member, Executive Council, 14 Oct. 1802; member and Speaker, Legislative Council, 4 Jan. 1803. MHA, Durham, Simcoe and East York, 1800–4.

See DCB 5.

ALWAY, Robert *b* 1790, Gloucester, England; *d* 6 Aug. 1840, Texas, USA. Son of Robert Alway; *m* [Sarah] ——— ; seven children. Anglican. Farmer, [teacher]. Bought 620 acres. Lived in (1) Townsend Twp. (2) (W.) Oxford Twp. (3) E. Nissouri Twp. 1816–38. Capt., 1st Regt., Oxford Militia, 24 Jan. 1834 (dismissed 1838). MHA, Oxford, 1834–41. Reformer.

See PAC, RG 1, L 3, vol. 7, A 12/16; RG 5, A 1, vol. 46, p. 22915; RG 9, IB 5, vols. 1,5; AO, abstract index to deeds, E. Nissouri Twp.; MTCL, Shenston Papers; UC, House of Assembly *Journals* (1825, 1835, 1836, 1837, 1839–40); B. Dawe, *Old Oxford is Wide Awake! Pioneer Settlers and Politicians in Oxford County, 1793–53* (n.p. 1980), 32, 65.

ARMSTRONG, James Rogers, *b* 17 Apr. 1787, Dorchester (Iberville), Que.; *d* 13 July 1873, Whitby, Ont. Son of John Armstrong and Mary Rogers (*dau* James Rogers, maj., King's Rangers; sister of David McGregor Rogers, *q.v.*); *m* Hannah Dougall (*dau* William Dougall, UE); one son, three daughters.

Educated in Vermont. Methodist. Farmer, merchant, manufacturer. Granted 400 acres. Lived in (1) Hallowell Twp. [1807–?] (2) Picton (3) Kingston 1822–8 (4) Toronto 1828–57. JP, Home Dist., 15 Sept. 1837. MHA, Prince Edward, 1836–41. Conservative.

See DCB 10.

ATKINSON, James, *b* 1793, England; *d* 1836. Son of William Atkinson, UE, (capt., Associated Loyalists) and Mary Badgley; *m* Mary Pember (*dau* Philip Pember, UE); one son, two daughters. Anglican. "Gentleman," shipowner. Granted a town lot in Kingston. Lived in Kingston. Served 1812–14 as a militia pvt.; ens., 1st Regt. Frontenac Militia, 25 Aug. 1831; lt., 19 Apr. 1836; capt., 30 May 1833. MHA, Frontenac, 1824–8.

See PAC, RG 1, l 3, vol. 5, A 10/64; vol. 6, A 11/55; vol. 274, K 18/49; RG 5, A 1, p. 41854; RG 9, IB 5, vols. 1, 2, 5.

BABY, François (Francis), *b* 16 Dec. 1768; *d* 27 Aug. 1852, Sandwich, CW. Son of Jacques Duperron Baby and Suzanne Réaume; brother of Hon. Jacques (James) Baby (member of the Executive and Legislative councils of UC, inspector general, UC) and Jean-Baptiste Baby (*q.v.*).; *m* Frances Abbot. Roman Catholic. Farmer, developer. Granted 2,400 acres, and two water lots in Sandwich. Lived in Sandwich. Lt. col., Kent Militia, 1812–14; asst. quartermaster general of militia, Western Dist. JP Western Dist., 15 July 1796; member, Heir and Devisee Committee, Western Dist., 22 Aug. 1800; lt., County of Essex, 1 Oct. 1807. MHA, Kent, 1792–6; Essex, 1820–30. Reformer.

See DCB 8.

BABY, Jean-Baptiste, *b* 10 Jan. 1770; *d* 1856, Sandwich, CW. Son of Jacques Duperron Baby and Suzanne Réaume; brother of François (Francis) Baby (*q.v.*) and Hon. Jacques (James) Baby; *m* Ann Hand (*dau* William Hand, JP, sheriff, treasurer, etc., Western Dist.). Roman Catholic. Merchant, farmer, public servant. Granted 2,400 acres. Lived in Sandwich Twp. Lt. col., 2d Regt., Essex Militia, [1806], 1812–14. JP, Western Dist., 17 May 1816; treasurer, Western Dist., 1837. MHA, Essex, 1808–12.

See PAC, RG 1, L 3, vol. 27, B 1/117; vol. 34, B 7/54; vol. 51, B 16/45; L 7, vol. 52; RG 8, C 661, p. 11; C 676, p. 180; RG 68, General Index to Commissions; F.H. Armstrong, "The Oligarchy of the Western District of Upper Canada," CHA *Historical Papers* (1977): 93, 100–1; J.B. Casgrain, *Mémorial des familles Casgrain, Baby et Perrault* (Québec 1878), 119–20.

BALDWIN, Robert, *b* 12 May 1804, York (Toronto); *d* 9 Dec. 1858, Toronto. Son of William Warren Baldwin (*q.v.*) and Phoebe Willcocks; *m* Augusta Elizabeth Sullivan (sister of Hon. Robert Baldwin Sullivan); two sons, two daughters. Educated at the Home Dist. Grammar School under Rev. John

Strachan; studied law with his father. Anglican. Lawyer, public servant. Lived in Toronto. Lt., 1st Regt., N. York Militia, 10 Apr. 1822; capt., 2 Oct. 1836. Member, Executive Council of UC, 20 Feb – 12 Mar. 1836. MHA, York (town) 1829–30. Reformer.
See DCB 8.

BALDWIN, William Warren, *b* 25 Apr. 1775, Carrigaline, Co. Cork, Ireland; *d*, Toronto, 8 Jan. 1844. Son of Robert Baldwin and Barbara Spread; brother of Admiral Augustus Warren Baldwin; *m* Margaret Phoebe Willcocks; six sons, including Robert (*q.v.*). Educated at the University of Edinburgh (MD 1796). Anglican. Physician, lawyer, public servant. Granted 1,200 acres and a town lot in York (Toronto); bought or inherited much property in Toronto and elsewhere. Lived in Toronto. Lt. col., Durham Militia Bttn. by 1807; lt. col., 1st Regt., Durham Militia, 26 June 1812. JP, Home Dist. 1 Jan. 1800; judge, District Court, Home Dist., 22 July 1809; Surrogate Court, Home Dist., 26 Dec. 1816; registrar, Court of Probate, Home Dist., 11 Nov. 1808. MHA, York and Simcoe, 1820–4; Norfolk, 1828–30. Reformer.
See DCB 7.

BEARDSLEY, Bartholomew Crannell, *b* 21 Oct. 1775, Poughkeepsie, NY (13 Cols); *d* 24 Mar. 1855, Oakville, CW. Son of Rev. John Beardsley (chaplain, Loyal American Regt.) and Gertrude Crannell; *m* Mary Jenkins; six sons, one daughter. Studied law in NB. Anglican. Lawyer. Granted 1,200 acres plus town lots in Niagara and York (Toronto). Lived at Niagara and at Oakville. MHA, Lincoln (2d and 3d ridings), 1824–8, 1830–4. Reformer.
See DCB 8.

BEASLEY, Richard, *b* 21 July 1761, Hudson Valley, NY (13 Cols); *d* 16 Feb. 1842, Hamilton. Son of Henry Beasley; cousin of Hon. Richard Cartwright; *m* Henrietta Springer; four sons, six daughters, including Catherine (*m* C.C. Ferrie, *q.v.*). Anglican. Miller, fur trader, merchant, land developer/speculator. Granted 1,200 acres. Bought Block 2 of the Grand River Tract (94,012 acres) from the Six Nations Indians, plus 13,000 acres in Norwich Twp. and other scattered holdings. Lived in (1) Niagara [1781]–90 (2) Burlington Heights (Hamilton) 1790–1842. Served for 2 years as acting commissary during the American Revolution; lt., Lincoln Militia, 28 July 1794; col., 2d Regt., York Militia, 2 Jan. 1809. JP Home Dist., 1 July 1796; commissioner to arrest persons suspected of high treason, 24 Mar. 1814. MHA, Durham, York and Lincoln (1st riding) 1797; Lincoln (1st riding), West York and Haldimand, 1800–4; York West, 1808–9; Halton, 1824–8.
See DHB 1; *DCB* 7.

BEIKIE, John, *b* 14 Feb. 1766, Gibraltar; *d* 20 Mar. 1839, Toronto; *m* Penelope Macdonell (*dau* "Spanish John" Macdonell [Scotus], capt., King's Royal Regt. of NY; sister of John Macdonell, *q.v.*; aunt of Donald Aeneas

Macdonell, *q.v.*). Anglican. Merchant, public servant. Granted 2,000 acres and a town lot in York (Toronto); bought at least 8,600 acres in Loyalist rights. Lived in (1) Cornwall [1794–1801] (2) York (Toronto) [1801]–39. Capt., Stormont Militia, 3 Oct. 1796; capt., 3d Regt., York Militia, 1813; volunteer with 8th (Regular) Regt. at the siege of York, 27 Apr. 1813; lt. col., 1st Regt., W. York Militia, 19 Mar. 1832; col., 1826. JP, Eastern Dist., 1 July 1796; Home Dist., 3 June 1822; sheriff, Home Dist., 2 May 1810 to 1815; junior clerk, Executive Council Office, UC, [1801]; first clerk, 10 June 1803; clerk, 17 Dec. 1832. MHA, Stormont and Russell, 1812–16.

See PAC, RG 1, L 3, vol. 28, B 2/101; vol. 32, B 5/103; vol. 47, B 14/194; vol. 50, B 15/111; RG 8, C 1170, p. 235; RG 9, IB 5, vol. 1; RG 68, General Index to Commissions; L.F. Gates, *Land Policies of Upper Canada* (Toronto 1968), 333; H.P. Gundy, "The Family Compact at Work" *OH* 66, no. 3 (Sept. 1974): 131; Henry Scadding, *Toronto of Old,* ed. F.H. Armstrong (Toronto 1965), 82; J.H. Harkness, *History of Stormont, Dundas and Glengarry* (Ottawa 1946), 90–1.

BERCZY, William Bent, *b* 6 Jan. 1791, London, England; *d* 9 Dec. 1873, Ste.-Mélanie d'Ailleboust, Québec. Son of William Berczy von Moll (the painter and colonizer) and Charlotte Allemand; *m* Louise-Amélie Panet (*dau* Pierre-Louis Panet, MHA, member of the Executive Council, judge, LC). [Anglican.] Farmer, contractor, shipowner, merchant, public servant. Granted 2,400 acres and a town lot in Chatham. Lived at (1) Amherstburgh and (2) Sandwich, UC 1818–3 [4]. Capt., Lower Canadian Militia, 26 Sept. 1813; adj. gen., 20 July 1813; at Crysler's Farm, 1813. JP, Western Dist., 23 Sept. 1826; judge, Western Dist. Court, 25 Apr. 1826. MHA, Kent, 1828–34. [Conservative.]

See DCB 10.

BETHUNE, Donald, *b* 11 July 1802, Williamstown, UC; *d* 19 June 1869, Toronto. Son of Rev. John Bethune, UE (chaplain to the 84th [Royal Highland Emigrants] Regt.) and Véronique Waddin; *m* Janet Smith (*dau* Peter Smith, UE). Educated by his brother John at a school in Augusta Twp. and at Rev. John Strachan's School at Cornwall; studied law with Jonas Jones (*q.v.*) in Brockville. Lawyer, public servant, shipowner. Granted 200 acres. Lived at (1) Kingston 1824–[40] (2) Cobourg 1840–3. Capt., 2d Regt., Frontenac Militia, 24 Mar. 1823; on duty with the rank of lt. col., 1837–8. JP Prince Edward Dist., 15 Mar. 1834; judge. Bathurst Dist. Court, 22 Nov. 1826; Prince Edward Dist. Court, 15 Mar. 1834, MHA, Kingston, 1828–30. Conservative.

See DCB 9.

BIDWELL, Barnabas, *b* 23 Aug. 1763, Monterey, Mass. (13 Cols); *d* 1833, Kingston; *m* Mary Gray, one son, Marshall Spring Bidwell (*q.v.*). Educated

at Yale (BA 1785) and studied law. Presbyterian. Lawyer, teacher. Lived at (1) Bath, UC (2) Kingston. MHA, Lennox and Addington, 1821.
See DCB 6.

BIDWELL, Marshall Spring, *b* 16 Feb. 1799, Stockbridge, Mass., USA; *d* 24 Oct. 1872, New York, NY. Son of Barnabas Bidwell (*q.v.*) and Mary Gray; *m* Clara Willcox; four children. Educated by his father and in local schools; studied law with Daniel Hagerman and Daniel Washburn. Presbyterian. Lawyer. Lived in (1) Bath (2) Kingston to [1835] (3) Toronto [1835]–7. MHA, Lennox and Addington, 1824–36. Reformer.
See DCB 10.

BLACKLOCK, Ambrose, *b* 17 May 1784, Dumfries, Scotland; *d* 5 Oct. 1866, St. Andrews, CW; *m* Catherine Macdonell (*dau* Ronald Macdonell, UE, lt., King's Royal Regt. of NY). Studied medicine in Scotland. Presbyterian. Farmer, physician. Granted 800 acres; bought [100] acres. Lived at (1) Cornwall (2) St. Andrews. Commissioned as surgeon, Royal Navy, 26 Dec. 1807; served on Lakes Ontario and Champlain, 1812–15 (HP [1820]). JP, Eastern Dist., 8 Jan. 1820; coroner, Eastern Dist., 30 July 1824. MHA, Stormont, 1828–30. Reformer.
See PAC, RG 1, L 3, vol. 44, B 13/33; vol. 62, B 21/53; RG. 8, C 736, p. 31a; RG 68, General Index to Commissions; J.H. Harkness, *History of Stormont, Dundas and Glengarry* (Ottawa 1946), 153; L.H. Irving, *Officers of the British Forces in Canada During the War of 1812–15* (Welland 1908), 233.

BOCHUS, Charles, *b* 30 Dec. 1802; *d* 10 Jan. 1878, Picton, Ont.; *m* Caroline Mallory. Anglican. Merchant. Lived in Picton, 1829–43. Capt., 4th Regt., Prince Edward Militia, 26 Mar. 1838. MHA, Prince Edward, 1836–41. Conservative.
See PAC, RG 9, IB 5, vol. 4; *Upper Canada Herald*, 9 Aug. 1836; *Dominion Annual Register* (1878), 331; J. Plomer, *Desperate Venture: Central Ontario Railway* (Belleville 1979), 12.

BOOTH, Joshua, *b* [1759], Orange Co., NY (13 Cols) *d* 27 Oct. 1813, Ernesttown Twp., UC Son of Benjamin Booth, UE; *m* Margaret Fraser (*dau* Daniel Fraser, UE, capt., McAlpine's Corps); five sons, five daughters. Presbyterian. Miller. Granted at least 2,500 acres, including several mill sites. Lived in Ernesttown Twp. Pvt., Delancey's Corps during the Revolution; capt., Addington Militia by 1807; capt., 1st Regt., Addington Militia, 1812–13 (died on duty). JP, Midland Dist., 15 July 1796. MHA, Addington and Ontario, 1792–6.
See DCB 5.

BOSTWICK, John, *b* 1780, Mass.; *d* 9 Sept. 1849, [Port Stanley], CW Son

of Rev. Gideon Bostwick; *m* Mary Ryerson (*dau* Joseph Ryerson, UE, lt., New Jersey Volunteers; niece of Rev. Egerton Ryerson); four sons, three daughters. Anglican. Surveyor, farmer, public servant. Granted 1,400 acres and received at least 1,218 acres as payment for surveys. Lived at Port Stanley, 1804–[49]. Capt., 1st Regt., Norfolk Militia by 1807; maj., 1 Aug. 1816; col., 3d Regt., Middlesex Militia, 18 June 1822, 1837–8. JP, London Dist., 6 Nov. 1806; collector of customs, Port Stanley, 20 July 1831. MHA, Middlesex, 1820–4.
See DCB 7.

BOULTON, D'Arcy, *b* 20 May 1759, Moulton, Lincolnshire; *d* 23 May 1834, Toronto. Son of Henry Boulton and Mary Preston; *m* Elizabeth Forster; five sons, including Henry John (*q.v.*) and George Strange (*q.v.*). Read law at the Middle Temple. Anglican. Lawyer, public servant. Granted 2,200 acres; bought a two-acre lot in York and 31,000 acres in Loyalist rights with H.J. Boulton. Lived in (1) Augusta Twp. 1802–5 (2) York (Toronto) 1805–34. Solicitor general of UC, 19 Feb. 1805; attorney general, 31 Dec. 1814; judge, Court of King's Bench, 12 Feb. 1818. MHA, Stormont and Russell, 1805–8.
See DCB 6.

BOULTON, George Strange, *b* 11 Sept. 1797, Greenbush, NY; *d* 13 Feb. 1869, Cobourg, Ont. Son of D'Arcy Boulton (*q.v.*) and Elizabeth Forster; brother of H.J. Boulton (*q.v.*); *m* (1) Elizabeth ——— (2) Anna Maria Berk, née Walton; three children. Educated by Rev. John Strachan at Cornwall and at the Home Dist. School. Anglican. Lawyer, survey contractor, public servant. Granted 600 acres; received at least 1,867 acres in payment for surveys; bought 12,700 acres in Loyalist rights. Lived at (1) Port Hope 1818–24 (2) Cobourg 1824–69. Served as a militia private (at age 15) during 1812–14; capt., 1st Regt., Durham Militia, 4 Oct. 1820; maj. 2d Regt., Durham Militia, 28 June 1825; lt. col., 3 May 1830. Registrar, Northumberland County, July 1824–69. MHA, Durham, 1824–5, 1830–41. Conservative.
See DCB 9.

BOULTON, Henry John, *b* 1790, Kensington, England; *d* 18 June 1870, Toronto. Son of D'Arcy Boulton (*q.v.*) and Elizabeth Forster; brother of G.S. Boulton, (*q.v.*); *m* Eliza Jones (*dau* of Ephraim Jones, *q.v.*); three sons, five daughters. Attended Rev. John Strachan's school in Cornwall; studied law with his father and at Lincoln's Inn and Oxford. Anglican. Lawyer, public servant. Bought 31,000 acres in Loyalist rights with his father. Lived in (1) Toronto to 1833 (2) St. John's Nfld., 1833–8 (3) Toronto 1838–70. Acting solicitor general of UC, 11 Mar. 1818; solicitor general, 2 Dec. 1819; attorney general, 13 July 1829. MHA Niagara (town) 1830–4. Conservative.
See DCB 9.

BRANT, John, *b* 27 Sept. 1794, Mohawk Village (near Brantford), UC; *d* 27 Aug. 1832, Brantford. Son of Joseph Brant (leader of the Six Nations) and Catherine Brant. Educated by private tutors and at Ancaster and Niagara. Anglican. Public servant. Granted 700 acres. Lived at (1) Burlington Beach and (2) Brantford. Lt., Indian Dep., Apr. 1813 to 1816. Superintendent, Six Nations, 1828–32. MHA, Haldimand, 1830–1. Conservative.
See DCB 6.

BROUSE, George, *b* 1790, Matilda Twp. UC; *d* 12 Feb. 1860, Iroquois, CW Son of Peter Brouse, UE, and Eliza Brouse; *m* Catherine Carman (*dau* Michael Carman, UE); five daughters, two sons. Methodist. Farmer, miller, merchant, [lumberman]. Granted 200 acres; bought 700 acres. Lived at Iroquois, Matilda Twp. [Lt., 2d Regt., Dundas Militia, 29 Apr. 1837; capt., 30 Jan. 1839.] MHA, Dundas, 1828–30. Reformer.
See DCB 8.

BROWN, John, *b* [1791], Ireland; *d* 28 Jan. 1842, Port Hope, CW; three children. [Anglican.] Merchant. Granted 200 acres. Lived in Port Hope [1818]–42. JP, Newcastle Dist., 26 July 1823. MHA, Durham, 1830–6. Conservative.
See PAC, RG 1, L 3, vol. 43, B 12/271; vol. 259, I–J 8/56; RG 68, General Index to Commissions; W.D. Reid, *Death Notices of Ontario* (Lambertville, NJ 1980), 264.

BROWNELL, John, *b* [1765, Duchess County NY (13 Cols)]; *d* 27 Dec. 1809, Osnabruck Twp.,UC; *m* Hannah Hogoboam. Presbyterian. [Farmer.] Lived in Osnabruck Twp. Taken prisoner at age 16 during the American Revolution. JP, Eastern Dist., 15 July 1796. MHA, Stormont and Russell. 1808–9.
See PAC, RG 1, L 3, vol. 35, B 8/65; RG 5, A 1, pp. 4577, 4582; J.G. Harkness, *History of Stormont, Dundas and Glengarry* (Ottawa 1946), 89; J.F. Pringle, *Lunenburgh, or the Old Eastern District* (Cornwall 1890), 409.

BRUCE, William, *b*, UC; *d* 20 Sept. 1838, Cornwall, UC. Son of William Bruce (son of Alexander Bruce, UE, pvt., 84th Regt.) and Mary Alguire (*dau* John Alguire, UE). Educated at Rev. John Strachan's school, Cornwall; studied medicine. Physician. Granted 100 acres. Lived in Cornwall. Served 1812–14 as pvt., 1st Regt., Stormont Militia; lt., 21 Feb. 1822. JP, Eastern Dist., 15 Dec. 1833; coroner, 16 Mar. 1835. MHA, Stormont, 1834–6. Reformer.
See PAC, RG 1, L 3, vol. 49, B 15/30; L 7, vol. 52; RG 9, IB 5, vol. 1; RG 68, General Index to Commissions; J.G. Harkness, *History of Stormont, Dundas and Glengarry* (Ottawa 1946), 144, 165–6; W. Canniff, *The Medical Profession in Upper Canada* (Toronto 1894), 53.

BUELL, William (senior), *b* 5 Oct. 1751, Hebron, Conn. (13 Cols); *d* 8 Aug.

1832, Brockville, UC. Son of Timothy Buell (major, King's Rangers) and Mercy Peters; *m* (1) Martha Naughton (*dau* Andrew Naughton, UE) (2) Margaret Bernard; four daughters, three sons, including William junior (*q.v.*). Anglican. Farmer, developer. Granted 2,000 acres, including 400 acres in Elizabethtown Twp. which were subdivided as the town of Brockville. Lived in Brockville. Ens., King's Rangers, 1777–84 (HP 1784). JP Lunenburg Dist., 24 July 1788; Midland Dist., 15 July 1796. MHA Leeds, 1800–4.
See DCB 6.

BUELL, William (junior), *b* 28 Feb. 1792, Elizabethtown Twp., UC; *d* 29 Apr. 1862, Brockville. Son of William Buell (*q.v.*) and Martha Naughton; *m* (1) Mary Ann Angelica Story (2) Deborah Dockstader (3) Catherine Dockstader; four daughters, three sons. Attended schools in Elizabethtown Twp. and Les Cedres, LC. Presbyterian. Journalist, merchant, farmer, miller. Lived in Brockville. Sgt., 1st Regt., Leeds Militia, 22 Feb. 1813–15 (wounded and pensioned); lt., 16 Apr. 1822; capt., 19 Apr. 1830; lt. col., 19 Dec. 1845; on active service 1837–8. JP, Johnstown Dist., 20 Feb. 1840; MHA, Leeds, 1828–34, 1836. Reformer.
See DCB 9.

BURKE, George Thew, *b* 1776, Ballyartella, Co. Tipperary, Ireland; *d* 2 Feb. 1854, Bytown, CW; *m* Lydia Grant; four daughters, two sons. Anglican. Soldier, merchant, distiller, public servant. Granted [700] acres and a town lot in Richmond. Bought 100 acres in Goulborn Twp. Lived in (1) Richmond and (2) Bytown. Capt., 100th (Regular) Regt., on duty in Canada 1811–18; maj. of brigade at Chambly, 21 July 1813; deputy asst. adj. gen., 15 June 1814 (HP 1818); secretary and storekeeper, Richmond military settlement, 10 Nov. 1818; col., 1st Regt., Carleton Militia, 10 Jan. 1822. JP Johnstown Dist., 2 June 1819; Bathurst Dist., 27 Nov. 1822; registrar, Lanark Co., 23 May 1824. MHA, Carleton, 1824–8.

See PAC, RG 1, E 13 (1822); RG 8, C 189, p. 9; C 212, p. 109; C 1179, p. 85; C 1218, p. 61; RG 9, IB 5, vol. 6; RG 68, General Index to Commissions; UC, House of Assembly, *Journals* (1825–6), Appendix; Ottawa *Citizen* 4 Feb. 1854; L.H. Irving, *Officers of the British Forces in Canada During the War of 1812–15* (Welland 1908), 6–7, 13–14.

BURNHAM, Zaccheus, *b* 20 Feb. 1777, Dunbarton, NH; *d* 25 Feb. 1857, Cobourg, CW. Son of Asa Burnham and Elizabeth Cutler; one son, five daughters. Anglican. Farmer, distiller, miller, public servant, survey contractor, businessman. Granted 1,500 acres plus 4,970 acres as payment for surveys. Lived in Cobourg, 1799–1857. Capt. 1ST Regt., Northumberland Militia, 1812–14; maj., 18 June 1822; lt. col., 27 June 1825; col., 3 Mar. 1837. JP Newcastle Dist., 29 Mar. 1813; treasurer, Newcastle Dist., 1815; judge, Newcastle Dist. Court, 16 July 1839; member of the Legislative Council of UC, 26 Jan. 1831. MHA, Northumberland and Durham, 1816–20; Northumberland, 1824–8. Conservative.

See DCB 8.

BURRITT, Henry, *b* 26 Aug. 1791, [Augusta Twp.] UC; *d* 4 Nov. 1872, Burritt's Rapids, Ont. Son of Stephen Burritt (*q.v.*). Anglican. Farmer, Granted 700 acres. Lived in Marlborough Twp. Lt., Volunteer Incorporated Bttn. of Militia, 1812–14; lt., 2d Regt., Grenville Militia, 18 Feb. 1812; maj., 19 Oct. 1815; lt. col., 17 Apr. 1830; lt. col., 3d Regt., Grenville Militia, 2 Apr. 1840. JP Johnstown Dist., 27 Mar. 1821. MHA, Grenville, 1839–41. Conservative.

See PAC, RG 1, L 3, vol. 51, B 16/19; L 7, vol. 52; RG 9, IB 5, vols. 1, 6; RG 68, General Index to Commissions; L.H. Irving, *Officers of the British Forces in Canada During the War of 1812–15* (Welland 1908), 37–8, 49.

BURRITT, Stephen, *b* [1759], 13 Cols; *d* 13 Jan. 1844, Marlborough Twp., UC. Son of Daniel Burritt, UE; *m* [Martha] Stevens (*dau* Roger Stevens, ens., King's Rangers); five sons, including Henry Burritt (*q.v.*), one daughter. Farmer. Granted 1,300 acres. Lived in Marlborough Twp., 1793–1844. Pvt. and sgt., King's Rangers, 1777–83; capt., Grenville Militia by 1803; maj. commanding flank companies of the Dundas and Grenville Militia, 1812–14; lt. col., 2d Regt., Grenville Militia, 5 June 1813. JP, Johnstown Dist., 30 June 1800; commissioner to arrest persons suspected of high treason, 24 Mar. 1814. MHA, Grenville, 1808–12.

See PAC, RG 1, L 3, vol. 31, B 4/81; vol. 32, B 5/76; vol. 56, B 18/188; L 7, vol. 52; RG 68, General Index to Commissions; L.H. Irving, *Officers of the British Forces in Canada During the War of 1812–15* (Welland 1908), 36, 49; W.D. Reid, *Death Notices of Ontario* (Lambertville, NJ 1980), 219.

BURWELL, Mahlon, *b* 18 Feb. 1783, NJ; *d* 25 Jan. 1846 near Port Talbot, CW. Son of Adam Burwell; *m* Sarah Hawn; seven sons, two daughters. Anglican. Surveyor, farmer, public servant, Granted 600 acres plus 24,169 acres as payment for surveys. Lived in (1) Bertie Twp. (2) Port Talbot (3) Port Burwell. Lt., 3d Regt., Lincoln Militia, 1810; lt. col., 1st Regt., Middlesex Militia, 13 Feb. 1812; col., 2d Regt., Middlesex Militia, 18 June 1822. JP, London Dist., 5 Apr. 1813; commissioner to arrest persons suspected of high treason, 24 Mar. 1814; registrar, Middlesex County, 20 Dec. 1809; collector of customs, Port Talbot, 10 Jan. 1822; coroner, London Dist., 30 July 1824. MHA, Oxford and Middlesex, 1812–20; Middlesex, 1820–4; London (town) 1836–41. Conservative.

See DCB 7.

CALDWELL, Francis, *b* 4 May 1792, [Detroit]; *d* 5 June 1851, Malden Twp.,

UC. Son of William Caldwell (Indian Dept., capt., Butler's Rangers, 1777–83) and Suzanne Baby; *m* Frances Réaume; one son. Roman Catholic. Farmer, public servant. Granted 700 acres; bought 2,600 acres in Loyalist rights. Lived in Malden Twp. Ens., 1st Regt., Essex Militia, 12 July 1812; at Detroit, Frenchtown, Moraviantown (wounded); capt., 15 July 1819; capt., Amherstburgh Volunteers, 8 Jan. 1838. JP, Western Dist., 11 Nov. 1833; collector of customs, Amherstburgh, 15 Apr. 1831. MHA, Essex, 1834–41 [Conservative.]

See DCB 8.

CAMERON, Duncan, *b* [1764], Glenmoriston, Inverness-shire, Scotland; *d* 15 May 1848, Williamstown, CW. Son of Alexander Cameron (pvt., King's royal Regt. of NY) and Margaret Macdonell; *m* Margaret McLeod; at least two sons. Presbyterian. Fur trader in the northwest, farmer. Lived at Williamstown, 1820–48. Served "under Sir John Johnson," 1780–83. JP Eastern Dist., 18 Apr. 1825. MHA, Glengarry, 1824–8.

See PAC, RG 1, L 3, vol. 107, C 14/252; RG 68, General Index to Commissions; W.L. Scott, "Glengarry's Representatives in the Legislative Assembly of Upper Canada," (part 2, 1812–41) CCHA, *Report* (1939–40) 35–6.

CAMERON, John, *b* 1778, Mohawk Valley, NY; *d* 7 Aug. 1829. Son of John Cameron (pvt., King's Royal Regt. of NY) and Elizabeth Ferguson; *m* Elizabeth Summers (*dau* Jacob Summers, UE); [two] sons. Presbyterian. Farmer. Granted 700 acres; bought 3,800 acres in many parts of UC. Lived at Fairfield, Charlottenburgh Twp. Lt., Glengarry Militia by 1807; lt., 1st Regt., Glengarry Militia, 15 Apr. 1812. JP, Eastern Dist., 17 June 1814. MHA, Glengarry, 1816–20.

See PAC, RG 1, L 3, vol. 93, C 5/43; vol. 100, C 11/185; L 7, vol. 52; RG 19, E 5a, vol. 3758, no. 1922; RG 68, General Index to Commissions; L.H. Irving, *Officers of the British Forces in Canada during the War of 1812–15* (Welland 1908), 41; J.G. Harkness, *History of Stormont, Dundas and Glengarry* (Ottawa 1946), 138; W.L. Scott, "Glengarry's Representatives in the Legislative Assembly of Upper Canada," (part 2, 1812–41) CCHA *Report* (1939–40): 33–35.

CAMERON, Malcolm, *b* 25 Apr. 1808, Trois Rivières, LC; *d* 1 June 1876, Ottawa. Son of Angus Cameron (sgt., Canadian Fencible Regt.) and Euphemia McGregor; *m* Christina McGregor; one (adopted) son, Malcolm Colin (MP; lt. gov., Northwest Territories), (one) daughter. Educated at a local school in Perth, UC. Presbyterian (Church of Scotland). Merchant, lumberman, developer, miller, shipbuilder, contractor, journalist. Granted a town lot in Perth. Bought 6,500 acres including 1,900 acres in Loyalist rights, 100 acres of which was subdivided to become Sarnia; bought 4,000 acres of Indian reserve land, as part of a syndicate. Lived at (1) Perth [1825]–37 (2) Sarnia 1837–63. MHA, Lanark, 1836–41. Reformer.

See DCB 10.

CAMPBELL, Alexander, *b* [1770], NY (13 Cols), *d* [18 Jan. 1834 in Edwardsburgh Twp., UC], Son of [Duncan] Campbell; *m* Abigail Brown; eleven children, including five sons, three daughters. Farmer, public servant. Granted 3,000 acres. Lived in Edwardsburgh Twp. 1795–[1834]. Lt., Loyal (Jessup's) Rangers, 1777–83 (HP 1784). JP, Johnstown Dist., 1 Jan. 1800; registrar, Leeds, Dundas and Grenville cos., 1795–1801. MHA, Dundas, 1792–6.

See PAC, RG 1, L 3, vol. 80, C 1/20, 49, 105, 104; vol. 91, C 3/130; vol. 126, Misc. 1788–95, 33, 35; RG 5, A 1, vol. 1a, p. 129; RG 68, General Index to Commissions; MG 21, B 167, pp. 56, 102, 156a, 283; PRO, Audit Office 12, vol. 21, p. 276; W.D. Reid, *Death Notices of Ontario* (Lambertville, NJ 1980), 101; T. Leavitt, *History of Leeds and Grenville* (Brockville 1879), 110, 118, 162.

CAMPBELL, John, *b* [1789], Scotland; *d* [9 Aug. 1834, Kingston, UC]. [Farmer.] Granted 500 acres. Lived in Kingston. Served 1812–14 as midshipman and mate, RN, on Lake Erie; commanded HMS *Chippawa* (wounded, POW). JP Midland Dist., 12 Sept. 1829. MHA, Frontenac, 1830–4. [Reformer.]

See PAC, RG 1, L 3, vol. 99, C 11/130; vol. 109, C 16/12; RG 8, C 730, p. 150, 161; C 692, p. 269; RG 68, General Index to Commissions; W.D. Reid, *Death Notices of Ontario* (Lambertville, NJ 1980), 110.

CARTWRIGHT, John Solomon, *b* 17 Sept. 1804, Kingston, UC; *d* 15 Jan. 1845, Kingston. Son of Hon. Richard Cartwright, UE (member of the Legislative Council) and Magdalen Secord; *m* Sarah Hayter Macaulay (*dau* Dr James Macaulay, Queen's Rangers; sister of Hon. John Simcoe Macaulay and Sir James Buchanan Macaulay); three sons, including Sir Richard J. Cartwright, and three daughters. Educated by Rev. John Strachan; studied law, Toronto, Oxford and Lincoln's Inn. Anglican. Lawyer, public servant, businessman. Granted 881 acres plus two acres in Kingston. Lived in Kingston. Lt., 2d Regt., East York Militia, 27 Nov. 1824; capt., 2d Regt., West York Militia, 23 May 1827; lt. col., 2d Regt., Lennox Militia, 3 May 1837. JP Midland Dist., 22 Oct. 1836; judge, Midland Dist. Court, 14 Jan. 1834. MHA, Lennox and Addington, 1836–41. Conservative.

See DCB 7.

CASEY, Samuel, *b* 14 Aug. 1788, Adolphustown Twp, UC. Son of Willet Casey (*q.v.*); *m* Cynthia Sharp[e] (*dau* Guisbert Sharp, lt., Loyal [Jessup's] Rangers). Farmer. Granted 700 acres. Lived in Adolphustown Twp. Sgt., troop of dragoons, 1st Regt., Lennox Militia, 1812–14; lt., 22 Jan. 1823; capt., cavalry troop, 13 Mar. 1834. JP, Midland Dist., 12 Sept. 1829. MHA, Lennox and Addington, 1820–4.

See PAC, RG 1, L 3, C 3/189; L 7, vol. 52; RG 9, IB 5, vols. 1, 6; RG 68 General Index to Commissions; T.W. Casey, "The Casey Scrapbooks," Lennox and Addington Historical Society, *Papers and Records* 4 (1912); OHS, *Papers and Records* 1:77.

CASEY, Willet, *b* 14 Feb. [1762]; *d* 7 Apr. 1848, Adolphustown Twp., UC. Son of Samuel Casey and Martha ——— ; *m* Jane Niles; four sons, including Samuel Casey (*q.v.*) and six daughters. Quaker. Farmer. Granted 300 acres. Lived in Adolphustown Twp. [1790]–1848. MHA, Lennox and Addington, 1810–12, 1816–20.

See PAC, RG 1, L 3, vol. 87C[a], part 1/12; C Misc, 1788–95, 89; MG 9, D 8, vol. 18, pp. 11936, 11975–7, 13934–8; T.W. Casey, "The Casey Scrapbooks," Lennox and Addington Historical Society, *Papers and Records* 4 (1912).

CAWTHRA, John, *b* 1789, England; *d* 1851, Newmarket, CW. Son of Joseph Cawthra and Mary Turnpenny. Married Ann ———; three sons, one daughter. Merchant, distiller. Granted 100 acres. Lived in Newmarket [1806]–51. Pvt., 3d Regt., York Militia, 1812–14; at Detroit, 1812. MHA, Simcoe, 1828–30. Reformer.

See PAC, RG 1, L 7, vol. 52; RG 8, C 1202, p. 2; UC, House of Assembly, *Journal* (1825) Appendix 10; *The Commercial and Biographical Record of York County* (Toronto 1907), 32.

CHESSER, John *b*, LC. Son of John Chesser; grandson of John Chesser, UE. Innkeeper. Lived in Caledonia Twp. and in L'Orignal. Lt., 7th Bttn., Incorporated Militia (LC), 1812–13; lt., 1st Regt., Prescott Militia, 9 Mar. 1824; capt., 26 Sept. 1826; capt., 2d Regt., Prescott Militia, 23 Apr. 1839. [Coroner, Ottawa Dist., 30 July 1824.] MHA, Prescott, 1835–6. [Reformer.]

See PAC, RG 8, C 1694, 37; RG 9, IB 5, vols. 1, 2, 6; RG 68, General Index to Commissions; MG 30, D 62, vol. 7; Upper Canada, House of Assembly, *Journals* (1825) Appendix 10.

CHISHOLM, Alexander, *b*, Scotland; *d* 19 Oct. 1854, Alexandria, CW. Son of Duncan Chisholm and Janet Chisholm; *m* Janet Macdonell; "numerous" children. Roman Catholic. Farmer, Granted [500] acres. Lived in (1) Lochiel Twp. (2) Alexandria. Lt., Royal African Corps (HP 1817); lt. col., 3d Regt., Glengarry Militia, 18 June 1822; col., 27 June 1825. JP, Eastern Dist., 18 Apr. 1825. MHA, Glengarry, 1834–41. Reformer.

See PAC, RG 1, L 3, vol. 101, C 12/19; RG 9, IB 5, vols. 1, 2, 6; RG 68, General Index to Commissions; UC, House of Assembly *Journals* (1835) Appendix;

and (1838); W.L. Scott, "Glengarry's Representatives in the Legislative Assembly of Upper Canada" (part 2 1812–41) CCHA *Report* (1939–40): 42.

CHISHOLM, William, *b* 15 Oct. 1788, NS; *d* 4 May 1842, Oakville, CW. Son of George Chisholm (UE) and Barbara McKenzie; *m* Rebecca Silverthorn. Attended common school in Flamborough East Twp. Anglican. Farmer, merchant, shipbuilder, lumberman, public servant. Granted 500 acres. Lived in (1) Flamborough East (2) Nelson Twp. [1816–27], (3) Oakville 1827–42. Ens., 2d Regt. York Militia, 8 May 1811; lt., flank company, 25 Oct. 1812; at Detroit, Queenston Heights, Lundy's Lane; lt., 2d Regt., Gore Militia, 19 June 1824; lt. col., 4th Regt., Gore Militia, 12 Aug. 1824; col., 2d Regt., Gore Militia, 3 May 1830; commanded the left wing of the loyalist force, Toronto, 7 Dec. 1837. JP, Gore Dist., 14 July 1829; collector of customs, Oakville, 10 Aug. 1834. MHA, Halton, 1820–4, 1830–4, 1836–41. Conservative.

See PAC, RG 1, L 3, vol. 97, C 9/79; vol. 108, C 15/109; vol. 120, C 20/174; L 7, vol. 52; RG 8, C 691, p. 18; C 1203½, p. 68; RG 9, IB 5, vols. 1, 3, 6; UC, House of Assembly, *Journals* (1825) Appendix 10; (1826) Appendix; (1828) Appendix; (1836) Appendix; A.C. Casselman, ed., *Richardson's War of 1812* (Toronto 1902), 56, 198, 123; L.H. Irving, *Officers of the British Forces in Canada During the War of 1812–15* (Welland 1908), 65–6.

CLARK, John, *b* 178[3 or 6?], Kingston, UC; *d* 12 July 1862, Grantham Twp., CW. Son of James Clark (8th [Regular] Regt., Commissariat Dept.; sherriff, Niagara Dist. 1800–3) and Jemima Mason; *m* Sarah Adams; six sons, four daughters. Educated by Rev. John Strachan [Kingston], at the garrison school, Niagara, and at Richard Cockerell's school, Niagara. [Presbyterian.] Merchant, farmer, Indian trader, manufacturer, land speculator, public servant. Granted 200 acres. Lived in Louth Twp. Adj., flank companies, 1st and 4th Regts., Lincoln Militia; capt. and asst. adj. gen. of militia, 25 Jan. 1813; lt. col., 1st Regt., Lincoln Militia, 5 Apr. 1834; lt. col., Frontier Light Infantry, 13 Jan. 1838. Collector of customs, Port Dalhousie, 1835–52. MHA, Lincoln (1st riding) 1820–8, 1830–4. Gourlayite, 1818; Conservative.

See PAC, RG 1, L 3, vol. 88, C^b/97; RG 9, IB 5, vol. 8; *Journal of Education For Upper Canada* (1862); L.H. Irving, *Officers of the British Forces in Canada During the War of 1812–15* (Welland 1908), 72, 74; Niagara Historical Society, *Publications*, no. 19:50; Grimsby Historical Society, *Annals of the Forty*, no. 4 (1953).

CLARK, Matthew, *b* 3 Oct. 1771, Duchess County, NY (13 Cols); *d* 8 June 1849, Ernesttown, CW. Son of Robert Clark (pvt., Loyal [Jessup's] Rangers) and Isobel Ketchum; *m* Ann (or Anna) McCoy (or McKay); twelve sons.

Farmer. Granted 1,200 acres. Lived in Ernesttown Twp. Capt., Addington Militia by 1807; capt., 1st Regt., Addington Militia, 1812–13; lt col., 1817. JP Midland Dist., 15 May 1814. MHA, Lennox and Addington, 1822–3.

See PAC, RG 1, L 3, vol. 106, C 11/106; vol. 126, C Misc., 1/69; vol. 18, C 19/136; L 7, vol. 52; RG 8, C 167, p. 12, C 1203½, p. 17; RG 68, General Index to Commissions; L.H. Irving, *Officers of the British Forces in Canada During the War of 1812–15* (Welland 1908), 53–5; D.A. McKenzie, *Death Notices in the Christian Guardian* (Lambertville, NJ 1982), 64–5.

CLENCH, Ralph or Ralfe, *b* [1762] "in America"; *d* 19 Jan. 1828; *m* Elizabeth Johnson (*dau* Lt. Brant Johnson, Indian Dept., UE); six sons, six daughters. Presbyterian. Auctioneer, farmer, public servant. Granted 2,800 acres. Lived at Niagara. Ens., 8th (Regular) Regt., [1776]; lt., Butler's Rangers, 17 July 1782 (HP, 1784); capt. and adj., Lincoln Militia, 28 July 1794; lt. col., 2d Regt., Lincoln Militia, 1803; col., 1st Regt., Lincoln Militia, 1811; asst. quartermaster general of militia, 13 Mar. 1813. Clerk of the Peace, Niagara Dist., May 1790; clerk, Court of Common Pleas, Niagara Dist., 17 June 1790; registrar, Surrogate Court, Home Dist., 13 Apr. 1798; clerk, Niagara Dist. Court, 1 Jan. 1800; judge, Niagara Dist. Court, 15 Nov. 1815. MHA, Lincoln (2d, 3d and 4th ridings) 1800–8; Lincoln (2d riding) 1812–20.

See DCB 6.

COLEMAN, Thomas; *m* Sarah Ann Everitt (*dau* John Everitt, UE, capt., Associated Loyalists). Anglican. Miller. Granted [800] acres plus a small gore of land in Belleville. Lived in (1) Thurlow Twp. (2) Belleville. Raised his own troop (Capt. Coleman's Light Dragoons) 29 April 1813, disbanded 1816; col., 1st Regt., Hastings Militia, 1 Sept. 1830. MHA, Hastings, 1824–8.

See PAC, RG 1, L 3, vol. 98, C 10/175, vol. 105, C 13/172; RG 8, C 687, p. 187; C 679, p. 315; C 703, p. 81; C 704, p. 12; C 1170, p. 189; RG 9, IB 5, vol. 5; L.H. *Irving, Officers of the British Forces in Canada During the War of 1812–15* (Welland 1908), 112; W.D. Reid, *The Loyalists of Ontario* (Lambertville, NJ 1973), 103.

COOK, John, *b* 28 Nov. 1791, Williamsburgh Twp., UC; *d* 8 Nov. 1877. Son of George Cook, UE; *m* Catherine ———. Lutheran. Farmer, merchant, miller, lumberman. Granted 300 acres; bought or inherited at least 350 acres. Lived in Williamsburg Twp. Cpl., 1st Regt., Dundas Militia, 1812–14; capt., 1 May 1837; capt., 3d Regt., Dundas Militia, 9 May 1839. JP, Eastern Dist., 12 May 1835. MHA, Dundas, 1830–41. Reformer.

See PAC, RG 1, vol. 117, C 19/6; vol. 138, C 5/117; L 7, vol. 52; RG 9, IB 5, vols. 5, 6; RG 19, E 5a, vol. 3746, no. 430; vol. 3754, no. 1283; RG 68, General Index to Commissions; UC, House of Assembly, *Journals*, (1832–3) Appendix. J.G. Harkness, *A History of Stormont, Dundas and Glengarry* (Ottawa 1946), 160; J.S. Carter, *The Story of Dundas* (Iroquois 1905), 215.

CORNWALL, John, *b*, Danbury, Conn. (13 Cols). Son of [John] Cornwall; *m* Mary Benedict; [one daughter and three sons], including Joshua (*q.v.*) and Mary (*m* William McCormick, *q.v.*). Farmer. Granted 1,850 acres. Lived in Colchester Twp. Pvt., Butler's Rangers, 1777–8. JP, Western Dist., 1797. MHA, Suffolk and Essex, 1797–1800.

See PAC, RG 1, L 3, vol. 127, C Misc. 1788–94, 257; vol. 99, C 3/97; vol. 93, C 5/63; RG 19, E 5a, vol. 3747, no. 492; F.C. Hamil, *The Valley of the Lower Thames* (Toronto 1951), 342, 347.

CORNWALL, Joshua, *b*, BNA; *d* 16 Mar. 1826, Raleigh Twp., UC. Son of John Cornwall (*q.v.*) and Mary Benedict. Farmer, miller. Granted 200 acres. Lived at (1) Detroit (2) Camden Twp. MHA, Kent 1816–20.

See PAC, RG 1, L 3, vol. 127; C Misc./262; RG 19, E 5a, vol. 3749, no. 698; F.C. Hamil, *The Valley of the Lower Thames* (Toronto 1951), 60, 222, 338, 342, 347.

CORNWALL, Nathan, *b*, UC, *d* 21 Jan. 1849, Chatham, CW. Anglican. Miller. Lived in Camden Twp. Commanded a company of militia volunteers in Camden and Howard Twps., Dec. 1838. JP Western Dist., 30 Mar. 1837. MHA, Kent, 1834–41. Conservative.

See PAC, RG 1, L 3, vol. 118, C 19/126; RG 68, General Index to Commissions; *Upper Canada Herald*, 9 Aug. 1836; F.C. Hamil, *The Valley of the Lower Thames* (Toronto 1951), 237.

COTTER, James, *b* 1772, NY (13 Cols), *d* 18 Jan. 1849, Sophiasburg Twp. UC. Son of James Cotter, UE; *m* Magdalene Hoffman; seven children. Farmer, public servant. Granted 600 acres. Lived in (1) Adolphustown Twp. [1794–1817] (2) Sophiasburgh Twp. Lt., Prince Edward Militia by 1807; capt. 1st Regt., Prince Edward Militia, 4 June 1811; on duty at Kingston, June–Dec. 1813; maj., 5 Nov. 1827; lt. col., 26 Jan. 1830; col., 3d Regt., Prince Edward Militia, 2 July 1833. JP, Midland Dist., 16 Mar. 1808; Prince Edward Dist., 15 Mar. 1834; judge, Prince Edward Dist. Court, 29 Sept. 1837. MHA, Prince Edward, 1816–20.

See PAC, RG 1, L 3, vol. 99, C 11/138; vol. 101, C 12/21; vol. 127, C Misc./ 274, 275; RG 9, IB 5, vols. 1, 3, 4; RG 68, General Index to Commissions; W.D. Reid, *Death Notices of Ontario* (Lambertville, NJ 1980), 252; B.M. Hudson, *Pride of Place: A Story of the Settlement of Prince Edward County* (Belleville 1982), 76.

COWAN, David, *d* 24 Sept. 1808, Fort Erie, UC. One son, one daughter.

Farmer, ferry operator, naval officer. Granted 2,007 acres; bought two town lots in Kingston. Lived at (1) Fort Erie (2) Amherstburgh. Served in the Royal Navy for four years during the American Revolution (HP 1786) and for seventeen years in the Provincial Marine, UC. MHA, Essex, 1804–8.

See PAC, RG 1, L 3, vol. 91, C 3/127, 204; vol. 93, C 5/6; vol. 203, G 1/45; RG 8, C 511, p. 159; C 728, pp. 23, 31, 33; RG 19, E 5a, vol. 3756, no. 1690.

CROOKS, James, *b* 15 Apr. 1778, Kilmarnock, Scotland; *d* 2 Mar. 1860, Flamborough West Twp., CW. Son of William Crooks and Margaret Ramsay; brother of William Crooks (*q.v.*); *m* Jane Cummings (*dau* Thomas Cummings, UE); eight sons, including Hon. Adam, five daughters. Presbyterian (Church of Scotland). Merchant, shipowner, paper manufacturer, miller, distiller, public servant. Granted 2,370 acres; bought at least 40,000 acres. Lived in (1) Niagara (2) Flamborough West Twp. (3) Hamilton. Ens., 1st Regt., Lincoln Militia, 3 Sept. 1794; lt., 24 June 1797; capt., 13 May 1807; capt., flank company at Queenston Heights; POW 1813; col., 2 Apr. 1822. JP, Niagara Dist., 17 May 1814; member of the Legislative Council of UC, 16 Mar. 1831. MHA, Halton, 1820–4, 1830–1. Conservative.

See DCB 8.

CROOKS, William, *b* 6 Aug. 1776, Kilmarnock, Scotland, *d* 31 Dec. 1836, Niagara. Son of William Crooks and Margaret Ramsay; brother of James Crooks (*q.v.*); *m* Mary Butler (*dau* John Butler, UE, col., Butler's Rangers); eight sons, four daughters. Anglican. Miller, merchant, shipowner, distiller. Granted 2,000 acres, Lived at (1) Niagara, [1794–1808] (2) Grimsby. Capt., 4th Regt., Lincoln Militia, 25 June 1802; capt., flank company, 1812–14. JP, Niagara Dist., 11 Dec. 1800; Gore Dist., 2 Apr. 1833. MHA, Lincoln (2d riding), 1830–4. Conservative.

See PAC, RG 1, L 3, vol. 89, C 1/88, C 2/20; vol. 91, C 3/95; L 7, vol. 52; RG 8, C 1203½, p. 3; c 1701, p. 153; RG 9, IB 5, vol. 1; RG 68, General Index to Commissions; UC, House of Assembly, *Journals* (1825) Appendix 10; Grimsby Historical Society, *Annals of the Forty*, no. 4 (1953); Niagara Historical Society, *Publications*, no. 19; L.H. Irving, *Officers of the British Forces in Canada During the War of 1812–15* (Welland 1908), 80.

CRYSLER, John, *b* [1768], 13 Cols; *d* 18 Jan. 1852, Crysler, CW. Son of John Crysler (Johannes Krausler) and Dorothy Meyers; *m* Nancy Loucks (*dau* Richard Loucks, UE); eight sons, seven daughters. Anglican. Farmer, merchant, miller, public servant, lumberman. Granted [1,000] acres; bought 60,200 acres in Loyalist rights. Lived in (1) Matilda Twp. (Crysler's Farm) (2) Finch Twp. Drummer boy, Butler's Rangers 1783; lt., Dundas Militia by 1803; capt., bttn, company, 1st Regt., Dundas Militia, 28 Jan. 1813; maj., 11 Aug. 1828; col., 29 Apr. 1837. JP, Eastern Dist., 11 Dec. 1804; collector of customs, Cornwall, Jan. 1817. MHA, Dundas, 1804–8, 1812–20, 1824–8.

See PAC, RG 1, L 3, vol. 127, C Misc., 1788–94, 321; L 7, vol. 52; RG 8, C 1202, p. 2; RG 9, IB 5, vols. 1, 4, 5, 6; RG 19, E 5a, vol. 3754, no.1385; MG 21, B 105, p. 39; B 105[a]; B 168, p. 92; MG 25, no. 199; OA, *Report* (Toronto 1904), 48; L.H. Irving, *Officers of the British Forces in Canada During the War of 1812–15* (Welland 1908), 46–7; L.F. Gates, *Land Policies of Upper Canada* (Toronto 1968), 333.

CUMMING, John, *b* [1764], Scotland; *d* 28 Feb. 1829, Kingston, UC. [Anglican.] Merchant, miller, public servant. Granted 1,200 acres plus three town and water lots in Kingston. Lived in Kingston. Capt., Frontenac Militia by 1811; col., 2d Regt., Frontenac Militia, 21 Aug. 1821. JP, Midland Dist., 1 Jan. 1800; inspector of licences, Midland Dist., 31 Mar. 1803. MHA, Kingston, 1824–8.

See PAC, RG 1, L 3, vol. 89, C 1/5; vol. 91, C 3/193; vol. 92, C 4/98; vol. 94, C 6/18, 28; vol. 96, C 8/99; vol. 271A, K 13/142; RG 9, IB 5, vol. 1; RG 68, General Index to Commissions; *Colonial Advocate*, 12 Mar. 1829; A.H. Young, ed., *The Parish Register of Kingston* (Kingston 1921), 57–8.

DALTON, Thomas, *b* 29 Apr. 1792, Birmingham, England; *d* 26 Oct. 1840, Toronto; *m* Sophia Simms; three sons, four daughters. Anglican. Brewer, journalist. Lived in (1) Kingston 1814–32 (2) Toronto 1832–40. Lt., 1st Regt., Frontenac Militia, 23 Aug. 1821; capt. (on reserve list) 30 May 1833. MHA, Frontenac, 1828–30. Reformer (to 1832).

See DCB 7.

DETLOR, George Hill, *b* 1794, UC. Son of John Detlor, UE, and Jerusha Simons (*dau* Titus Simons, UE); *m* Maria Roblin. Attended the Home Dist. School under Rev. John Strachan. Methodist. Merchant. Granted [200] acres plus a town lot in Kingston and located 20,400 acres in Loyalist rights. Lived at (1) Kingston (2) Fredericksburg Twp. (3) Napanee (4) Brighton. Ens., 2d Regt., York Militia, 26 Oct. 1812; lt., 1st Regt., Lennox Militia, 20 June 1823; capt., 1 May 1826. JP, Midland Dist., 13 Dec. 1834; coroner, Midland Dist., 16 Mar. 1835. MHA, Lennox and Addington, 1836–41. Conservative.

See PAC, RG 1, L 3, vol. 154, D 11/38; vol. 156, D 13/32; vol. 165, D 1/46; RG 9, IB 5, vols. 1, 6; RG 68, General Index to Commissions; OA, Strachan Papers, M 535; *Upper Canada Herald*, 9 Aug. 1836; W. Canniff, *The Settlement of Upper Canada* (Toronto 1869), 647; W.D. Reid, *The Loyalists of Ontario* (Lambertville, NJ 1973), 89; L.F. Gates, *Land Policies of Upper Canada* (Toronto 1968), 333.

DICKSON, Robert, *b* 1796, Niagara; *d* 28 Nov. 1846, Livorno. Italy. Son of Hon. William Dickson (member of the Legislative Council of UC) and

Charlotte Adlem; nephew of Thomas Dickson (*q.v.*); *m* (1) Margaret McKay (2) Jane Jones. Educated in Edinburgh. Lawyer. Lived at Niagara. Lt., 1st Regt., Lincoln Militia, 3 Feb. 1825; capt., 4 Sept. 1829. MHA, Niagara (town), 1828–30. [Conservative.]

See PAC, RG 9, IB 5, vols. 3, 4; "Weddings at Niagara," OHS, *Papers and Records* 3 (1901): 62; Niagara Historical Society, *Publications*, no. 19; Waterloo Historical Society, *Report*, no. 4.

DICKSON, Thomas, *b* 1775, Dumfries, Scotland; *d* 22 Jan. 1825, Queenston, UC. Son of John Dickson and Helen Wright; brother of Hon. William Dickson; uncle of Robert Dickson (*q.v.*); *m* (1) Eliza —— (2) Archange Grant (*dau* Alexander Grant, member of the Executive and Legislative Councils of UC, administrator of the Province of UC, 1805–6). Merchant, forwarder, ferry operator, public servant. Granted 1,200 acres plus town lots in Niagara and Fort Erie. Lived at (1) Fort Erie (2) Queenston. Lt. col., 2d Regt., Lincoln Militia, 5 Jan. 1814; wounded at Chippawa, 5 July 1814. JP, Niagara Dist., 30 June 1800; collector of customs, Queenston, Apr. 1803. MHA, Lincoln (3d riding) 1812–16.

See DCB 6.

DORLAND, Phillip, *b* [1756, Duchess Co., NY (13 Cols)]. Son of Samuel Dorland; brother of Thomas Dorland (*q.v.*); three sons, three daughters. Quaker. Farmer. Granted 2,000 acres. Lived in Adolphustown Twp. Lt. in Col. Cuyler's Loyalist Refugees during the American Revolution. JP, Midland Dist., 1813. MHA, Prince Edward and Adolphustown, 1792; unseated for refusing to take the oath.

See PAC, RG 1, L 3, vol. 150, D 3/34; RG 8, C 691, p. 203; MG 21, B 168, p. 68; W.D. Reid, *Loyalists of Ontario* (Lambertville, NJ 1973), 93.

DORLAND, Thomas, *b* [1760, Duchess Co., NY (13 Cols)]; *d* 15 Mar. 1832, Adolphustown Twp., UC. Son of Samuel Dorland; brother of Phillip Dorland (*q.v.*); two sons, one daughter. Anglican. Farmer, ferry operator. Granted 2,000 acres. Lived in Adolphustown Twp. Sgt., Associated Loyalists during the American Revolution; capt., 1st Regt., Lennox Militia, 3 Jan. 1801; on duty at Kingston, 1813–14; maj., 18 June 1823; lt. col., 22 Aug. 1825; col., 15 Apr. 1838. JP, Midland Dist., 1 Jan. 1800. MHA, Lennox and Addington, 1804–12.

See DCB 6.

DRAPER, William Henry, *b* 11 Mar. 1801 near London, England; *d* 3 Nov. 1877, Yorkville (Toronto). Son of Rev. Henry Draper; *m* Mary White. Educated privately and studied law with George S. Boulton (*q.v.*). Anglican. Lawyer, public servant. Lived in (1) Hamilton Twp. (2) Port Hope (3) Toronto, 1829–77. Capt. and adj., 1st Regt., Durham Militia, 30 Jan. 1823; maj., 4 Mar. 1827; lt. col., 30 May 1835; col., 2d Regt., North York Militia, 22 Jan. 1838. Reporter, Court of King's Bench, 1829; member of the Executive Council of UC, 27 Dec. 1836; solicitor general, 23 Mar. 1837; attorney general, 14 Feb. 1840. MHA., Toronto, 1836–41. Conservative.

See DCB 10.

DUNCOMBE, Charles, *b* 28 July 1792, Stratford, Conn. USA; *d* 1 Oct. 1867, Hicksville, Calif. Son of Thomas Duncombe and Rhoda Tyrell; brother of David Duncombe (*q.v.*); *m* (1) Nancy Haines (2) Lucy Millard; two sons, three daughters. Educated by his mother and studied medicine in New York City. Methodist. Physician, contractor. Bought "large holdings" of land. Lived in (1) Delaware Twp. 1819–22 (2) St. Thomas 1822–8 (3) Burford Twp. 1828–37. Surgeon, 2d Regt., Middlesex Militia, 19 Jan. 1824. Coroner, London Dist., 16 Mar. 1835. MHA, Oxford, 1830–8. Reformer.

See DCB 9.

DUNCOMBE, David, *b*, [NY], USA; *d* 1887, Waterford, Ont. Son of Thomas Duncombe and Rhoda Tyrell; brother of Charles Duncombe (*q.v.*) Studied medicine with his brother Charles and at Fairfield Academy, Herkimer, NY. Methodist. Physician. Lived in Townsend Twp. Coroner, Talbot Dist., 13 Apr. 1840. MHA, Norfolk, 1834–41. Reformer.

See PAC, RG 68, General Index to Commissions; *Upper Canada Herald*, 9 Aug. 1836; W. Canniff, *The Medical Profession in Upper Canada* (Toronto 1894), 350–1.

DUNLOP, Robert Graham, *b* [1791], Scotland; *d* 28 Feb. 1841, Goderich, CW. Son of Alexander Dunlop and Janet Graham; *m* Louisa McColl. Educated in Glasgow and Edinburgh. Presbyterian (Church of Scotland). Farmer, public servant. Granted [1,425] acres. Lived in Colborne Twp. 1833–41. Served in the Royal Navy for thirty years as lt. (1812) and commander (1822), (HP 1823); col., 3d Regt., Huron Militia, 13 Jan. 1838. JP, London Dist., 31 May 1833; registrar, Huron County, 30 May 1835. MHA, Huron, 1835–41. Conservative.

See DCB 7.

DURAND, James (senior), *b* 1775, Wales; *d* 22 Mar. 1833, Hamilton UC; *m* (1) ——— (2) Kezia Morrison; six sons, including James Durand, junior (*q.v.*), three daughters. Anglican. Farmer, merchant, miller, distiller, newspaper owner, public servant. Granted 1,800 acres; bought and sold land in Ancaster, Delaware, Barton, Townsend, Dorchester, and Toronto Gore twps. and in Brantford, London and Sarnia. Lived in (1) Barton Twp. 1805–13 (2) Belleville 1813–6 (3) [Hamilton] 1816–33. Capt., 5th Reg., Lincoln

Militia, 1 May 1812. Registrar, Halton and Wentworth cos., 10 May 1816. MHA, York West, 1815–16; Wentworth 1816–20.
See DHB 1.

DURAND, James (junior), *b* 1799, London, England; *d* 1872, Kingston, Ont. Son of James Durand (*q.v.*); *m* (1) Maria Rolph (*dau* John Rolph, *q.v.*) (2) ——— Cattrell. [Anglican.] Merchant. Lived at Dundas. Ens., 1st Regt., Gore Militia, 8 Apr. 1823. MHA, Halton, 1834–6. Reformer.
See PAC, RG 1, L 3, vol. 157, D 14/158; RG 9, IB 5, vol. 1; *Journal of Education in Ontario* (1872).

ELLIOTT, George, *b*, Ireland; *d* July 1844, Monaghan Twp., CW. Anglican. [Farmer.] Granted 200 acres. Lived in Monaghan Twp. Capt., 2d Regt., Durham Militia, 9 Jan. 1828; maj., Durham Volunteers, 8 Nov. 1838; maj., 2d Regt., Durham Militia, 13 July 1839. JP, Newcastle Dist., 2 June 1837. MHA, Durham, 1836–41. Conservative.
See PAC, RG 9, IB 5, vol. 6; RG 68, General Index to Commissions; W.D. Reid, *Death Notices of Ontario* (Lambertville, NJ 1980), 222.

ELLIOTT, Matthew, *b* [1739], Co. Donegal, Ireland; *d* 7 May 1814, Burlington, UC; *m* Sarah Donovan; four sons. Farmer, fur trader, public servant. Granted 3,000 acres; bought at least 1,000. Lived in Malden Twp. Capt., Indian Dept., 1778–83 (HP [1784]); lt. col., Essex Militia by 1807; col., 1st Regt., Essex Militia, 1812–14 (died on active service). JP, Hesse Dist., 24 July 1788; Western Dist., 15 July 1796. Assistant agent for western Indians, 1790; superintendent, Indian Dept. at Amherstburgh, 1796–9, 1808–13. MHA, Essex, 1800–12.
See DCB 5.

ELLIOTT, William, *b* 1775, England; *m* Sophia Bouchette; ten children. Lawyer, farmer. Granted 1,400 acres plus a town lot in Sandwich (Windsor). Lived at Sandwich, UC. Lt. and adj., Essex Militia by 1807; capt., 1st Regt., Essex Militia, 1812; capt., Indian Dept., 25 June 1813; col., 2d Regt., Essex Militia, 1 Apr. 1822. MHA, Essex, 1830–4. Conservative.
See PAC, RG 1, L 3, vol. 176, E 7/21, 23; vol. 177, E 11/44; RG 9, IB 5, vol. 6; L.H. Irving, *Officers of the British Forces in Canada During the War of 1812–15* (Welland 1908), 90, 95, 210; R. Horsmann, *Matthew Elliott, British Indian Agent* (Detroit 1964), 214, 218–9, 242.

EWING, Benjamin, *b* [1776], Mass. (13 Cols); five sons, two daughters. [Presbyterian.] Farmer, businessman. Granted 500 acres. Lived in Haldimand Twp. Quartermaster, 1st Regt., Northumberland Militia, 20 June 1810; lt., 3 July 1816; capt., 14 June 1826. Coroner, Newcastle Dist., 30

July 1824. MHA, Northumberland, 1825, 1828–30. [Conservative.]

See PAC, RG 1, L 3, vol. 104, E Leases 126; vol. 180, E 21/30; RG 9, IB 5, vols. 1, 3, 6; RG 68, General Index to Commissions; *Historical Atlas of Northumberland and Durham* (Toronto 1878), vii–viii.

FAIRFIELD, Benjamin, *b* [1772, Charlotte co., Vt. (13 Cols]; *d* 9 May 1842, Bath, CW. Son of William Fairfield, UE, and Abigail Baker; brother of William Fairfield (*q.v.*); *m* Abigail Hawley (*step-dau* Lt. Jeptha Hawley, UE). Presbyterian. Shipowner, merchant. Granted 200 acres. Lived in Ernesttown Twp. Lt., 1st Regt., Frontenac Militia, 25 Aug. 1821; capt., 20 Apr. 1826. JP, Midland Dist., 25 June 1818. MHA, Lennox and Addington, 1812–16.

See PAC, RG 1, L 3, vol. 271, K 11/45; RG 9, IB 5, vols. 1, 3, 5; RG 19, E 5a, vol. 3755, no. 517; RG 68, General Index to Commissions; T.W. Casey, "The Pioneers of Ernesttown," Lennox and Addington Historical Society, *Papers and Records* 14 (1972): 92; *DCB* 5.

FAIRFIELD, William, *b* [1770, Charlotte Co., Vt. (13 Cols)]; *d* 6 Feb. 1816, Ernesttown, UC. Son of William Fairfield, UE, and Abigail Baker; brother of Benjamin Fairfield (*q.v.*); *m* (1) Elizabeth Billings (2) Clarissa Fulton; seven children. Miller, shipbuilder, merchant. Granted 200 acres. Lived in Ernesttown Twp. JP, Midland Dist., 16 Mar. 1808. MHA, Lennox and Addington, 1799–1800.

See DCB 5.

FANNING, John, *b*, 13 Cols; *d* 19 Jan. 1813; *m* Sarah Willson (*dau* Benjamin Wilson, UE; sister of Crowell Wilson, *q.v.*) Innkeeper, miller, stagecoach operator, farmer. Granted 600 acres. Lived at Niagara and Chippawa. MHA, Lincoln (4th riding), 1812–13.

See PAC, RG 1, L 3, vol. 185, F 1/11; RG 5, A 1, p. 7112; AO, W.G. Rieve Collection, Street Papers; P. Wilson, "Irish John Willson and Family, Loyalists," OHS, *Papers and Records* 21 (1936): 228–42; Welland County Historical Society, *Papers and Records*, 5:49–50.

FERGUSON, John, *b* 1756; *d* 1830; *m* Helena Magdalene Johnson (*dau* Sir William Johnson and Molly Brant). Anglican. Farmer, merchant, public servant. Granted 3,200 acres plus town lots in Niagara and Kingston. Lived in (1) Sidney Twp. (2) Kingston. Deputy barrack master at Oswegatchie, 1772; commissary, 1778; barrackmaster and commissary, Fort Ontario, 1782; commissary, Kingston, [1783] (HP, 1787); col., 1st Regt., Hastings Militia, 1 Nov. 1804; capt., Indian Dept., 1 Sept. 1812. JP, Montreal Dist., 22 May 1799; Bathurst Dist., 18 Apr. 1825, lt., Hastings County, 23 Nov. 1798; judge, Midland Dist. Court, 3 Nov. 1798. MHA, Frontenac, 1800–4.

See PAC, RG 1, L 3, vol. 186, F 3/5, 29; vol. 195a, F Misc./21; vol. 268, JK 4/

8; RG 8, C 122, pp. 340–60; C 258, pp. 233–7; RG 9, IB 5, vol. 1; RG 68, General Index to Commissions; W. Canniff, *The Settlement of Upper Canada* (Toronto 1889), 94, 486; R.A. Preston, ed., *Kingston Before the War of 1812* (Toronto 1959), 241.

FERRIE, Colin Campbell, *b* May 1808, Glasgow, Scotland; *d* 9 Nov. 1856, Hamilton. Son of Hon. Adam Ferrie and Rachel Campbell; *m* Catherine Beasely (*dau* Richard Beasely, *q.v.*); two sons. Presbyterian (Church of Scotland). Merchant, banker. Lived in Hamilton. JP, Gore Dist., 2 Apr. 1833. MHA, Hamilton, 1836–41. Conservative.
See DCB 8.

FOTHERGILL, Charles, *b* 23 May [1782], Yorkshire, England; *d* 22 May 1840, Toronto; *m* Eliza Richardson. Quaker. Merchant, journalist, miller, survey contractor, farmer, public servant. Granted 1,200 acres; bought [600] acres. Lived at (1) York (Toronto) (2) Pickering Twp. JP Newcastle Dist., 15 June 1818; Home Dist., 27 Mar. 1833; king's printer, 1 Jan. 1822–26. MHA, Durham, 1825–30 [Reformer.]
See DCB 7.

FRASER, Alexander, *b* 18 Jan. 1786, near Fort Augustus, Scotland; *d* 12 Nov. 1853 near Williamstown, CW; *m* (1) Catharine Grant (2) Anne Macdonell (*dau* Archibald Macdonell, capt., King's Royal Regt. of NY); two sons, four daughters. Roman Catholic. Farmer, soldier, public servant. Granted 500 acres; bought at least 2,200 acres. Lived in Charlottenburgh Twp. Quartermaster, Canadian Fencible Regt. 1812–14 (HP 1816); col., 1st Regt., Glengarry Militia, 1 Apr. 1822; on active service in Lower Canada, Jan.–Mar., Nov. 1838). JP, Eastern Dist., 8 Jan. 1820; registrar, Glengarry County, Jan. 1837; member of the Legislative Council of UC, 3 Dec. 1839. MHA, Glengarry, 1828–34. Conservative.
See DCB 8.

FRASER, Donald. Farmer. Granted 500 acres. Lived at Perth. Served in the British Army for 30 years; lt., 1st (Royal Scots) Regt. of Foot, 3 July 1813; wounded at Lundy's Lane, 1814 (HP); maj., 2d Regt., Lanark Militia, 13 June 1822; lt. col., 10 Dec. 1829. JP, Johnstown Dist., 27 Mar. 1821; Bathurst Dist., 7 Feb. 1826. MHA, Lanark, 1832. [Conservative.]
See PAC, RG 1, L 3, vol. 192, F 16/54; RG 8, C 684, p. 233; C 694, p. 50; C 1171, p. 69; RG 9, IB 5, vols. 2, 6; RG 68, General Index to Commissions.

FRASER, Isaac, *b* 19 Sept. 1779, Albany Co., NY (13 Cols); *d* 2 July 1858. Son of Daniel Fraser, UE, and Sarah Conklin; *m* Nancy Storing (or Stawring); nine children. Presbyterian. Farmer, miller, public servant. Granted 1,000 acres. Lived in Ernesttown Twp. Cornet, Addington Militia, by 1807; lt., light dragoons, 1st Regt., Addington Militia, 1812–14; lt. col., 1 Apr. 1822; col., 6 July 1832. JP, Midland Dist., 25 June 1818; registrar, Surrogate Court, Midland Dist.; member of the Legislative Council of UC, 16 July 1839. MHA, Lennox and Addington, 1816–20.

See PAC, RG 1, L 3, vol. 186a, F 5/12; vol. 189a, F 11/79; L 7, vol. 52; RG 9, IB 5, vols. 5, 6; RG 68, General Index to Commissions; MG 9, D 8, Lennox and Addington Historical Society Collection, T.W. Casey papers, p. 11851; L.H. Irving, *Officers of the British Forces in Canada During the War of 1812–15* (Welland 1908), 56.

FRASER, Richard Duncan, *b* 1782, BNA; *d* 1 Apr. 1857, Edwardsburg Twp. CW. Son of Hon. Thomas Fraser (*q.v.*) and Mary McBean; *m* Mary Macdonell (*dau* Allan Macdonell [Leek] UE); two sons, four daughters. Educated by Rev. John Strachan. Fur trader, merchant, farmer, public servant. Granted 100 acres and bought [800] acres. Lived in Edwardsburg Twp. Lt., 2d Regt., Grenville Militia, 17 Feb. 1812; capt., light dragoons, 2d Regt., Grenville Militia, 1812–15; assistant quartermaster general of militia, 25 Feb. 1815; maj., 1st Regt., Dundas Militia, 21 Jan. 1822; lt. col., 2d Regt., Grenville Militia, 1827; col., 17 Apr. 1830; commanded militia at Battle of the Windmill, Prescott, Nov. 1838. JP, Johnstown Dist., 25 Mar. 1816; collector of customs, Brockville, 31 Dec. 1831. MHA, Grenville, 1830–4. Conservative.
See DCB 8.

FRASER, Thomas, *b* 1749, Stratherrick, Scotland; *d* 13 Oct. 1821, Matilda Twp., UC. Son of William and Grace Fraser; *m* (1) Mary McBean (2) Mary Macdonell (daughter of John Macdonell [Leek], UE) (3) Cornelia (Munro) Paterson (*dau* [Hon.] John Munro, UE); five sons, including Richard Duncan Fraser (*q.v.*), and four daughters. Presbyterian. Farmer, public servant. Granted at least 6,350 acres plus town lots in York and Cornwall and four town lots in Johnstown; bought "over 20,000" acres. Lived in (1) Edwardsburg Twp. 1784–[1804] (2) Matilda Twp. 1804–21. Capt., Loyal (Jessup's) Rangers, serving for 6½ years (HP 1783); lt. col., Grenville Militia by 1807; lt. col., 1st Regt., Dundas Militia, 15 Feb. 1812; commanded militia at Ogdensburg, 1813. JP, Eastern Dist., 1793; Johnstown Dist., 30 June 1800; sheriff, Johnstown Dist., 1 Jan. 1800; commissioner to arrest suspected traitors, 24 Mar. 1814. MHA, Dundas, 1797–1800; Glengarry, 1808–12.
See DCB 6.

FRENCH, Jeremiah, *b* 8 May 1743, Vt. (13 Cols); *d* 5 Dec. 1820, Cornwall, UC. Son of Jeremiah French; *m* Elizabeth Wheeler; three sons, five daughters. Farmer. Granted 2,000 acres plus a town lot in Cornwall. Lived in Cornwall. Capt., Peter's Corps of Rangers, 1777; lt., King's Royal Regt. of

NY, 1781 (HP 1784). JP, Lunenburg Dist., 24 July 1788; Eastern Dist., 1 July 1796. MHA, Stormont, 1792–6.

See PAC, RG 1, L 3, vol. 185, F 1/37, F 2/73; vol. 188, F 9/51, F 10/13; RG 5, A 1, vol. 5, p. 2192; RG 8,C 200 , PP. 85–8; RG 68, General Index to Commissions; J.H. Harkness, *A History of Stormont, Dundas and Glengarry* (Ottawa 1946), 69.

GAMBLE, John William, *b* 5 July 1799, York (Toronto), UC; *d* 12 Dec. 1873, Vaughan Twp., Ont. Son of John Gamble, UE, and Isabella Elizabeth Clarke; *m* (1) Mary Macaulay (2) Matilda Atkinson (3) Minerva Ann (Wenham) Niles; one son, six daughters. Anglican. Merchant, miller, distiller, manufacturer. Lived in (1) York (Toronto) 1815–23 (2) Etobicoke Twp. 1823–43. Lt., 1st Regt., E. York Militia, 19 Dec. 1821; capt., 1 Feb. 1826; lt. col. 27 Dec 1837; lt. col., 3d Regt. W. York Militia, 21 Nov. 1838. JP, Home Dist., 27 Mar. 1833. MHA York (1st riding) 1838–41. Conservative.

See DCB 10.

GAMBLE, Moses, *b* USA. Farmer. Granted 200 acres. Lived in Markham Twp. MHA, Halton, 1816–17; declared ineligible, 3 Mar. 1817.

See PAC, RG 1, L 3, vol. 204, G 7/15; vol. 220a, G Leases/33; UC, House of Assembly, *Journals*, 25 Feb., 3 Mar. 1817; J. Garner, *The Franchise and Politics in British North America* (Toronto 1969), 87.

GATES, Walter Freeman, *d* 5 Feb. 1828, Johnstown, UC. Educated by Rev. John Strachan. Presbyterian. Merchant, "gentleman." Granted two town lots in Johnstown. Lived at Johnstown. Capt., cavalry troop, 1st Regt., Grenville Militia, 21 Jan. 1822. JP, Johnstown Dist., 19 Mar. 1818. MHA, Grenville, 1820–4.

See PAC, RG 1, L 3, vol. 205, G 10/39; RG 9, IB 5, vols. 1, 3; RG 68, General Index to Commissions; *Colonial Advocate*, 21 Feb. 1828.

GIBSON, David, *b* 9 Mar. 1804, Glamis, Forfarshire, Scotland; *d* 25 Jan. 1864, Quebec City; *m* Eliza Milne; four sons, three daughters. Learned surveying in Scotland. Presbyterian. Farmer, surveyor, miller. Lived in North York Twp. (Willowdale). MHA, York (1st riding) 1834–7; expelled 15 Jan. 1837 as a rebel. Reformer.

See DCB 9.

GILCHRIST, John, *b* 5 Feb. 1792, Bedford, NH, USA; *d* 15 Sept. 1859, Port Hope, CW. Son of Samuel Gilchrist and Sarah Aitken; *m* Lucretia Gore (niece of Zaccheus Burnham, *q.v.*); nine children. Studied medicine at Yale and Dartmouth. Physician, farmer, merchant, miller. Lived (1) Hamilton Twp. [1817]–25 (2) Otonabee Twp. (Keene) 1825–31 (3) Cobourg 1831–4 (4)

Peterborough 1834–49. Surgeon, 1st Regt., Northumberland Militia, 1822. JP, Newcastle Dist., 9 Jan. 1835; coroner, Newcastle Dist., 3 Jan. 1833. MHA, Northumberland, 1834–6. Reformer.

See DCB 8.

GORDON, James, *b* 26 Aug. 1786, Inverness, Scotland; *d* 10 Apr. 1865, Toronto. Son of Rev. Alexander Gordon; *m* Arabella Gilkison Innes. Educated at Inverness Royal Academy. [Presbyterian]. Merchant, public servant. Granted 1,100 acres plus two water lots in Anderdon Twp. Bought [400] acres plus two town and water lots in Amherstburgh. Lived in Amherstburgh. Ens., Essex Militia by 1807; lt., 1st Regt., Essex Militia, 6 June 1809; militia paymaster, Western Dist., 1813; lt., Marine Dept. in charge of gunboats at Detroit and Frenchtown; lt. col., 1st Regt. Essex Militia, 1 Apr. 1822. JP Western Dist., 6 June 1822; member of the Legislative Council of UC, 8 Jan. 1829. MHA, Kent, 1820–8.

See PAC, RG 1, L 3, vol. 206, G 11/65; vol. 210, G 17/107; vol. 214, G 22/23; L 7, vol. 52; RG 8, C 678, p. 48; RG 9, IB 5, vol. 1; RG 68, General Index to Commissions; *Journal of Education for Upper Canada* (1865); L.H. Irving, *Officers of the British Forces in Canada During the War of 1812–15* (Welland 1908), 14, 33, 89.

GOUGH, Thomas Barnes, *b* 1760, Ireland; *d* Apr. 1815, York (Toronto). Educated in Bristol, England. Merchant. Granted 1,200 acres. Lived in York (Toronto) 1801–15. MHA, York East and Simcoe, 1808–12.

See PAC, RG 1, L 3, vol. 204a, G 8/34; York *Gazette*, 22 Apr. 1815; E.G. Firth, ed., *The Town of York, 1793–1815* (Toronto 1962), 178.

GOWAN, Ogle Robert, *b* 13 July 1803, Mt. Nebo, Co. Wexford, Ireland; *d* 21 Aug. 1876, Toronto. Son of John Hunter Gowan and Margaret Hogan; *m* (1) Frances Anne Turner (2) Alice Hitchcock; eleven children. Educated at home. Anglican. Farmer, journalist. Lived in Brockville 1829–52. Capt., 2d Regt., Leeds Militia, 12 Jan. 1838; lt. col. commanding a provisional battalion at the Battle of the Windmill, Prescott, Nov. 1838. MHA, Leeds, 1834–5, 1836–41. Conservative.

See DCB 10.

GRAY, Robert Isaac Dey, *b* [1772, NY (13 Cols)]; *d* 8 Oct. 1804 in the loss of the *Speedy* on Lake Ontario. Son of James Gray (maj., King's Royal Regt. of NY) and Elizabeth Low. Never married. Educated at Quebec and studied law in Cornwall. Lawyer, public servant. Granted 1,200 acres; bought at least 10,000 acres, mostly in Loyalist rights. Lived in (1) Cornwall 1784–97 (2) York (Toronto) 1797–1804. Registrar, Surrogate Court, Eastern Dist., 5 Sept. 1793; judge, Home Dist. Court, 7 June 1796, solicitor general, 21

Mar. 1797. MHA, Stormont, 1796–1800; Stormont and Russell, 1800–4.
See DCB 5.

HAGERMAN, Christopher Alexander, *b* 28 Mar. 1792, Adolphustown Twp, UC; *d* 14 May 1847, Toronto. Son of Nicholas Hagerman, UE, and Anne Fisher; brother of Daniel Hagerman (*q.v.*) *m* (1) Elizabeth Macaulay (sister of Sir James Buchanan, judge, Court of King's Bench of UC and Hon. John Simcoe Macaulay, member of the Legislative Council of UC) (2) Emily Merry (*dau* William Merry, deputy secretary at war, London) (3) Caroline Tysen; two daughters, one son. Educated at Adolphustown; studied law with his father. Anglican. Lawyer, public servant. Granted 2,400 acres plus a town lot in Kingston. Lived at Kingston and Toronto. Ens. 1st Regt., Lennox Militia, 24 Feb. 1812; on duty at Kingston, June–Dec., 1813, lt. col. and provincial aide-de-camp to Sir Gordon Drummond, 13 Dec. 1813; col., 2d Regt., Lennox Militia, 5 Apr. 1825. Collector of customs. Kingston, 1813; judge, Court of King's Bench of UC, 16 June 1828 (appointment not confirmed); solicitor general, 13 July 1829; attorney general, 23 Mar. 1837; judge, Court of King's Bench, 15 Feb. 1840. MHA, Kingston, 1820–4, 1830–41. Conservative.
See DCB 7.

HAGERMAN, Daniel, *b* 1794, [Adolphustown Twp.], UC, *d* 30 June 1821, Bath, UC. Son of Nicholas Hagerman, UE, and Anne Fisher; brother of Christopher Alexander Hagerman (*q.v.*). Educated in Adolphustown Twp. and studied law with his father. Lawyer, public servant. Granted 700 acres and a town lot in Kingston. Lived in Kingston and Fredericksburg Twp. Quartermaster, 1st Regt., Lennox Militia, 25 May 1813. Registrar, Surrogate Court, Midland Dist., 1814. MHA, Lennox and Addington, 1820–1.
See PAC, RG 1, L 3, vol. 227, H 11/9; vol. 228, H 11/57; vol. 287a, L 11/93; RG 5, B 7, vol. 3; Kingston *Chronicle*, 6 July 1821; L.H. Irving, *Officers of the British Forces in Canada During the War of 1812–15* (Welland 1908), 56.

HALL, George Benson, *d* 9 Jan. 1821, Amherstburgh, UC; *m* Angelica Fortier; at least one son. Anglican. Naval officer, [farmer]. Granted 1,200 acres plus a town lot in Chatham; bought three water lots in Amherstburgh. Joined the Royal Navy as a midshipman, 1798; mate, UC Provincial Marine, 1802; lt., 26 Apr. 1806; commanding snow *Camden*, 1808; commander, 25 Apr. 1812; senior naval officer on Lake Erie, 1813; superintendent, Amherstburgh dockyard, Sept. 1813; naval storekeeper, Montreal, Dec. 1813 (HP 1814); maj. 1st Regt., Essex Militia, 21 Sept. 1818. JP, Western Dist., 9 Nov. 1816. MHA, Essex, 1816–20.
See PAC, RG 1, L 3, vol. 15, A 23/13; vol. 226a, H 10/36; vol. 228 H 11/66; L 7, vol. 52; RG 8, C 78, p. 2; C 728, p. 31; C 729, pp. 1, 117, 121; C 730,

p. 125; C 1168, p. 136; C 1171, p. 149; C 1224, p. 166; C 1700, p. 294; RG 68, General Index to Commissions; Irving, *Officers of the British Forces in Canada During the War of 1812–15* (Welland 1908), 89, 204–6.

HAM, George, *b* [1797, Ernesttown Twp.], UC; *d* [7 Feb. 1834, Cobourg, CW]. Son of John Ham, UE; *m* Hester Hawley (*dau* Sheldon Hawley, UE and Elizabeth Densbaugh). Merchant. Granted 200 acres. Lived in [(1) Ernesttown twp., (2) South Fredericksburg twp. (3) Cobourg]. Sgt., later adj., 1st Regt., Addington Militia, 1812–14; lt. col., 1st Regt., Northumberland Militia, 21 Apr. 1838; on duty 1838. JP, Midland Dist., 3 Aug. 1821; Newcastle Dist., 9 Jan. 1835. MHA, Lennox and Addington, 1824.

See PAC, RG 1, L 3, vol. 228, H 11/68; L 7, vols. 10, 52; RG 9, IB 5, vols. 4, 5; RG 68, General Index to Commissions; UC, Canada, House of Assembly, *Journals* (1833–4) Appendix; L.H. Irving, *Officers of the British Forces in Canada During the War of 1812–15* (Welland 1908), 55.

HAMILTON, George, *b* [1788] Queenston, UC; *d* 20 Feb. 1836, Hamilton. Son of Hon. Robert Hamilton (member of the Legislative Council of UC) and Catharine (Askin) Robertson, brother of Robert Hamilton, junior (*q.v.*); *m* Maria Lavinia Jarvis (*dau* William Jarvis, provincial secretary of UC); three sons, five daughters. Educated in Edinburgh. [Presbyterian.] Farmer, developer, merchant, public servant. Granted 800 acres; bought 257 acres in Barton Twp., which later became Hamilton, 1,200 acres in Washingham Twp., and 14,000 acres on the Grand River. Lived at (1) Queenston to 1815 (2) Hamilton 1815–36. Capt., Niagara Light Dragoons, 28 June 1812; capt., 1st Regt., Lincoln Militia, 1812–14. JP, Gore Dist., 25 Mar. 1816; treasurer, Gore Dist., 1822; member of the Legislative Council of UC, 23 Jan. 1836. MHA, Wentworth, 1820–30. Reformer.

See DCB 7.

HAMILTON, Robert, *b* 1787, Fort Niagara, UC; *d* 1856, [Queenston], UC. Son of Hon. Robert Hamilton (member of the Legislative Council of UC) and Catharine (Askin) Robertson, brother of George Hamilton (*q.v.*); *m* Mary Biggar; three sons, four daughters. Merchant, shipbuilder, farmer. Granted [800] acres. Lived at Queenston. Capt., 2d Regt., Lincoln Militia by 1808; capt., flank company, 1812–14; lt. col., 18 June 1823. JP, Niagara Dist., 9 May 1823. MHA, Lincoln (3d riding) 1820–4.

See PAC, RG 1, L 7, vol. 52; RG 8, C 91, pp. 208–9; RG 9, IB 5, vol. 6; RG 68, General Index to Commissions; L.H. Irving, *Officers of the British Forces in Canada During the War of 1812–15* (Welland 1908), 77; H.F. Gardiner, "The Hamiltons of Queenston, Kingston and Hamilton," OHS *Papers and Records* 8 (1907): 24.33.

HAMILTON, William, *b*, Ireland, *d* 1822. Son of Charles Hamilton and Elizabeth Chetwood. Lumberman, merchant. Granted 1,200 acres. Lived at Hawkesbury. Capt., 1st Regt., Prescott Militia, 25 Feb. 1812. JP, Eastern Dist., 24 Mar. 1812; Ottawa Dist., 25 Mar. 1816. MHA, Prescott and Russell, 1820–1.

See PAC,RG 1, L 3, vol. 227, H 10/96; vol. 259, H Misc. Leases/199; RG 5, A 1, p. 6003; B 7, vol. 12; RG 68, General Index to Commissions; E.M. Chadwick, *Ontarian Families* (Toronto 1894), 1:137; A.R.M. Lower, *Great Britain's Woodyard* (Montreal 1973), 177–8; L.H. Irving, *Officers of the British Forces in Canada During the War of 1812–15* (Welland 1908), 263; M.A. Higginson and J.T. Brock, *The Village of Hawkesbury, 1808–1888* (Hawkesbury [1961]), 1–23.

HARDISON, Benjamin, *b* 1761, Berwick, Mass. (13 Cols); *d* May 1825, Fort Erie, UC. Farmer, miller, distiller. Granted 1,200 acres; bought at least 200 acres. Lived at Fort Erie, Bertie Twp. Served in the Royal Highland Emigrants (84th Regt. of Foot) [1775–6]; capt., 3d Regt., Lincoln Militia by 1808. JP, Niagara Dist., 1 Jan. 1800. MHA, Lincoln and Norfolk, 1797–1800.

See PAC, RG 1, L 3, vol. 222a, H 1/35; vol. 224a, H 4/9; L 7, vol. 52; RG 9, IB 5, vols. 1, 2; RG 19, E 5a; vol. 3750, no. 803; RG. 68, General Index to Commissions.

HATT, Richard, *b* 10 Sept. 1769, London England; *d* 26 Sept. 1819, Dundas, UC. Son of Richard and Mary Hatt; *m* Mary (Polly) Cooley; six sons, three daughters. Merchant, miller, distiller, speculator, farmer, shipowner, public servant. Granted 1,200 acres. Bought at least 9,750 acres. Lived at (1) Niagara 1793–6 (2) Ancaster Twp. 1796–1800 (3) Dundas 1800–19. Major, 1st Regt., Lincoln Militia by 1803; maj., 5th Regt., Lincoln Militia, 18 June 1812; wounded at Lundy's Lane. JP, Home Dist., 1 Jan. 1810; Gore Dist., 15 June 1818; judge, Gore Dist. Court, 15 Apr. 1816. MHA, Halton, 1817–19.

See DHB 1.

HENDERSON, Rufus C., *b* [1779]; *d* 5 Apr. 1847, Augusta Twp., CW; *m* Ann Jones (*dau* Solomon Jones, *q.v.*). Presbyterian. Physician, merchant. Granted [500] acres. Surgeon, 2d Regt., Grenville Militia, 1812–14. JP, Johnstown Dist., 27 Mar. 1821. MHA, Grenville, 1828–30. Conservative.

See PAC, RG 1, L 3, vol. 244a, H 3/104; RG 9, IB 5, vols. 1, 4; RG 68, General Index to Commissions; Brockville *Recorder*, 8 Apr. 1847; L.H. Irving, *Officers of the British Forces in Canada During the War of 1812–15* (Welland 1908), 34.

HILL, Solomon, *b* 30 Aug. 1756, Duchess County, NY (13 Cols); *d* 30 Aug. 1807, Grimsby Twp., UC. Son of William Hill and Bethia Smith; *m* Bethiah

Griffin; eight sons, three daughters. Farmer. Granted 500 acres. Lived in Grimsby Twp. Cpl., Loyal American Regt., 1777–83. MHA, West York, Lincoln (1st riding) and Haldimand, 1804–7.

See PAC, RG 1, L 3, vol. 222a, H 1/20; RG 5, A 1, vol. 6, p. 2681; RG 8, C 867, p. 5; W.D. Reid, *Loyalists of Ontario* (Lambertville, NJ 1973), 149–50.

HOPKINS, Caleb, *b* [1785], NJ, USA; *d* 8 Oct. 1880, Toronto. Son of Silas Hopkins, UE, and Mary Swayze (or Swazie); *m* Hannah Green (*dau* John Green, UE). Methodist. Farmer, merchant, innkeeper, stagecoach operator. Granted 200 acres. Lived in Nelson Twp. Pvt., 2d Regt., York Militia, 1812–14; quartermaster, 2d Regt., Gore Militia, 18 Oct. 1827. MHA, Halton, 1828–30, 1834–36. Reformer.

See DCB 10.

HORNOR, Thomas, *b* 17 Mar. 1767, Bordenston NJ (13 Cols); *d* 5 Aug. 1834, Burford Twp, UC. "Not a church member." Farmer, miller, survey contractor, public servant. Granted 600 acres plus 3,773 acres as payment for surveys. Lived in Blenheim and Burford twps. Capt. Oxford Militia by 1808; on active service in charge of "a party of Indians," Aug. 1812; col., 1st Regt., Oxford Militia, 18 June 1822. JP, London Dist., 1 Jan. 1800; registrar, Oxford and Middlesex counties, 11 July 1800. MHA, Oxford, 1820–30, 1832–4. Reformer.

See DCB 6.

HOTHAM, Richard Phillips, *b*, England; *d* 10 Oct. 1840 at sea en route to England; three sons. Anglican. Lawyer, public servant. Lived at L'Orignal, 1820–40. Registrar, Prescott and Russell counties, 5 Dec. 1820; clerk of the Peace, Ottawa Dist., 1 May 1821; registrar, Surrogate Court, Ottawa Dist., 1 May 1821; clerk, District Court, Ottawa Dist., 1 Aug. 1835; inspector of licences, Ottawa Dist., Dec. 1837. MHA, Prescott, 1836–40. Conservative.

See PAC, RG 1, E 13, Blue Books, 1821, 1835, 1839; L 3, vol. 241a, H 22/133; *Upper Canada Herald*, 9 Aug. 1836; Toronto *Patriot*, 25 Dec. 1840; Upper Canada, House of Assembly, *Journals* (1839) Appendix 5.

HOWARD, Matthew Munsell, *b* 1794, UC; *d* 6 Sept. 1879. Son of Peter Howard (*q.v.*) and Sarah Munsell; *m* Harriet Nichols. Miller, farmer. Lived in (1) Yonge Twp. (2) Elizabethtown Twp. Served [as a militia pvt.] 1812–14; lt., 1st Regt., Leeds Militia, 21 June 1823; capt., 30 Mar. 1835. MHA, Leeds, 1830–4, 1836. Reformer.

See PAC, RG 9, IB 5, vols. 1, 6; T. Leavitt, *A History of Leeds and Grenville* (Brockville 1879), 41; H.M. Brown, "The Howards of Leeds County," Ontario Genealogical Society, *Ottawa Branch News* 14, no 6, (Nov.–Dec. 1981): 68.

HOWARD, Peter, *b* 21 May 1772, Albany Co., NY (13 Cols); *d* 24 Nov. 1843, [Brockville], UC. Son of Matthew Howard, UE (ens. in a corps of Rangers under Capt. Samuel McKay); *m* Sarah Munsell. Physician, farmer, innkeeper, merchant, miller. Granted 400 acres. Lived in (1) Matilda Twp. (2) Elizabethtown Twp. (3) Yonge Twp. (4) Brockville. JP, Johnstown Dist., 11 Dec. 1806. MHA, Leeds, 1804–12, 1816–20.

See DCB 7.

HUNTER, Roger Rollo, *b*, Scotland. Presbyterian. Farmer. Bought [200] acres. Lived in Blandford Twp., [1834–40]. Lt., East Indian (Bengal) Artillery; capt., 2d Regt., Oxford Militia, 1838; lt. col., 5th Regt., Oxford Militia, 8 Feb. 1838; on active duty Dec., 1838. JP, London Dist., 12 June 1835; Brock Dist., 20 Feb. 1840. MHA, Oxford, 1839–41. Conservative.

See PAC, RG 1, L 3, vol. 248a, H 8/47; RG 8, C 1476, p. 8; RG 9, IB 1, vol. 30; IB 5, vol. 6; RG 68, General Index to Commissions; B. Dawe, *Old Oxford is Wide Awake! Pioneer Settlers and Politicians in Oxford County, 1793–1853* (n.p. 1980), 71, 89.

INGERSOLL, Charles Fortescue, *b* 1791, Mass., USA; *d* [Aug.] 1832. Son of Thomas Ingersoll; *m* Anna Maria Merritt (sister of William Hamilton Merritt, *q.v.*); three sons, five daughters. Merchant, distiller, miller. Granted 900 acres. Lived in (1) Grantham Twp. [?]–1818 (2) (N.) Oxford Twp. 1818–32. Quartermaster, Niagara Light Dragoons, 1812; cornet, 24 Oct. 1812; lt., 1813; lt. col., 1st Regt., Oxford Militia, 15 Dec. 1823. JP, London Dist., 31 July 1821. MHA, Oxford, 1824–8, 1830–2. Conservative.

See PAC, RG 1, L 3, vol. 259, I 17/8; L 7, vol. 52; RG 9, IB 5, vol. 1; RG 68, General Index to Commissions; R. McKenzie, *Laura Secord, the Legend and the Lady* (Toronto 1971), 31–2, 34–5, 75; L.H. Irving, *Officers of the British Forces in Canada During the War of 1812–15* (Welland 1908), 70–1.

JAMESON, Robert Sympson, *b* 1796, Hampshire, England; *d* 1 Aug. 1854, Toronto. Son of Thomas Jameson and Mary Sympson; *m* Anna Brownell Murphy. Read law at the Middle Temple. Anglican. Lawyer, public servant. Bought 1,500 acres in Loyalist rights plus "considerable" land in Toronto. Lived in Toronto. Attorney General of UC, 31 June 1833; vice-chancellor, Court of Chancery of UC, 23 Mar. 1837. MHA, Leeds, 1834–5. Conservative.

See DCB 8.

JARVIS, George Stephen, *b* 21 Apr. 1797, Federicton, NB; *d* 15 Apr. 1878, Cornwall, Ont. Son of Stephen Jarvis, UE, and Amelia Glover; brother of William Botsford Jarvis (*q.v.*); *m* (1) Julia Sherwood (*dau* Adiel Sherwood, sheriff of Johnstown Dist.) (2) Anna Maria Mountain (*dau* Rev. Salter Mountain, Anglican rector of Cornwall); five sons, eight daughters. Educated in

Federicton and York (Toronto); studied law with Hon. Jonas Jones (*q.v.*). Anglican. Lawyer, public servant. Granted [700 acres] plus a town lot in Cornwall. Lived at (1) York (Toronto) 1809–[25] (2) Cornwall [1825]–78. Gentleman volunteer, 49th (Regular) Regt., 14 Sept. 1812; ens. 8th (Regular) Regt., 16 Nov. 1813; lt., 104th (Regular) Regt. 1815–17 (HP 1817); capt., 1st Regt., Stormont Militia, 5 Jan. 1838; maj., 1839. Judge, Ottawa Dist. Court, 21 Dec. 1825; Johnstown Dist. Court, 30 June 1837; collector of customs, Cornwall, 30 July 1836. MHA, Cornwall, 1836–41. Conservative.
See DCB 10.

JARVIS, William Botsford, *b* 4 May 1799, Fredericton, NB; *d* 26 July 1864, Toronto. Son of Stephen Jarvis (UE) and Amelia Glover; brother of George Stephen Jarvis (*q.v.*); *m* Mary (Powell) Boyles; two sons, three daughters. Educated in Toronto by Rev. George Okill Stuart and Rev. John Strachan. Anglican. Public servant, land developer. Lived at York (Toronto) 1809–64. Lt., 1st Regt., East York Militia, 2 Apr. 1823; capt., 5 Feb. 1826; Capt., Queen's Rangers, 8 Dec. 1837; commanded a loyalist picket on Yonge Street, 5 Dec. 1837; lt. col., 1st Regt., East York Militia, 21 July 1841. Sheriff, Home Dist., 1 May 1827. MHA, York (town) 1830–4. Conservative.
See DCB 9.

JESSUP, Edward (senior), *b* 26 May 1766, Albany, NY (13 Cols); *d* 4 Nov. 1815, Prescott, UC. Son of Edward Jessup, UE (maj., Loyal [Jessup's] Rangers); *m* Susannah Covell (*dau* Simeon Covell, capt., Loyal [Jessup's] Rangers); seven children, including Edward Jessup (junior) (*q.v.*). [Anglican.] Farmer, public servant. Granted 600 acres. Bought "a number" of Loyalist rights. Lived in Augusta Twp. Lt., Loyal (Jessup's) Rangers (HP 1783); lt. col., 1st Regt., Leeds Militia by 1809. JP, Johnstown Dist., 30 June 1800; clerk of the Peace, Johnstown Dist., 1 Jan. 1800. MHA, Grenville, 1796–1800.
See PAC, RG 1, L 3, vol. 254a, J 4/18; RG 19, E 5a, vol. 3757, no. 1863; RG 68, General Index to Commissions; MG 25, Jessup Papers, no. 59.

JESSUP, Edward (junior), *b* UC; *d* [10] Sept. 1831, Brockville, UC. Son of Edward Jessup (*q.v.*) and Susannah Covell. [Anglican.] [Farmer.] Lived at Prescott. Lt., 1st Regt., Grenville Militia, 22 Jan. 1822; capt., 1 Oct. 1828. MHA, Grenville, 1830–1. [Conservative.]
See PAC, RG 9, IB 5, vols. 1, 4; MG 25, Jessup Papers, no. 59.

JONES, Charles, *b* 28 Feb. 1781, [Montreal]; *d* 27 Aug. 1840, Brockville, UC. Son of Ephraim Jones (*q.v.*) and Charlotte Coursol; brother of Jonas Jones (*q.v.*); *m* (1) Mary Stuart (*dau* Rev. John Stuart, UE, chaplain, King's Royal Regt. of NY) (2) Florella Smith; six sons, one daughter. Educated by

Rev. John Strachan, Cornwall. Merchant, miller, land speculator, public servant. Granted 2,000 acres; bought up to 5,000 acres. Capt., troop of dragoons, 1st Regt., Leeds Militia, 1812–14; col., 2d Regt., Leeds Militia, 10 Jan. 1822. JP, Johnstown Dist., 25 Mar. 1816; clerk, Johnstown Dist. Court, 1 Jan. 1800; treasurer, Johnstown Dist., 1804; member of the Legislative Council of UC, 7 Jan. 1829. MHA, Leeds, 1820–8.

See DCB 7.

JONES, David, *b* 1792, Montreal; *d* 26 June 1870, Brockville. Son of Daniel Jones, UE, and Margaret Hartley; *m* Catherine Eliza Hayes. Anglican. Lawyer, public servant. Granted 700 acres. Lived in Brockville. Maj. 4th Regt., Leeds Militia, 9 Mar. 1824; lt. col., 23 Mar. 1840. JP, Eastern Dist., 15 Dec. 1834; Johnstown Dist., 20 Feb. 1840; registrar, Leeds County, 21 Sept. 1838; judge, Eastern Dist. Court, 21 Dec. 1825. MHA, Leeds, 1824–8; Brockville, 1834–6. Conservative.

See PAC, RG 9, IB 5, vol. 6; RG 68, General Index to Commissions; Oakland Cemetery, Brockville, records and gravestone inscription.

JONES, Ephraim, *b* 27 Apr. 1750, Weston, Mass. (13 Cols); *d* 24 Jan. 1812, Augusta Twp., UC. Son of Elisha Jones and Mary Allen; *m* (1) Charlotte Coursol (2) Margaret Beke; six sons (including Charles Jones, *q.v.*), six daughters. [Farmer], miller, merchant, manufacturer, public servant. Granted 2,746 acres; owned a total of 11,260 acres in 1811. Lived in Augusta Twp. Ens., Loyal (Jessup's) Rangers, 1781–3 (HP 1783). JP, Montreal Dist., 18 Feb. 1786; Lunenburg Dist., 24 July 1788; Johnstown Dist., 1 Jan. 1800; judge, Surrogate Court, Eastern Dist., 6 June 1796. MHA, Grenville, 1792–6.

See DCB 5.

JONES, Henry, *b* 1790, [USA]; *d* 21 Jan. 1860 in [Brockville]. Son of Joseph and Sophia Jones; *m* Lucy Catherine Macdonell; five sons, two daughters. Merchant. Granted 1,100 acres. Lived in Brockville. Cornet, troop of dragoons, 1st Regt., Leeds Militia, 1812–14. JP, Johnstown Dist., 23 July 1822. MHA, Brockville, 1830–4. [Conservative.]

See PAC, RG 1, L 3, vol. 259, J 18/7; L 7, vol. 52; RG 68. General Index to Commissions; T. Leavitt, *A History of Leeds and Grenville* (Brockville 1879) 184; E.M. Chadwick, *Ontarian Families* (Toronto 1894), 1:170–1.

JONES, Jonas, *b* 19 May 1791, [UC]; *d* 8 July 1848. Son of Ephraim Jones (*q.v.*) and Charlotte Coursol; brother of Charles Jones (*q.v.*); *m* Mary Elizabeth Ford; eight sons, three daughters. Educated by Rev. John Strachan, Cornwall. Anglican. Lawyer, public servant. Granted 1,500 acres. Lived in (1) Brockville to 1837 (2) Toronto. Lt., troop of dragoons, 1st Regt.,

Leeds Militia, 22 June 1812; capt., flank company, [1813]; col., 3d Regt., Leeds Militia, 18 June 1822. JP, Bathurst Dist., 27 Nov. 1822; Eastern Dist., 23 Apr. 1830; Johnstown Dist., 22 July 1833; judge, Bathurst Dist. Court, 6 Dec. 1822; Midland Dist. Court, 21 Dec. 1825; Johnstown Dist. Court, 18 Oct. 1828; Surrogate Court, Bathurst Dist., 6 Dec. 1822; Surrogate Court, Johnstown Dist., 21 Dec. 1824; Court of King's Bench of UC, 23 Mar. 1837; registrar, Dundas County, 20 June 1837; member of the Legislative Council of UC, 27 Feb. 1839. MHA, Grenville, 1816–28; Leeds, 1836–7. Conservative.

See DCB 7.

JONES, Solomon, *b* 1756, Conn. (13 Cols), *d* 1822, [Augusta Twp.], UC; *m* Mary Tunnicliffe; three sons, one daughter (Ann, who married Rufus C. Henderson, *q.v.*). Studied medicine in Albany, NY. Physician, merchant, public servant. Granted 4,000 acres, including lands inherited from his brother, Lt. David Jones. Lived in Augusta Twp. Surgeon's mate, Loyal (Jessup's) Rangers (HP 1783); capt., Grenville Militia by 1807. JP, Eastern Dist., 1 July 1796; JP, Johnstown Dist., 23 July 1802; judge, Johnstown Dist. Court, 1 Jan. 1800. MHA, Leeds and Frontenac, 1796–1800;

See DCB 6.

KEARNS, John, *b* 1784, Ireland; *d* 1864, [Plantagenet Twp.], UC. Roman Catholic. Farmer. Granted 500 acres. Lived in Plantagenet Twp. Lt., 68th (Regular) Regt. (HP 1819); capt., 1st Regt., Prescott Militia, 6, May 1820; lt. col., 2d Regt., Prescott Militia, 23 Apr. 1839. JP, Ottawa Dist., 5 June 1822. MHA, Prescott, 1836–41. Conservative.

See PAC, RG. 5, A 1, vol. 48, pp. 23662–7; RG 8, C 190, pp. 68, 181; RG 9, IB 5, vol. 6; RG 68, General Index to Commissions; C. Thomas, *History of the Counties of Argenteuil, Quebec and Prescott, Ontario* (Belleville 1981), 640.

KERR, William Johnson, *b* 1781, UC; *d* 24 Apr. 1845, Wellington Square (Burlington), CW. Son of Robert Kerr (UE, surgeon, King's Royal Regt. of NY) and Elizabeth Johnson (*dau* Sir William Johnson, superintendent of Northern Indians, 1756–74, and Molly Brant); *m* Elizabeth Brant (*dau* Joseph Brant, captain, Indian Dept., War Chief of the Six Nations). Merchant, lumberman. Granted 1,800 acres. Lived at (1) Niagara to [1820] (2) Wellington Square [1820]–1845. Capt., Indian Dept., 1812–14. JP, Niagara Dist., 5 Dec. 1817; Gore Dist., 12 July 1828. MHA, Lincoln (2d riding), 1820–4.

See DCB 7.

KETCHUM, Jesse, *b* 31 Mar. 1782, Spencertown, NY; *d* 7 Sept. 1867, Buffalo, NY. Son of Jesse Ketchum and Mollie Robbins; *m* (1) Anne Love (2) Mary Ann Rubergall; three sons, four daughters. Methodist. Tanner, land speculator, farmer. Granted 200 acres. Bought and sold urban and farm properties in the Home Dist. Lived in (1) York Twp. 1799–1812 (2) York (Toronto) 1812–45. [Pvt.], 3d Regt., York Militia, 1812–13. MHA, York, 1828–34. Reformer.

See DCB 9.

KILBORN, John, *b* 27 June 1794, Elizabethtown Twp., UC. Son of David Kilborn and Hannah White (*dau* Joseph White, UE); *m* Elizabeth Baldwin; eight sons, one daughter. Attended local school near Brockville, Merchant, lumberman. Granted 500 acres. Lived at (1) Brockville 1811–6 (2) Elizabethtown Twp. 1816–30 (3) Kilmarnock 1830–[?] Sgt., 1st Regt., Leeds Militia, 1812; ens., Volunteer Incorporated Militia Bttn., 1813–14 (HP 1825); ensign, 1st Regt., Leeds Militia, 1818; capt. 4th Regt. Leeds Militia, 30 Apr. 1830; major, 2d Regt., Leeds Militia, 1841; on duty, 1837–8, at Gananoque. JP Johnstown Dist., 22 July 1833. MHA, Leeds, 1828–30. [Reformer.]

See PAC, RG 1, L 7, vol. 52; RG 9, IB 5, vol. 6; RG 68, General Index to Commissions; L.H. Irving; *Officers of the British Forces in Canada During the War of 1812–15* (Welland 1908), 38–9; T. Leavitt, *History of Leeds and Grenville* (Brockville 1879), 68–72.

LEFFERTY, John Johnson, *b* 1774, 13 Cols; *d* 26 Oct. 1842, Lundy's Lane, CW. Presbyterian. Medical doctor. Granted 500 acres. Lived in Stamford Twp. Lt., 3d Regt., Lincoln Militia, 1812; capt., 25 Jan. 1813; surgeon, 2d Regt., Lincoln Militia, 26 Apr. 1824. JP, Niagara Dist., 31 May 1833. MHA, Lincoln (2d and 3d ridings) 1824–8; Lincoln (3d riding) 1828–30, 1834–5. Reformer.

See DCB 7.

LEWIS, John Bower, *b* Apr., 1785, Babcary, Somersetshire, England; *d* 19 Sept. 1849 in Bytown (Ottawa), CW; *m* Henrietta Jones. Anglican. Merchant, distiller. Granted 800 acres. Bought at least 500 acres plus three town lots in Richmond. Lived in Richmond. Capt., 88th (Regular) Regt.; served 15 years. JP Bathurst Dist., 12 Nov. 1833. MHA, Carleton, 1830–41. Conservative.

See PAC, RG 1, L 3, vol. 290a, L 15/17; vol. 295, L 20/59; vol. 296a, L 22/51; vol. 297a, L 3/19; vol. 299, L 4/7; RG 68, General Index to Commissions; UC, House of Assembly, *Journals*, (1825) Appendix 10; *Upper Canada Herald*, 9 Aug. 1836; W.D. Reid, *Death Notices of Ontario* (Lambertville, NJ 1980), 256.

LEWIS, Levi, *b* 1762, NJ (13 Cols); *d* [Dec.] 1828 near Grimsby, UC. Son of Levi Lewis; *m* Mary Beemer; three sons, three daughters. Farmer. Granted 800 acres; bought at least 400 acres. Lived in (1) Grimsby Twp. (2) Townsend Twp. (3) Saltfleet Twp. Joined a Loyalist unit in NJ but never actually served.

JP, Gore Dist., 25 Mar. 1816. MHA, Lincoln (1st riding) and Haldimand, 1808–12.

See PAC, RG 1, L 3, vol. 283, L 1/56; vol. 306a, L Misc./5; RG 68, General Index to Commissions; *Colonial Advocate*, 4 Dec. 1828; J. Powell, *Annals of the Forty*, no. 6 (1955); D.P. Gagan, *Hopeful Travellers: Families, Land and Social Change in Mid-Victorian Peel County* (Toronto 1981), 27.

LOCKWOOD, Joseph N. Distiller, farmer. Granted 200 acres. Lived in Sydney Twp. Sgt., 1st Regt., Addington Militia, 1812–14. MHA, Hastings, 1828–30. Reformer.

See PAC, RG 1, L 7, vol. 52; MG 9, B 8–12; UC, House of Assembly, *Journals* (1826–7) Appendix; C. Lindsey, *Life and Times of W.L. Mackenzie* (Toronto 1862), 2:324.

LONGLEY, George, *b* 1788, Newbiggin, Westmoreland, England; *d* 1842 at sea near the English coast; *m* Ruth Wells (sister of William Benjamin Wells, *q.v.*); two sons, one daughter. Lumberman, farmer, merchant, miller. Lived at Maitland, Augusta Twp., 1826–42. JP, Johnstown Dist., 22 July 1833. MHA, Grenville, 1828–30. [Reformer.]

See DCB 7.

LOUNT, Samuel, *b* 24 Sept. 1791, Cattawissa, Penn., USA; *d* 12 Apr. 1838, Toronto. Son of Gabriel Lount; *m* Elizabeth ——— ; seven children. Methodist. Blacksmith, shipowner, farmer. Lived in (1) Whitchurch Twp. (2) Holland Landing. MHA, Simcoe, 1834–6. Reformer.

See DCB 7.

LYON, George, *b* 1790, Inverary, Scotland; *d* 26 Mar. 1851, Richmond, CW. Son of George Lyon and Elizabeth Philips; *m* Catherine Radenhurst (sister of Thomas Mabom Radenhurst, *q.v.*); six sons, five daughters. Anglican. Miller, distiller, merchant. Granted [1400] acres; bought at least 9,600 acres. Lived at Richmond. Ens., 40th (Regular) Regt., 4 Sept. 1806; lt., 10 Feb. 1808, lt., 100th (Regular) Regt., 25 May 1809; fought in Canada, 1812–14 (HP 1818); capt., 1st Regt., Carleton Militia, 2 Aug. 1821. JP, Bathurst Dist., 12 Apr. 1825. MHA, Carleton, 1833–4. Conservative.

See DCB 8.

LYONS, James. Methodist. Merchant. Granted 500 acres. Lived in (1) Niagara Dist. (2) Cramahe Twp. (3) Murray Twp. Ens., 2d Regt., Lincoln Militia, 1812–14; capt., 1st Regt., Northumberland Militia, 6 Sept. 1822; capt., 3d Regt., Northumberland Militia, 6 Nov. 1822. JP, Newcastle Dist., 13 July 1829. MHA, Northumberland, 1824–34. Reformer.

See PAC, RG 1, L 3, vol. 556, Leases and Licences of Occupation, 26; L 7, vol. 52; RG 9, IB 2, vol. 31; IB 5, vols. 1, 2; RG 68, General Index to Commissions; L.H. Irving, *Officers of the British Forces in Canada During the War of 1812–15* (Welland 1908), 77; E.C. Guillet, ed., *The Valley of the Trent* (Toronto 1957), 306.

LYTLE, Nicholas, *d* 2 Oct. 1825; *m* Elizabeth Little (*dau* John Little, UE); four children. [Farmer], "gentleman". Granted 500 acres. Lived in Colchester Twp., 1800–25. Private, Caldwell's Rangers (1812); Ens., 1st Regt., Essex Militia, 12 July 1812; capt., 16 July 1819. [MHA, Essex, 1824] (tied in the election with Francis Baby).

See PAC, RG 1, L 3, vol. 290a, L 15/12; vol. 296, L 21/8; vol. 305, L Leases/56; L 7, vol. 52; RG 9, IB 5, vols. 1, 2; RG 19, E 5a, vol. 3756, no. 1670; L.H. Irving, *Officers of the British Forces in Canada During the War of 1812–15* (Welland 1908), 89.

McBRIDE, Edward, *b* [1792]; *d* 3 Sept. 1834, Niagara, UC. Son of Peter McBride (UE) and Mary Bradshaw. "Not a church member." Merchant, journalist, auctioneer, innkeeper. Granted 300 acres plus a town lot in Niagara. Lived at Niagara. Sgt., 3d Regt., York Militia; promoted to quartermaster sgt.; Ens., 1st Regt., Lincoln Militia 1812–14; sgt. major, 4 June 1818; ens., 23 Apr. 1823; lt., 14 Aug. 1824; capt., 17 Feb. 1831. MHA, Niagara (town) 1824–8.

See DCB 6.

McCALL, Duncan, *b* 1768, Baskingridge, NJ (13 Cols); *d* 25 Nov. 1832, Toronto; *m* (1) Jemina Fairchild (2) ——— Lockwood; [one daughter, two sons]. Presbyterian. Merchant, fur trader, farmer. Granted [200] acres; bought or leased [600] acres. Lived in Charloteville Twp. Capt., 1st Regt., Norfolk Militia, 14 Feb. 1812. JP, London Dist., 13 June 1829. MHA, Norfolk, 1824–32. Reformer.

See DCB 6.

McCARGER, Milo, *b* [1798, UC]; *d* 14 Jan. 1860, Kemptville, CW. Son of Thomas McCarger. Farmer. Lived in (1) S. Gower Twp. (2) Mountain Twp. Fought with the Grenville Militia at the Battle of the Windmill, Nov. 1838; capt., 1st Regt., Grenville Militia, 14 June 1839. JP, Johnstown Dist., 20 Feb. 1840; coroner, Johnstown Dist., 16 Mar. 1835. MHA, Grenville, 1839–41. Reformer.

See PAC, RG 5, A 1, vol. 125, p. 68831; RG 9, IB 5, vol. 6; RG 68, General Index to Commissions; MTCL, Baldwin Papers, W.B. Wells to Baldwin, 31 July 1843; Ottawa *Citizen*, 20 Jan. 1860; T. Leavitt, *History of Leeds and Grenville* (Brockville 1879) 77; J.R. Robertson, *History of Freemasonry in Canada* (Toronto 1899), 1:1157.

McCORMICK, William, *b* 30 May 1784, near the Maumee river (Ohio); *d* 18 Feb. 1840. Son of Alexander McCormick (UE) and Elizabeth Twiner; *m* Mary Cornwall (*dau* John Cornwall, *q.v.*); four daughters, eight sons. Anglican. Farmer, merchant, lumberman, quarry operator. Granted 900 acres, plus a town lot in Amherstburgh; leased 600 acres. Lived in (1) Malden Twp. 1795–? (2) Colchester Twp. (3) Pelee Island 1834–40. Ens., Essex Militia by 1807; lt., 1st Regt., Essex Militia, promoted to capt., 1812–14; wounded at Frenchtown and POW, 1814; major, 1 Apr. 1822; lt. col., 30 Jan. 1816. MHA, Essex, 1812–24.

See DCB 7.

McCRAE, Thomas, *d* 11 June 1814, [Raleigh Twp.] UC; three sons. Farmer, tailor, innkeeper. Granted 400 acres. Lived at (1) Detroit 1779–? (2) Raleigh Twp. 1789–[1814]. Served as steward, HM brig *Gage* on Lake Erie for three years during the American Revolution; capt., Kent Militia by 1807; capt., 1st Regt., Kent Militia, 1812–14. JP, Western Dist., 11 Dec. 1806. MHA, Kent, 1800–4.

See PAC, RG 1, L 3, vol. 323a Mc Misc/28; RG 68, General Index to Commissions; F.C. Hamil, *The Valley of the Lower Thames* (Toronto 1951), 353–4; L.H. Irving, *Officers of the British Forces in Canada During the War of 1812–15* (Welland 1908), 94; V. Lauriston, *Romantic Kent* (Chatham 1952), 99.

McCRAE, William, *b*, Detroit, [Son of Thomas McCrae, *q.v.*]. Anglican, Farmer. Granted 200 acres. Lived in Raleigh Twp. JP, Western Dist., 9 Nov. 1816. MHA, Kent, 1834–41. Conservative.

See PAC, RG 1, L 3, vol. 339a, M 12/14; RG 19, E 5a, vol. 3747, no. 534; RG 68, General Index to Commissions; V. Lauriston, *Romantic Kent* (Chatham 1952), 99; F.C. Hamil, *The Valley of the Lower Thames* (Toronto 1951), 187, 224.

MACDONALD, Archibald, *b* about 1787; *d* 1872. [Farmer.] Granted 800 acres. Lived near Cobourg. Capt., 35th (Regular) Regt. of Foot 1813; fought in the Napoleonic Wars, 1805–14 (HP 1817); col., 2d Regt., Northumberland Militia, 27 June 1825. JP, Newcastle Dist., 31 July 1827. MHA, Northumberland, 1830–4. Conservative.

See PAC, RG 9, IB 5, vol. 5; RG 68, General Index to Commissions; *The Seventh Report from the Committee on Grievances* (Toronto 1835); R.S. Sorrell, "1828 Upper Canada Election Results Table," *OH* 63, no. 1 (Mar. 1971): 68, McMaster University Library, *Research News* (July 1980).

MACDONALD, Donald, *b*, Scotland. Roman Catholic. Public servant. Lived in [South Plantagenet Twp.]. Treasurer, Ottawa Dist., 1822; inspector of licences, Ottawa Dist., 8 Mar. 1834; coroner, Ottawa Dist., 16 May 1835. MHA, Prescott and Russell, 1824–34. [Reformer.]

See PAC, RG 68, General Index to Commissions; *The Seventh Report from the Committee on Grievances* (Toronto 1835); C. Thomas, *History of Argenteuil, Quebec and Prescott, Ontario* (Belleville 1981), 664; R.S. Sorrel, "1828 Upper Canada Election Results Table," *OH* 63, no. 1 (Mar. 1971): 67.

MACDONELL, Alexander (Collachie), *b* 1762, Scotland; *d* 18 Mar. 1842, Toronto. Son of Allan Macdonell, UE (Capt., 84th [Royal Highland Emigrant] Regt.) and Helen MacNab; brother of Angus Macdonell (Collachie) (*q.v.*); *m* Annie Smith (sister of Hon. Samuel Smith, member of the Executive Council of UC, administrator); two daughters, five sons. Roman Catholic. Public servant, superintendent of settlement at Lord Selkirk's Baldoon settlement. Granted 2,100 acres. Lived in (1) York (Toronto) (2) Baldoon 1805–12. Ens., 84th (Royal Highland Emigrant) Regt., 1778; lt., Butler's Rangers, 6 Sept. 1781 (HP 1784); deputy paymaster general of militia, 1812; POW 1813. Sheriff, Home Dist., 1 Mar. 1792; inspector of licences, Home Dist., Oct. 1808; superintendent, Military Settling Dept. 1815; assistant secretary, Indian Dept., June 1816; member of the Legislative Council of UC, 27 Jan. 1831. MHA, Glengarry and Prescott, 1800–8; Glengarry, 1808–16.
See DCB 7.

MACDONELL, Alexander (Greenfield), *d* 23 Feb. 1835 in Toronto. Son of Alexander Macdonell (Greenfield) and Janet Macdonell (*dau* Alexander Macdonell, UE, capt., King's Royal Regt. of NY); brother of John Macdonell (Greenfield) (*q.v.*) and Donald Macdonell (Greenfield) (*q.v.*); *m* —— McAuley. Educated by Rev. John Strachan, Cornwall. Roman Catholic. Fur trader, farmer, public servant. Lived in [(1) Charlottenburgh Twp. (2) L'Orignal]. [Lt., Stormont Militia, 1807.] Sheriff, Ottawa Dist., 6 Dec. 1822; JP, Ottawa Dist., 17 Mar. 1834. MHA, Glengarry, 1820–8; Prescott, 1834–5. [Conservative.]
See DCB 6.

MACDONELL, Alexander, *b* 1786, Scotland; *d* 29 Nov. 1861, Peterborough, CW. Nephew of Bishop Alexander Macdonell. Roman Catholic. Public servant, lumberman. [Bought 1,600 acres in Loyalist rights.] Lived in (1) Eastern Dist. [1804]–1825 (2) Peterborough 1825–61. Capt., 1st Regt., Glengarry Militia, 25 Apr. 1812; ens., Glengarry Light Infantry Fencible Regt., 8 Oct. 1812; capt. and adj., 2d Regt., Northumberland Militia, 30 Aug. 1822; major, 9 Mar. 1831; col., 5 Jan. 1838; on active duty 1838. JP, Newcastle Dist., 27 June 1837. MHA, Northumberland, 1834–41. Conservative.
See DCB 9.

MACDONELL, Angus (Sandaig), *b* [1751], Scotland; *d* 1812; *m* Marie-Anne Picoté de Belestre. Roman Catholic. [Farmer, fur trader.] Granted 2,000 acres. Lived in Charlottenburgh Twp. Ens. 71st (Regular) Regt., 6 Dec. 1775; lt., 14 Oct. 1778; served in the American Revolution (HP 1784). MHA, Glengarry and Prescott, 1800–4.

See PAC, RG 1, L 3, vol. 323a, Mc Misc/44; vol. 332, M 6/9; W.L. Scott, "Glengarry's Representatives in the Legislative Assembly of Upper Canada" (Part 1) CCHA *Report* (1938–39): 32–4; "Jean-Francois-Marie-Joseph Macdonell," *DCB* 9.

MACDONELL, Angus (Collachie), *b* in Inverness-shire, Scotland; *d* 8 Oct. 1804 in the loss of the *Speedy* on Lake Ontario. Son of Allan Macdonell UE, (Capt., 84th [Royal Highland Emigrant] Regt.) and Helen MacNab; brother of Alexander Macdonell (Collachie) (*q.v.*). Roman Catholic. Lawyer, public servant. Granted 1,300 acres plus a town lot in York (Toronto). Lived in York (Toronto). Clerk, House of Assembly, 12 Dec. 1792. MHA, Durham, Simcoe and East York, 1801–4.

See DCB 5.

MACDONELL, Donald (Greenfield), *b* 17 Jan. 1788, Scotland; *d* 13 June 1861, Quebec City. Son of Alexander Macdonell and Janet Macdonell (*dau* Capt. Alexander Macdonell, UE); brother of John Macdonell (Greenfield) (*q.v.*); nephew of John Macdonell (Aberchalder) (*q.v.*); *m* Elizabeth Macdonell (*dau* Ronald Macdonell [Leek], UE); five sons, two daughters. Attended Rev. John Strachan's school, Cornwall. Roman Catholic. Public servant. Lived in Cornwall 1792–1846. Capt., 2d Regt., Glengarry Militia, 15 Apr. 1812; lt. col. and assistant quartermaster general of militia, 1814; col., 1 Jan. 1822; on active service for six months, 1838. Sheriff, Eastern Dist., 13 Aug. 1819, MHA, Glengarry, 1834–41. Conservative.

See DCB 9.

MACDONELL, Donald AEneas, *b* 31 July 1794, UC; *d* 11 Mar. 1879, Brockville. Ont. Son of Miles Macdonell (capt., King's Royal Regt. of NY) and Isabella Macdonell; *m* Mary Macdonell (*dau* Archibald Macdonell [Leek], Lt., 84th [Royal Highland Emigrant] Regt.); four daughters, two sons. Attended Rev. John Strachan's school, Cornwall. Roman Catholic. Soldier, [farmer]. Granted 500 acres. Lived at St. Andrew's, Cornwall Twp. Ens., 8th (Regular) Regt., [7 Aug.] 1813; lt., 98th (Regular) Regt., 29 Nov. 1815 (HP 1817); major, 1st Regt., Stormont Militia, 7 Feb. 1822; lt. col., 28 June 1830; commanded a militia detachment sent to Beauharnois, LC, 1838. JP, Eastern Dist., 15 Dec. 1834. MHA, Stormont, 1834–41. Reformer.

See DCB 10.

MACDONELL, Hugh (Aberchalder), *b*, Scotland; *d* [in Firenze, Italy]. Son of Alexander Macdonell, UE (capt., King's Royal Regt. of NY); brother of John Macdonell (*q.v.*); *m* (2) Louise Ulrich, (*dau* Admiral Ulrich, Danish

Consul General at Algiers); eight daughters, two sons. [Roman Catholic.] Surveyor, soldier, public servant. Granted 2,000 acres plus a town lot in Niagara. Lived in the Eastern Dist. Ens., lt., 1780, King's Royal Regt. of NY (HP [1784]); capt., Royal Canadian Volunteers Regt., 1796–1802; adj. gen. of militia, UC, 1 June 1794; lt. col., Glengarry Militia, 1803. JP, Lunenburg Dist., 10 June 1793; assistant commissary general, Gibraltar, 1805–12, consul general, Algiers, Mar. 1812. MHA, Glengarry, 1792–6.

See PAC, RG 68, General Index to Commissions; W.L. Scott, "Glengarry's Representatives in the Legislative Assembly of Upper Canada" (Part 1) CCHA *Report* (1938–39): 26–9; J.A. Macdonell, *Sketches Illustrating the Early Settlement and History of Glengarry in Canada* (Montreal 1893), 104–10.

MACDONELL, John (Aberchalder), *b* [1758], Scotland; *d* 21 Nov. 1809, Quebec City. Son of Alexander Macdonell, (UE capt., King's Royal Regt. of NY); brother of Hugh Macdonell (*q.v.*); *m* Helen Yates; one son, two daughters. Educated in Scotland. Roman Catholic. Farmer, soldier, public servant. Granted 5,000 acres plus town lots in York (Toronto) and Niagara. Lived in Cornwall Twp. Ens., 84th (Royal Highland Emigrant) Regt., 14 June 1775; lt., 1777; Capt., Butler's Rangers, 1 Aug. 1778 (HP 1784); lt. col., Royal Canadian Volunteer Regt., 1 July 1796–1802; paymaster, 10th Royal Veteran Bttn., 1807–9. JP, Lunenburg Dist., 24 July 1788; judge, court of Common Pleas, Lunenburg Dist., 7 Jan. 1790; lieutenant, Glengarry Co., 2 Nov. 1792. MHA, Glengarry, 1792–1800.

See DCB 5.

MACDONELL, John (Greenfield), *b* 19 Apr. 1785, Scotland; *d* 4 Oct. 1812, Queenston Heights. Son of Alexander Macdonell and Janet Macdonell (*dau* Alexander Macdonell, UE, capt., King's Royal Regt. of NY); brother of Alexander Macdonell (Greenfield) (*q.v.*) and Donald Macdonell (*q.v.*). Studied law in York (Toronto). Roman Catholic. Lawyer, public servant. Granted 1,200 acres. Lived in York (Toronto). Lt. col. and aide-de camp to General Brock, 1812. Acting attorney general of UC, 28 Sept. 1811; attorney general, 18 June 1812. MHA, Glengarry, 1812.

See DCB 5.

MACDONELL, John (Scotus), *b* 30 Nov. 1768, Scotland; *d* 17 Apr. 1850, Point Fortune, CW. Son of "Spanish" John Macdonell (UE capt., King's Royal Regt. of NY); *m* Magdeliene Poitras; six sons, two daughters. Roman Catholic. Fur trader, merchant, forwarder, miller, public servant. Granted 1,020 acres; bought at least 1,000 acres. Ens., Cornwall and Osnabruck Militia, 20 June 1788; capt., Corps of Canadian Voyageurs, 2 Oct. 1812; lt. col., 1st Regt., Prescott Militia, 21 May 1821. JP, Ottawa Dist., 25 Mar. 1816; judge, Ottawa Dist. Court, 25 Mar. 1816. MHA, Prescott, 1816–20.

See PAC, RG 1, L 3, vol. 337, M 11/95; vol. 360, M 19/47; RG 9, IB 5, vols. 2, 6; RG 68, General Index to Commissions; L.H. Irving, *Officers of the British Forces in Canada During the War of 1812–15* (Welland 1908), 114–5; A.G. Morice, "A Canadian Pioneer, Spanish John," "Sidelights on the Careers of Miles Macdonell and his brothers," *CHR* 10 (1939): 212–35, 308–32.

McGREGOR, John, *d* 1 Feb. 1828, Sandwich, UC; *m* Martha Scott; [three sons, two daughters]. Merchant, miller, farmer. Granted 600 acres plus a town lot in Amherstburgh. Lived at Sandwich, 1785–1828. Ens., 1st Regt., Kent Militia, 1812–14. JP, Western Dist., 30 June 1800. MHA, Kent, 1804–16.

See DCB 6.

McINTOSH, John, *b* 4 Mar. 1796, Colarich, Scotland; *d* 3 July 1853, Toronto. Son of John McIntosh and Ann Ferguson; *m* (1) Catharine Stewart (2) Helen (Baxter) Ferguson (sister of Isabel Baxter, *m* William Lyon MacKenzie, *q.v.*); six daughters, four sons. Educated by Rev. John Strachan, Toronto. Presbyterian. Sailor, shipowner, ship's captain. Granted 300 acres. Lived in York (Toronto), 1803–53. Private, 3d Regt., York Militia, 1812; also served as a pilot on Lake Ontario. MHA, York (4th riding), 1836–41. Reformer.

See DCB 8.

MacKAY, Thomas, *b* 1 Sept. 1792, Perth, Scotland; *d* 9 Oct. 1855 in Ottawa. Son of John and Christina MacKay; *m* Ann Chrichton: sixteen children. Presbyterian (Church of Scotland). Contractor, miller, merchant. Bought 10 acres at the mouth of the Rideau River as a mill site. Lived in Bytown (Ottawa) 1826–55. Lt. col., 1st Regt., Russell Militia, 16 Apr. 1836; col., 19 Feb. 1838. JP, Bathurst Dist., 12 Nov. 1833; Ottawa Dist., 17 Mar. 1834. MHA, Russell, 1836–41. Conservative.

See DCB 8.

McKEE, Thomas, *b* [1770, 13 Cols]; *d* 20 Oct. 1814, near Île des Cascades, LC. Son of Col. Alexander McKee, UE (Indian Dept.); *m* Thérèse Askin; four children. Soldier, farmer, public servant. Granted 1,200 acres; held Pelee Island on a 999-year lease. Lived at Sandwich. Ens., 60th (Regular) Regt., 29 Mar. 1791; lt., 5 Feb. 1795; Capt., 20 Feb. 1796; major, Essex Militia, 1807; major, 2d Regt., Essex Militia, 1812–14. Superintendent, Indian Affairs, St. Joseph's Island, 1797; superintendent at Amherstburgh, 1799–1808. MHA, Kent, 1796–1800; Essex, 1800–04.

See DCB 5.

MACKENZIE, William Lyon, *b* 12 Mar. 1795, Dundee, Forfarshire, Scotland; *d* 28 Aug. 1861, Toronto. Son of Daniel Mackenzie and Elizabeth

Chalmers; *m* Isabel Baxter; thirteen children. Educated at the Dundee parish school and Mr. Adie's school. [Presbyterian.] Journalist. Lived at (1) Queenston, 1823–4 (2) York (Toronto) 1824–37. MHA, York, 1828–34; York (2d riding) 1834–6. Reformer.

See DCB 9.

McLEAN, Alexander, *b* 14 Feb. 1793, St. Andrew's, Cornwall Twp., UC; *d* 16 Apr. 1875, Cornwall, Ont. Son of Hon. Neil McLean, UE (ens., 84th [Royal Highland Emigrant] Regt., member of the Legislative Council of UC) and Isabella Macdonell; brother of Archibald McLean (*q.v.*); *m* ——— Dallas. Educated by Rev. John Strachan. Presbyterian. Merchant, farmer, public servant. Granted 500 acres; bought 200 acres and two town lots in Cornwall. Lived in Cornwall. Lt., 1st Regt., Stormont Militia, 1812–13; wounded 1813; lt., Royal Newfoundland Regt., 24 June 1813 (HP 1818); on active service Nov. 1838 at Beauharnois, LC. JP, Eastern Dist., 15 Dec. 1834; treasurer, Eastern Dist., 10 Feb. 1832. MHA, Stormont, 1837–41. Conservative.

See PAC, RG 1, L 3, vol. 311, MC 1/51; vol. 311a, MC 1/90, 112; vol. 341, M 12/179; RG 68, General Index to Commissions; L.H. Irving, *Officers of the British Forces in Canada During the War of 1812–15* (Welland 1908), 44–5; J.G. Harkness, *A History of Stormont, Dundas and Glengarry* (Ottawa 1946), 176.

McLEAN, Allan, *b* 1752, [Scotland]; *d* 8 Oct. 1847, Kingston, CW.; *m* Harriet McLean [daughter of (Hon.) Neil McLean]. Anglican. Lawyer, forwarder, public servant. Granted [3,000] acres. Bought 36,100 acres in Loyalist rights. Lived in Kingston. Lt., 29th (Regular) Regt.; served 17 years in America and during the American Revolution; lt. col., 1st Regt., Frontenac Militia, 1812; lt. col., Volunteer Incorporated Militia Bttn., 1813–14. Registrar, Frontenac, Lennox and Addington, Prince Edward and Hastings counties, 4 June 1796; clerk of the Peace, Midland Dist., 1 Jan. 1800. MHA, Frontenac, 1804–24.

See DCB 7.

McLEAN, Archibald, *b* 15 Apr. 1791, St. Andrews, UC, *d* 24 Oct. 1865, Toronto. Son of Hon. Neil McLean, UE (ens., 84th [Royal Highland Emigrant] Regt., member of the Legislative Council, UC) and Isabella Macdonell; brother of Alexander McLean (*q.v.*); *m* Joan Macpherson; seven children. Attended Rev. John Strachan's school, Cornwall; studied law in York (Toronto) with Attorney General William Firth. Presbyterian (Church of Scotland). Lawyer, public servant. Granted 1,400 acres plus a town lot in Cornwall. Bought 400 acres [plus 1,600 acres in Loyalist rights]. Lived in (1) Cornwall to 1837 (2) Toronto, 1837–65. Capt., 3d Regt., York Militia, 18 May 1812; wounded at Queenston Heights; assistant quartermaster general of militia; capt., Volunteer Incorporated Militia Bttn. (HP); col., 2d Regt.,

Stormont Militia, 1 Apr. 1822; col., 1st Regt., Stormont Militia, [29 Feb.] 1836; on active service at Toronto, Dec. 1837. JP, Johnstown Dist., 27 Mar. 1821; clerk of the Peace, Eastern Dist., 25 Jan. 1817; registrar, Stormont and Dundas co., 10 Feb. 1817; registrar, Surrogate Court, Eastern Dist., 3 Apr. 1817; judge, Court of King's Bench, 23 Mar. 1837; coroner, Eastern Dist., 4 Dec. 1837. MHA, Stormont, 1820–37. Conservative.

See DCB 9.

McMARTIN, Alexander, *b* 1788, Charlottenburgh Twp., UC; *d* 12 July 1853, Martintown, CW. Son of Malcolm McMartin, UE (lt., King's Royal Regt., of NY) and Margaret McIntyre; *m* Mary Carlyle; four sons, two daughters. Presbyterian. Merchant, [farmer], miller, contractor, public servant. Granted 200 acres. Lived at Martintown, Charlottenburgh Twp. Ens., 2d Regt., Glengarry Militia, 24 Apr. 1812; major, 1st Regt., Glengarry Militia, 15 July 1822; lt. col. 6 Mar. 1837; on duty in LC Feb.–Mar., Nov. 1838. JP, Eastern Dist., 8 Jan. 1820; sheriff, Eastern Dist., 18 Dec. 1838. MHA, Glengarry, 1812–24, 1830–4. Conservative.

See DCB 8.

McMICKING, Gilbert, *b* [1790], UC. Son of Peter McMicking, UE (Private, Butler's Rangers). Presbyterian. Merchant, public servant. Granted 700 acres; bought 100 acres plus 1,900 acres in Loyalist rights. Lived in Stamford Twp. Quartermaster, 2d Regt., Lincoln Militia by 1809 and 1812–14. Coroner, Niagara Dist., 26 Apr. 1811; collector of customs, Queenston, 1 Aug. 1838. MHA, Lincoln (4th riding), 1834–41. Reformer.

See PAC, RG 1, L 3, vol. 335a, M 10/45; vol. 362, M 19/213; L 7, vol. 52; RG 5, B 7, vol. 3; RG 9, IB 5, vol. 1; RG 68, General Index to Commissions; UC, House of Assembly, *Journals* (1839–40) Appendix 1; L.H. Irving, *Officers of the British Forces in Canada During the War of 1812–15* (Welland 1908), 34; L.F. Gates, *Land Policies of Upper Canada* (Toronto 1968), 374.

MacNAB, Allan Napier, *b* 19 Feb. 1798, Niagara, UC; *d* 8 Aug. 1862, Hamilton, CW. Son of Allan MacNab, UE (lt., Queen's Rangers) and Anne Napier; *m* (1) Elizabeth Brooke (2) Mary Stuart; three daughters, one son. Educated at the Home Dist. School under Rev. John Strachan and Rev. G.O. Stuart. Anglican. Lawyer, developer, public servant. Granted 500 acres; bought at least 10,500 acres and 3,500 acres in Loyalist rights. Lived in Hamilton. Volunteer with the 8th (Regular) Reg., 1813; midshipmen on HMS *Wolfe*, 1813; ens., 49th (Regular) Regt., 1814 (HP); capt., 1st Regt., West York Militia, 1 Dec. 1820; lt., 68th (Regular) Regt., 11 May 1826; lt. col., 4th Regt., Gore Militia, 24 May 1830; col., 3d Regt., Gore Militia, 14 May 1836; on duty at Toronto, Dec. 1837, and commanded the militia in the London Dist. and on the Niagara frontier, 1838. JP, Gore Dist., 17 Mar.

1838; registrar, Wentworth County, 23 Mar. 1840. MHA, Wentworth, 1830–4; Hamilton, 1834–6; Wentworth, 1836–41. Conservative.

See DCB 9; D.R. Beer, *Sir Allan Napier MacNab* (Hamilton, 1984).

McNABB, James, *b* [1776 in the 13 Cols]; *d* 5 Apr. 1820. Son of James McNabb, UE (surgeon, McAlpine's Corps); *m* Mary Ann Fraser; one son. [Anglican.] Farmer, merchant, miller. Granted 660 acres plus two town lots in Belleville. Bought 100 acres. Lived (1) in Thurlow Twp. (2) in Belleville. Served as billeting, transport and commissariat agent, Bay of Quinte region, 1812–14. JP, Midland Dist., 10 Mar. 1808. MHA, Hastings and Ameliasburgh Twp., 1808–12, 1816–20.

See DCB 5.

McNEILLEDGE, Colin, *b* [1798 in Scotland]; *d* 16 Oct. 1839, Port Dover, UC. [Miller, merchant.] Lived in Port Dover. Ens., 2d Regt., Lincoln Militia, 27 Apr. 1824; lt., 1 May 1828; capt., 2d Regt., Norfolk Militia, 17 Feb. 1831. JP, London Dist., 31 May 1833. MHA, Norfolk, 1833–4. [Conservative.]

See PAC, RG 9, IB 5, vols. 1, 3, 6; RG 68, General Index to Commissions; MG 9, D 8–35; W.D. Reid, *Death Notices of Ontario* (Lambertville, NJ 1980), 183.

MACOMB, William, *b*, 13 Cols; *d* 1796, Detroit. Son of John Macomb and Jane Gordon; *m* (1) Sarah Jane Dring (2) ——— Gallant. [Anglican.] Merchant, miller, farmer. Obtained Grosse Isle (6,180 acres) from the Indians. Lived at Detroit. JP, Hesse Dist., 24 July 1788. MHA, Kent, 1792–6.

See PAC, RG 68, General Index to Commissions; AO, *Report* (1929) 44–5; C.C. James, "The First Legislature of Upper Canada," *Transactions of the Royal Society of Canada* (1902).

MAÇON, Jean-Baptiste, [Roman Catholic.] Merchant. Granted 400 acres. Lived at Amherstburgh. Capt., 2d Regt., Essex Militia, 18 Aug. 1818. JP, Western Dist., 23 Sept. 1826. MHA, Essex, 1830–4. Conservative.

See PAC, RG 1, L 3, vol. 368, M 3/110; RG 5, A 1, vol. 115, p. 64470; RG 9, IB 5, vol. 5; RG 68, General Index to Commissions; *The Seventh Report From the Committee on Grievances* (Toronto 1835).

MALCOLM, Finlay, *b* 20 June 1779, Maine (13 Cols); *d* Mar. 1862. Son of Finlay Malcolm, UE; *m* Fanny Taylor; four daughters, three sons. Congregationalist. Farmer, tavern keeper. Granted [200] acres. Lived in Oakland Twp. Lt., 1st Regt., Oxford Militia, 1812–14. MHA, Oxford, 1828–30. Reformer.

See C. Read, *The Rising in Western Upper Canada 1837–8* (Toronto 1982), 68, 227; C. Read and R. Stagg, eds., *The Rebellion of 1837* (Toronto 1985), 194.

MALLOCH, Edward, *b*, Scotland; *d* 1867. Son of Edward Malloch; *m* ——— Hill. Anglican. Merchant, land speculator. Bought at least 8,000 acres plus 5,100 acres in Loyalist rights. Lived in (1) Richmond (2) Bytown (Ottawa). Ens., 1st Regt., Carleton Militia, 27 Jan. 1826; capt., 1 Dec. 1837. MHA, Carleton, 1834–41. Conservative.

See PAC, RG 1, L 3, vol. 305, M 22/118; vol. 363, M 20/88, 90; RG 9, IB 5, vols. 6, 8; UC, House of Assembly, *Journals* (1825–6) Appendix; *Journal of Education for Ontario* (1870); *Canada Directory* (1854–5); Beechwood Cemetery, Ottawa, gravestone inscription; L.F. Gates, *Land Policies of Upper Canada* (Toronto 1968), 334.

MALLORY, Benajah, *b* about 1764, 13 Cols; *d* 9 Aug. 1853, Lockport, NY; *m* (1) Abia Dayton (2) Sally Bush; five children. Methodist. Farmer, innkeeper, tanner, distiller. Granted 1,200 acres; leased [350] acres from Joseph Brant. Lived in Burford Twp. Capt., York Militia, 1798; capt., 1st Regt., Oxford Militia, 1799. JP, London Dist., 11 Dec. 1806. MHA, Norfolk, Oxford and Middlesex, 1804–8; Oxford and Middlesex, 1808–12.

See DCB 8.

MANAHAN, Anthony, *b* 1794, Mount Bellew, County Galway, Ireland; *d* 21 Jan. 1849, Kingston, CW; *m* Sarah Phoebe Nugent (*dau* Hon. John Nugent, member of the Council of Trinidad). Roman Catholic. Merchant, businessman, lumberman. Lived in (1) Kingston 1820–26 (2) Marmora 1826–31 (3) Kingston 1831–49. Major, 2d Regt., Hastings Militia, 20 Oct. 1826; lt. col., 3 May 1830; col., 18 Sept. 1830; on active service 1837–8. JP, Midland Dist., 12 Sept. 1829. MHA, Hastings, 1836–41. Conservative.

See DCB 7.

MARKLE, Abraham, *b* 26 Oct. 1770, Ulster County, NY (13 Cols); *d* 26 Mar. 1826, Terre Haute, Indiana; *m* (1) ——— Vrooman (2) Catherine ———; eight sons, two daughters. Miller, innkeeper, distiller, farmer. Granted 200 acres; bought at least 200 acres. Lived in Ancaster Twp., 1802–13. MHA, York West, Saltfleet and Ancaster Twps., 1812–14.

See DCB 6.

MARKS, John Bennet, *b* 1777, Plymouth, England; *d* 7 Mar. 1872, Kingston, Ont.; *m* Ann ———. Anglican. Naval Clerk, purser, farmer. Lived in Pittsburgh Twp. Purser, Kingston dockyard, 1812–14; agent, naval hospital, 1816; agent and victualler, 1817; secretary to Commodore Barrie, 1819–34; naval storekeeper, Kingston, 1834–44; col., 3d Regt., Frontenac Militia, 13 Jan. 1838. JP, Midland Dist., 18 Apr. 1825. MHA, Frontenac, 1836–41. Conservative.

See PAC, RG 9, IB 5, vol. 6; RG 68, General Index to Commissions; Kingston *Daily News*, 8 Mar. 1872; T.L. Brock, "H.M. Dock Yard, Kingston, Under

Commissioner Robert Barrie, 1819–34" *Historic Kingston*, no. 16 (Jan. 1968): 6, 11, 18.

MARSH, Abraham, *d* 1833; *m* Catherine French; six daughters, two sons. "Gentleman." Granted a town lot in Cornwall. Lived in Cornwall. Private, 84th (Royal Highland Emigrant) Regt., 1776–84; lt., Stormont Militia by 1808. JP, Eastern Dist., 17 Oct. 1810. MHA, Stormont and Russell, 1810–12.

See PAC, RG 1, L 3, vol. 335, M 9/158; vol. 376, M Misc. 1/17; RG 68, General Index to Commissions; W.D. Reid, *The Loyalists in Ontario* (Lambertville, NJ 1973), 217.

MATTHEWS, John, *b*, England; *d* [1833], England. Unitarian. Farmer. Granted 800 acres. Lived in Lobo Twp., 1820–[29]. Capt., Royal Invalid Artillery; aide-de-camp to the Duke of Richmond, 1819. JP, London Dist., 31 July 1821. MHA, Middlesex, 1824–30. Reformer.

See DCB 6.

MATHEWSON, James, *b*, County Antrim, Ireland; *d* 9 Jan. 1843, Pittsburgh Mills, Pittsburgh Twp., CW. Anglican. Lumberman, miller. Lived at Pittsburgh Mills. JP, Midland Dist., 22 Oct. 1836. MHA, Frontenac, 1836–41. Conservative.

See PAC, RG 68, General Index to Commissions; *Upper Canada Herald*, 9 Aug. 1836; W.D. Reid, *Death Notices In Ontario* (Lambertville, NJ 1980), 257.

MEARS, Thomas, *b* [1775], 13 Cols; *d* 16 Oct. 1832, West Hawkesbury Twp., UC. Merchant, lumberman, miller, brewer, shipowner, public servant. Lived in West Hawkesbury Twp. JP, Eastern Dist., 11 Dec. 1806; Ottawa Dist., 25 Mar. 1816; commissioner to arrest persons suspected of high treason, Eastern Dist., 24 Mar. 1814; sheriff, Ottawa Dist., 25 Mar. 1816; inspector of licences, Ottawa Dist., 28 Mar. 1816. MHA, Prescott, 1808–16.

See PAC, RG 68, General Index to Commissions; UC, House of Assembly, *Journals* (1825) Appendix 10; M.A. Higginson, *The Village of Hawkesbury 1808–1888* (1961), 1–23, A.R.M. Lower, *Great Britain's Wood Yard* (Montreal 1973), 177; W.D. Reid, *Death Notices in Ontario* (Lambertville, NJ 1980), 164.

MERKLEY, Henry, *b* [1758], 13 Cols; *d* [1840]. Son of Christopher Merkley. Lutheran. Farmer. Granted [100] acres. Lived in Williamsburgh Twp. Private, King's Royal Regt. of NY (wounded); capt. Dundas Militia by 1807; Major, 1st Regt., Dundas Militia, 20 Feb. 1812; lt. col., 21 Jan. 1822. MHA, Dundas, 1808–12.

See PAC, RG 1, L 3, vol. 339a, M 12/3; RG 8, C 633d, p. 26; RG 9, IB 5, vol. 1; M.B. Fryer and W.A. Smy, *Rolls of the Provincial (Loyalist) Corps* (Toronto 1981), 36; J.F. Pringle, *Lunenburgh, or the Old Eastern District* (Cornwall 1890), 202; L.H. Irving, *Officers of the British Forces in Canada During the War of*

1812–15 (Welland 1908), 46–7; M.R. Dow, "The Markells and Merkleys of Upper Canada," *Canadian Genealogist* 2, no. 2 (1980).

MERRITT, William Hamilton, *b* 3 July 1793, Bedford, NY; *d* 5 July 1862, Cornwall, CW. Son of Thomas Merritt, UE (lt., Queen's Rangers) and Mary Hamilton; *m* Catharine Prendergast; four sons, two daughters. Attended Richard Cockrel's school and Rev. John Burns' school at Niagara. Anglican. Farmer, miller, distiller, businessman, promoter, merchant, lumberman, land agent, public servant. Granted 1,000 acres. Lived at St. Catharines. Lt., Niagara Dragoons; capt., troop of provincial dragoons, 1812–14. JP, Niagara Dist., 5 Dec. 1817; collector of customs, Port Dalhousie, 2 Dec. 1829. MHA, Haldimand, 1832–41. [Conservative.]
See DCB 9.

MOORE, Elias, *b* [1776], NJ (13 Cols). Quaker. Farmer. Owned or rented about 900 acres. Lived in Yarmouth Twp. [1812–?]. MHA, Middlesex, 1834–41. Reformer.
See PAC, RG 1, L 3, vol. 379a, M Leases/225; C. Read, *The Rising in Western Upper Canada* (Toronto 1982), 54, 90, 121, 235.

MORRIS, James, *b* 1 Nov. 1798, Paisley, Scotland; *d* 29 Sept. 1865, Brockville, CW. Son of Alexander Morris and Janet Lang; brother of William Morris (*q.v.*); *m* Emily Rosamund Murney (sister of Edmund Murney, *q.v.*); four daughters, four sons. Attended Mr. Nelson's academy, Sorel, LC. Presbyterian (Church of Scotland). Merchant, banker. Lived in Brockville. Capt., 3d Regt., Leeds Militia, 19 June 1822; lt. col., 30 Jan. 1836. JP, Johnstown Dist., 18 Apr. 1825. MHA, Leeds, 1837–41. Reformer.
See DCB 9.

MORRIS, William, *b* 31 Oct. 1786, Paisley, Scotland; *d* 29 June 1858, Montreal. Son of Alexander Morris and Janet Lang; brother of James Morris (*q.v.*); *m* Elizabeth Cochran; four daughters, three sons. Attended a grammar school in Paisley. Presbyterian (Church of Scotland). Merchant, miller, distiller, businessman, speculator, public servant. Granted 1,000 acres; bought at least 4,120 acres, including 1,400 acres in Loyalist rights. Lived in (1) Elizabethtown Twp. 1806–16 (2) Perth 1816–45. Ens., 1st Regt., Leeds Militia, 1812–14; lt. col., 2d Regt., Lanark Militia, 18 Jan. 1822; col., 14 Feb. 1831. JP, Johnstown Dist., 19 Mar. 1818; Bathurst Dist., 24 Feb. 1830; member of the Legislative Council of UC, 22 Jan. 1836. MHA, Carleton, 1820–24; Lanark, 1824–36. Conservative.
See DCB 8.

MORRISON, Thomas David, *b* [1796], Quebec City; *d* 19 Mar. 1856,

Toronto. Son of William Morrison; *m* Effie Gilbert. Studied medicine in the USA. Methodist. Physician. Granted 200 acres. Lived in York (Toronto) 1816–38. Clerk, Purveyor's Branch, British Army Medical Dept., 1812–14. MHA, York (3d riding) 1834–9, Reformer.
See DCB 8.

MOUNT, Roswell, *b* [1797], Delaware Twp., UC; *d* 19 Jan. 1834, Toronto. Son of Moses Mount UE (sgt., Butler's Rangers) and Jane Burtch, (*dau* Charles Burtch, UE); one daughter, one son. Learned surveying with Mahlon Burwell (*q.v.*). [Anglican.] Surveyor. Granted 200 acres plus at least 2,003 acres in payment for surveys. Lived in Delaware Twp. [Private] on duty 1812–14; capt., 4th Regt., Middlesex Militia, 10 Apr. 1823; lt. col., 5th Regt., Middlesex Militia, 18 Feb. 1832. MHA, Middlesex, 1830–4. Conservative.
See DCB 6.

MURNEY, Edmund, *b* 11 Nov. 1812, Kingston, UC; *d* 15 Aug. 1861, Belleville, CW. Son of Henry Murney (commander, Provincial Marine). Attended Upper Canada College; studied law with M.S. Bidwell (*q.v.*). Anglican. Lawyer, public servant. Bought at least 1,000 acres in Loyalist rights. Lived in Belleville. Major, 1st Regt., Hastings Militia, 3 Jan. 1838. Clerk of the Peace, Victoria Dist., 18 Oct. 1839. MHA, Hastings, 1836–41. Conservative.
See PAC, RG 8, C 84, p. 176; RG 9, IB 5, vol. 6; Toronto *Globe*, 17 Aug. 1861; L.F. Gates, *Land Policies of Upper Canada* (Toronto 1968), 334.

NELLES, Robert, *b* 6 Oct. 1761, NY (13 Cols); *d* 27 July 1842, Grimsby, CW. Son of Henry William Nelles, UE (capt., Indian Dept.); brother of Abraham Nelles, member of the Legislative Council of UC; *m* (1) Elizabeth Moore (2) Maria Jane Waddell; seven daughters, seven sons. Anglican. Farmer, miller, distiller, shipowner. Granted [3,200] acres. Lived in Grimsby Twp. Lt., Indian Dept., during the American Revolution (HP 1784); capt., Lincoln Militia, 28 July 1794; lt. col., 4th Regt., Lincoln Militia, 1814; col., 12 Jan. 1822. JP, Home Dist., 1 July 1796; Niagara Dist., 11 Dec. 1800. MHA, West York, Lincoln (1st riding) and Haldimand, 1800–8; Lincoln (1st riding) 1816–20.
See DCB 7.

NICHOL, Robert, *b* [1774], Scotland; *d* 3 May 1824, accidentally in the Niagara River; *m* Theresa Wright. Miller, distiller, merchant, public servant. Granted 2,400 acres plus a town lot in Niagara; bought [200] acres. Lived in (1) Amherstburgh (2) Fort Erie (3) Woodhouse Twp. Lt., Lincoln Militia by 1803; lt. col., 2d Regt., Lincoln Militia, 12 Feb. 1812; quartermaster general of militia, 1812–14. JP, Niagara Dist., 11 Dec. 1806; judge, Surrogate Court, Niagara Dist., 11 Mar. 1824. MHA, Norfolk, 1812–24.
See DCB 6.

NORTON, Hiram, *b* Vt., USA; *d* 1875; *m* Rhoda Morey. Methodist. Merchant, manufacturer, stage proprietor. Lived in Prescott. JP, Johnstown Dist., 22 July 1833; JP, Eastern Dist., 4 Dec. 1837. MHA, Grenville, 1831–8. Reformer.
See PAC, RG 68, General Index to Commissions; Toronto *Herald,* 2 Aug. 1836; T. Leavitt, *History of Leeds and Grenville* (Brockville 1879), 128, 148.

PARKE, Thomas, *b* 1793, Co. Wicklow, Ireland; *d* 29 Jan. 1864, St. Catharines, CW; *m* (1) Sarah —— (2) Harriet Rose Wilkes; [four sons, three daughters]. Methodist. Carpenter, builder, developer, newspaper publisher. Granted 100 acres; bought and subdivided land near London; bought Loyalist rights. Lived in (1) York (Toronto) 1820–32 (2) London 1832–[45]. JP, London Dist., 7 July 1840. MHA, Middlesex, 1834–41. Reformer.
See DCB 9.

PATTEE, David, *b* 30 July 1778, Goffstown, NH; *d* 5 Feb. 1851, Hawkesbury, CW. Son of John Pattee and Mary Hadley; *m* Clarissa Thomas; five daughters, three sons. Studied medicine. Anglican. Miller, farmer, public servant. Bought 300 acres. Lived in Hawkesbury [1803]–51. Capt., 1st Regt., Prescott Militia, 29 Feb. 1812. JP, [Eastern Dist.], 24 Mar. 1812; Ottawa Dist., 25 Mar. 1816; judge, Surrogate Court, Ottawa Dist., 25 Mar. 1816. MHA, Prescott and Russell, 1821–4.
See DCB 8.

PATTINSON, Richard, *b* [1773, 13 Cols]; *d* 1 Jan. 1818, Albany, NY: *m* Julie [Chabert]. Merchant, shipowner, lumberman. Granted 1,200 acres plus town, water and park lots in Sandwich. Lived in Sandwich [1796–?]. Capt., Essex Militia by 1807; capt., 2d Regt., Essex Militia, 1812–14. JP, Western Dist., 11 Dec. 1806. MHA, Essex, 1812–16.
See PAC, RG 1, L 3, vol. 400a, P 4/6; vol. 401, P 5/16.; vol. 402, P 9/16; RG 8, C 257, pp. 196–7; C 728, p. 61a; RG 19, E 5a, vol. 3744, no. 262; RG 68, General Index to Commission; L.H. Irving, *Officers of the British Forces in Canada During the War of 1812–15* (Welland 1908), 92, W.D. Reid, *Death Notices of Ontario* (Lambertville, NJ 1980), 22.

PAWLING, Benjamin, *b* [1750], Penn. (13 Cols); *d* 12 Dec. 1818, Grantham Twp., UC; *m* Susan ——; four sons, one daughter. [Anglican.] Farmer, public servant. Granted 3,000 acres. Lived in Grantham Twp. Lt., Butler's Rangers, 25 Oct. 1778; capt. (HP 1784); major, Lincoln Militia, 28 July 1794. JP, Nassau Dist., 19 Jan. 1788; Home Dist., 1 July 1796; Niagara Dist., 1 Jan. 1800; judge, Court of Common Pleas, Nassau Dist., 24 Oct. 1788. MHA, Lincoln (2d riding) 1792–6.
See DCB 5.

PERRY, Peter, *b* 14 Nov. 1792, Ernesttown Twp., UC; *d* 24 Aug. 1851, Saratoga, NY. Son of Robert Perry, UE, (sgt., Loyal [Jessup's] Rangers) and Jemima Gary Washburn (sister of Ebeneezer Washburn, *q.v.*); *m* Mary Ham (*dau* John Ham, UE); seven daughters, two sons. Methodist. Farmer, merchant, land speculator. Granted 200 acres; bought 5,800 acres in Loyalist rights. Lived in (1) South Fredericksburg Twp. to 1836 (2) Whitby, 1836–51. On duty 1812–14 as [private], 1st Regt., Addington Militia. JP, Midland Dist., 30 Sept. 1829, MHA, Lennox and Addington, 1824–36. Reformer.

See DCB 8.

PETERSON, Paul, *b* [1791, UC]. Son of [Nicholas Peterson, UE]. Methodist. Farmer. Granted [200] acres. Lived in [Adolphustown Twp.] MHA, Prince Edward, 1820–30. Reformer.

See PAC, RG 1, L 3, vol. 402a, P 10/30; UC, House of Assembly, *Journals* (1828) Appendix; W. Canniff, *The Settlement of Upper Canada* (Toronto 1869), 116–7.

PETTIT, Nathaniel, *b* 12 June 1724, NJ (13 Cols); *d* 9 Mar. 1803, Ancaster Twp., UC. Son of Nathaniel Pettit and Elizabeth Heath; *m* Margaret McFarland; six daughters, one son. Farmer, public servant. Granted 2,000 acres. Lived in (1) Grimsby Twp., [1787–1800] (2) Ancaster Twp., [1800]–3. Commissioned to raise loyal forces, 1776; POW, 1777–8. JP Nassau Dist., 19 Jan. 1789; Home Dist., 1 July 1796; judge, Court of Common Pleas, Nassau Dist., 4 Oct. 1788. MHA, Durham, York and Lincoln (1st riding) 1792–6.

See DCB 5.

PINHEY, Hamnet Kirkes, *b* 11 Dec. 1784, Plymouth, England; *d* 3 Mar. 1857, Ottawa. Son of William Pinhey and Mary Townley; *m* Mary Ann Tasker; two daughters, two sons. Attended Christ's Hospital School, London. Anglican. Farmer, miller. Granted 1,000 acres. Lived in March Twp. JP Bathurst Dist., 24 Feb. 1830. MHA, Carleton, 1832–3. Conservative.

See DCB 8.

PLAYTER, Ely, *b* 1775, [NJ (13 Cols)]. Son of Capt. George Playter, UE; *m* Sophia Beeman. Farmer, tavern keeper. Granted 500 acres. Lived in York Twp. Adj., York Militia by 1807; lt., 3d Regt., York Militia, 30 June 1812; commissary of transport, Port of York, 1812–15; capt., 1st Regt., East York Militia, 13 July 1816. MHA, York and Simcoe, 1824–7.

See PAC, RG 1, L 3, vol. 400a, P 4/26; vol. 404, P 12/31; RG 8, C 690, p. 166; RG 9, IB 5, vol. 1; E.G. Firth, ed., *The Town of York, 1793–1815* (Toronto 1962), 17, 99; L.H. Irving, *Officers of the British Forces in Canada During the*

War of 1812–15 (Welland 1908), 67; *Commercial and Biographical Record of the County of York* (Toronto 1907), 198.

POWELL, John Ambrose Hume, *b*, Ireland; *d* 20 July 1843, Perth, CW. Son of col. James Hamilton Powell (superintendent and secretary, Perth military settlement). Anglican. Public servant. Granted 600 acres. Lived in Perth. Capt., 1st Regt., Lanark Militia, 5 Feb. 1823. Sherriff, Bathurst Dist., 14 Nov. 1831–[2]; reappointed, 2 May 1834. MHA, Lanark, 1836–41. Conservative.

See PAC, RG 1, L 3, vol. 410, P 21/8; RG 9, IB 5, vols. 2, 6; *Upper Canada Herald*, 9 Aug. 1836; Chatham *Journal*, 5 Aug. 1843.

PRINCE, John, *b* 12 Mar. 1796, England; *d* 30 Nov. 1870, Sault Ste. Marie, Ont. Son of Richard Prince and Mary ——— ; *m* Mary Ann Millington; eight sons, one daughter. Educated by his uncle and at the Collegiate Grammar School, Hereford, England, and studied law. Anglican. Farmer, lawyer, brewer, ferry operator, mine and railway promoter. Bought at least 200 acres. Lived in Sandwich Twp., 1833–60. On active service Jan.–Dec. 1838; col., 3d Regt., Essex Militia, 24 Apr. 1838. JP, Western Dist., 11 Nov. 1833. MHA, Essex, 1836–41. Conservative.

See DCB 9.

RADENHURST, Thomas Mabon, *b* 6 Apr. 1803, Fort St. John, LC; *d* 7 Aug. 1854, Perth, CW. Son of Thomas Radenhurst and Ann Campbell; *m* Lucy Edith Ridout (*dau* Hon. Thomas Ridout, *q.v.*); six daughters, five sons. Attended the Home District Grammar School under Rev. John Strachan and studied law with George Ridout. Anglican. Lawyer. Lived in Perth [1823]–54. Ens., 1st Regt., East York Militia, 20 Dec. 1820. MHA, Carleton, 1828–30. Reformer.

See DCB 8.

RANDALL, Robert, *b* [1768], Va. (13 Cols); *d* 1 May 1834, Niagara Falls, UC. Anglican. Merchant, manufacturer, miller, land speculator. Granted 1,000 acres; bought "valuable lands in various parts of the province." Lived in Chippawa. MHA, Lincoln (4th riding) 1820–34. Reformer.

See DCB 6.

RICHARDSON, Charles, *b* 6 Mar 1805, UC; *d* 11 Mar. 1848, Niagara, CW. Son of Dr. Robert Richardson (assistant surgeon, Queen's Rangers) and Madeleine Askin; *m* (1) Elizabeth Euretta Clench (*dau* Ralph Clench, *q.v.*) (2) Jane Clarke; [two daughters, one son]. Studied law with John Beverley Robinson (*q.v.*). Anglican. Lawyer, public servant. Lived at Niagara. Lt., 1st

Regt., West York Militia, 21 June 1823. Clerk of the Peace, Niagara Dist., 21 Feb. 1828. MHA, Niagara (town) 1834–41. Conservative.

See PAC, RG 9, IB 5, vol. 1; RG 68, General Index to Commissions; A.C. Casselman, ed., *Richardson's War of 1812* (Toronto 1902), xlvii; E.G. Firth, ed., *The Town of York 1815–1834* (Toronto 1966), 97; W.D. Reid, *Death Notices of Ontario* (Lambertville, NJ 1980), 348.

RIDOUT, Thomas, *b* [4 Sept.] 1754, England; *d* 8 Feb. 1829, York (Toronto). Son of George Ridout and Mary Gibbs; *m* Isabella ——— (2) Mary Campbell (*dau* Alexander Campbell, UE); eight sons, five daughters. Anglican. Public servant. Granted 3,750 acres plus two town lots in York (Toronto). Lived at (1) Niagara 1792–96 (2) York (Toronto) 1796–1829. Capt., York Militia by 1807. JP, Home Dist., 11 Dec. 1806; clerk, Surveyor General's Office, 1793; registrar York County, 14 Sept. 1796; clerk of the Peace, Home Dist., 1 Jan. 1800; joint acting surveyor general, 6 Jan. 1807; surveyor general, 12 Sept. 1810; commissioner to arrest persons suspected of high treason, 20 Mar. 1814; member of the Legislative Council of UC, 11 Oct. 1823. MHA, York East and Simcoe, 1812–16.

See DCB 6.

ROBINSON, Christopher, *b* 1763, Va. (13 Cols); *d* 21 Nov. 1798, York (Toronto). Son of [Peter Robinson and Sarah Lister]; *m* Esther Sayre (*dau* Rev. John Sayre, UE); three sons (Peter Robinson, *q.v.*; Sir John Beverley Robinson, *q.v.*; William Benjamin Robinson, *q.v.*) and three daughters. Attended William and Mary College. Anglican. Lawyer, farmer, public servant. Granted [2,000] acres plus town lots in York (Toronto) and Niagara. Lived in (1) Kingston 1792–98 (2) York (Toronto) 1798. Ens., Queen's Rangers, 1781–3 (HP 1783). Inspector of woods in UC, 1 June 1792. MHA, Addington and Ontario, 1796–98.

See DCB 4.

ROBINSON, Sir John Beverley, *b* 26 July 1791, Berthier, LC; *d* 31 Jan. 1863, Toronto. Son of Christopher Robinson (*q.v.*) and Esther Sayre; brother of Peter Robinson (*q.v.*) and William Benjamin Robinson (*q.v.*); *m* Emma Walker; four sons, three daughters. Educated at the schools of Rev. John Stuart, Kingston and Rev. John Strachan, Cornwall; studied law with D'Arcy Boulton (solicitor general) and John Macdonell (attorney general); read law at Lincoln's Inn. Anglican. Lawyer, public servant. Granted 1,700 acres. Bought land in York, Ontario and Peel co. and "29 parcels elsewhere." Lived in Toronto. Lt., promoted to capt., 25 Dec. 1812, 3d Regt., York Militia; col., 2d Regt., East York Militia, 1 Jan. 1823. Acting attorney general of UC, 19 Nov. 1812 (at age 21); attorney general, 11 Feb. 1818; member of the

Executive Council of UC, 25 April 1829; member of the Legislative Council of UC, 1 Jan. 1830; chief justice, Court of King's Bench, 13 July 1829. MHA, York (town) 1820–30. Conservative.
See DCB 9.

ROBINSON, Peter, *b* 1785, NB, *d* 8 July 1838, Toronto. Son of Christopher Robinson (*q.v.*) and Esther Sayre; brother of Sir John Beverley Robinson (*q.v.*) and William Benjamin Robinson (*q.v.*). Attended Rev. John Strachan's school, Cornwall. Anglican. Miller, fur trader, innkeeper, public servant. Granted 1,000 acres. Lived at (1) Newmarket (2) Holland Landing (3) York (Toronto). Capt., 1st Regt., York Militia, 1812–14; col., 1st Regt., North York Militia, 1 Jan. 1822. JP, Home Dist., 11 May 1818; member of the Executive Council of UC, 24 Dec. 1823; commissioner of Crown Lands, 30 Aug. 1827; member of the Legislative Council of UC, 6 Jan. 1829. MHA, York (east riding) and Simcoe, 1816–20; York and Simcoe, 1820–4.
See DCB 7.

ROBINSON, William Benjamin, *b* 22 Dec. 1797, Kingston, UC, *d* 18 July 1873, Toronto. Son of Christopher Robinson (*q.v.*) and Esther Sayre, brother of Hon. Peter Robinson (*q.v.*) and Sir John Beverley Robinson (*q.v.*); *m* Elizabeth Ann Jarvis (*dau* William Jarvis, UE, provincial secretary). Attended Rev. John Strachan's school, Cornwall. Anglican. Merchant, fur trader, miller, distiller, public servant. Granted 200 acres. Lived in (1) Newmarket (2) Holland Landing (3) St. Catharines, 1837–43. Capt., 1st Regt., East York Militia, 2 Apr. 1823; maj. 2d Regt., North York Militia, 7 June 1825; lt. col., 2 Apr. 1827. JP, Home Dist., 3 June 1822; superintendent, Welland Canal, 1833–43. MHA, Simcoe, 1830–41. Conservative.
See DCB 10.

ROBLIN, John, *b* 3 June 1774, [NJ, 13 Cols], *d* 28 Feb. 1813, Adolphustown Twp., UC. Son of Philip Roblin, UE, and Elizabeth Miller; uncle of John Phillip Roblin (*q.v.*); *m* Mary Moore. Methodist. Farmer. Granted 200 acres. Lived in Adolphustown Twp., 1786–1813. MHA, Lennox and Addington, 1808–10.
See PAC, RG 1, L 3, vol. 423, R 3/4; vol. 446, R Misc./85; MG 25, no. 254.

ROBLIN, John Phillip, *b* 16 Aug. 1799, Sophiasburghh Twp., UC; *d* 12 Nov. 1874, Picton, Ont. Son of Philip Roblin, UE, and Prudence Platt; nephew of John Roblin (*q.v.*); *m* Nancy Conger. Attended a local common school. Methodist. Farmer. Granted 200 acres. Bought 1,400 acres in Loyalist rights. Lived in Ameliasburg Twp. Ens., 1st Regt., Prince Edward Militia, 5 Dec. 1827; capt., cavalry troop, 1st Regt., Prince Edward Militia, 1837–8. JP, Prince Edward Dist., 15 Mar. 1834. MHA, Prince Edward 1830–6. Reformer.
See DCB 10.

ROGERS, David McGregor, *b* 23 Nov. 1772, [13 Cols]; *d* 18 July 1824, Haldimand Twp., UC. Son of James Rogers, UE (major, King's Rangers) and Margaret McGregor; *m* Sarah Playter (*dau* George Playter, UE, sister of Ely Playter, *q.v.*). Farmer, public servant. Granted 2,200 acres; bought or inherited [600] acres. Lived in (1) Fredericksburg Twp. (2) Cramahe Twp. (3) Haldimand Twp. Major, 1st Regt., Northumberland Militia on "special service," 1812–14. JP, Newcastle Dist., 29 Mar. 1813; registrar, Northumberland County, 3 July 1799; clerk, District Court, Newcastle Dist., 16 July 1802; clerk of the Peace, Newcastle Dist., 16 July 1802; registrar, surrogate Court, Newcastle Dist., 16 July 1802; judge, District Court and Surrogate Court, Newcastle Dist., 16 May 1815; commissioner to arrest persons suspected of high treason, Newcastle Dist., 24 Mar. 1814. MHA, Prince Edward and Adolphustown, 1796–1800; Hastings and Northumberland, 1800–8; Northumberland and Durham, 1808–16; Northumberland, 1820–4.
See DCB 6.

ROLPH, George, *b* 7 Apr. 1794, Thornbury, Gloucestershire, England; *d* 25 July 1875, Dundas Ont. Son of Thomas Rolph and Frances Petty; brother of John Rolph (*q.v.*); *m* Georgianna Clement; two daughters. Educated in England; studied law in York (Toronto). [Anglican.] Lawyer, public servant. Granted 500 acres; bought at least 400 acres. Lived at Vittoria 1808–[16], Dundas, [1816]–75. Lt., 1st Regt., Norfolk Militia, 1812–14; capt., 1st Regt., Gore Militia, 23 Apr. 1823. Clerk, District Court, Gore Dist., 4 Apr. 1816; registrar, Surrogate Court, Gore Dist., 4 Apr. 1816; clerk of the Peace, Gore Dist., [1] Apr. 1816. MHA, Halton, 1828–30. Reformer.
See DHB 1.

ROLPH, John, *b* 4 Mar. 1793, Thornbury, Gloucestershire, England; *d* 19 Oct. 1870, Mitchell, Ont. Son of Thomas Rolph and Frances Petty; brother of George Rolph (*q.v.*); *m* Grace Haines; three sons, one daughter. Read law at the Inner Temple; read law and medicine at St. John's College, Cambridge; studied medicine at St. Thomas and St. George Hospital, London. Anglican. Physician, lawyer, public servant. Granted 200 acres. Lived in (1) Charlotteville Twp. [1821]–31 (2) York (Toronto) 1831–7. Militia paymaster, London Dist., 1813–15; major, 2d Regt., Middlesex Militia, 24 Mar. 1823. Member of the Executive Council of UC, 20 Feb. 1836. MHA, Middlesex, 1824–30; Norfolk, 1836–8. Reformer.
See DCB 9.

RUTTAN, Henry, *b* 12 June 1792, Adolphustown Twp., UC; *d* 31 July 1871, Cobourg, Ont. Son of William Ruttan, UE (Lt., New Jersey Volunteers) and Margaret Steele; *m* Mary Jones; nine children. Educated in Adolphustown Twp. Anglican. Farmer, inventor, survey contractor, merchant, distiller, public servant. Granted 700 acres plus land as payment for surveys. Lived in (1) Kingston (2) Cramahe Twp. (3) Hamilton Twp. (4) Cobourg. Lt., Volunteer Incorporated Militia, 1812–14 (HP 1815); capt., 1st Regt., Northumberland Militia, 28 June 1825. JP, Newcastle Dist., 15 June 1818; sheriff, Newcastle Dist., 24 Oct. 1827. MHA, Northumberland, 1820–4, 1836–41. Conservative.

See DCB 10.

RYKERT, George, *b* 8 June 1797, Rhinebeck, NY, USA; *d* 1 Nov. 1857, St. Catharines, CW. Son of Zachesius Rykert (Reickert) and Catherine ——; *m* Ann Maria Mittleberger; three sons, one daughter. Anglican. Merchant, miller, distiller, surveyor. Lived in St. Catharines. [Private], 1st Regt., Lincoln Militia, 1812–14; capt., St. Catharines Cavalry Troop, 1838. JP, Niagara Dist., 31 May 1833. MHA, Lincoln (2d riding) 1834–41. Conservative.

See DCB 8.

RYMAL, Jacob, *b* 1790, UC; *d* 1868 in [Barton Twp., CW]. Son of Jacob Rymal; *m* Christine Horning. [Presbyterian.] Carpenter, [farmer]. Granted 400 acres. Lived in Barton Twp. Sgt., 1st Regt., York Militia, 1812–14. MHA, Wentworth, 1834–6. Reformer.

See PAC, RG 1, L 3, vol. 430, R 14/25; L 7, vol. 52; RG 5, A 1, vol. 212, pp. 6932–71; J. Powell, *Annals of the Forty*, no. 8, (1957).

SALMON, William, *b* 1802, Alveston, England; *d* 8 Feb. 1868, Simcoe, CW. Lawyer. Lived at Simcoe. Major, 2d Regt., Norfolk Militia, 6 Oct. 1828, MHA, Norfolk, 1838–41. [Conservative.]

See PAC, RG 9, IB 5, vol. 4; C. Read and R. Stagg, eds., *The Rebellion of 1837* (Toronto 1985), 361.

SAMSON, James Hunter, *b* [1800], Ireland; *d* 20 Mar. 1836, Belleville, UC. Son of Lt. —— Samson (adjutant, 70th [regular] Regt.). Studied law with C.A. Hagerman (*q.v.*). Lawyer. Lived in Belleville. Lt., 1st Regt., Frontenac Militia, 23 Nov. 1824; capt., 2d Regt., Hastings Militia, 15 Jan. 1827; major, 3 May 1830; lt. col., 18 Sept. 1830. MHA, Hastings, 1828–36. Conservative.

See DCB 7.

SCOLLICK, William, *d*, [Preston, UC]. Anglican. Farmer. Lived in Dumfries Twp. JP, Gore Dist., 14 July 1827. MHA, Halton, 1824–8.

See PAC, RG 1, L 3, vol. 467a, S 8/22; RG 68, General Index to Commissions; J.M. Young, *Reminiscences of the Early History of Galt and Dumfries* (Galt 1967), 147.

SECORD, David, *b* 10 Aug. 1759, NY (13 Cols); *d* 9 Aug. 1844, St. Davids, CW. Son of James Secord, UE (Lt., Indian Dept.) and Magdelana Badeau; *m*

(1) ——— Millard (2) Catharine Smith (3) Mary Dunn; ten sons, three daughters. Methodist. Miller, merchant, farmer. Granted 4,200 acres; bought [600] acres. Lived at St. Davids, 1786–1844. Sgt., Butler's Rangers (wounded) 1776–83; capt., Lincoln Militia, 28 July 1794; major, 2d Regt., Lincoln Militia, 1812–14. JP, Home Dist., 1 July 1796; Niagara Dist., 30 June 1800. MHA, Lincoln (2d riding) 1816–20.

See DCB 7.

SHADE, Absalom, *b* 1793, USA; *d* 15 Mar. 1862, Galt, CW; *m* (1) ——— Andrews (2) Jemima Davidson. Anglican. Miller, distiller, builder, contractor, farmer, merchant, businessman. Bought 900 acres. Lived in Galt, 1816–62. JP, Gore Dist., 2 Apr. 1833. MHA, Halton, 1831–4, 1836–41. Conservative.

See DCB 9.

SHAVER, Peter, *b* Oct. 1777, NY (13 Cols); *d* 21 June 1866, Iroquois, CW. Son of Philip Shaver (Schaeffer), UE (Private, King's Royal Regt., of NY). Methodist. Farmer, merchant, lumberman. Granted 700 acres; bought 200 acres. Lived in Matilda Twp. Ens., Dundas Militia by 1811; lt., 1st Regt., Dundas Militia, 1812–14; capt., 21 Jan. 1822; lt. col., 29 Apr. 1837. JP, Eastern Dist., 18 Apr. 1825. MHA, Dundas, 1820–4, 1828–41. Reformer.

See PAC, RG 1, L 7, vol. 52; RG 9, 1C 6, vols. 7, 9; RG 19, E 5a, vol. 3746, no. 416; RG 68, General Index to Commissions; J. Croil, *Dundas, or a Sketch of Canadian History* (Montreal 1861), 281–2; L.H. Irving, *Officers of the British Forces in Canada During the War of 1812–15* (Welland 1908), 46, 49.

SHERWOOD, Henry, *b* 1807, Augusta Twp., UC; *d* 7 July 1855, Bad Kessinger, Germany. Son of Levius Peters Sherwood (*q.v.*) and Charlotte Jones (*dau* Ephraim Jones, *q.v.*; nephew of Jonas Jones (*q.v.*); *m* Mary Graham Smith (*dau* Peter Smith, UE). Attended the Home Dist. Grammar School under Rev. John Strachan, studied law with H.J. Boulton (*q.v.*). Anglican. Lawyer. Lived in (1) Brockville (2) Toronto 1835–55. Ens., 4th Regt., Leeds Militia, 15 Mar. 1824; lt., 1st Regt., West York Militia, 16 May 1827; lt. col., 2d Regt., North York Militia, 22 Jan. 1838; aide-de-camp to Lt.-Gov. Sir Francis Bond Head, Dec., 1837. MHA, Brockville, 1836–41. Conservative.

See DCB 8.

SHERWOOD, Levius Peters, *b* 1777, St. John's, Quebec; *d* May 1850, [Toronto]. Son of Justus Sherwood, UE (capt., Loyal [Jessup's] Rangers) and Sarah Bottum; brother of Samuel Sherwood (*q.v.*); *m* Charlotte Jones (*dau* Ephraim Jones, *q.v.*); four sons, including Henry Sherwood (*q.v.*) three daughters. Lawyer, miller, land speculator, public servant. Granted 1,900 acres; bought over 1,000 acres. Lived in Brockville. Capt., Leeds Militia by 1808; lt. col. commanding the incorporated militia of the Eastern and Johnstown dists., 1812–14; col., 1st Regt., Leeds Militia, 21 Jan. 1820. Collector of customs, Brockville, 1801; registrar, Leeds and Carleton cos., 20 May 1801; judge, Surrogate Court, Johnstown Dist., 16 Mar. 1812; District Court, Johnstown Dist., 15 Nov. 1820; Eastern Dist. Court, 19 Mar. 1821; Court of King's Bench of UC, 17 Oct. 1825. MHA, Leeds, 1812–16, 1820–4.

See DCB 7.

SHERWOOD, Samuel, *b*, [13 Cols]. Son of Justus Sherwood, UE (capt., Loyal [Jessup's] Rangers) and Sarah Bottum; brother of Levius Peters Sherwood (*q.v.*); uncle of Henry Sherwood (*q.v.*). Studied law in Montreal. Lawyer, public servant. Granted 4,000 acres; bought 10,800 acres in Loyalist rights with R. Sherwood. Lived in Augusta Twp. Scout "on secret service" with Jessup's Rangers during the American Revolution; capt., Grenville Militia by 1807. JP, Mecklenburg Dist., 16 Oct. 1790; Midland Dist., 15 July 1796; registrar, Surrogate Court, Eastern Dist., 7 June 1796; Surrogate Court, Johnstown Dist., 1 Jan. 1800. MHA, Grenville, 1800–8.

See PAC, RG 1, L 3, vol. 450, S 3/175, 190; vol. 493a, S Misc./197; RG 68, General Index to Commissions; MG 21, B 168, p. 86; T. Leavitt, *History of Leeds and Grenville* (Brockville 1879), 19, 161–2; L.F. Gates, *Land Policies of Upper Canada* (Toronto 1968), 333; W.D. Reid, *The Loyalists of Ontario* (Lambertville, NJ 1973), 286.

SHIBLEY, Jacob, *b* 31 Oct. 1778, 13 Cols; *d* 11 Nov. 1869. Son of John Shibley, UE (corp., Loyal [Jessup's] Rangers). Farmer, "gentleman." Lived in Portland Twp. Ens., 1st Regt., Frontenac Militia, 1812–14. JP, Midland Dist., 18 Apr. 1825. MHA, Frontenac, 1834–6. [Reformer.]

See PAC, RG 1, L 3, vol. 477, S 2/50; RG 68, General Index to Commissions; UC, House of Assembly, *Journals* (1825) Appendix; *Upper Canada Herald*, 19 Apr. 1836; H.C. Burleigh, *Loyalist Graves in the Bay of Quinte Region* (Bath 1972), 4.

SMALL, James Edward, *b* Feb. 1798, York (Toronto); *d* 27 May 1869, London, Ont. Son of John Small (clerk, Executive Council of UC) and Eliza Goldsmith; *m* Frances Elizabeth Ridout (*dau* Thomas Ridout, *q.v.*); four sons. Attended the Home Dist. School under Rev. John Strachan and Rev. George Okill Stuart; studied law with W.W. Baldwin. Anglican. Lawyer. Granted 1,700 acres. Lived in Toronto. Midshipman on ship *St. Lawrence* 1812–14; lt., 1st Regt., East York Militia, 2 May 1820; capt., 30 Jan. 1826; lt. col., 30 May 1835. MHA, Toronto 1834–6; York (3d riding) 1839–41. Reformer.

See DCB 9.

SMITH, David William, *b* 4 Sept. 1764, England; *d* 9 May 1837, England. Son of John Smith (major, 5th [Regular] Regt.) and Anne ———; *m* (1) Anne O'Reilly (2) Mary Tyler; nine children. Soldier, miller, public servant.

Granted 1,450 acres; bought [200] acres. Lived at (1) Detroit (2) Niagara (3) York (Toronto). Ens., 5th (Regular) Regt., 8 Sept. 1779; lt. and assistant deputy quartermaster, Niagara, 2 Apr. 1792; capt., 2 Sept. 1795; col., Lincoln Militia, 7 Jan. 1797; col., York Militia, 1 June 1798. JP, Nassau Dist., 27 Aug. 1792; acting surveyor general of UC, 23 Sept. 1792; member of the Executive Council of UC, 2 Mar. 1796; lieutenant, York County, 3 Dec. 1798; master in Chancery, 17 July 1799. MHA, Suffolk and Essex, 1792–6; Lincoln (2d riding) 1796–1800; Norfolk, Oxford and Middlesex, 1800–4.

See DCB 7.

SMITH, Harmannus, *b* 13 Nov. 1790, Louth Twp., UC; *d* 1 July 1872. Son of Joseph Smith, UE, and Anna Margaret House (*dau* Hermanns House, UE); *m* Elizabeth Fillman; four sons, three daughters. Attended school at Niagara; studied medicine with a Dr. Allen. Anglican. Physician, farmer, developer. Bought [300] acres. Lived in (1) Barton Twp. (2) Ancaster Twp. Private, 1st Regt., Lincoln Militia, 27 June 1812; assistant surgeon, 14 May 1813. MHA, Wentworth, 1834–6. Reformer.

See PAC, RG 8, C 1701, pp. 87, 103; L.H. Irving, *Officers of the British Forces in Canada During the War of 1812–15* (Welland 1908), 34; J. Powell, *Annals of the Forty*, no. 8 (1957); V.M. Spack, "The Story of a Pioneer Doctor, Harmannus Smith," *Wentworth Bygones* 5 (1964); W. Caniff, *The Medical Profession in Upper Canada* (Toronto 1894), 620.

SMITH, John David, *b* 1786, NY (13 Cols); *d* 30 Mar. 1849, Port Hope, CW. Son of Elias Smith, UE, and Catherine ———; *m* (1) Susan ——— (2) Augusta Louisa Woodward; fourteen children. [Merchant.] Granted 200 acres; bought [200] acres. Lived in Port Hope. Ens., Durham Militia by 1808; capt., 1st Regt., Durham Militia, 1812–14. JP, Newcastle Dist., 29 Mar. 1813. MHA, Durham, 1828–30. Reformer.

See PAC, RG 1, L 3, vol. 454, S 9/4, vol. 456a; S 10/187; vol. 474, S 22/137; RG 68, General Index to Commissions; D.A. McKenzie, *Death Notices in the Christian Guardian* (Lambertville, NJ 1982), 286, L.H. Irving, *Officers of the British Forces in Canada During the War of 1812–15* (Welland 1908), 62; W.D. Reid, *The Loyalists of Ontario* (Lambertville, NJ 1973), 294; M. McBurney and M. Byers, *Homesteads: Early Buildings and Families from Kingston to Toronto* (Toronto 1979), 189.

SMITH, Thomas, *b* [1754], Wales; *d* 3 Mar. 1833, Sandwich UC. Merchant, surveyor, soldier, public servant. Granted 1,200 acres plus at least 4,455 acres as payment for surveys; bought at least 800 acres. Lived in Sandwich. Capt., Indian Dept., 1776–7; lt., later capt., Essex Militia, 1787–95. JP, Western Dist., 15 July 1796; clerk, Court of Common Pleas, Hesse Dist., 24 July 1788. MHA, Kent, 1796–1800.

See PAC, RG 1, L 3, vol. 448a, s 2/36; L 4, vol. 2, pp. 128–92; RG 19, E 5a, vol. 3752, no. 1155; MG 19, F 1, vol. 6; E. Lajeunesse, ed., *The Windsor Border Region* (Toronto 1960), 202; R.W. Widdis, "Speculation and the Surveyor," *HS/SH* 15, no. 30 (Nov. 1982): 450.

SOVEREIGN, Philip, *b* [1779, 13 Cols]; *d* 2 July 1833, Trafalgar Twp., UC. Son of Leonard Sovereign and Ruhannah ———. Farmer, public servant. Granted 200 acres. Lived in (1) Townsend Twp. 1800–14 (2) Trafalgar Twp. 1814–33. JP, Gore Dist., 22 June 1818; judge, Surrogate Court, London Dist. 13 Mar. 1811. MHA, Norfolk, 1808–12.

See PAC, RG 1, L 3, vol. 453, s 7/27; vol. 456a, s 10/144; RG 5, B 7, vol. 3; RG 68, General Index to Commissions; W.D. Reid, *Death Notices of Ontario* (Lambertville, NJ 1980), 94; E.A. Owen, *Pioneer Sketches of Long Point Settlement* (Toronto 1898), 493.

SPENCER, Hazelton, *b* 29 Aug. 1757, East Greenwich, Rhode Island (13 Cols); *d* 6 Feb. 1813, Fredericksburg Twp., UC. Son of Benjamin Spencer, UE, and Mercy Potter; *m* Margaret Richards (*dau* John Richards, UE); six sons, three daughters. Anglican. Farmer, soldier, public servant. Granted 3,200 acres; bought at least 2,600 acres. Lived in Fredericksburg Twp. Lt., King's Royal Regt. of NY 1776–83 (HP 1784); capt., 2d Bttn., Royal Canadian Volunteers, 1795; major, 1797; col., 1st Regt., Lennox Militia, 1794. JP, Mecklenburg Dist., 16 Oct. 1790; Midland Dist., 1 Jan. 1800; judge, Surrogate Court, Midland Dist., 5 Sept. 1793; lieutenant, Lennox County, 23 June 1794. MHA, Lennox, Hastings and Northumberland, 1792–6.

See DCB 5.

STINSON, John, *b* 17 Mar. 1764, NH (13 Cols); *d* 7 Jan. 1842, Hallowell Twp., CW. Son of John Stinson, UE (capt., King's Rangers); *m* Jane ———. [Farmer.], "gentleman." Granted 2,000 acres. Lived in (1) Sophiasburg Twp. 1786–[1802] (2) Hallowell Twp. [1802]–42. Capt., 1st Regt. Prince Edward Militia, 14 July 1807; capt. (Stinson's) troop of light dragoons, 1812–14. JP, Midland Dist., 15 July 1796. MHA, Prince Edward, 1811–16.

See PAC, RG 1, L 3, vol. 494, s Misc./294; vol. 450, s 3/120; L 7, vol. 52; RG 9, IB 5, vols. 1, 3; RG 68, General Index to Commissions; W.D. Reid, *Death Notices of Ontario* (Lambertville, NJ 1980), 305–6; H.C. Burleigh, *Loyalist Graves in the Bay of Quinte Region* (Bath 1972), 31.

STRANGE, John, *b* 2 Sept. 1788, Kilbryde Scotland; *d* 14 Oct. 1840, Caledonia Springs, CW. Son of Maxwell Strange and Catherine Warlock; *m* Mary McGill; three sons, two daughters. Presbyterian. Merchant, auctioneer. Lived in Kingston. Capt., 1st Regt., Frontenac Militia, 18 June 1822. JP, Midland Dist., 13 Dec. 1834. MHA, Frontenac, 1834–6. Conservative.

See PAC, RG 1, L 3, vol. 271, K 11/45; RG 5, A 1, vol. 46, p. 22901; RG 9, IB 5, vol. 5; RG 19, E 5a, vol. 3756, no. 1615; RG 68, General Index to Commissions; private communication from Dr. Margaret Angus, Kingston.

STREET, Samuel, *b* 2 Jan. 1753, Wilton, Conn. (13 Cols); *d* 3 Feb. 1815, Thorold, UC. Son of Samuel Street and Elizabeth Smith; *m* Phoebe Van Camp; one daughter. Presbyterian. Merchant, farmer, miller, speculator, public servant. Granted 1,200 acres; bought at least 9,800 acres in Loyalist rights. Lived in Willoughby Twp. Supplied provisions to the British forces during the American Revolution; capt., 3d Regt., Lincoln Militia, 2 Jan. 1809; deputy paymaster of militia, 1813–15. JP, Nassau Dist., 24 July 1788; judge, Niagara Dist. Court, 7 Jan. 1807. MHA, Lincoln (3d riding) 1796–1800, 1808–12.

See DCB 5.

SWAYZE, Isaac, *b* 1751, [Roxbury] NJ (13 Cols); *d* 24 Mar. 1828, Niagara, UC. Son of Caleb Swayze; *m* (1) [Bethia Luce] (2) Sarah Secord (3) Elenor Ferris; four daughters, three sons. [Presbyterian.] Farmer, public servant. Granted 2,000 acres; bought 400 acres. Lived in Niagara Twp. "Pilot to the New York Army" during the American Revolution; capt., Provincial Artillery Drivers, 1812–14; col., 1st Regt., Lincoln Militia. JP, Home Dist., 1 July 1796; inspector of licences, Niagara Dist., 1 Mar. 1803. MHA, Lincoln (3d riding) 1792–6; Lincoln (2d, 3d and 4th ridings) 1800–8; Lincoln (4th riding) 1814–20.

See DCB 6.

TAYLER, Josias, *b* 1787, England. Merchant, public servant. Granted 700 acres. Lived in Perth. Ens., 3d (Regular) Regt., 9 July 1803; lt., 1805; capt., 24 Feb. 1813; capt., Canadian Fencible Regt., 17 Oct. 1813 (HP 1816); col., 3d Regt., Lanark Militia, 10 Jan. 1822. JP, Johnstown Dist., 27 Mar. 1821; Bathurst Dist., 12 Nov. 1833; registrar, Surrogate Court, Bathurst Dist., 24 June 1830; judge, Bathurst Dist. Court, 25 July 1835. MHA, Lanark, 1834–6. [Conservative.]

See PAC, RG 1, L 3, vol. 497, T 10/30; vol. 500, T 15/16; vol. 512, T Misc./47; RG 5, A 1, vol. 114, p. 64152; vol. 178, p. 98414; RG 8, C 1171, p. 74; RG 9, IB 5, vol. 2; RG 68, General Index to Commissions; *Upper Canada Herald*, 19 Apr. 1836; UC, House of Assembly, *Journals* (1825) Appendix 10.

TERRY, Parshall, *b* 1756, Orange County, NY (13 Cols); *d* 20 July 1808 by drowning in the Don River; *m* Rhoda Skinner; ten daughters and three sons, including William Terry (*q.v.*). Miller, merchant. Granted 1,200 acres; bought 500 acres. Lived in (1) Niagara [1784]–98 (2) York (Toronto) 1798–1808. Sgt., Butler's Rangers, 1777–84. JP, Home Dist., 1 July 1796. MHA, Lincoln (4th riding) and Norfolk, 1792–6.

See PAC, RG 1, L 3, vol. 495, T 1/10, T 3/10; RG 68, General Index to Commissions; Henry Scadding, *Toronto of Old*, ed. F.H. Armstrong (Toronto, 1966), 381; W.D. Reid, *The Loyalists of Ontario* (Lambertville, NJ 1973), 316.

TERRY, William, *b* [1798], Niagara, UC. Son of Parshall Terry (*q.v.*) and Rhoda Skinner. Innkeeper, apothecary. Granted 200 acres. Lived in Thorold Twp. [Private], 2d Regt., Lincoln Militia, 1812–14. MHA, Lincoln (1st and 2d ridings) 1828–30. [Conservative.]

See PAC, RG 1, L 3, vol. 498, T 12/80; vol. 500, T 15/17; W.D. Reid, *The Loyalists of Ontario*, (Lambertville, NJ 1973), 316.

THOM, Alexander, *b* [1775], Scotland; *d* 26 Sept. 1845, Perth, CW; *m* (1) Harriet Smythe (2) Eliza Graves. [Anglican.] Physician, miller, farmer, public servant. Granted [800] acres. Lived in Perth. Surgeon, 41st (Regular) Regt., 30 Aug. 1799; acting staff surgeon to the British forces in UC, 31 July 1812; surgeon to the British forces in UC, 7 July 1813; resident medical officer, rideau Military Settlement, 19 Aug. 1815 (HP 1817). JP, Johnstown Dist., 25 Mar. 1816; Bathurst Dist., 27 Nov. 1822; judge, Bathurst Dist. Court, 23 Apr. 1835. MHA, Lanark, 1836. Conservative.

See DCB 7.

THOMPSON, Timothy, *b* 1762, 13 Cols; *d* 23 Apr. 1823. Son of John Thompson; *m* Elizabeth Fraser (*dau* John Ferguson, UE; widow of William Fraser, UE, adj., 2d Bttn., King's Royal Regt., of NY). Anglican. Farmer, laywer, public servant. Granted 2,000 acres plus two town lots in Kingston. Lived in South Fredericksburg Twp. Ens., King's Royal Regt. of NY, 1781–4 (HP 1784); lt. col., 1st Regt., Lennox Militia; col., 29 May 1813. JP, Midland Dist., 1 Jan. 1800; judge, Midland Dist. Court, 30 Apr. 1798; collector of customs, Port of Newcastle, 6 Aug. 1801; judge, Newcastle Dist. Court, 16 July 1802; Surrogate Court, Newcastle Dist., 16 July 1802; commissioner to arrest persons suspected of high treason, 24 Mar. 1814. MHA, Lennox, Hastings and Northumberland, 1796–1800; Lennox and Addington, 1800–4, 1812–16.

See PAC, RG 1, L 3, vol. 495, T 3/2; vol. 495a, T 6/4, vol. 511, T Misc./21; RG 5, A 1, vol. 5, pp. 2180, 3636, 4071, 4275; B 7, vol. 3; RG 68, General Index to Commissions; L.H. Irving, *Officers of the British Forces in Canada During the War of 1812–15* (Welland 1908), 56, 58, C.C. James, "The Second Legislature of Upper Canada," *Transactions of the Royal Society of Canada* (1903); H.C. Burleigh, *Loyalist Graves in the Bay of Quinte Region* (Bath 1972), 15.

THOMPSON, William, *b* 17 June 1786, NB; *d* 18 Jan. 1860, Toronto Twp., CW. Son of Cornelius Thompson, UE (lt., New Jersey Volunteers) and

Rebecca ——— ; *m* Jane Garden (*dau* [William] Garden, UE); six sons, three daughters. Anglican. Farmer. Granted 400 acres. Lived in (1) Markham Twp. 1809–[15] (2) Toronto Twp. [1815]–60. Capt., 2d Regt., York Militia, 16 Apr. 1812; major, 1st Regt., West York Militia, 18 June 1823; lt., col., 3d Regt., West York Militia, 18 Aug. 1826; col., 17 May 1830; on active duty 1837–8. JP Home dist., 13 Mar. 1820. MHA, York and Simcoe, 1824–8.

See DCB 8.

THOMSON, Edward William, *b* Jan. 1794, Kingston, UC; *d* 20 Apr. 1865, York Twp., CW. Son of Archibald Thomson, UE, and Elizabeth McKay; brother of Hugh C. Thomson (*q.v.*); *m* (1) Sarah Maria Terry (*dau* Parshall Terry, *q.v.*) (2) Mary Ketchum (daughter of Jesse Ketchum, *q.v.*) (3) Selina Lee; ten children. Presbyterian. Farmer, contractor, businessman. Granted 300 acres. Lived in (1) Scarborough Twp. 1808–[26] (2) [Montague Twp.] [1826]–30 (3) York Twp., 1830–65. Private, 3d Regt., York Militia, 1812; ensign, 25 Dec. 1812; capt., 1st Regt., East York Militia, 10 Apr. 1822; capt., 3d Regt., West York Militia, 2 Apr. 1827; major, Queen's Light Infantry, 11 Dec. 1837 (on active service 1837–8); lt. col., 7th Regt., North York Militia, 17 May 1839. JP, Home Dist., 27 Mar. 1833. MHA, York (2d riding) 1836–41. Conservative.

See DCB 9.

THOMSON, Hugh Christopher, *b* 1791, Kingston, UC; *d* 23 Apr. 1834, Kingston. Son of Archibald Thomson, UE, and Elizabeth McKay; brother of Edward W. Thomson (*q.v.*); *m* (1) Elizabeth Spafford (2) Elizabeth Ruttan (*dau* William Ruttan, UE, lt., New Jersey Volunteers; sister of Henry Ruttan, *q.v.*); two sons, one daughter. Anglican. Merchant, journalist. Granted 500 acres plus a town and a water lot in Kingston. Lived in Kingston. Sgt., Frontenac Militia, 1812–14; lt., 1st Regt., Frontenac Militia, 30 Aug. 1821; capt., 30 May 1833. JP, Midland Dist., 30 Sept. 1829. MHA, Frontenac, 1824–34. Reformer.

See DCB 6.

THORBURN, David, *b* [1790], Roxburghshire, Scotland; *d* Nov. 1862, Queenston, CW. Presbyterian. Merchant. Bought 1,600 acres in Loyalist rights. Lived in Queenston. Private, 1st Regt., Lincoln Militia, 1824. JP, Niagara Dist., Aug. 1838. MHA, Lincoln (3d Riding) 1835–41. Reformer.

See PAC, RG 5, A 1, vol. 203, pp. 111730–1; RG 8, C 1702, p. 228; RG 68, General Index to Commissions; Toronto *Globe*, 29 Nov. 1862; *Journal of Education of Upper Canada* (1862); UC, House of Assembly, *Journals* (1825) Appendix 10; L.F. Gates, *Land Policies of Upper Canada* (Toronto 1968), 334; Niagara Historical Society *Publications*, no. 19, 54.

THORPE, Robert, *b*, Ireland; *d* 14 May 1836, [England]. Studied law. Public servant. Lived in York (Toronto) 1805–7. JP, Home Dist., 11 Dec. 1806; judge, Court of King's Bench of UC, 1 Jan. 1805. MHA, Durham, Simcoe and East York, 1806–8.

See DCB 7.

VANALSTINE, Peter, *b* 1743, Kinderhook, Albany Co., NY (13 Cols); *d* 1811, Adolphustown Twp., UC; *m* Abida Van Alen; [two sons, one daughter]. Miller, farmer. Granted 5,000 acres. Lived in (1) Adolphustown Twp. (2) Marysburgh Twp. Capt., Associated Loyalists, 1777–84 (HP 1784). JP, Montreal Dist., 18 Apr. 1785; Mecklenburg Dist., 24 July 1788; Midland Dist., 1 Jan. 1800; lieutenant, Prince Edward County, 2 Nov. 1792. MHA, Prince Edward and Adolphustown, 1793–6.

See PAC, RG 1, L 3, vol. 513, U–V Misc./24; vol. 514, U–V 1/22; RG 68, General Index to Commissions; MG 14, AO 12, vol. 54; AO 13, bundle 16; T.W. Casey, "The Casey Scrapbooks, Part II," Lennox and Addington Historical Society *Papers and Records* 4 (1912); W.D. Reid, *The Loyalists of Ontario* (Lambertville, NJ 1973), 322.

VANKOUGHNET, Philip, *b* 2 Apr. 1790, Cornwall, UC; *d* 7 May 1873. Son of Michael VanKoughnet, UE (sgt., King's Royal Regt. of NY) and Eve Empey; *m* Harriet Sophia Scott. Attended Rev. John Strachan's School, Cornwall. Anglican. Merchant, manufacturer, public servant. Granted 700 acres. Lived in Cornwall. Lt., 1st Regt., Stormont Militia, 1812–14; lt. col., 2d Regt., Stormont Militia, 1 Apr. 1822; col., 29 Feb. 1836; lt. col. commanding Cornwall volunteers at Prescott, Nov., 1838; lt. col., 5th Incorporated Bttn. of Militia, 1839. JP, Eastern Dist., 18 Apr. 1825; inspector of licences, Eastern Dist., 10 Oct. 1832; member of the Legislative Council of UC, 23 Jan. 1836. MHA, Stormont and Russell, 1816–20; Stormont, 1820–8, 1830–4. Conservative.

See DCB 10.

WALKER, Hamilton, *b* 1782, BNA; *d* 8 Sept. 1830, Prescott, UC. Son of James Walker and Abigail Jessup (*dau* Major Edward Jessup, UE); *m* Jane ———. Lawyer, public servant. Granted 800 acres. Lived in Prescott. Ens., Grenville Militia by 1807; capt., 2d Regt., Grenville Militia; capt., Volunteer Incorporated Militia Bttn., 1812–14 [HP 1815]; lt. col., 2d Regt., Grenville Militia, 1 Apr. 1822; col., 1 Aug. 1828. JP, Bathurst Dist., 18 Apr. 1825; judge, Bathurst and Johnstown Dist. Courts, 18 Nov. 1823. MHA, Grenville, 1824–8.

See PAC, RG 1, L 3, vol. 547, W Misc./91; L 7, vol. 52; RG 9, IB 5, vols. 1, 3, 4; RG 68, General Index to Commissions; MG 25, G 59; L.H. Irving, *Officers of the British Forces in Canada During the War of 1812–14* (Welland 1908), 37, 49.

WALSH, Francis Leigh, *b* 12 Mar. 1789, Hartford Co., Maryland, USA; *d* 14 Oct. 1884, Simcoe, Ont. Son of Thomas Welch (clerk, Dist. Court, registrar, judge, Surrogate Court, London Dist.) and Mary Mitchell; *m* Elsie Fairchild. Anglican. Public servant. Granted 200 acres; bought 1,200 acres in Loyalist rights. Lived in (1) Vittoria, Charlotteville Twp. (2) London. Quartermaster, 1st Regt., Norfolk Militia by 1808 and 1812–14; capt., 13 Aug. 1824. JP, London Dist., 31 July 1821; Talbot Dist., 22 Mar. 1838; registrar, Norfolk County, 4 Apr. 1810; Surrogate Court, London Dist., 29 May 1810. MHA, Norfolk, 1820–8, 1834–6. Conservative.

See PAC, RG 1, L 3, vol. 525a, W 9/62; RG 8, C 681, p. 146; RG 9, IB 5, vol. 6; RG 68, General Index to Commissions; W.D. Reid, *The Loyalists of Ontario* (Lambertville, NJ 1973), 355, L.F. Gates, *Land Policies of Upper Canada* (Toronto 1968), 334; L.H. Irving, *Officers of the British Forces in Canada During the War of 1812–15* (Welland 1908), 35.

WARREN, John, *d* 5 Sept. 1832. Son of John Warren (collector of customs, Fort Erie). Merchant, ferry Operator, public servant. Granted 2,000 acres. Lived in Bertie Twp. Capt., 3d Regt., Lincoln Militia by 1808; major, 25 Jan. 1813; col., 1 Apr. 1822. JP, Niagara Dist., 9 May 1823; collector of customs, Fort Erie (succeeding his father) 16 May 1815. MHA, Haldimand, 1831–2. [Conservative.]

See PAC, RG 1, L 3, vol. 522, W 2/21; vol. 524, W 6/23; vol. 526, W 10/49; L 7, vol. 52; RG 5, B 7, vol. 3; RG 9, IB 1, vol. 18; IB 5, vol. 1; RG 19, E 5a, vol. 3751, no. 1139; RG 68, General Index to Commissions; L.H. Irving, *Officers of the British Forces in Canada During the War of 1812–15* (Welland 1908), 79; Niagara Historical Society, *Publications*, no. 19 (1910).

WASHBURN, Ebenezer, *b* [1753], 13 Cols; *d* 12 Nov. 1826, Hallowell, UC; *m* (1) Sarah DeForest (2) Hannah McBride. [Methodist.] Merchant, lumberman. Granted 200 acres plus a town lot in Kingston; bought 2,200 acres. Lived in (1) Fredericksburg Twp. (2) Hallowell Twp. Sgt., Loyal (Jessup's) Rangers, 1777–84. JP, Midland Dist., 10 Mar. 1808; commissioner to arrest persons suspected of high treason, Midland Dist., 24 Mar. 1814. MHA, Prince Edward, 1800–8.

See DCB 6.

WATERS, Charles, *b* [1791], BNA; *d* 9 Sept. 1869, L'Orignal, CW. Son of Abel Waters (cornet, King's American Dragoons); *m* Maria Frost. [Methodist.] Farmer, merchant, public servant. Lived in L'Orignal. "Did his duty,"

1812–14; ens., 1st Regt., Prescott Militia, 29 Nov. 1820; lt., 27 Sept. 1826. JP, Ottawa Dist., 5 June 1822; coroner, Ottawa Dist., 30 July 1824. MHA, Prescott, 1834–6. Reformer.

See PAC, RG 1, L 3, vol. 534, W 19/78; vol. 548, W Misc., 1816–45/9; RG 5, A 1, vol. 114, p. 64036; RG 9, IB 5, vols. 1, 3, 5; RG 68, General Index to Commissions; UC House of Assembly, *Journals* (1825) Appendix 19; *Upper Canada Herald* 19 Apr. 1836; Cassburn United Church (Methodist) cemetery records.

WEAGER, Jacob, *b* 1756, 13 Cols. Son of Everhart Weager; *m* Mary Hare (*dau* Henry Hare, UE, lt., Indian Dept.); six daughters, three sons. [Farmer.] Granted 200 acres. Lived in Williamsburgh Twp. Sgt., King's Royal Regt. of NY, 1777–84; adj., Dundas Militia by 1807; capt. 1st Regt., Dundas Militia, 29 Jan. 1810 and 1812–14. JP, Eastern Dist., 30 June 1800. MHA, Dundas, 1800–4.

See PAC, RG 1, L 3, vol. 525, W 8/53; RG 68, General Index to Commissions; MG 13, WO 28, vol. 10; MG 14, AO 12, vol. 29; W.D. Reid, *Loyalists of Ontario* (Lambertville, NJ 1973), 333; L.H. Irving, *Officers of the British Forces in Canada During the War of 1812–15* (Welland 1908), 46–7.

WEEKES, William, *b*, Ireland; *d* 11 Oct. 1806, [Niagara], UC. Lawyer. Granted 1,200 acres. Lived in York (Toronto). MHA, Durham, Simcoe and East York, 1805–6.

See DCB 5.

WELLS, William Benjamin, *b* 3 Oct. 1809, Augusta Twp., UC; *d* 8 Apr. 1881, Toronto, Ont. Son of William Wells and Sarah Clough; *m* Mary Julia Hogan; five daughters, four sons. Attended a school in Augusta Twp. taught by Rev. John Bethune; studied law with M.S. Bidwell (*q.v.*). Anglican. Lawyer, journalist. Lived in Prescott. MHA, Grenville, 1834–8. Reformer.

See DCB 11.

WERDEN, Asa, *b* 1779, Stonington, Conn. (13 Cols), *d* 1866, Athol Twp., UC. Son of (Dr.) Isaac Werden; *m* Elizabeth Ellsworth; [eight] daughters, [four] sons. Farmer, businessman, tanner, lumberman, land speculator. Granted 100 acres; bought land in the Prince Edward, Home, Newcastle, and [Western] districts. Lived in Athol Twp. Pvt., 1st Regt., Prince Edward Militia, 1812–14. JP, Midland Dist., 3 Aug. 1821. MHA, Prince Edward, 1830–41. Conservative.

See PAC, RG 1, L 3, vol. 533, W 18/96; L 7, vol. 52; RG 68, General Index to Commissions; *Pioneer Life on the Bay of Quinte* (Toronto 1904), 876–8.

WHITE, John, *b* [1761], England, *d* 4 Jan. 1800, York (Toronto). Son of

John White; *m* Marrianne Lynne; two sons, one daughter. Read law at the Inner Temple. Lawyer, public servant. Granted 1,400 acres. Lived in York (Toronto). Attorney general of UC, 31 Dec. 1791; judge, Home Dist. Court, 9 July 1794. MHA, Leeds and Frontenac, 1792–6.
See DCB 4.

WHITE, Reuben, *b*, Scoharie County, NY; *d* 1857; *m* Esther (or Hester) March; eight daughters, four sons. Quaker. Miller, merchant. Granted a town lot in Belleville. Lived in Sidney Twp. MHA, Hastings, 1820–8, 1830–4. Reformer.
See PAC, RG 1, L 3, vol. 529, W 13/13; MG 9, B 8–12; *Pioneer Life on the Bay of Quinte* (Toronto 1904), 857–9; C. Read and R. Stagg, eds. *The Rebellion of 1837 in Upper Canada* (Toronto 1985), 284.

WICKENS, James, *b* [1776], England; *d* 20 May 1847, [Vespra Twp.]. Anglican. Farmer, miller. Granted [500] acres. Lived at (1) Penetanguishene (2) Vespra Twp. Lt., Royal Waggon Train, 10 Feb. 1809; deputy assistant commissary general (HP 1814); on duty, 1838. JP, Home Dist., 13 Sept. 1837. MHA, Simcoe, 1836–41. Conservative.
See PAC, RG 1, L 3, vol. 537a, W 22/72; RG 68, General Index to Commissions; *Upper Canada Herald*, 9 Aug. 1836; Great Britain. War Office, Army List, 1810–15; A.F. Hunter, *A History of Simcoe County* (Barrie 1948), 102–3.

WILKINSON, John Alexander, *b* 14 Sept. 1789, Dublin, Ireland; *d* 17 Sept. 1862; *m* Frances Hands (*dau* William Hands, sheriff, treasurer etc., Western Dist.) Anglican. Granted 500 acres and a town lot in Sandwich. Lived in Sandwich. Lt., 37th (Regular) Regt. on duty in Canada, 1814–15; lt., 24th (Regular) Regt. (HP 1818); capt., Sandwich Volunteers, 8 Jan. 1838. JP, Western Dist., 20 Mar. 1837; judge, Surrogate Court, Western Dist., 9 Mar. 1836. MHA, Essex, 1824–30, 1834–6. Conservative.
See PAC, RG 1, L 3, vol. 530, W 14/174; vol. 530a, W 15/36; RG 8, C 258, p. 449; C 698, pp. 73–8; RG 9, IB 5, vol. 8; RG 68, General Index to Commissions; *The Seventh Report from the Committee on Grievances* (Toronto 1835); G.M. Rose, *A Cyclopedia of Canadian Biography* (Toronto 1886), 1:690.

WILKINSON, Richard Norton, *b*, [Scotland]; *d* 1804 [Cornwall, UC]; *m* (1) Amelia Everitt (sister of Peter Everitt, UE, lt., King's Royal Regt. of NY) (2) Eleanor Macdonell (sister of John Macdonell [Aberchalder] *q.v.*); four daughters, two sons, including W.B. Wilkinson (*q.v.*) [Presbyterian.] Farmer, merchant, public servant. Granted 200 acres plus a town lot in York. Lived in Charlottenburgh Twp. [1786]–1804. Lt., King's Royal Regt. of NY; lt., Indian Dept., 1778–84 (HP 1784); capt., Royal Canadian Volunteers [1796–

1802]; capt., Glengarry Militia, 1803. JP, Lunenburg Dist., 24 July 1788; Eastern Dist., 18 Oct. 1804; judge, Surrogate Court, Eastern Dist., 5 Sept. 1793; Eastern Dist. Court, 9 July 1794. MHA, Glengarry, 1796–1800.

See PAC, RG 1, L 3, vol. 523, W 3/10; vol. 523a, W 4/73; RG 8, C 106, p. 31; C 546, p. 105; C 724, pp. 5, 45; RG 68, General Index to Commissions; W.L. Scott, "Glengarry's Representatives in the Legislative Assembly of Upper Canada," (Part 1) CCHA *Report* (1938–39): 29–31, J.G. Harkness, *A History of Stormont, Dundas and Glengarry* (Ottawa 1946), 74.

WILKINSON, Walter Butler, *b* [1781], BNA; *d* Sept. 1807. Son of Richard Norton Wilkinson (*q.v.*) and Amelia Everitt; *m* Cecilia Bethune (*dau* Rev. John Bethune, UE). Presbyterian. Lawyer. Granted 200 acres. Lived in Cornwall. MHA, Glengarry and Prescott, 1804–8.

See PAC, RG 1, L 3, vol. 524, W 6/40; W.D. Reid, *The Loyalists of Ontario* (Lambertville, NJ 1973) 337; W.L. Scott, "Glengarry's Representatives in the Legislative Assembly of Upper Canada" (Part 1) CCHA *Report* (1938–39): 34–5.

WILLCOCKS, Joseph, *b* 1773, Palmerston (near Dublin), Ireland; *d* 4 Sept. 1814, Fort Erie, UC. Son of Robert Willcocks and Jane Powell. Journalist, public servant. Granted 1,200 acres. Lived in York (Toronto). Sheriff, Home Dist., 4 Sept. 1804. MHA, West York, Lincoln (1st riding) and Haldimand, 1808; Lincoln (1st riding) and Haldimand, 1808–12; Lincoln (1st riding), 1812–14.

See DCB 5.

WILLSON, Crowell, *b* 17 Sept. 1762, Sussex County, NJ (13 Cols); *d* 11 Aug. 1832, Crowland Twp., UC. Son of Benjamin Willson, UE; *m* (1) Hannah Crane (2) ——— Wiley; seven daughters, five sons. Farmer. Granted 1,000 acres. Lived in (1) Bertie Twp. 1787–1801 (2) Willoughby Twp. (3) Crowland Twp. Procured provision for British forces, 1776–83. JP, Niagara Dist., 30 June 1800. MHA, Lincoln (4th riding) 1808–12.

See PAC, RG 1, L 3, vol. 525a, W 9/24; vol. 526, W 10/30; RG 68, General Index to Commissions; *Ontario Register*, no. 1 (1968): 94; T.B. Wilson, *Descendants in Canada and the United States of Benjamin and Sarah Willson* (Madison, NJ 1967), 7–8.

WILLSON, John, *b* 5 Aug. 1776, NJ (13 Cols); *d* 26 May 1860, Saltfleet Twp., CW; *m* Elizabeth Bowlby; nine children including Ann (*m* Michael Aikman, *q.v.*). Methodist. Farmer, merchant, public servant. Granted 400 acres. Lived at (1) Niagara 1793–7 (2) Saltfleet Twp. 1797–1860. Capt., 3d Regt., York Militia, 1812–14. JP, Home Dist., 1 July 1796; Gore Dist., 25 Mar. 1811; inspector of licences, Gore Dist., 1 Apr. 1816; judge, Surrogate

Court, Gore Dist., 21 June 1838; member of the Legislative Council of UC, 11 Dec. 1839. MHA, York West, 1800–12; Wentworth, 1820–34. [Conservative.]

See DCB 8.

WILMOT, Samuel Street, *b* 1773, NY (13 Cols); *d* 1856. Son of Lemuel Wilmot, UE, (capt., Loyal American Regt.); *m* Mary Stegman; [four] sons. Surveyor, tanner. Granted 600 acres; bought 400 acres. Lived in Markham Twp., Clarke Twp. Major, 1st Regt., York Militia, 1812–14. JP, Newcastle Dist., 4 Aug. 1821. MHA, Durham, 1820–4.

See PAC, RG 1, L 3, vol. 523a, W 5/27; RG 8, C 682, p. 67; C 686, p. 248; C 703E, p. 20; C 1717, p. 84; RG 68, General Index to Commissions; J. Squair, *The Townships of Darlington and Clarke* (Toronto 1927) 53, 64.

WILSON, James, *b* [1770, England]; *d* 1 Sept. 1847. Methodist. Farmer. Granted 200 acres. Lived in Sophiasburgh Twp. MHA, Prince Edward, 1808–10, 1820–30, 1834–6. Reformer.

See PAC, RG 1, L 3, vol. 522, W 1/32; vol. 525, W 8/79; vol. 530, W 14/73; vol. 547, W Misc./125; W.D. Reid, *Death Notices of Ontario* (Lambertville, NJ 1980), 245.

WILSON, William, *b*, UC; *d* 29 July 1847, Simcoe, CW. Miller, distiller. Lived in Simcoe. Served [as pvt.] 1812–14; capt., 2d Regt. Norfolk Militia, 21 June 1823. JP, London Dist. 13 June 1829; Talbot Dist., 22 Mar. 1838. MHA, Norfolk, 1830–4. [Conservative.]

See PAC, RG 9, IB 5, vol. 1; RG 68, General Index to Commissions; MG 9, D 8–35; D.A. McKenzie, *Death Notices from the Christian Guardian* (Lambertville, NJ 1982), 334.

WOODRUFF, Richard, *b* 1784, USA; *d* 1872. Brother of William Woodruff (*q.v.*); *m* Anne Clement (*dau* Joseph Clement, UE); five sons, two daughters. [Methodist.] Merchant, miller. Granted 200 acres. Lived at St. David's. Pvt., promoted to sgt., 1st Regt., Lincoln Militia, 1812; ens., 1813; lt., 20 Feb. 1827; capt., 7 June 1835. JP, Niagara Dist., 31 May 1833. MHA, Lincoln (1st riding) 1836–41. Reformer.

See PAC, RG 1, L 7, vol. 52; RG 9, IB 5, vols. 1, 6; RG 68, General Index to Commissions; L.H. Irving, *Officers of the British Forces in Canada During the War of 1812–15* (Welland 1908), 73, 75; J. Carnochan, *Inscriptions and Graves in the Niagara Peninsula* (Niagara n.d.), 46.

WOODRUFF, William, *b* 1 Oct. 1793, USA; *d* June, 1860. Brother of Richard Woodruff (*q.v.*). Methodist. Merchant, miller. Granted 100 acres. Lived at (1) Queenston (2) Stamford Twp. (3) St. David's 1812–60. Pvt., promoted to ens., 1st Regt., Lincoln Militia, 1812–14; lt., 23 Aug. 1824; capt., 14 Mar. 1827. MHA, Lincoln (1st and 2d ridings) 1828–30. Reformer.

See PAC, RG 1, L 3, vol. 528, W 12/174; L 7, vol. 52; RG 9, IB 5, vol. 1; L.H. Irving, *Officers of the British Forces in Canada during the War of 1812–15* (Welland 1908), 73, 75; *Journal of Education for Upper Canada* (1860).

WOOLVERTON, Dennis, *b* 1 Jan. 1790, NJ (USA); *d* 23 May 1875. Son of Jonathan Woolverton and Mary Barcroft; *m* (1) Catherine Nixon (2) Mary Ann Nelles (*dau* Robert Nelles, *q.v.*). Baptist. Farmer. Granted 100 acres. Lived in Grimsby Twp. Sgt., 4th Regt., Lincoln Militia, 1812–14. MHA, Lincoln (1st riding) 1834–6. Reformer.

See PAC, RG 1, L 3, vol. 527a, W 11/161; RG 8, C 1701, p. 240; J. Carnochan, *Inscriptions and Graves in the Niagara Peninsula* (Niagara n.d.), 99; Grimsby Historical Society, *Annals of the Forty*, no. 9 (1958).

YAGER, Henry W., *b*, USA. Farmer. Lived in Thurlow Twp. Acting quartermaster of militia, 1837–8. MHA, Hastings, 1834–6. [Reformer.]

See PAC, RG 1, L 3, vol. 556, Leases and Licences, 1798–1839/123; MG 9, B 8–12.

YOUNG, James, *b* [1777], NS; *d* 1 July 1831, Carrying Place, UC. Son of Robert Young and Jean McGregor; *m* Catherine Weller. Farmer. Granted 700 acres. Lived in Ameliasburgh Twp. Ens., Prince Edward Militia by 1807; lt., capt., 1st Regt., Prince Edward Militia, 1812–14; maj., 2d Regt., Prince Edward Militia, 1823; lt. col., 12 Aug. 1824. JP, Midland Dist., 16 Mar. 1808; commissioner to arrest persons suspected of high treason, Newcastle Dist., 24 Mar. 1814. MHA, Hastings, and Ameliasburgh, 1812–16.

See PAC, RG 1, L 3, vol. 549, Y 3/9, Y 10/12; L 7, vol. 52; RG 9, IB 5, vol. 5; RG 68, General Index to Commissions; L.H. Irving, *Officers of the British Forces in Canada During the War of 1812–15* (Welland 1908) 53, 58–9, *Pioneer Life on the Bay of Quinte*, 998–1001; W.D. Reid, *Death Notices of Ontario* (Lambertville, NJ 1980) 65.

Notes

INTRODUCTION

1 This form of abbreviation is the standard form adopted by the *Dictionary of Canadian Biography* (Toronto: University of Toronto Press, 1965–).
2 F.H. Armstrong, "The Oligarchy of the Western District of Upper Canada 1788–1841," CHA *Historical Papers* (1977): 91.
3 D.H. Akenson, *Being Had: Historians, Evidence and the Irish in North America* (Port Credit: P.D. Meany 1985), 43.

CHAPTER ONE

1 It is worth noting that the proportion of "gentlemen" among the MHAS was about the same (a little over two percent) as the proportion of "gentlemen" listed in the Toronto *Directory* of 1837.
2 R.W. Widdis, "Speculation and the Surveyor: An Analysis of the Role played by Surveyors in the Settlement of Upper Canada," *Hs/SH* 15, no. 30 (Nov. 1982): 444–5.
3 Ibid., 455–8.
4 See for example E. Pessen, *Riches, Class and Power Before the Civil War* (Lexington, Mass.: D.C. Heath 1973), 46. A survey of the occupations of one hundred members of the Nova Scotia Legislature who sat during the period 1792–1841 produced a very similar pattern — that is a wide variety of overlapping occupations. *See* C.B. Fergusson, ed., *A Directory of the Legislative Assembly of Nova Scotia, 1758–1958* (Halifax: Public Archives of Nova Scotia 1958). A similar observation has been made about another elite group, Canadian authors. *See* M.L. MacDonald, "*Literature and Society in the Canadas, 1830–1850*" (PHD thesis, Carleton University 1984), 126.

5 J. Jarvis, *Three Centuries of Robinsons* (Toronto: T.H. Best 1967), 115–24; PAC, RG 1, E 13, Blue Books, 1828.

6 L.F. Gates, *Land Policies of Upper Canada* (Toronto: University of Toronto Press 1968), 97, 228.

7 D.J. Brock "Thomas Parke," *DCB* 9:618–9.

8 A.G. Morice, "Sidelights on the Careers of Miles Macdonell and his Brothers," *CHR* 10, no. 4 (Dec. 1929): 323–2; OA, John Macdonell Papers, Assessment Rolls, Hawkesbury Township; L.R. Masson, *Les Bourgeois de la Compagnie du Nord Ouest,* 2 vols. (Quebec: A. Coté 1889) 1:267–95.

9 P. Baskerville, "Donald Bethune's Steamboat Business: A Study of Upper Canadian Commerical and Financial Practice," *OH* 67, no. 3 (Sept. 1975): 135–49.

10 H.J. Morgan, *Sketches of Celebrated Canadians* (Quebec: Hunter Rose 1862), 378–9; J. Petryshyn, ed., *Victorian Cobourg: A Nineteenth Century Profile* (Belleville: Mika Publishing 1976), 13; E. Ermatinger, *Life of Colonel Talbot and the Talbot Settlement* (St. Thomas: McLachlin's Home Journal Office 1859), 122–7; PAC, RG 1, L 3, vol. 47, B 14/125; L 7, vol. 10.

11 J.K. Johnson "George Brouse," *DCB* 8:104–5.

12 J.K. Johnson "George Lyon," *DCB* 8:509–10.

13 Grimsby Historical Society, *Annals of the Forty* (1953): 16–17; Niagara Historical Society, *Publications* 19:50; *Journal of Education in Upper Canada* 15, no. 9 (Sept. 1862): 137.

14 H. Mathews, *Oakville and the Sixteen* (Toronto: University of Toronto Press 1953), 174.

15 Cited in R.F. Hirsch, "William Stewart and the Square Timber Trade on the Upper Ottawa in the 1840s," research essay, Carleton University (1983), 23.

16 R.E. Ankli and K.J. Duncan, "Farm Making Costs in Early Ontario," in Donald H. Akenson, ed., *Canadian Papers in Rural History* (Gananoque: Langdale Press, 1984), 4:48.

17 I. MacPherson, *Matters of Loyalty: The Buells of Brockville 1830–1850* (Belleville: Mika Publishing 1981), 73.

18 A. MacKenzie, "Edward William Thomson," *DCB* 9:788–9.

19 J. Croil, *Dundas or A Sketch of Canadian History* (Montreal: B. Dawson & Son 1861), 282; *The Canada Directory for 1857–58.*

20 PAC, RG 5, A 1, 30696, 4488–9.

21 MacPherson, *Matters of Loyalty*, 10.

22 D. McCalla, "The 'Loyalist' Economy of Upper Canada 1784–1806," *Hs/SH* 17, no. 32 (Nov. 1983): 303–4. *See also* D. McCalla, "The Wheat Staple and Upper Canadian Development," CHA *Historical Papers* (1978): 39–40.

23 E.H. Jones, "Joseph Willcocks," *DCB* 5:856.
24 PAC, RG 1, E 13, Blue Books.
25 UC, House of Assembly, *Journals of the House of Assembly*, (1835) appendix 1, no. 1, 100.
26 R.J. Burns, "William Botsford Jarvis," *DCB* 9:411–12.
27 PAC, RG 1, L 3, vol. 458, S 11/332.
28 Toronto *Patriot*, 25 Dec. 1840.
29 Between 1821 and 1839 the public service increased about two and one-half times. In the same period the population increased three and one-half times. In the 1830s, when immigration was high, the population increased by about 73 percent, and the public service grew by about 24 percent. *Census of Canada* (1931) 1:148–9; PAC, RG 1, E 13, vols. 141, 155.
30 The major source for patronage requests is the extensive Upper Canada Sundries Series, PAC, RG 5, A 1. *See also* PAC, RG 5, B 7, Applications for Appointment.
31 *Census of Canada* (1871) 4:92–131.
32 Ibid., 140.
33 Ibid., 103, 113, 126, 131. *See also* McCalla, "Wheat Staple," 37.
34 McCalla, "Wheat Staple," 41.
35 W. Canniff, *The Settlement of Upper Canada* (Toronto: Dudley & Burns 1869), 486.
36 PAC, RG 19, E 5 (a) vol. 3740, no. 46.
37 UC, House of Assembly, *Journals* (1839–40) *appendix* 1:2.
38 P.A. Russell, "Attitudes to Social Structure and Social Mobility in Upper Canada, 1815–1840," (PH.D. thesis, Carleton University, 1981, 129.
39 D.R. Beer, *Sir Allan Napier MacNab* (Hamilton: *DHB* 1984) 18–21.
40 See for example D.S. MacMillan "The Scot as Businessman", in W.S. Reid, ed., *The Scottish Tradition in Canada* (Toronto: McClelland and Stewart 1976), 199; F.H. Armstrong, "Ethnicity in the Formation of the Family Compact," in J. Dahlie and T. Fernando, eds., *Ethnicity, Power and Politics in Canada* (Toronto: Methuen 1981), 34; J.M. Bumsted, *The Scots in Canada* (Ottawa: CHA 1982), 5.
41 *Census of Canada*, 1871, 4:136.
42 Ibid.
43 Ibid.
44 Ibid.
45 Ibid., 135.
46 F.H. Armstrong, *Handbook of Upper Canadian Chronology and Territorial Legislation* (London, Ontario: Dundurn Press 1985), 128.
47 Ibid.
48 G.B. Baker, "Legal Education in Upper Canada 1785–1889: The Law

Society as Educator," in D.H. Flaherty, ed., *Essays in the History of Canadian Law*, 2 vols. (Toronto: The Osgoode Society 1983), 2:69.

49 Armstrong, *Handbook of Upper Canadian Chronology*, 122–31. R.I.D. Gray, Archibald McLean, A.N. MacNab, W.B. Wilkinson and Robert Dickson are examples.

50 T.C. Smout, *A History of the Scottish People 1560–1830* (New York: Charles Scribner & Sons 1969), 373.

51 E.G. Firth, ed., *The Town of York, 1815–1834* (Toronto: Champlain Society 1966), xlvi, xlix.

52 Baker, "Legal Education," 69.

CHAPTER TWO

1 E.G. Firth, ed., *The Town of York, 1793–1815* (Toronto: Champlain Society 1962), 178.

2 OA, Abstract Index to Deeds. As E.C. Gray and B.E. Prentice have pointed out in "Exploring the Price of Farmland in two Ontario localities since Letters Patenting," (in Donald H. Akenson, ed.), *Canadian Papers in Rural History* (Gananoque: Langdale Press 1984), 4:226–39, the abstract index is not a reliable guide to land prices since the amount paid or acreage involved is often unrecorded. This information is only systematically available by the use of actual deeds kept in the county land titles offices.

3 OA, RG 21, Ontario Township Assessment Rolls. See also M. Doucet and John C. Weaver, "Town Fathers and Urban Continuity: The Roots of Community Power and Physical Form in Hamilton, Upper Canada in the 1830s" *Urban History Review* 13, no. 2 (October, 1984): 77–9.

4 H. Perkin, *The Age of the Railway* (London: Panther Books 1970), 34.

5 PAC, RG 8, C Series, vol. C405, 122–5.

6 Ibid., vol. 190, 34.

7 PAC, RG 5, A1, Upper Canada Sundries, 3636, 4071, 4275; B 7, vol. 3.

8 PAC, RG 8, C Series, vol. 405, 35.

9 J.D. and M. Stewart, "John Solomon Cartwright: Upper Canadian Gentleman and Regency 'Man of Taste'," *Historic Kingston*, 27 (Jan. 1979): 65.

10 J. Weaver, "Adam Ferrie," and "Colin Campbell Ferrie," DHB 1:73–5.

11 B.G. Wilson, "Robert Hamilton," *DCB* 5:402–6.

12 J.K. Johnson "William Benjamin Wells," *DCB* 9:914.

13 W.L. Scott, "Glengarry's Representatives in the Legislative Assembly of Upper Canada," CCHA *Report* (1939–40), 33.

14 Ibid., 40.

15 *Pioneer Life on the Bay of Quinte* (Toronto: Rolph and Clark 1904), 877; information supplied by John B. Aikens, Grimsby, Ontario.
16 H.J. Morgan, *Sketches of Celebrated Canadians and Persons Connected with Canada* (Quebec: Hunter, Rose, 1862), 379.
17 Patrick Campbell, *Travels in the Interior Inhabited Parts of North America*, ed. H.H. Langton, (Toronto: Champlain Society 1937), 133–5; F.J. Audet, "The Honourable Thomas McKay, M.L.C., Founder of New Edinburgh, 1792–1855," CHA *Report* (1932): 67; J.K. Johnson "Joshua Booth," *DCB* 5:92; I.B. Wells, "A Short Sketch of the History of Wm. Wells and his Family," ms. in the possession of Ruth McKenzie, Ottawa, 3; C.M. Johnston, *The Head of the Lake* (Hamilton: Wentworth County Council 1967), 153; L.A. Johnson "Absalom Shade," *DCB* 9:717.
18 J.B. Robinson, *Canada and the Canada Bill* (London: J. Hatchard and Son 1840), 145.
19 M. Katz, *The People of Hamilton, Canada West* (Cambridge, Mass: Harvard University Press 1975), 188–92. See also D. McCalla, *The Upper Canada Trade 1834–1872* (Toronto: University of Toronto Press 1979), 126–7, 142.
20 PAC, RG 1, E 13, Blue Books, 1821–64.
21 Ibid., vol. 141, 1821.
22 P.A. Russell, "Attitudes to Social Structure and Social Mobility in Upper Canada, 1815–1840," (PHD thesis, Carleton University 1981) 28.
23 PAC, RG 1, E 13, vols. 141, 155.
24 Ibid.
25 T. Cook, "John Beverley Robinson and the Conservative Blueprint for the Upper Canadian Community," *OH* 64, no. 2 (June 1972): 94.
26 PAC, RG 1, E 14, vol. 155.
27 J.K. Johnson, "Anthony Manahan and the Status of Irish Catholics in Upper Canada," *Historic Kingston* 31 (Jan. 1983): 32–44.
28 R. McKenzie, "James FitzGibbon," *DCB* 9:265–6.
29 PAC, RG 19, E 5a, Losses Claims, 1813–48.
30 Ibid., vol. 3747, no. 509.
31 Ibid., vol. 3740, no. 7.
32 Ibid., vol. 3746, no. 423.
33 Ibid., vol. 3752, no. 146.
34 Ibid., vol. 3747, no. 503.
35 Ibid., vol. 3752, no. 1210. See also R.L. Fraser "Richard Hatt," *DHB* 1:96–100.
36 PAC, RG 19, E 5a, vol. 3744, no. 262.
37 Ibid., vol. 3740, no. 46.
38 See for example the petitions of L.P. Sherwood, who acquired mill sites on the Ottawa at the Chaudière Falls. PAC, RG 1, L 3, vol. 475,

S 1/29; vol. 478, S 3/8.

39 PAC, RG 19, E 5a, vol. 3750, no. 803.

40 Ibid., vol. 3744, no. 262.

41 Ibid., vol. 3745, no. 354; vol. 3749, no. 698; vol. 3756, no. 1690; vol. 3748, no. 633; vol. 3741, no. 72.

42 Ibid., vol. 3752, no. 1155.

43 I.B. Wells, "a Short Sketch," 1.

44 Ibid., 3.

45 PAC, MG 25, vol. 6, no. 14; J.G. Harkness, *Stormont, Dundas and Glengarry, A History 1784–1945* (Ottawa: Mutual Press 1946), 154.

46 Harkness, *Stormont, Dundas and Glengarry*, 160; J.K. Johnson, "James William Cook," *DCB* 10:195.

47 *Pioneer Life on the Bay of Quinte*, 877–8.

48 Brockville *Recorder*, 23 Feb. 1860.

49 D.P. Gagan, *Hopeful Travellers* (Toronto: University of Toronto Press 1981), 96.

50 F.H. Armstrong, "Ethnicity in the Formation of the Family Compact: A Case Study in the Growth of the Canadian Establishment" in J. Dahlie and T. Fernando, eds., *Ethnicity, Power and Politics in Canada* (Toronto: Methuen 1981), 29–30.

51 Beasely, Booth, Brouse, Burnham, J. Cameron, Cartwright, Cook Joshua Cornwall, J. Crooks, T. Dickson, M. Elliott, Ferrie, A. Fraser, I. Fraser, T. Fraser, Gordon, G. Hamilton, R. Hamilton, Hardison, Hatt, Jessup, sr., C. Jones, J. Jones, Longley, McGregor, MacKay, W. Morris, Nichol, Pattinson, J. Robinson, G. Rolph, Shade, Shaver, T. Smith, VanKoughnet, Wells, Werden, J. Willson.

52 Gore, 8; Eastern, 7; Western, 6; Johnstown, 5; Niagara, 3; Midland, 3; Bathurst, 2; Newcastle, 1; Home, 1; London, 1; Prince Edward, 1.

53 Jonas Jones, at age forty-six.

54 PAC, RG 1, L 3, vol. 381a, N Misc/12; vol. 382, N 4/13, N 8/13, N 8/1; W.S. Wallace, *The Macmillan Dictionary of Canadian Biography* (Toronto: Macmillan 1963), 549.

55 L.A. Johnson, *History of the County of Ontario* (Whitby: County of Ontario 1973), 97.

56 For example, Henry Allcock, after being appointed a judge of the Court of King's Bench, was granted 1,200 acres for himself and 1,200 each for his wife and daughter before he even arrived in the province. *See* E.A. Cruikshank, ed., *The Correspondence of the Honourable Peter Russell*, 3 vols. (Toronto: Ontario Historical Society 1936), 3:15; F.H. Armstrong "Henry Allcock," *DCB* 5:17.

57 PAC, RG 1, L 3, vol. 458, S 11/332; vol. 43, B 12/371; vol. 189a, F 11/79; vol. 450, S 3/120.

58 Ibid., vol. 189, F 11/27.

59 P. Romney, "A Conservative Reformer in Upper Canada: Charles Fothergill, Responsible Government and the 'British Party', 1824–1840," CHA *Historical Papers* (1984): 44.
60 PAC, RG 1, L 3, vol. 227, H 10/96.
61 Ibid., vol. 222a, H 1/66; vol. 224, H 3/161.
62 Ibid., vol. 426a R 10/47; L 7, vol. 52.
63 PAC, RG 1, L 3, vol. 48, B 14/250.
64 PAC, RG 19, E 5a, vol. 3742, no. 163.
65 PAC, RG 8, C Series, vol. 506, 9–28.
66 PAC, RG 19, E 5a, vol. 3752, no. 1155.
67 P. Campbell, *Travels in the Interior*, 133–5.
68 R.L. Fraser, "John Willson," *DHB* 1:214.
69 J.K. Johnson, "The Businessman as Hero: The Case of William Warren Street," *OH* 65, no. 3 (Sept. 1973): 128.
70 R.W. Widdis, "Identifying Land Speculators in Upper Canada," *Canadian Geographer* 23, no. 4 (winter 1979): 338, 343–4.
71 PAC, RG 1, L 3, vol. 450a, S 4/16. Street and his nephew are identified as "long term" speculators in B.G. Wilson, *The Enterprises of Robert Hamilton* (Ottawa: Carleton University Press 1983), 98.
72 PAC, RG 1, L 3, vol. 198, F 2/41.
73 Ibid., vol. 305, M 22/118; vol. 363, M 20/88, M 20/90 (and fourteen other petitions).
74 Ibid., vol. 203a, G 4/75.
75 L.F. Gates, *Land Policies of Upper Canada* (Toronto: University of Toronto Press 1968), 333.
76 C.M. Johnston, "An Outline of Early Settlement in the Grand River Valley," *OH* 54, no. 1 (March 1962): 53–5.
77 C. Thomas, *Love and Work Enough: The Life of Anna Jameson* (Toronto: University of Toronto Press 1967), 195; PAC, RG 1, L 3, vol. 261a, J 22/29.
78 R.E. Saunders "John Beverley Robinson," *DCB* 9:677.
79 Brockville *Recorder* 12 Jan. 1830.
80 Bathurst *Courier*, 25 Dec. 1840.
81 Toronto *Patriot*, 24 Nov. 1840.
82 D.R. Beer, *Sir Allan Napier MacNab* (Hamilton: *DHB* 1984), 17–21.
83 Wilson, *Enterprises of Robert Hamilton*, 97–8.
84 Ibid., 174.
85 G.F. Macdonald, "How Windsor got its name," Essex County Historical Society, *Papers and Addresses* 3 (1921): 38.
86 A.N. Buell, "was always struggling to maintain a decent standard of living." I. MacPherson, *Matters of Loyalty*, 57. For a somewhat contrary argument see Doucet and Weaver, "Town Fathers and Urban Continuity," 89.

87 R.L. Fraser "Richard Hatt," *DHB* 1:97.

CHAPTER THREE

1 F.H. Armstrong, "The Oligarchy of the Western District of Upper Canada 1788–1841," CHA *Historical Papers* (1977), 91, 93; C. Read, "The London District Oligarchy in the Rebellion Era," *OH* 72, no. 4 (Dec. 1980): 196; J.H. Aitchison, "The Municipal Corporation Act of 1849," *CHR* 30, no. 2 (June 1949): 108; G.M. Craig, *Upper Canada, The Formative Years 1784–1841* (Toronto: McClelland and Stewart 1963), 30.

2 J.M. Beattie, *Attitudes Towards Crime and Punishment in Upper Canada, 1830–1850* (Toronto: Working Paper of the Centre of Criminology, University of Toronto 1977), 1.

3 J.H. Aitchison, "The Court of Requests in Upper Canada," *OH* 41, no. 3 (Sept. 1949): 125–32.

4 One estimate put assault and battery at 90 percent of all cases. A. Shortt, "Early Records of Ontario," *Queen's Quarterly* 7 (July 1899: 55.

5 OA, *Report of the Department of Public Records and Archives of Ontario* (Toronto: 1933), 63, 129.

6 Ibid., 14, 93, 125, 175, 187.

7 Ibid., 71.

8 The definitive study is J.H. Aitchison, "The Development of Local Government in Upper Canada, 1783–1850," 2 vols. (PHD thesis, University of Toronto, 1953).

9 Shortt, "Early Records of Ontario," 137–8.

10 J.H. Aitchison, "The Municipal Corporation Act of 1849" *CHR*, 30, no. 2 (June 1949): 110–1.

11 PAC, RG 68, General Index to Commissions, Upper and Lower Canada, 1651–1841.

12 Ibid.

13 Ibid.; PAC, RG 5, A 1, 30696, 37110.

14 Armstrong, "Oligarchy of the Western District," 84.

15 S.F. Wise, "The Rise of Christopher Hagerman," *Historic Kingston* 45 (1965): 12–23.

16 Aitchison, "*Development of Local Government*," 112–3.

17 S.F. Wise, "Upper Canada and the Conservative Tradition," in E.G. Firth, ed., *Profiles of a Province* (Toronto: OHS 1967), 30.

18 R.L. Jones, *History of Agriculture in Ontario, 1613–1880* (Toronto: University of Toronto Press 1946), 26.

19 Quoted in C.P. Stacey, "The War of 1812 in Canadian History," in M. Zaslow, ed., *The Defended Border: Upper Canada and the War of 1812* (Toronto: Macmillan 1964), 334.

20 S.F. Wise, "God's Peculiar Peoples," in W.L. Morton, ed., *The Shield of Achilles* (Toronto: McClelland and Stewart 1968), 52–3.
21 See Charles A. Stewart, *The Service of British Regiments in Canada and North America* (Ottawa: Department of National Defence Library 1962), 120, 148, 283, 289, 295, 316, 334.
22 Actually the age limits varied. The Militia Act of 1793 (33 Geo. 2, c. 1) established sixteen to fifty as the ages of service. In 1808 (48 Geo. 3, c. 1) it became sixteen to sixty and by the Act of 1839 (2 Vict., c. 9) the ages were changed to eighteen to sixty.
23 Anna Jameson, *Winter Studies and Summer Rambles in Canada*, 3 vols. (London: Saunders and Otley 1838), 1:302–3.
24 PAC, RG 9, IB 5, vols. 5, 7.
25 R.A. Douglas, ed., *John Prince, 1796–1870: A Collection of Documents* (Toronto: Champlain Society 1980), 53.
26 PAC, RG 9, IB 1, vol. 18, French to Coffin, 28 Sept. 1832.
27 Ibid., vol. 21, McLean to Coffin, 13 Feb. 1836.
28 Cornwall *Observer*, 8 Aug. 1836.
29 PAC, RG. 9, IB 1, vol. 18, Beikie to Rowan, 31 Dec. 1832.
30 Ibid., vol. 19, Macdonell to Coffin, 1 Jan. 1833, 13 May 1833.
31 Ibid., vol. 21, VanKoughnet to Coffin, 7 Feb. 1836.
32 Ibid., J. Joseph to Coffin, 13 Feb. 1836.
33 Ibid., VanKoughnet to Coffin, 7 Feb. 1836.
34 Ibid., Macdonell to Head, 9 Feb. 1836.
35 Ibid., McLean to Coffin, 13 Feb. 1836.
36 Ibid., Macdonell to Coffin, 19 Feb. 1836.
37 Ibid., Macdonell to Head, 26 Feb. 1836.
38 Ibid., VanKoughnet to Coffin, 14 Apr. 1836.
39 Ibid., VanKoughnet to Coffin, 14 Mar. 1836.
40 Ibid., vol. 22, Macdonell to FitzGibbon, 13 Dec. 1837.
41 PAC, RG 1, L 3, vol. 549, Y 12/8.
42 Cited in G.M. Craig, *Upper Canada* (Toronto: McClelland and Stewart 1963), 89.
43 The Militia Act of 1839 (2 Vict., c. 9) set fees which ranged from 30 shillings for lieutenant colonels to 10 shillings for ensigns.
44 D.P. Gagan, *The Denison Family of Toronto, 1792–1925* (Toronto: University of Toronto Press 1973), 17.
45 PAC, RG 9, IB 1, vol. 18, Tayler to Coffin, 7 April 1832.
46 H.B. Timothy in *The Galts: A Canadian Odyssey, John Galt, 1779–1839* (Toronto: McClelland and Stewart 1977), 117–8, Timothy records that although John Galt never actually received the militia commission which was promised him, he later had his portrait painted in the uniform of a colonel in the Upper Canadian militia.
47 PAC, RG 5, B 3, vol. 12.

CHAPTER FOUR

1 OA, *Report* (1931), 109.

2 The collectors were regulated by an Imperial Act, (3 & 4 Will. 4, c. 59) and by two provincial acts (4 Geo. 4, c. 10 and 4 & 5 Vict., c. 14. For an example of the collectors' powers of seizure, see J.K. Johnson, "Anthony Manahan and the Status of Irish Catholics in Upper Canada" *Historic Kingston* 31, (Jan. 1983): 33.

3 PAC, RG 1, L 3, vol. 343, M 13/75.

4 PAC, RG 5, A 1, vols. 114, 115, 64036–65150.

5 D.R. Beer, *Sir Allan Napier MacNab* (Hamilton: *DHB* 1984), 143.

6 R.A. Douglas, ed., *John Prince, 1796–1870: A Collection of Documents* (Toronto: Champlain Society 1980) xxvi–xxvii.

7 PAC, RG 68, Index to Commissions, Upper and Lower Canada, 1651–1841.

8 C. Durand, *Reminiscences of Charles Durand of Toronto, Barrister* (Toronto: Hunter Rose 1897), 403.

9 Johnson, "Anthony Manahan and the Status of Irish Catholics in Upper Canada," *Historic Kingston* 31 (Jan. 1983): 33.

10 PAC, RG 1, L 3, vol. 161, D 19/46.

11 B.G. Wilson, *The Enterprises of Robert Hamilton* (Ottawa: Carleton University Press) 35–47, 128–65; F.H. Armstrong, "The Oligarchy of the Western District of Upper Canada," CHA *Historical Papers* (1977), 86–103; C.F. Read, "The London District Oligarchy in the Rebellion Era" *OH* 72, no. 4 (Dec. 1980) 195–209; H.V. Nelles, "Loyalism and Local Power—the District of Niagara, 1792–1837," *OH* 58, no. 2 (June 1966): 97–114; E.M. Richards, "The Joneses of Brockville and the Family Compact," *OH* 60, no. 4 (Dec. 1968): 169–84; S.F. Wise, "Tory Factionalism: Kingston Elections and Upper Canadian Politics, 1820–1836," *OH* 57, no. 4 (Dec. 1965): 205–25.

12 S.F. Wise, "Upper Canada and the Conservative Tradition," in E.G. Firth, ed., *Profiles of a Province* (Toronto: OHS 1967), 20–30.

13 Richards, "Joneses of Brockville," 169–84.

14 PAC, RG 5, A 1, vol. 202, 112138–9, 112356.

15 Richards, "Joneses of Brockville," 178–9.

16 Ibid., 179.

17 Wise, "Upper Canada and the Conservative Tradition," 27.

18 PAC, RG 1, E 3, vol. 70, Duncan Macdonell to Powell, 28 June 1819, John Macdonell to Hillier, 18 June 1819.

19 S.F. Wise, "The Rise of Christopher Hagerman" *Historic Kingston* 14 (1965): 12–23.

20 J.A. Macdonell, *Sketches Illustrating the Early Settlement and History of Glengarry in Canada* (Montreal: W. Foster, Brown 1893), 108.

21 PAC, RG 5, A 1, vol. 125, 68857–9, 68880.

22 PAC, RG 5, C 1, vol. 78, no. 2488, Macdonell to S.B. Harrison, 6 Dec. 1841.

23 Richards, "Joneses of Brockville," 183.

24 PAC, RG 9, IB 1, vol. 43, Bullock to Jones, 1 Feb. 1838.

25 Ibid., vol. 22, VanKoughnet to Coffin, 15 May 1837.

26 PAC, RG 9, IB 5, vol. 5.

27 PAC, RG 5, A 1, vol. 114, 63734–7.

28 Wise, "Upper Canada and the Conservative Tradition," 31.

29 H.C. Pentland, *Labour and Capital in Canada, 1650–1860* (Toronto: James Lorimer 1981), 181.

30 L.F. Gates, *Land Policies of Upper Canada* (Toronto: University of Toronto Press 1968), 228.

31 J. Lownsborough, *The Privileged Few* (Toronto: Art Gallery of Ontario 1980), 27.

32 F.H. Armstrong, review of A.S. Thompson, *Jarvis Street: A Story of Triumph and Tragedy*, *OH* 74, no. 1 (March 1982): 58.

33 D. Leighton, "The Compact Tory as Bureaucrat: Samuel Peters Jarvis and the Indian Department, 1837–1845," *OH* 73, no. 1 (March 1981): 46.

34 A.S. Thompson, *Jarvis Street: A Story of Triumph and Tragedy* (Toronto: Personal Library 1980), 126.

35 See R.J. Burns, "George Herchmer Markland," *DCB* 9:534–6.

36 PAC, RG 5, A 1, vol. 125, 68831.

37 MTPL, Baldwin Papers, W.B. Wells to Baldwin, 31 July 1843.

38 Wise, "Upper Canada and the Conservative Tradition," 28.

39 Wise, "The Rise of Christopher Hagerman," 14.

40 G.M. Craig, "John Strachan," *DCB* 9:755.

41 R. Baldwin, Bethune, G.S. Boulton, H.J. Boulton, Bruce, Cartwright, J. Clark, Detlor, R.D. Fraser, Gates, W.B. Jarvis, C. Jones, J. Jones, A. Macdonell (Greenfield), D. Macdonell (Greenfield) D.A. Macdonell, McIntosh, Alexander McLean, Archibald McLean, A.N. MacNab, Radenhurst, J.B. Robinson, P. Robinson, W.B. Robinson, H. Sherwood, Small, VanKoughnet.

42 Beasely, Beikie, Bethune, M. Bidwell, Brant, W. Buell, W. Buell junior, H. Burritt, S. Burritt, Burwell, Cartwright, W. Chisholm, Clench, J. Crooks, W. Crooks, Cumming, Dalton, Draper, C. Duncombe, D. Duncombe, B. Ewing, B. Fairfield, R.D. Fraser, C. Hagerman, D. Hagerman, Ham, W. Hamilton, Hornor, P. Howard, Jameson, G. Jarvis, W. Jarvis, E. Jessup, sr., S. Jones, Ketchum, Kerr, McBride, McCall, McCarger, Angus Macdonell (Collachie) MacNab, Markle, Mears, Nelles, Prince, Ridout, J. Rolph, H. Sherwood, L.P. Sherwood, S. Sherwood, H. Smith, Spencer, Swayze, P. Terry, T. Thompson,

H.C. Thomson, W.B. Wilkinson.

43 H.T. Smith, *History of St. Andrew's Lodge A.F. and A.M. no. 6 G.R.C.* (Toronto: Bryant Press 1901), 1.

44 B.D. Palmer, *A Culture in Conflict* (Montreal: McGill-Queen's University Press 1979), 41.

45 S.F. Wise, "Kingston Elections and Upper Canadian Politics, 1820–1836" *OH* 57, no. 4 (Dec. 1965): 214.

46 J.R. Robertson, *History of Freemasonry in Canada*, 2 vols. (Toronto: Hunter Rose 1899) 2:373.

47 I. MacPherson, *Matters of Loyalty: The Buells of Brockville* 1830–1850 (Belleville: Mika 1981), 82–3.

48 Hamilton *Spectator* 22 March 1881.

49 UC, House of Assembly, *Journals of the House of Assembly* (1828), appendix 18.

50 F.C. Hamil, *Lake Erie Baron* (Toronto: Macmillan 1955), 172.

51 Most of the witnesses examined by a select committee of the assembly in 1828 believed the Methodists to be the most numerous denomination. See UC, House of Assembly, *Journals* (1828) appendix 18. See also A. Dunham, *Political Unrest in Upper Canada, 1815–1836* (Toronto: McClelland and Stewart 1963), 88.

52 He was buried at St. Andrew's Anglican Church in Grimsby. *See* Grimsby Historical Society, *Annals of the Forty* (1958) 9:69. He is said to have opposed "the spoliation of the Church property"; PAC, MG 24, K 2, Coventry Manuscripts, vol. 13.

53 F.H. Armstrong, "Ethnicity in the Formation of the Family Compact: A Case Study in the Growth of the Canadian Establishment" in J. Dahlie and T. Fernando, eds. *Ethnicity, Power and Politics in Canada* (Toronto: Methuen 1981), 31.

54 J. Garner, *The Franchise and Politics in British North America* (Toronto: University of Toronto Press 1969), 151–2.

55 UC, House of Assembly *Journals* (1810) 6 Feb., 3 March, 7 March.

56 R.E. Saunders, "What was the Family Compact?" *OH* 49 no. 4 (Autumn 1957): 167.

57 *Lord Durham's Report: An Abridgement of Report of the Affairs of British North America*, ed. G.M. Craig (Toronto: McClelland and Stewart 1963), 84, 93.

58 J.H. Aitchison, "The Municipal Corporations Act of 1849" *CHR* 30, no. 2 (June 1949): 112.

59 Armstrong, "Ethnicity ... Family Compact," 34–6.

60 H.I. Cowan, *British Emigration to British North America* (Toronto: University of Toronto Press 1967), 289.

61 D.H. Akenson, "Ontario: Whatever Happened to the Irish?" in D.H. Akenson, ed., *Canadian Papers in Rural History*, (Gananoque: Langdale

Press), 3:209.

62 Aitchison, "Municipal Corporations Act," 112.

63 J.S. Moir, *Church and State in Canada West 1841–1867* (Toronto: University of Toronto Press 1959), 186.

64 E.G. Firth ed., *The Town of York 1815–1834* (Toronto: Champlain Society 1966) 196.

65 Toronto *Patriot*, 2 Aug. 1836.

66 Moir, *Church and State*, 187.

67 Armstrong, "Ethnicity ... Family Compact," 34.

68 *Census of Canada*, 1871, 4:136. The figures for the Irish are based upon Akenson's calculation of the ratio of Protestant to Catholic Irish as two-to-one.

69 W.C. Crofton, *Sketches of the Thirteenth Parliament of Upper Canada* (Toronto: Rogers and Thomson 1840), 30.

70 John George Lambton, 1st Earl of Durham, *Report Upon the Affairs of British North America* (London: 1839) Appendix A, no. 7.

71 J.K. Johnson, "Anthony Manahan and the Status of Irish Catholics in Upper Canada," *Historic Kingston* 31 (Jan. 1983): 40.

72 *Canadian Freeman*, 28 Oct. 1830.

73 R.L. Fraser, "John Willson," *DHB* 1:212.

74 The six were Barnabas and M.S. Bidwell, John McIntosh, William Weekes, W.B. Wells and W.B. Wilkinson.

75 W.J. Rattray, *The Scot in British North America*, 4 vols. (Toronto: Maclear 1880) 1: 189; J.M. Bumsted, *The Scots in Canada* (Ottawa: CHA 1982), 5; D.S. Macmillan, "The 'New Men' in Action: Scottish Mercantile and Shipping Operations in the North American Colonies, 1760–1825," in D.S. Macmillan ed., *Canadian Business History* (Toronto: McClelland and Stewart 1972), 103; D. McCalla, *The Upper Canada Trade* (Toronto: University of Toronto Press 1979), 38–9; Wilson, *Enterprises of Robert Hamilton*, 58–67; H.I. Cowan, *British Immigration Before Confederation* (Ottawa: CHA), 7.

76 K.J. Duncan, "Patterns of Settlement in the East" in W.S. Reid, ed., *The Scottish Tradition in Canada*, (Toronto: Methuen 1981) 72.

77 G.W. Spragge ed., *The John Strachan Letter Book: 1812–1834* (Toronto: OHS 1946), 186.

78 Armstrong, "Ethnicity ... Family Compact," 35.

79 P.A. Russell, "Attitudes to Social Structure and Social Mobility in Upper Canada, 1815–1840," (PHD thesis, Carleton University, 1981), 290.

80 Akenson, "Ontario: Whatever happened to the Irish?," 206, 219.

81 J.K. Johnson, "Colonel James FitzGibbon and the Suppression of Irish Riots in Upper Canada," *OH* 58, no. 3 (Sept. 1966): 139–155; H.J. Graff, "The Reality Behind the Rhetoric: The Social and Economic Meanings of Literacy in the Mid-Nineteenth Century: The Example

of Literacy and Criminality," in N. McDonald and A. Chaiton, eds., *Egerton Ryerson and his Times* (Toronto: Macmillan 1978), 203–16; J. Burnet, *Ethnic Groups in Upper Canada* (Toronto: OHS 1972), 78–81.

82 G.J. Lockwood, "Irish Immigrants and the 'Critical Years' in Eastern Ontario: The Case of Montague Township 1821–1881," in Akenson, *Canadian Papers in Rural History* 4:153–76. Akenson's own study of the Irish of Leeds and Lansdowne Township, *The Irish In Ontario, A Study in Rural History* (Montreal: McGill-Queen's University Press 1984), presents a contrary case study of Irish success.

83 Pentland, *Labour and Capital*, 105.

84 See for example, *Colonial Advocate*, 8 July and 5 August 1824; J. MacTaggart, *Three Years in Canada* (London: N. Colburn 1829) 2: 243–4; Anna Jameson, *Winter Studies and Summer Rambles in Canada* 3 vols. (London: Saunders and Otley 1838), 1:269; S. Strickland, *Twenty Seven Years in Canada West* (London: Richard Bentley 1853), 1:138, J. McGregor, *British America* (Edinburgh: W. Blackwood 1833), 2: 540.

85 Irish Catholics of some prominence who can be identified in the 1820s and 1830s for Toronto alone include: James King, lawyer; John King, doctor and alderman; William Bergin, merchant; Francis Collins, journalist; Michael and Robert Meighan, merchants; Ulick Howard, hotel owner; Patrick McGan, auctioneer; Maurice Scollard, clerk of the Bank of Upper Canada; and Edward McMahon, chief clerk in the lieutenant governor's office, 1812–41. See Firth, *Town of York*, 56, 95, 103, 111, 200, 238; Brother Alfred, "Francis Collins — First Catholic Journalist in Upper Canada," CCHA *Report* (1938–9), 51–66. Owen McMahon, sheriff of the Prince Edward District, also an Irish Catholic, was probably a relative of Edward McMahon.

86 *Census of Canada*, 1871, 4:136.

87 F. Landon, *Western Ontario and the American Frontier* (Toronto: McClelland and Stewart 1967), 47.

CHAPTER FIVE

1 E.A. Cruikshank ed., *The Correspondence of Lieut. Governor John Graves Simcoe*, 5 vols. (Toronto: Ontario Historical Society 1923) 1:249.

2 Ibid., 232.

3 Maitland to Sir George Murray, 12 Aug. 1828, cited in A. Dunham, *Political Unrest in Upper Canada*, (Toronto: McClelland and Stewart 1963), 115.

4 W. Wood, ed., *Select British Documents of the Canadian War of 1812*, 4 vols. (Toronto: Champlain Society 1920) 1:305.

5 Strachan to James Brown, 9 Oct. 1808, cited in G.M. Craig, *Upper*

Canada, The Formative Years (Toronto: McClelland and Stewart 1963), 58.

6 R.L. Fraser, "Like Eden in her Summer Dress: Gentry, Economy and Society: Upper Canada, 1812–1840" (PHD thesis, University of Toronto, 1979) 221.

7 D.C. MacDonald, "Honourable Richard Cartwright 1759–1815," in G.W. Spragge, ed., *Three History Theses* (Toronto: OA 1961), 161; E.H. Jones "Joseph Willcocks" *DCB* 5:855–6.

8 MTCL, Baldwin Papers, W.B. Wells to Robert Baldwin, 31 July 1843.

9 E.A. Cruikshank and A. F. Hunter eds., *The Correspondence of the Honourable Peter Russell*, 3 vols. (Toronto: OHS 1936) 3:217.

10 *Canadian Freeman*, 28 Oct. 1830.

11 H.T. Manning, *The Revolt of French Canada, 1800–1835* (London: Macmillan 1962), 31.

12 Dunham, *Political Unrest in Upper Canada*, 116.

13 S.F. Wise "Upper Canada and the Conservative Tradition," in E.G. Firth, ed., *Profiles of a Province* (Toronto: OHS 1967), 22–3.

14 Fraser, "Like Eden in Her Summer Dress," 163–5.

15 Cruikshank and Hunter, *Peter Russell*, 217.

16 Ibid.

17 G.S. French, *Parsons and Politics* (Toronto: Ryerson Press 1962), 47; Robert Gourlay, *Statistical Account of Upper Canada*, ed. S.R. Mealing (Toronto: McClelland and Stewart 1974), 111.

18 UC, House of Assembly, *Journals of the House of Assembly* (1810), 6 Feb., 3 March, 8 March.

19 M. Smith, *A Geographical View of the Province of Upper Canada* (Hartford: P. Mauro 1813), 62–3; Craig, *Upper Canada: The Formative Years*, 47.

20 Akenson has concluded that all population figures for the province before the war are "shaky."; D.H. Akenson, *The Irish in Ontario, A Study in Rural History* (Montreal: McGill-Queen's University Press 1984) 112.

21 *Census of Canada*, 1871 4:136.

22 UC, House of Assembly, *Journals* (1828) appendix 18.

23 Akenson, *Irish in Ontario*, 26.

24 E. Jackson, "The Organization of Upper Canadian Reformers, 1818–1867," *OH* 53, no. 2 (June 1961): 95–115; Wise "Upper Canada and the Conservative Tradition," 27.

25 Some historians have found the first symptoms of partyism in Upper Canada in the period 1805–12. See H.H. Guest, "Upper Canada's First Political Party," *OH* 54 no. 4 (Dec. 1962): 275–93 and Jones, "Joseph Willcocks," *DCB* 5:856–7.

26 P. Romney, "The Spanish Freeholder Imbroglio of 1824: Inter-Elite and Intra-Elite Rivalry in Upper Canada," *OH* 76, no. 1 (March 1984): 44.
27 See R.S. Sorrell, "1828 Upper Canada Election Results Table," *OH* 63, no. 1 (March 1971): 67–9.
28 Kingston *Chronicle and Gazette,* 25 Oct. 1834.
29 Toronto *Patriot,* 2 Aug. 1836.
30 J. Ward, *The Hansard Chronicles* (Ottawa: Deneau and Greenberg 1980), 34.
31 M.S. Cross, "1837: The Necessary Failure," in M.S. Cross and G.S. Kealey, eds., *Pre-Industrial Canada, 1760–1849* (Toronto: McClelland and Stewart 1982), 156–7.
32 M. Fairley, ed., *The Selected Writings of William Lyon Mackenzie* (Toronto: Oxford University Press 1960), 216–7.
33 A.G. Doughty, ed., *The Elgin-Grey Papers, 1846–1852* (Ottawa: PAC 1937), 833.
34 Canada (Province), Legislative Assembly, *Debates of the Legislative Assembly of United Canada,* ed. E. Gibbs (Montreal: Presse de l'École des hautes études commerciales 1973) vol. 4, part 2 (1844–5), 1940.
35 Craig, *Upper Canada, The Formative Years,* 112.
36 T. Leavitt, *History of Leeds and Grenville* (Brockville: Recorder Press 1879), 68; M. Rubincam, ed., *The Old United Empire Loyalist List* (Baltimore: Genealogical Publishing Co. 1969), 201.
37 PAC, RG 1, L 3, vol. 106, C 11/106; vol. 118 C 19/136; vol. 130, C 2/244.
38 Ibid., vol. 548, W Misc. 1816–45/9; vol. 534, W 19/78.
39 Ibid., vol. 438, R 2/55, R 3/13.
40 D.R. Beer, *Sir Allan Napier MacNab* (Hamilton: *DHB* 1984), 22–5.
41 PAC, RG 19, E 5a, vol. 3747, no. 520.
42 Ibid., vol. 3753, no. 1237; vol. 3746, nos. 416, 430, 354; C. Read, *The Rising in Western Upper Canada, 1837–8* (Toronto: University of Toronto Press 1982), 68.
43 PAC, RG 19, E 5a, vol. 3746, no. 440.
44 Wise, "Upper Canada and the Conservative Tradition," 28.
45 F.H. Armstrong, "James Edward Small," *DCB* 9:724.
46 Ibid.
47 W. Canniff, *The Medical Profession in Upper Canada, 1783–1850* (Toronto: William Briggs 1894), 522.
48 J.M.S. Careless, "Robert Baldwin," in J.M.S. Careless, ed., *The Pre-Confederation Premiers: Ontario Government Leaders, 1841–1867* (Toronto: University of Toronto Press 1980), 97.
49 P. Brode, *Sir John Beverley Robinson: Bone and Sinew of the Compact* (Toronto: The Osgoode Society 1984), 146.

50 D.H. Akenson, *Being Had: Historians, Evidence and the Irish in North America* (Port Credit: P.D. Meany Publishers 1985), 77–90.
51 John George Lambton, 1st Earl of Durham, *Report Upon the Affairs of British North America* (London: 1839) appendix A, no. 7.
52 Wise, "Upper Canada and the Conservative Tradition," 21.
53 Ibid.
54 P.G. Cornell, *The Alignment of Political Groups in Canada, 1841–1867* (Toronto: University of Toronto Press 1962), 95, 98, 100, 103, 106, 108, 109, 110.
55 S.F. Wise, "Tory Factionalism: Kingston Elections and Upper Canadian Politics, 1820–1836," *OH* 57, no. 4 (Dec. 1965): 225.
56 M.S. Cross, "The Age of Gentility: The Formation of an Aristrocracy in the Ottawa Valley," CHA *Historical Papers* (1967): 116.
57 C.G. Karr, *The Canada Land Company: The Early Years* (Toronto: OHS 1974), x.
58 Wise, "Upper Canada and the Conservative Tradition," 24.
59 For one example of an urban electorate see E.G. Firth, ed., *The Town of York, 1815–1834* (Toronto: Champlain Society 1966), 126–9.
60 L.A. Johnson, "The Settlement of Western District, 1749–1850" in F.H. Armstrong *et al.*, eds., *Aspects of Nineteenth-Century Ontario* (Toronto: University of Toronto Press 1974), 31.
61 Cross, "Age of Gentility," 114.

CHAPTER SIX

1 R.L. Fraser, "Like Eden in her Summer Dress: Gentry, Economy and Society: Upper Canada, 1812–1840" (PHD thesis, University of Toronto, 1979), 5, 11.
2 Cited in G.M. Craig, ed. *Discontent in Upper Canada* (Toronto: Copp Clark 1974), 152.
3 Fraser, "Like Eden in her Summer Dress," 218–9.
4 S.F. Wise, "Upper Canada and the Conservative Tradition," in E.G. Firth, ed., *Profiles of a Province* (Toronto: OHS 1967), 21.
5 J. Porter, *The Vertical Mosaic: An Analysis of Social Class and Power in Canada* (Toronto: University of Toronto Press 1965), 558.
6 J.O. Coté, *Political Appointments and Elections in the Province of Canada* (Ottawa: Lowe Martin 1918), 52, 81, 89, 91, 95, 99, 101, 104, 115, 117.
7 J.K. Johnson, "William Thompson," *DCB* 8:885.
8 J.K. Johnson "James William Cook," *DCB* 10:195.
9 D. Swainson, "The Personnel of Politics; A Study of the Ontario Members of the Second Federal Parliament," (PHD thesis, University of Toronto, 1968).

10 Ibid., 478.
11 Ibid., 474.
12 Ibid., 463.
13 Ibid.
14 Ibid., 514, 525–6.
15 Ibid., 421.

A Note on Sources

DOCUMENTARY SOURCES

The specific sources of the biographical information in the Appendix are found at the end of each entry or (in some cases) at the end of the relevant entries in the *Dictionary of Canadian Biography*. Nonetheless some general comments on the major sources and their relative usefulness for the purposes of this study, or for similar studies, may be in order.

A number of series of government records relating to the period, held at the Public Archives of Canada, have been searched in every individual case. The first of these is Record Group (RG) 68, General Index to Commissions, Upper and Lower Canada, 1651–1841. These invaluable registers are a generally complete record of all the government appointments made in the period. They are, for example, the only reliable centralized source for magistrates' commissions as well as for more (or less) exalted offices. A less comprehensive record of public service appointments may be found in RG 1, E 13 (the Blue Books), which do not include unpaid offices such as magistracies but do have other advantages; they contain details of the revenue arising from paid or fee-generating positions and often specify the duties involved.

A companion source for the military is RG 9, IB 5, Registers of Militia Officers in Upper Canada. These registers are complete only from 1824 on, but they often provide earlier dates at which officers were commissioned. A less obvious biographical source is RG 1, L 3, Upper Canada Land Petitions. This series not only provides details of who received grants of land and in what amounts, but it almost invariably includes statements of personal past histories, including place of birth, length of residence in Upper Canada, previous military or civil offices, and much more.

An almost equally rich source is RG 5, A 1, Upper Canada Sundries, which consists of correspondence of all sorts received by the province's civil secretaries from 1792 to 1841. The Sundries include, among much else, innumerable applications for government positions or favours, which also ordinarily involved a recitation of past history and accomplishments. Sadly, unlike the land petitions, which are nominally indexed, the Sundries must be approached via a calendar which is maddeningly unwieldy and notoriously inaccurate.

A number of other primary sources which have been extensively consulted deal with more specific groups or periods. RG 8, C Series, British Military Records, is particularly relevant to the War of 1812, as is RG 19, E 5a, War of 1812 Losses Claims. Similarly Manuscript Group (MG) 21, G 2 (Haldimand Papers), vols. 166–8, contains lists of military Loyalists and refugees, including some details of families. A source which ought to be of general biographical use, RG 31, Census Records for 1825–81, is in fact of very limited value in this case. The closest Upper Canadian census, that of 1842, lists only heads of households by name and does not provide individual details of place of birth, religious denomination, etc. Subsequent censuses beginning in 1851 do yield such information but naturally became increasingly less relevant for Upper Canadian purposes.

PRINTED SOURCES

There are a number of helpful compilations of a biographical sort. E.M. Chadwick's *Ontarian Families* (2 vols, Toronto: Rolph, Smith 1894) has its merits but is confined to the "best" families. For Loyalists, there are good standard works, especially W.D. Reid's *The Loyalists in Ontario* (Lambertville, N.J.: Hunterdon House 1973) and M. Rubicam, ed., *The Old United Empire Loyalists List* (Baltimore: Genealogical Publishing 1969). For military Loyalists there is M.B. Fryer's and W.A. Smy's very thorough *Rolls of the Provincial (Loyalist) Corps, Canadian Command, American Revolutionary Period* (Toronto: Dundurn Press 1981). A similar work on the War of 1812 is L.H. Irving's *Officers of the British Forces in Canada During the War of 1812–15* (Welland: Tribune Printing 1908), although, as the title suggests, it does not list people who served only in the ranks. Three publications providing a different category of information are the result of an exhaustive combing of Upper Canadian newspapers; W.D. Reid's *Death Notices of Ontario* and his *Marriage Notices of Ontario* and D.A. McKenzie's *Death Notices from the Christian Guardian, 1836–1850* (all published by Hunterdon House in Lambertville N.J.)

SECONDARY SOURCES

There are few good modern biographies of Upper Canadian figures. For the MHAS themselves the main examples are W. Kilbourn's *The Firebrand: William Lyon Mackenzie and the Rebellion in Upper Canada* (Toronto: Clark Irwin 1956), R. Horsman's *Matthew Elliott, British Indian Agent* (Detroit: Wayne State University Press 1964), P. Brode's *Sir John Beverley Robinson, Bone and Sinew of the Family Compact* (Toronto: The Osgoode Society 1984) and D.R. Beer's *Sir Allan Napier MacNab* (Hamilton: Dictionary of Hamilton Biography 1984).

Local histories are sometimes good sources of biographical data though their reliability varies greatly. In general, with local histories and collective biography the rule is "the older the better". Many early local histories have extensive sections devoted to prominent individuals or families, a practice which more recent local historians evidently consider old-fashioned and antiquarian. The most biographically oriented local histories also tend to deal with the areas of earliest settlement, such as J. Carnochan's *History of Niagara* (Toronto: William Briggs 1914), W. Canniff's *The Settlement of Upper Canada (Ontario) with Special Reference to the Bay of Quinte* (Toronto: Dudley and Burns 1869), J.F. Pringle's *Lunenburgh, or the Old Eastern District* (Cornwall: Standard Printing 1890), J. Croil's *Dundas; A Sketch of Canadian History* (Montreal: B. Dawson & Son 1861), W.S. Herrington's *History of the County of Lennox and Addington* (Toronto: Macmillan 1913), T.W.H. Leavitt's *History of Leeds and Grenville* (Brockville: Recorder Press 1879) and two anonymous compilations, *Commemorative Biographical Record of the County of York, Ontario* (Toronto: J.H. Beers 1907) and *Pioneer Life on the Bay of Quinte* (Toronto: Rolph and Clark 1904).

A number of leadership groups in Upper Canada, from the central "Family Compact" to a variety of local oligarchies, have been the subjects of recent analysis by historians. These studies have greatly helped to provide models, and sometimes points of disagreement, for this book. The most thoughtful of these are probably S.F. Wise's "Upper Canada and the Conservative Tradition," in E.G. Firth, ed., *Profiles of a Province* (Toronto: Ontario Historical Society 1967) and F.H. Armstrong's "The Oligarchy of the Western District of Upper Canada, 1788–1841," in the Canadian Historical Association's *Historical Papers* 1977). But there are quite a few others, including E.M. Richards's "The Joneses of Brockville and the Family Compact" (*Ontario History* 60, no. 4 [Dec. 1968]), R.E. Saunders's "What was the Family Compact?" (*Ontario History*, 49, no. 4 [Autumn, 1957]), H.V. Nelles's "Loyalism and Local Power: The District of Niagara, 1792–1837" *Ontario History* 58, no. 2 [June 1966], S.F. Wise's "Tory Factionalism: Kingston Elections and Upper Canadian Politics, 1820–1836" *Ontario History* 57, no. 4 [Dec. 1965], C.F. Read's "The London District Oligarchy in the Rebellion Era" *Ontario History* 72, no. 4 [Dec. 1980] and M.S. Cross's "The Age of Gentility: The Formation of an Aristocracy in the

Ottawa Valley," in the Canadian Historical Association's *Report* (1966).

F.H. Armstrong has written an article which for the first time attempts to analyze the central elite in ethnic terms; his "Ethnicity in the Formation of the Family Compact: A Case Study in the Growth of the Canadian Establishment" appears in J. Dahlie and T. Fernando, eds., *Ethnicity, Power and Politics in Canada* (Toronto: Methuen 1981). A more ambitious and thought-provoking study of the role of ethnicity in the history of Upper Canada and Ontario is D.H. Akenson's *The Irish in Ontario: A Study in Rural History* (Montreal: McGill-Queen's University Press 1984).

Index